Submanifolds in Metric Manifolds

Submanifolds in Metric Manifolds

Editor

Cristina-Elena Hretcanu

Basel • Beijing • Wuhan • Barcelona • Belgrade • Novi Sad • Cluj • Manchester

Editor
Cristina-Elena Hretcanu
Faculty of Food Engineering,
University Stefan cel Mare
Suceava
Romania

Editorial Office
MDPI
St. Alban-Anlage 66
4052 Basel, Switzerland

This is a reprint of articles from the Special Issue published online in the open access journal *Mathematics* (ISSN 2227-7390) (available at: https://www.mdpi.com/journal/mathematics/special_issues/Submanifolds_in_Metric_Manifolds).

For citation purposes, cite each article independently as indicated on the article page online and as indicated below:

Lastname, A.A.; Lastname, B.B. Article Title. *Journal Name* **Year**, *Volume Number*, Page Range.

ISBN 978-3-7258-0893-9 (Hbk)
ISBN 978-3-7258-0894-6 (PDF)
doi.org/10.3390/books978-3-7258-0894-6

© 2024 by the authors. Articles in this book are Open Access and distributed under the Creative Commons Attribution (CC BY) license. The book as a whole is distributed by MDPI under the terms and conditions of the Creative Commons Attribution-NonCommercial-NoDerivs (CC BY-NC-ND) license.

Contents

Cristina E. Hretcanu
Preface to: Submanifolds in Metric Manifolds
Reprinted from: *Mathematics* **2024**, *12*, 1102, doi:10.3390/math12071102 1

Cornelia-Livia Bejan, Şemsi Eken Meriç and Erol Kılıç
Contact-Complex Riemannian Submersions
Reprinted from: *Mathematics* **2021**, *9*, 2996, doi:10.3390/math9232996 4

Yanlin Li, Pişcoran Laurian-Ioan, Akram Ali and Ali H. Alkhaldi
On the Topology of Warped Product Pointwise Semi-Slant Submanifolds with Positive Curvature
Reprinted from: *Mathematics* **2021**, *9*, 3156, doi:10.3390/math9243156 14

Ali H. Alkhaldi, Pişcoran Laurian-Ioan, Izhar Ahmad and Akram Ali
Vanishing Homology of Warped Product Submanifolds in Complex Space Forms and Applications
Reprinted from: *Mathematics* **2022**, *10*, 3884, doi:10.3390/math10203884 27

Mohabbat Ali, Abdul Haseeb, Fatemah Mofarreh and Mohd Vasiulla
Z-Symmetric Manifolds Admitting Schouten Tensor
Reprinted from: *Mathematics* **2022**, *10*, 4293, doi:10.3390/math10224293 44

Rongsheng Ma and Donghe Pei
The $*$-Ricci Operator on Hopf Real Hypersurfaces in the Complex Quadric
Reprinted from: *Mathematics* **2023**, *11*, 90, doi:10.3390/math11010090 54

Hristo Manev
First Natural Connection on Riemannian Π-Manifolds
Reprinted from: *Mathematics* **2023**, *11*, 1146, doi:10.3390/math11051146 68

Siraj Uddin, Esmaeil Peyghan, Leila Nourmohammadifar and Rawan Bossly
On Nearly Sasakian and Nearly Kähler Statistical Manifolds
Reprinted from: *Mathematics* **2023**, *11*, 2644, doi:10.3390/math11122644 84

Cristina E. Hretcanu and Mircea Crasmareanu
The (α, p)-Golden Metric Manifolds and Their Submanifolds
Reprinted from: *Mathematics* **2023**, *11*, 3046, doi:10.3390/math11143046 103

Cristina-Liliana Pripoae, Iulia-Elena Hirica, Gabriel-Teodor Pripoae and Vasile Preda
Holonomic and Non-Holonomic Geometric Models Associated to the Gibbs–Helmholtz Equation
Reprinted from: *Mathematics* **2023**, *11*, 3934, doi:10.3390/math11183934 116

Simona-Luiza Druta-Romaniuc
Quasi-Statistical Schouten–van Kampen Connections on the Tangent Bundle
Reprinted from: *Mathematics* **2023**, *11*, 4614, doi:10.3390/math11224614 136

Feyza Esra Erdoğan, Selcen Yüksel Perktaş, Şerife Nur Bozdağ and Bilal Eftal Acet
Lightlike Hypersurfaces of Meta-Golden Semi-Riemannian Manifolds
Reprinted from: *Mathematics* **2023**, *11*, 4798, doi:10.3390/math11234798 156

Editorial

Preface to: Submanifolds in Metric Manifolds

Cristina E. Hretcanu

Faculty of Food Engineernig, University Stefan cel Mare, 720229 Suceava, Romania; cristina.hretcanu@fia.usv.ro

Citation: Hretcanu, C.E. Preface to: Submanifolds in Metric Manifolds. *Mathematics* **2024**, *12*, 1102. https://doi.org/10.3390/math12071102

Received: 25 March 2024
Accepted: 2 April 2024
Published: 7 April 2024

Copyright: © 2024 by the author. Licensee MDPI, Basel, Switzerland. This article is an open access article distributed under the terms and conditions of the Creative Commons Attribution (CC BY) license (https://creativecommons.org/licenses/by/4.0/).

The present editorial contains 11 research articles, published in the Special Issue entitled *"Submanifolds in metric manifolds"* of the MDPI *mathematics* journal, which cover a wide range of topics from differential geometry in relation to the theory and applications of the structure induced on submanifolds by the structure defined on various ambient manifolds. The geometry of some particular manifolds and their submanifolds, with examples and applications (characterization properties and inequality or equality cases), is studied.

The concept of Riemannian submersion between Riemannian manifolds is very popular in theoretical physics, as well as in differential geometry. In Contribution **1**, the authors consider a contact-complex Riemannian submersion, which puts the almost-contact-metric structure from the domain manifold to the almost-Hermitian structure of the target manifold. The authors provide several new results, showing mainly when the base manifold admits a Ricci soliton when it is Einstein, when the fibres are η-Ricci solitons, and when they are η-Einstein.

A classical challenge in Riemannian geometry is to discuss the geometrical and topological structures of submanifolds. In Contribution **2**, the authors obtain some topological characterizations for the warping function of a warped product pointwise semi-slant submanifold in a complex projective space (where the constant sectional curvature c = 4). Some important applications of this theory can be found for the singularity structure in liquid crystals, in the system in statistical mechanics with low dimensions, and physical phase transitions. Since paper **2** considers both the warped product manifold and the homotopy–homology theory, its results can be used as part of physical applications.

In Contribution **3**, the authors prove the non-existence of stable integral currents in a compact oriented warped product pointwise semi-slant submanifold of a complex space form, under extrinsic conditions, which involve the Laplacian, the squared norm gradient of the warped function, and pointwise slant functions. The authors investigate the curvature and topology of submanifolds in a Riemannian manifold and the usual sphere theorems in Riemannian geometry. The second target of paper **3** is to establish topological sphere theorems from the viewpoint of warped product submanifold geometry with positive constant sectional curvature and pinching conditions in terms of the squared norm of the warping function and the Laplacian of the warped function as extrinsic invariants.

The importance of spaces with constant curvature is well understood in cosmology. A cosmological model of the universe is obtained by assuming that the universe is isotropic and homogeneous. In Contribution **4**, the authors focus on the *Z-symmetric manifold* admitting certain types of Schouten tensor and they find some properties of Z-symmetric spacetime admitting Codazzi-type Schouten tensor.

The Kähler manifold is the subject of symplectic geometry. Contact geometry appears as the odd dimensional counterpart of symplectic geometry, in which the almost-contact manifold corresponds to the almost-complex manifold. In Contribution **5**, the authors study the $*$-Ricci operator on Hopf real hypersurfaces in the complex quadric. As the correspondence to the semi-symmetric Ricci tensor, the authors give a classification of real hypersurfaces in the complex quadric with the semi-symmetric $*$-Ricci tensor.

In Contribution **6**, the author studies the geometry of the almost-paracontact and almost-paracomplex Riemannian manifolds. The author defines the first natural connection and constructs a relation between this connection and the Levi–Civita connection. Moreover, some properties of curvature tensors, torsion tensors, Ricci tensors and scalar curvatures using these connections are given, along with an explicit five-dimensional example.

A statistical manifold can be considered as an expanse of a Riemannian manifold, such that the compatibility of the Riemannian metric is developed to a general condition. In Contribution 7, the authors present nearly Sasakian and nearly Kähler structures on statistical manifolds and show the relation between these geometric notions. Moreover, the authors study some properties of (anti-)invariant statistical submanifolds of nearly Sasakian statistical manifolds.

The geometry of submanifolds in Golden or metallic Riemannian manifolds was widely studied by many geometers. The notion of a Golden structure was introduced 15 years ago and has been a constant interest of several geometers. In Contribution 8, the authors propose a new generalization (apart from that called the metallic structure), named the almost (α, p)-Golden structure. By adding a compatible Riemannian metric, the authors focus on the study of the structure induced on submanifolds in this setting and its properties.

In Contribution 9, the authors study a new holonomic Riemannian geometric model, associated with the Gibbs–Helmholtz equation from classical thermodynamics, in a canonical way. Using a specific coordinate system, the authors define a parameterized hypersurface in R^4 as the graph of the entropy function. The main geometric invariants of this hypersurface are determined and some of their properties are derived. Using this geometrization, the authors characterize the equivalence between the Gibbs–Helmholtz entropy and the Boltzmann–Gibbs–Shannon, Tsallis and Kaniadakis entropies, respectively, by means of three stochastic integral equations. They prove that some specific (infinite) families of normal probability distributions are solutions for these equations. This particular case offers a glimpse of the more general equivalence problem between classical entropy and statistical entropy.

The background of Contribution 10 is the total space TM of the tangent bundle of a Riemannian manifold (M, g), endowed with a metric G, constructed as a general natural lift of the metric from the base manifold. The author studies the conditions under which the (pseudo-)Riemannian manifold (TM, G), endowed with the Schouten–Van Kampen connection and associated with the Levi Civita connection of G, is a statistical manifold admitting torsion. The results obtained in this work lead to new examples of (quasi-)statistical structures on the tangent bundle of a Riemann manifold.

In Contribution 11, the authors investigate the properties of the induced structure on a light-like hypersurface by a meta-Golden semi-Riemannian structure. Moreover, the authors study the properties of the invariant and anti-invariant light-like hypersurfaces, and screen semi-invariant light-like hypersurfaces of almost-meta-Golden semi-Riemannian manifolds. They also provide some useful examples.

As the Guest Editor of this Special Issue, I would like to thank the MDPI publishing editorial team, who gave me the opportunity to undertake the role of Guest Editor for the Special Issue "Submanifolds in metric manifolds". I am very grateful to all the authors who have contributed through their research articles. Also, I would like to express my gratitude to all the reviewers for their valuable suggestions and critical comments, which have improved the quality of the papers in this Issue.

We hope that the selected research studies will have a positive impact on the international scientific community, inspiring other researchers to study and expand on the topics covered in this book.

Conflicts of Interest: The author declares no conflicts of interest.

List of Contributions:

1. Bejan, C.L.; Meriç, S.E.; Kılıç, E. Contact-Complex Riemannian Submersions. *Mathematics* **2021**, *9*, 2996.

2. Yanlin, L.; Ali, H.A.; Akram, A.; Piscoran, L.I. On the Topology of Warped Product Pointwise Semi-Slant Submanifolds with Positive Curvature. *Mathematics* **2021**, *9*, 3156.
3. Ali, H.A.; Piscoran, L.I.; Izhar, A.; Akram, A. Vanishing Homology of Warped Product Submanifolds in Complex Space Forms and Applications. *Mathematics* **2022**, *10*, 3884.
4. Ali, M.; Haseeb, A.; Mofarreh, F.; Vasiulla, M. Z-Symmetric Manifolds Admitting Schouten Tensor. *Mathematics* **2022**, *10*, 4293.
5. Ma, R.; Pei, D. The $\star$-Ricci Operator on Hopf Real Hypersurfaces in the Complex Quadric. *Mathematics* **2023**, *11*, 90.
6. Manev, H. First Natural Connection on Riemannian Π-Manifolds. *Mathematics* **2023**, *11*, 1146.
7. Uddin, S.; Peyghan, E.; Nourmohammadifar, L.; Bossly, R. On Nearly Sasakian and Nearly Kähler Statistical Manifolds. *Mathematics* **2023**, *11*, 12644.
8. Hretcanu, C.E.; Crasmareanu, M. The (α, p)-Golden Metric Manifolds and Their Submanifolds. *Mathematics* **2023**, *11*, 3046.
9. Pripoae, C.L.; Hirica, I.E.; Pripoae, G.T.; Preda, V. Holonomic and Non-Holonomic Geometric Models Associated to the Gibbs–Helmholtz Equation. *Mathematics* **2023**, *11*, 3934.
10. Druta-Romaniuc, S.L. Quasi-Statistical Schouten–van Kampen Connections on the Tangent Bundle. *Mathematics* **2023**, *11*, 4614.
11. Erdogan, F.E.; Perktas, S.Y.; Bozdag, S.N.; Acet, B.E. Lightlike Hypersurfaces of Meta-Golden Semi-Riemannian Manifolds. *Mathematics* **2023**, *11*, 4798.

Disclaimer/Publisher's Note: The statements, opinions and data contained in all publications are solely those of the individual author(s) and contributor(s) and not of MDPI and/or the editor(s). MDPI and/or the editor(s) disclaim responsibility for any injury to people or property resulting from any ideas, methods, instructions or products referred to in the content.

Article

Contact-Complex Riemannian Submersions

Cornelia-Livia Bejan [1,2,*], Şemsi Eken Meriç [3] and Erol Kılıç [4]

[1] Department of Mathematics, Technical University Gheorghe Asachi Iasi, 700050 Iasi, Romania
[2] Seminar Matematic, Alexandru Ioan Cuza University, Bd. Carol I No. 11, 700506 Iasi, Romania
[3] Department of Mathematics, Faculty of Science and Arts, Mersin University, Mersin 33343, Turkey; semsieken@mersin.edu.tr
[4] Department of Mathematics, Faculty of Science and Arts, İnönü University, Malatya 42280, Turkey; erol.kilic@inonu.edu.tr
* Correspondence: cornelia-livia.bejan@academic.tuiasi.ro

Abstract: A submersion from an almost contact Riemannian manifold to an almost Hermitian manifold, acting on the horizontal distribution by preserving both the metric and the structure, is, roughly speaking a contact-complex Riemannian submersion. This paper deals mainly with a contact-complex Riemannian submersion from an η-Ricci soliton; it studies when the base manifold is Einstein on one side and when the fibres are η-Einstein submanifolds on the other side. Some results concerning the potential are also obtained here.

Keywords: Riemannian submersion; submanifold; almost-contact metric manifold; Ricci soliton

MSC: 53C40; 32Q15; 53D10

Citation: Bejan, C.-L.; Eken Meriç, Ş.; Kılıç, E. Contact-Complex Riemannian Submersions. *Mathematics* **2021**, *9*, 2996. https://doi.org/10.3390/math9232996

Academic Editor: Cristina-Elena Hretcanu

Received: 14 October 2021
Accepted: 15 November 2021
Published: 23 November 2021

Publisher's Note: MDPI stays neutral with regard to jurisdictional claims in published maps and institutional affiliations.

Copyright: © 2020 by the authors. Licensee MDPI, Basel, Switzerland. This article is an open access article distributed under the terms and conditions of the Creative Commons Attribution (CC BY) license (https://creativecommons.org/licenses/by/4.0/).

1. Introduction

The notion of Ricci flow was introduced by R. S. Hamilton in 1892 to find a desired metric on a Riemannian manifold. For the metrics on a Riemannian manifold, the Ricci flow is an evolution equation that is given by

$$\frac{\partial}{\partial t} g(t) = -2Ric,$$

and it is a heat equation. Moreover, he showed that the self-similar solutions of Ricci flows are Ricci solitons and that they are natural generalizations of Einstein metrics [1]).

Let (M, g) be a Riemannian manifold. If there exists a smooth vector field (so-called potential field) ν and it satisfies

$$\frac{1}{2}(\mathscr{L}_\nu g) + Ric + \lambda g = 0,$$

then (M, g) is said to be a Ricci soliton. Here, $\mathscr{L}_\nu g$ is the Lie-derivative of the metric tensor g with respect to ν, Ric is the Ricci tensor of M, and λ is a constant. A Ricci soliton is denoted by (M, g, ν, λ), and it is called or shrinking, steady, expanding, if $\lambda > 0$, $\lambda = 0$, or $\lambda < 0$, respectively.

In 2009, J.T. Cho and M. Kimura introduced a more general notion called the η-Ricci soliton. According to this definition, a Riemannian manifold (M, g) is an η-Ricci soliton if it satisfies

$$\frac{1}{2}(\mathscr{L}_\nu g) + Ric + \lambda g + \mu \eta \otimes \eta = 0, \qquad (1)$$

where λ, μ are functions and η is a 1-form. It is clear that if μ is zero, then the η-Ricci soliton becomes a Ricci soliton (see [2]).

Due to the geometric importance of Ricci solitons and their wide applications in theoretical physics, they have become a popular topic studied in the literature. So, the notion of the Ricci soliton has been studied on manifolds that are endowed with many different geometric structures, such as contact, complex, warped product, etc. (see [3–6]).

On the other hand, the concept of Riemannian submersion between Riemannian manifolds is very popular in theoretical physics, as well as in differential geometry, and particularly in general relativity and Kaluza–Klein theory. For this reason, Riemannian submersions have been studied intensively (see [7–13]).

In this paper, we consider a contact-complex Riemannian submersion π from an almost-contact metric manifold M onto an almost Hermitian manifold such that M admits an η-Ricci soliton. Firstly, we calculate the Ricci tensor of the almost-contact metric manifold M, and using it, we present some necessary conditions for which any fibre of π or base manifold B admits a Ricci soliton, η-Ricci soliton, Einstein, or η-Einstein. Moreover, we study a contact-complex Riemannian submersion with totally umbilical fibres whose total space M admits an η-Ricci soliton. Depending on whether the potential field v of the η-Ricci soliton is vertical or horizontal, we obtain some new results.

Now, we briefly describe the content of the paper. The purpose of the Preliminaries is to review some basic notions, such as almost contact metric structure, Riemannian submersion, some properties of the vertical and horizontal distributions, and of the fundamental tensor fields. Then the main notion of our paper, namely the contact-complex Riemannian submersion, from an almost contact metric manifold, onto an almost Hermitian manifold, is described in Section 3. Then, the main results of the paper are contained in Section 4, which deals with contact-complex Riemannian submersions from manifolds admitting an η-Ricci soliton. Here we obtain conditions under which the base manifold is Einstein, the fibres are η-Einstein, the base manifold admits a Ricci soliton, and some other related facts.

2. Preliminaries

The authors recall the following notations from [13,14].

A Riemannian manifold M of dimension $(2m+1)$ has an almost-contact structure (ϕ, ξ, η) if it admits a vector field ξ (the so-called characteristic vector field), a $(1,1)$–tensor field ϕ, and a 1–form η satisfying:

$$\eta(\xi) = 1, \quad \phi^2 = -I + \eta \otimes \xi. \tag{2}$$

As a consequence of (2), we note that $\phi(\xi) = 0$ and $\eta \circ \phi = 0$. If M is endowed with an almost-contact structure (ϕ, ξ, η), then it is called an almost-contact manifold. Moreover, if a Riemannian metric g on M satisfies

$$g(\phi X, \phi Y) = g(X, Y) - \eta(X)\eta(Y) \tag{3}$$

for any vector fields X, Y, then the metric g is said to be compatible with the almost-contact structure (ϕ, ξ, η). In this case, the manifold M is said to be endowed with the almost-contact metric structure (ϕ, ξ, η, g), and (M, ϕ, ξ, η, g) is called an almost-contact metric manifold.

Now, we recall the following concepts.

Let $\pi : (M^m, g) \to (B^n, g')$ be a submersion between two Riemannian manifolds and let $r = m - n$ denote the dimension of any closed fibre $\pi^{-1}(x)$ for any $x \in B$. For any $p \in M$, putting $\mathcal{V}_p = ker\,\pi_{*p}$, we have an integrable distribution $\mathcal{V}$ that corresponds to the foliation of M determined by the fibres of π. Therefore, one has $\mathcal{V}_p = T_p \pi^{-1}(x)$, and $\mathcal{V}$ is called the vertical distribution. Let $\mathcal{H}$ be the horizontal distribution, which means that $\mathcal{H}$ is the orthogonal distribution of $\mathcal{V}$ with respect to g, i.e., $T_p(M) = \mathcal{V}_p \oplus \mathcal{H}_p$, $p \in M$. We note that for any $X' \in \Gamma(TB)$, the basic vector field π-related to X' is named the horizontal lift of X'. Here, $\pi_* X$ is denoted by the vector field X' to which X is π-related.

A map π between Riemannian manifolds M and B is called a Riemannian submersion if the following conditions hold:

(i) π has a maximal rank;
(ii) The differential π_{*p} preserves the length of the horizontal vector fields at each point of M.

For any $E \in \Gamma(TM)$, we denote vE and hE as the vertical and horizontal components of E, respectively.

Proposition 1. *Let $\pi : (M,g) \to (B,g')$ be a Riemannian submersion. If X, Y are the basic vector fields, which are π-related to X', Y', one has*

(i) $g(X,Y) = g'(X',Y') \circ \pi$;
(ii) $h[X,Y]$ *is the basic vector field π-related to* $[X',Y']$;
(iii) $h(\nabla_X Y)$ *is the basic vector field π-related to* $\nabla'_{X'} Y'$;
(iv) *for any vertical vector field V, $[X,V]$ is vertical,*

where ∇ and ∇' denote the Levi–Civita connections of M and B, respectively (see [13]).

The tensor fields $\mathcal{T}$ and $\mathcal{A}$ are said to be the fundamental tensor fields on the manifold M that are defined by

$$\mathcal{T}(E,F) = \mathcal{T}_E F = h(\nabla_{vE} vF) + v(\nabla_{vE} hF),$$
$$\mathcal{A}(E,F) = \mathcal{A}_E F = v(\nabla_{hE} hF) + h(\nabla_{hE} vF),$$

for any $E, F \in \Gamma(TM)$.

The fundamental tensor fields $\mathcal{T}$ and $\mathcal{A}$ on M satisfy the following properties:

$$g(\mathcal{T}_E F, G) = -g(\mathcal{T}_E G, F) \tag{4}$$

and

$$\mathcal{T}_V W = \mathcal{T}_W V, \tag{5}$$

for any $E, F, G \in \Gamma(TM), V, W \in \Gamma(\mathcal{V})$.

Note the fact that the vanishing of the tensor field $\mathcal{T}$ or $\mathcal{A}$ has some geometric meanings. For instance, if the tensor $\mathcal{A}$ vanishes identically on M, the horizontal distribution $\mathcal{H}$ is integrable. If the tensor $\mathcal{T}$ vanishes identically, any fibre of π is a totally geodesic submanifold of M.

Using the fundamental tensor fields $\mathcal{T}$ and $\mathcal{A}$, one can see that

$$\nabla_V W = \mathcal{T}_V W + \hat{\nabla}_V W, \tag{6}$$
$$\nabla_V X = h(\nabla_V X) + \mathcal{T}_V X, \tag{7}$$
$$\nabla_X V = \mathcal{A}_X V + v(\nabla_X V), \tag{8}$$
$$\nabla_X Y = h(\nabla_X Y) + \mathcal{A}_X Y, \tag{9}$$

where ∇ and $\hat{\nabla}$ are the Levi–Civita connections of M and any fibre of π, respectively, for any $V, W \in \Gamma(\mathcal{V})$ and $X, Y \in \Gamma(\mathcal{H})$.

We recall the following from [11].

Definition 1. *A distribution D on a Riemannian manifold (M,g) is called parallel if $\nabla_X Y \in \Gamma(D)$ for any vector field X on M and any $Y \in \Gamma(D)$, where ∇ is the Levi–Civita connection of g.*

On the other hand, the mean curvature vector field H on any fibre of the Riemannian submersion π is given by

$$\mathcal{N} = rH, \tag{10}$$

such that

$$\mathcal{N} = \sum_{j=1}^{r} \mathcal{T}_{U_j} U_j \tag{11}$$

where r denotes the dimension of any fibre of π and $\{U_1, U_2, \ldots, U_r\}$ is an orthonormal basis of the vertical distribution $\mathcal{V}$.

Using the equality (11), we get

$$g(\nabla_E \mathcal{N}, X) = \sum_{j=1}^{r} g((\nabla_E \mathcal{T})(U_j, U_j), X)$$

for any $E \in \Gamma(TM)$ and $X \in \Gamma(\mathcal{H})$. We denote the horizontal divergence of the horizontal vector field X by $\check{\delta}(X)$, which is given by

$$\check{\delta}(X) = \sum_{i=1}^{n} g(\nabla_{X_i} X, X_i), \tag{12}$$

where $\{X_i\}_{1 \leq i \leq n}$ is an orthonormal frame of $\mathcal{H}$, where n is also the dimension of B. On the other hand, any fibre of π is totally umbilical if

$$\mathcal{T}_U W = g(U, W) H, \tag{13}$$

is satisfied. Here, H is the mean curvature vector field of π in M for any $U, W \in \Gamma(\mathcal{V})$.

Furthermore, the Ricci tensor Ric on M satisfies

$$Ric(X, Y) = Ric'(X', Y') \circ \pi - \frac{1}{2}\{g(\nabla_X \mathcal{N}, Y) + g(\nabla_Y \mathcal{N}, X)\} \tag{14}$$

$$+ 2\sum_{i=1}^{n} g(\mathcal{A}_X X_i, \mathcal{A}_Y X_i) + \sum_{j=1}^{r} g(\mathcal{T}_{U_j} X, \mathcal{T}_{U_j} Y)$$

$$Ric(U, W) = \hat{Ric}(U, W) + g(\mathcal{N}, \mathcal{T}_U W) - \sum_{i=1}^{n} g((\nabla_{X_i} \mathcal{T})(U, W), X_i)$$

$$- \sum_{i=1}^{n} g(\mathcal{A}_{X_i} U, \mathcal{A}_{X_i} W), \tag{15}$$

for any $X, Y \in \Gamma(\mathcal{H})$ and $U, W \in \Gamma(\mathcal{V})$, where Ric' and $\hat{Ric}$ are the Ricci tensors of the base manifold B and any fibre of π, and $\{X_i\}, \{U_j\}$ are some orthonormal bases of $\mathcal{H}$ and $\mathcal{V}$, respectively.

3. Contact-Complex Riemannian Submersions

We recall some notations of [13] in the following.

Let $(M^{2m+1}, \phi, \eta, g, \xi)$ be an almost-contact metric manifold and let $(B^{2n}, \mathcal{J}, g')$ be an almost-Hermitian manifold. A Riemannian submersion $\pi : M \to B$ is called a contact-complex Riemannian submersion if

$$\mathcal{J} \circ \pi_* = \pi_* \circ \phi.$$

We note here that the vertical distribution $\mathcal{V}$ and horizontal distribution $\mathcal{H}$ are of dimensions $2r + 1$ and $2n$, respectively, where $r = m - n$.

For the contact-complex Riemannian submersion $\pi : (M^{2m+1}, g) \to (B^{2n}, g')$, the following properties are satisfied:

(i) The distributions $\mathcal{V}$ and $\mathcal{H}$ are ϕ-invariant,
(ii) The characteristic vector field ξ is vertical,
(iii) $\mathcal{H} \subset \ker \eta$, i.e., $\eta(X) = 0$, for any horizontal vector field X.

Example 1. Let $\pi : S^{2n+1} \to P^n(C)$ be a projection from the total space of a principal fibre bundle S^{2n+1} onto an n-dimensional complex projective space $P^n(C)$. Then, $\pi : S^{2n+1} \to P^n(C)$ is a contact-complex Riemannian submersion with respect to the canonical metric g on S^{2n+1} and the Kaehler metric on $P^n(C)$ (for details, see [13]).

4. Contact-Complex Riemannian Submersions Whose Total Space Admits an η-Ricci Soliton

Now, we recall the following lemma from [15].

Lemma 1. Let $\pi : (M,g) \to (B,g')$ be a Riemannian submersion between Riemannian manifolds. The following statements are equivalent to each other:

(i) the vertical distribution $\mathcal{V}$ is parallel;
(ii) the horizontal distribution $\mathcal{H}$ is parallel;
(iii) the fundamental tensor fields $\mathcal{T}$ and $\mathcal{A}$ vanish identically.

Throughout this paper, we make the following assumptions.

Assumption: A contact-complex Riemannian submersion $\pi : M \to B$ is defined from an almost-contact metric manifold (M, ϕ, ξ, η, g) onto an almost-Hermitian manifold $(B, \mathcal{J}, g')$.

Using (14) and (15), for any local orthonormal frames $\{X_i\}_{1 \leq i \leq 2n}$ and $\{U_j, \xi\}_{1 \leq j \leq 2r}$ of $\mathcal{H}$ and $\mathcal{V}$, respectively, we give the following:

Lemma 2. Let $\pi : M \to B$ be a contact-complex Riemannian submersion between manifolds. For any $U, W \in \Gamma(\mathcal{V})$ and $X, Y \in \Gamma(\mathcal{H})$ that are π-related to X', Y', the Ricci tensor of M satisfies

$$Ric(U,W) = \hat{Ric}(U,W) + g(\mathcal{N}, \mathcal{T}_U W) - \sum_{i=1}^{2n} \Big\{ g((\nabla_{X_i}\mathcal{T})(U,W), X_i) \quad (16)$$
$$+ g(\mathcal{A}_{X_i}U, \mathcal{A}_{X_i}W) \Big\},$$

$$Ric(U,\xi) = \hat{Ric}(U,\xi) + g(\mathcal{N}, \mathcal{T}_U \xi) - \sum_{i=1}^{2n} \Big\{ g((\nabla_{X_i}\mathcal{T})(U,\xi), X_i) \quad (17)$$
$$+ g(\mathcal{A}_{X_i}U, \mathcal{A}_{X_i}\xi) \Big\},$$

$$Ric(\xi,\xi) = \hat{Ric}(\xi,\xi) + g(\mathcal{N}, \mathcal{T}_\xi \xi) - \sum_{i=1}^{2n} \Big\{ g((\nabla_{X_i}\mathcal{T})(\xi,\xi), X_i) \quad (18)$$
$$+ g(\mathcal{A}_{X_i}\xi, \mathcal{A}_{X_i}\xi) \Big\},$$

$$Ric(X,Y) = Ric'(X',Y') \circ \pi - \frac{1}{2}(\mathcal{L}_\mathcal{N} g)(X,Y) \quad (19)$$
$$+ 2\sum_{i=1}^{2n} g(\mathcal{A}_X X_i, \mathcal{A}_Y X_i) + \sum_{j=1}^{2r} g(\mathcal{T}_{U_j}X, \mathcal{T}_{U_j}Y) + g(\mathcal{T}_\xi X, \mathcal{T}_\xi Y).$$

Definition 2. Let $(M, g, \xi, \lambda, \eta)$ be an η-Ricci soliton and let $\pi : M \to B$ be a contact-complex Riemannian submersion. If v is vertical, we say that v is a vertical potential field. Similarly, if v is horizontal, we say that v is a horizontal potential field.

Using equalities (16)–(18) in Lemma 2, we have the following theorem.

Theorem 1. Let $(M, g, \xi, \lambda, \eta)$ be an η-Ricci soliton with vertical potential field v and let $\pi : M \to B$ be a contact-complex Riemannian submersion. If one of the conditions in Lemma 1 is satisfied, then we have the following:

(i) The base manifold B is Einstein.
(ii) Any fibre of π admits an η-Ricci soliton with potential field v.

Proof. (*i*) Since M admits an η-Ricci soliton, one has

$$\frac{1}{2}\{g(\nabla_X v, Y) + g(\nabla_Y v, X)\} + Ric(X,Y) + \lambda g(X,Y) \qquad (20)$$
$$+ \mu \eta(X) \eta(Y) = 0,$$

for any horizontal vector fields X, Y. Using (8) in (20) gives

$$\frac{1}{2}\{g(\mathcal{A}_X v, Y) + g(\mathcal{A}_Y v, X)\} + Ric(X,Y) + \lambda g(X,Y)$$
$$+ \mu \eta(X) \eta(Y) = 0.$$

Applying (19) to the last equality, we get

$$\frac{1}{2}\{g(\mathcal{A}_X v, Y) + g(\mathcal{A}_Y v, X)\} + Ric'(X', Y') \circ \pi - \frac{1}{2}(\mathcal{L}_{\mathcal{N}} g)(X, Y) \qquad (21)$$
$$+ 2\sum_{i=1}^{2n} g(\mathcal{A}_X X_i, \mathcal{A}_Y X_i) + \sum_{j=1}^{2r} g(\mathcal{T}_{U_j} X, \mathcal{T}_{U_j} Y) + g(\mathcal{T}_\xi X, \mathcal{T}_\xi Y) + \lambda g(X, Y)$$
$$+ \mu \eta(X) \eta(Y) = 0.$$

Since $\eta(X) = 0$, for any horizontal vector field X and if one of the conditions of Lemma 1 is satisfied, Equation (21) gives

$$Ric'(X', Y') \circ \pi + \lambda g(X, Y) = 0$$

which is equivalent to

$$\left(Ric'(X', Y') + \lambda g'(X', Y')\right) \circ \pi = 0$$

for any vector fields X', Y' on $\Gamma(TB)$. Hence,

$$Ric' + \lambda g' = 0$$

is satisfied, which means that (*i*) is obtained.

(*ii*) One proof is provided in the following.

Since the total space M admits an η-Ricci soliton with vertical potential field v, from (1), we can write

$$\frac{1}{2}\{g(\nabla_U v, W) + g(\nabla_W v, U)\} + Ric(U, W) + \lambda g(U, W) + \mu \eta(U) \eta(W) = 0, \qquad (22)$$

for any $U, W \in \Gamma(\mathcal{V})$. Using (6) in (22), it follows that

$$\frac{1}{2}\{g(\hat{\nabla}_U v, W) + g(\hat{\nabla}_W v, U)\} + Ric(U, W) + \lambda g(U, W) + \mu \eta(U) \eta(W) = 0. \qquad (23)$$

Applying (16) to Equation (23) gives

$$\frac{1}{2}(\mathcal{L}_v \hat{g})(U, W) + \hat{Ric}(U, W) + g(\mathcal{N}, \mathcal{T}_U W) - \sum_{i=1}^{2n}\left\{g((\nabla_{X_i}\mathcal{T})(U, W), X_i)\right.$$
$$\left. + g(\mathcal{A}_{X_i} U, \mathcal{A}_{X_i} W)\right\} - g((\nabla_\xi \mathcal{T})(U, W), \xi) - g(\mathcal{A}_\xi U, \mathcal{A}_\xi W) \qquad (24)$$
$$+ \lambda g(U, W) + \mu \eta(U) \eta(W) = 0.$$

Since one of the conditions in Lemma 1 is satisfied, Equation (24) is equivalent to

$$\frac{1}{2}(\mathcal{L}_v \hat{g})(U,W) + \hat{Ric}(U,W) + \lambda \hat{g}(U,W) + \mu \eta(U)\eta(W) = 0,$$

which means that any fibre of π is an η-Ricci soliton, and the proof is complete. □

Using Lemma 2, we give the following theorem.

Theorem 2. *Let $(M, g, \xi, \lambda, \eta)$ be an η-Ricci soliton with horizontal potential field v and let $\pi : M \to B$ be a contact-complex Riemannian submersion. If one of the conditions in Lemma 1 is satisfied, then any fibre of π is η-Einstein.*

Proof. Case I. For any vertical vector fields $U, W \neq \xi$, we can write

$$\frac{1}{2}(\mathcal{L}_v g)(U,W) + Ric(U,W) + \lambda g(U,W) + \mu \eta(U)\eta(W) = 0, \quad (25)$$

for any vertical vector fields U, W. Using (7) in the Lie-derivative of (25), one has

$$\begin{aligned}\frac{1}{2}(\mathcal{L}_v g)(U,W) &= \frac{1}{2}\{g(\nabla_U v, W) + g(\nabla_W v, U)\} \\ &= \frac{1}{2}\{g(\mathcal{T}_U v, W) + g(\mathcal{T}_W v, U)\} \\ &= 0,\end{aligned}$$

and since Lemma 1 is satisfied, the tensor field $\mathcal{T} \equiv 0$. In addition, putting (16) into Equation (25) gives

$$\hat{Ric}(U,W) + g(\mathcal{N}, \mathcal{T}_U W) - \sum_i \{g((\nabla_{X_i}\mathcal{T})(U,W), X_i) + g(\mathcal{A}_{X_i} U, \mathcal{A}_{X_i} W)\}$$
$$+ \lambda g(U,W) + \mu \eta(U)\eta(W) = 0,$$

which means that

$$\hat{Ric}(U,W) + \lambda \hat{g}(U,W) + \mu \eta(U)\eta(W) = 0. \quad (26)$$

Case II. For any vertical vector field $U \neq \xi$, Equation (1) gives

$$\frac{1}{2}\{g(\nabla_U v, \xi) + g(\nabla_\xi v, U)\} + Ric(U,\xi) + \lambda g(U,\xi) + \mu \eta(U)\eta(\xi) = 0.$$

Then, it follows that

$$Ric(U,\xi) + \lambda g(U,\xi) + \mu \eta(U)\eta(\xi) = 0. \quad (27)$$

Using (19) in (27) gives

$$\hat{Ric}(U,\xi) + g(\mathcal{N}, \mathcal{T}_U \xi) - \sum_i \{g((\nabla_{X_i}\mathcal{T})(U,\xi), X_i) + g(\mathcal{A}_{X_i} U, \mathcal{A}_{X_i} \xi)\}$$
$$+ \lambda g(U,\xi) + \mu \eta(U)\eta(\xi) = 0.$$

Since $\mathcal{T} \equiv 0$, the last equality is equivalent to

$$\hat{Ric}(U,\xi) + \lambda g(U,\xi) + \mu \eta(U)\eta(\xi) = 0. \quad (28)$$

Case III. Finally, choosing $U = W = \xi$, Equation (1) gives

$$g(\nabla_\xi v, \xi) + Ric(\xi,\xi) + \lambda g(\xi,\xi) + \mu \eta(\xi)\eta(\xi) = 0.$$

Through similar calculations, we have

$$Ric(\xi,\xi) + \lambda g(\xi,\xi) + \mu \eta(\xi)\eta(\xi) = 0.$$

Applying (18) to the last equality and using the vanishing of the tensor field $\mathcal{T}$ gives

$$\hat{Ric}(\xi,\xi) + \lambda \hat{g}(\xi,\xi) + \mu \eta(\xi)\eta(\xi) = 0 \qquad (29)$$

is obtained.

As a result of equalities (26), (28), and (29), we obtain that any fibre of π is η-Einstein. □

Considering Equation (29), we can give the following corollary.

Corollary 1. *Let $(M, g, \xi, \lambda, \eta)$ be an η-Ricci soliton with horizontal potential field v and let $\pi : M \to B$ be a contact-complex Riemannian submersion. If one of the conditions in Lemma 1 is satisfied, then the Ricci tensor of the distribution $Span\{\xi\}$ is given by*

$$\hat{Ric}(\xi,\xi) = -(\lambda + \mu).$$

Theorem 3. *Let $(M, g, \xi, \lambda, \eta)$ be an η-Ricci soliton with a horizontal potential field v and let $\pi : M \to B$ be a contact-complex Riemannian submersion. If one of the conditions in Lemma 1 is satisfied, then the base manifold B admits a Ricci soliton with potential field v' such that $\pi_* v = v'$.*

Proof. For any horizontal vector fields X, Y, we can write

$$\frac{1}{2}\{g(\nabla_X v, Y) + g(\nabla_Y v, X)\} + Ric(X,Y) + \lambda g(X,Y) + \mu \eta(X)\eta(Y) = 0. \qquad (30)$$

Since the vector fields X, Y are horizontal, we get $\eta(X) = \eta(Y) = 0$. Then, it follows that

$$\frac{1}{2}\{g(\nabla_X v, Y) + g(\nabla_Y v, X)\} + Ric(X,Y) + \lambda g(X,Y) = 0. \qquad (31)$$

In addition, using (19) in (31), one has

$$\frac{1}{2}\{g(\nabla_X v, Y) + g(\nabla_Y v, X)\} + Ric'(X',Y') \circ \pi + 2 \sum_{i=1}^{2n} g(\mathcal{A}_X X_i, \mathcal{A}_Y X_i)$$
$$+ \sum_{j=1}^{2r} g(\mathcal{T}_{U_j} X, \mathcal{T}_{U_j} Y) + g(\mathcal{T}_\xi X, \mathcal{T}_\xi Y) + \lambda g(X,Y) = 0.$$

Since Lemma 1 is satisfied, it follows that

$$\frac{1}{2}\{g(\nabla_X v, Y) + g(\nabla_Y v, X)\} + Ric'(X',Y') \circ \pi + \lambda g(X,Y) = 0. \qquad (32)$$

Moreover, considering Proposition 1, Equation (32) gives

$$\frac{1}{2}\{g'(\nabla'_{X'} v', Y') \circ \pi + g'(\nabla'_{Y'} v', X') \circ \pi\} + Ric'(X',Y') \circ \pi$$
$$+ \lambda g'(X',Y') \circ \pi = 0,$$

for any $X', Y' \in \Gamma(TB)$. Then, the last equation is equivalent to

$$\frac{1}{2}\left(\mathcal{L}_{v'} g'\right)(X',Y') + Ric'(X',Y') + \lambda g'(X',Y') = 0,$$

where the vector field v on M is π-related to v' on B. Therefore, the base manifold B admits a Ricci soliton with potential field v'. □

Theorem 4. *Let $(M, g, \xi, \lambda, \eta)$ be an η-Ricci soliton with horizontal potential field v and let $\pi : M \to B$ be a contact-complex Riemannian submersion with totally umbilical fibres. If the horizontal distribution $\mathcal{H}$ is integrable, then any fibre of π is η-Einstein.*

Proof. Since the total space M admits an η-Ricci soliton, one has

$$\frac{1}{2}\left(\mathcal{L}_v g\right)(U, W) + Ric(U, W) + \lambda g(U, W) + \mu \eta(U)\eta(W) = 0, \tag{33}$$

for any vertical vector fields U, W. Putting (16) into the last equation gives

$$\frac{1}{2}\Big(g(\nabla_U v, W) + g(\nabla_W U)\Big) + \hat{Ric}(U, W) + g(\mathcal{N}, \mathcal{T}_U W)$$
$$-\sum_{i=1}^{2n}\Big\{g((\nabla_{X_i}\mathcal{T})(U, W), X_i) + g(\mathcal{A}_{X_i}U, \mathcal{A}_{X_i}W)\Big\} + \lambda g(U, W)$$
$$+\mu\eta(U)\eta(W) = 0.$$

In addition, the horizontal distribution $\mathcal{H}$ is integrable, and it follows that

$$\frac{1}{2}\Big(g(\nabla_U v, W) + g(\nabla_W U)\Big) + \hat{Ric}(U, W) + g(\mathcal{N}, \mathcal{T}_U W)$$
$$-\sum_{i=1}^{2n}\Big\{g((\nabla_{X_i}\mathcal{T})(U, W), X_i) + \lambda g(U, W) + \mu\eta(U)\eta(W) = 0.$$

Since any fibre of π is totally umbilical and by using Equations (6), (12), and (13) in the last equality, one has

$$\frac{1}{2}\Big(g(\mathcal{T}_U v, W) + g(\mathcal{T}_W v, U)\Big) + \hat{Ric}(U, W) + (2r+1)\|H\|^2 g(U, W)$$
$$-\check{\delta}(H)g(U, W) + \lambda g(U, W) + \mu\eta(U)\eta(W) = 0.$$

Using (4) and (5), we get

$$\hat{Ric}(U, W) + \Big\{(2r+1)\|H\|^2 + \check{\delta}(H) - g(H, v) + \lambda\Big\}g(U, W)$$
$$+\mu\eta(U)\eta(W) = 0,$$

which gives that any fibre of π is η-Einstein. □

5. Conclusions

The paper deals with an interesting concept, of a contact-complex Riemannian submersion, which puts in relation the almost contact metric structure from the domain manifold, to the almost Hermitian structure of the target manifold. The fundamental properties of the Riemannian submersions are used here to link some geometric feature on the domain manifold, with the ones on fibres and with those on the base manifold. We provide several new results, showing mainly when the base manifold admits a Ricci soliton, when it is Einstein, when the fibres are η-Ricci solitons, and when they are η-Einstein. Our future study will be developed on certain well known manifolds on which we may apply the above theory.

Author Contributions: Conceptualization, C.-L.B., Ş.E.M. and E.K.; methodology, C.-L.B., Ş.E.M. and E.K.; software, C.-L.B. and Ş.E.M.; validation, C.-L.B., Ş.E.M. and E.K.; formal analysis, C.-L.B. and Ş.E.M.; investigation, C.-L.B., Ş.E.M. and E.K.; resources, C.-L.B., Ş.E.M. and E.K.; data curation, C.-L.B., Ş.E.M. and E.K.; writing—original draft preparation, C.-L.B. and Ş.E.M.; writing—review and editing, C.-L.B., Ş.E.M. and E.K.; visualization,C.-L.B. and Ş.E.M.; supervision, E.K.; project administration, E.K. All authors have read and agreed to the published version of the manuscript.

Funding: This research received no external funding.

Institutional Review Board Statement: Not applicable.

Informed Consent Statement: Not applicable.

Data Availability Statement: Not applicable.

Acknowledgments: The authors deeply thank all three referees for valuable suggestions, that are used here. To the memory of Aurel Bejancu (1946–2020).

Conflicts of Interest: The authors declare no conflict of interest.

References

1. Hamilton, R.S. The Ricci flow on surfaces, Mathematics and General Relativity (Santa Cruz, CA, 1986). *Contemp. Math. Am. Math. Soc.* **1988**, *71*, 237–262.
2. Cho, J.T.; Kimura, A. Ricci Solitons and Lagrangian Submanifolds in Kaehler Manifolds. *Mem. Fac. Sci. Eng. Shimane Univ. Ser. B Math. Sci.* **2010**, *43*, 27–32.
3. Chen, B.-Y.; Deshmukh, S. Ricci solitons and concurrent vector fields. *Balkan J. Geom. Appl.* **2015**, *20*, 14–25.
4. Chen, B.-Y. Concircular vector fields and pseudo-Kähler manifolds. *Kragujev. J. Math.* **2016**, *40*, 7–14. [CrossRef]
5. Yüksel Perktaş, S.; Keleş, S. Ricci solitons in 3-dimensional normal almost paracontact metric manifolds. *Int. Electron. J. Geom.* **2015**, *8*, 34–45. [CrossRef]
6. Yoldaş, H.I.; Eken Meriç, Ş.; Yaşar, E. On generic submanifold of Sasakian manifold with concurrent vector field. *Commun. Fac. Sci. Univ. Ank. Ser. A1 Math. Stat.* **2019**, *68*, 1983–1994. [CrossRef]
7. Bejan, C.-L.; Eken Meriç, Ş. Conformality on Semi-Riemannian Manifolds. *Mediterr. J. Math.* **2016**, *13*, 2185–2198. [CrossRef]
8. Bejan, C.-L.; Eken Meriç, Ş.; Kiliç, E. Gradient Weyl-Ricci soliton. *Turk. J. Math.* **2020**, *44*, 1137–1145. [CrossRef]
9. Gray, A. Pseudo-Riemannian almost product manifolds and submersions. *J. Math. Mech.* **1967**, *16*, 715–737.
10. O'Neill, B. The fundamental equations of a Riemannian submersions. *Mich. Math. J.* **1966**, *13*, 459–469.
11. Şahin, B. *Riemannian Submersions, Riemannian Maps in Hermitian Geometry, and Their Applications*; Elsevier Academic: Amsterdam, The Netherlands, 2017.
12. Yadav, A.; Meena, K. Riemannian maps whose total manifolds admit a Ricci soliton. *J. Geom. Phys.* **2021**, *168*, 104317. [CrossRef]
13. Falcitelli, M.; Ianus, S.; Pastore, A.M. *Riemannian Submersions and Related Topics*; World Scientific Publishing Co. Pte. Ltd.: Singapore, 2004.
14. Blair, D.E. *Contact Manifolds in Riemannian Geometry*; Lecture Notes in Mathematics, 509; Springer: Berlin, Germany, 1976.
15. Eken Meriç, Ş.; Kılıç, E. Riemannian submersions whose total manifolds admit a Ricci soliton. *Int. J. Geom. Methods Mod. Phys.* **2019**, *16*, 1950196. [CrossRef]

Article

On the Topology of Warped Product Pointwise Semi-Slant Submanifolds with Positive Curvature

Yanlin Li [1,†], Ali H. Alkhaldi [2,†], Akram Ali [2,*,†] and Pişcoran Laurian-Ioan [3]

1 School of Mathematics, Hangzhou Normal University, Hangzhou 311121, China; liyl@hznu.edu.cn
2 Department of Mathematics, College of Science, King Khalid University, Abha 61413, Saudi Arabia; ahalkhaldi@kku.edu.sa
3 Department of Mathematics and Computer Science, North University Center of Baia Mare, Technical University of Cluj Napoca, 430122 Baia Mare, Romania; Laurian.PISCORAN@mi.utluj.ro
* Correspondence: akali@kku.edu.sa
† These authors contributed equally to this work.

Abstract: In this paper, we obtain some topological characterizations for the warping function of a warped product pointwise semi-slant submanifold of the form $\Omega^n = N_T^l \times_f N_\phi^k$ in a complex projective space $\mathbb{C}P^{2m}(4)$. Additionally, we will find certain restrictions on the warping function f, Dirichlet energy function $\mathbb{E}(f)$, and first non-zero eigenvalue λ_1 to prove that stable l-currents do not exist and also that the homology groups have vanished in Ω^n. As an application of the non-existence of the stable currents in Ω^n, we show that the fundamental group $\pi_1(\Omega^n)$ is trivial and Ω^n is simply connected under the same extrinsic conditions. Further, some similar conclusions are provided for CR-warped product submanifolds.

Keywords: warped product submanifolds; complex projective spaces; homology groups; homotopy; sphere theorems; stable currents; kinetic energy

1. Introduction and Main Results

A classical challenge in Riemannian geometry is to discuss the geometrical and topological structures of submanifolds. The stable currents and homology groups are the most important characterizations of the Riemannian submanifolds because they control the behavior of the topology of submanifolds. The notion of non-existence stable current and vanishing homology on pinching the second fundamental form was introduced by Lawson-Simons [1]. Xin proved in [2] as the following important form:

Theorem 1 ([1,2]). *Suppose Ω^n is a compact n-dimensional submanifold in a space form $\widetilde{\Omega}(c)$ of curvature $c \geq 0$. Suppose l, k is any positive integer, that is, $l + k = n$, and the inequality*

$$\sum_{A=1}^{l} \sum_{B=l+1}^{n} \left\{ 2||h(e_A, e_B)||^2 - g(h(e_A, e_A), h(e_B, e_B)) \right\} < lkc \qquad (1)$$

holds for all orthonormal basis $\{e_i, \cdots, e_n\}$ of the tangent space $T\Omega^n$; then there are no stable l-currents in Ω^n and

$$\mathbb{H}_l(M^n, \mathbb{G}) = \mathbb{H}_{n-l=k}(\Omega^n, \mathbb{G}) = 0,$$

where $\mathbb{H}_i(\Omega^n, \mathbb{G})$ stands for i integral homology groups of Ω^n, while $\mathbb{G}$ is a finite abelian group with integer coefficients.

The generalized Poincaré conjecture for dimension $n \geq 5$ was proved by Smale [3] by using the nonexistence for the stable currents over compact submanifolds on a sphere. Then, Lawson and Simons obtained the striking sphere theorem in [1], in which they showed that an n-dimensional compact-oriented submanifold Ω^n in the unit sphere $\mathbb{S}^{n+k}$

is homeomorphic to the sphere $\mathbb{S}^n$ with $n \neq 3$, provided that the second fundamental form was bounded above by a constant that depends on the dimension n. Additionally, it was proved that Ω^3 is homotopic to the sphere $\mathbb{S}^3$. Using Theorem 1, Leung [4] proved that for a compact connected oriented submanifold Ω^n in the unit sphere $\mathbb{S}^{n+k}$ with $\|h(X,X)\|^2 < \frac{1}{3}$ thus Ω^n is homeomorphic to the sphere $\mathbb{S}^n$ in the case $n \neq 3$, and also that Ω^3 is homotopic to a sphere $\mathbb{S}^3$. More recently, geometric, topological, and differentiable rigidity theorems of the Riemannian submanifold connecting to parallel mean curvature in space forms such that $c + H^2 > 0$ have been obtained in terms of Ricci curvature in [5]. In some articles such as [3,6–17], several results have been derived on topological and differentiable structures of singular submanifolds and submanifolds with specific effective conditions for the second fundamental form, sectional curvatures, and Ricci curvatures.

However, very few topological obstructions to warped product submanifolds with positive sectional curvature are known; for example, Sahin et al. [13] verified some outcomes for the non-existence of the stable current and vanishing homology groups into a contact CR-warped product which immersed in a sphere with an odd dimension, by putting suitable restrictions on the Laplacian and the gradient of the warping function. Taking the benefits of the constant section curvature which could be zero or one, Sahin [13,14] extended this study on a class of CR-warped product in an Euclidean space and in the nearly Kaehler six-sphere. By assuming negative constant section curvature, Ali et al. [18–20] obtained various results on CR-warped product, especially on the complex hyperbolic spaces, and many structures about this subject remain open.

Therefore, we shall study the warped product pointwise semi-slant submanifolds of complex projective spaces where the constant sectional curvature $c = 4 > 0$ is positive. More specifically, our motivation comes from the studies of Sahin [21]. In that paper, Sahin investigated the warped product pointwise semi-slant submanifolds in a Kähler manifold, and also showed that the warped product pointwise semi-slant of form $N_T^l \times_f N_\phi^k$ is nontrivial. It was shown by the Ref. [21] that the warped product pointwise semi-slant submanifold $N_T^l \times_f N_\phi^k$ of Kähler manifold generalized the CR-warped products [22] and the angle ϕ is treated as a slant function. In this case, suppose $\mathbb{C}^* = \mathbb{C} - \{0\}$ and $\mathbb{C}_*^{m+1} = \mathbb{C}^{m+1} - \{0\}$. Additionally, assuming that the action $\mathbb{C}^*$ on $\mathbb{C}_*^{m+1}$ can be expressed using γ, which means $(z_0, z_1, \ldots, z_m) = (\gamma z_0, \gamma z_1, \ldots, \gamma z_m)$, then all equivalent classes set are produced from this idea are represented using $\mathbb{C}P^m$. If we denote with $\pi(z)$, the equivalent classes which contains z, then $\mathbb{C}_*^{m+1} \to \mathbb{C}P^m$ is a surjection, and it is well-known that $\mathbb{C}P^m$ endowed a complex structure derived by the complex construction of $\mathbb{C}^{m+1}$ with a Kähler metric such that the constant holomorphic sectional curvature is equal to 4 [23]. We can observe that the almost complex J on $\mathbb{C}P^m(4)$ is determined by the almost complex construction of $\mathbb{C}^{m+1}$ via the Hopf fibration. Let us now recall introduce the following Theorem 1.

Theorem 2. *Let $\Omega^n = N_T^l \times_f N_\phi^k$ be a compact warped product pointwise semi-slant submanifold with regard to the complex projective space $\mathbb{C}P^{2m}(4)$, which satisfies the following condition*

$$f\Delta f + (\csc^2 \phi + \cot^2 \phi + k)\|\nabla f\|^2 < \left(3l - \frac{\|h_\mu\|^2}{k}\right)f^2, \qquad (2)$$

where ∇f and Δf are the gradient and the Laplacian of the warped function f, respectively. Then we have the following:

(a) *The warped product submanifold Ω^n does not exist for any stable integral l-currents.*

(b) *The i integral homology groups of Ω^n with integer coefficients vanish; that is,*

$$\mathbb{H}_l(\Omega^n, \mathbb{G}) = \mathbb{H}_k(\Omega^n, \mathbb{G}) = 0.$$

(c) *The finite fundamental group $\pi_1(\Omega)$ is null, that is, $\pi_1(\Omega) = 0$. Moreover, Ω^n is a simply connected warped product manifold.*

Remark 1. To apply Theorem 2, suppose the slant function ϕ becomes globally constant, setting $\phi = \frac{\pi}{2}$ from [24]. Then, the pointwise slant submanifold N_ϕ^k turns into a totally real submanifold $N_\perp^k$. Thus, a warped product pointwise semi-slant submanifold $\Omega^n = N_T^l \times_f N_\phi^k$ turns to CR-warped products within a Kähler manifold of the type $\Omega^n = N_T^l \times_f N_\perp^k$ such that N_T^l, as well as $N_\perp^k$ are holomorphic and totally real submanifolds, respectively [22].

Therefore, we deduce the following result from Theorem 2 and Remark 1 for the non-existence of stable integrable l-currents and homology groups in the CR-warped product submanifolds of the complex projective space $\mathbb{C}P^{2m}(4)$.

Corollary 1. Let $\Omega^n = N_T^l \times_f N_\perp^q$ be a compact CR-warped product submanifold of the complex projective space $\mathbb{C}P^{2m}(4)$. In this case, the following conditions occur:

$$f\Delta f + (1+k)\|\nabla f\|^2 < \left(3l - \frac{\|h_\mu\|^2}{k}\right)f^2. \tag{3}$$

Then we have the following:

(a) For the CR-warped product submanifold, Ω^n does not have any stable integral l-currents.
(b) The i integral homology groups of Ω^n with integer coefficients vanish; that is,

$$\mathbb{H}_l(\Omega^n, \mathbb{G}) = \mathbb{H}_k(\Omega^n, \mathbb{G}) = 0.$$

(c) The finite fundamental group $\pi_1(\Omega)$ is null, that is, $\pi_1(\Omega) = 0$. Moreover, Ω^n is a simply connected warped product manifold.

Other important motivation for our study comes from the Ref. [25], where some geometric mechanics on Riemannian manifolds were studied. From that study, we found that for a positive differentiable function φ ($\varphi \in \mathcal{F}(\Omega^n)$) defined at a compact Riemannian manifold Ω, the *Dirichlet energy* of that function φ is given as in see [25] (p. 41), as follows:

$$\mathbb{E}(\varphi) = \frac{1}{2}\int_{\Omega^n} \|\nabla \varphi\|^2 dV \qquad 0 < E(\varphi) < \infty. \tag{4}$$

Using the Dirichlet energy Formula (4) for a compact manifold without a boundary, as well as Theorem 2, we give the next theorem:

Theorem 3. Under similar suppositions as in Theorem 2 with satisfied pinching condition

$$\mathbb{E}(f) < \frac{1}{(4\csc^2\phi + 2k)}\int_{\Omega^n}\left(3l - \frac{\|h_\mu\|^2}{k}\right)f^2 dV. \tag{5}$$

Thus, the following properties hold:

(a) For the warped product submanifold Ω^n, there are no stable integral l-currents.
(b) The i integral homology groups of Ω^n with integer coefficients vanished; that is,

$$\mathbb{H}_l(\Omega^n, \mathbb{G}) = \mathbb{H}_k(\Omega^n, \mathbb{G}) = 0,$$

(c) The finite fundamental group $\pi_1(\Omega)$ is null, that is, $\pi_1(\Omega) = 0$. Moreover, Ω^n is a simply connected warped product manifold.

Using the result of Theorem 3, we can now recall the next sphere theorem for the compact oriented CR-warped product submanifold of a complex projective space $\mathbb{C}P^{2m}(4)$ due to Chen [22], that is,

Corollary 2. Let $M^n = N_T^p \times_f N_\perp^q$ be a compact CR-warped product submanifold at a complex projective space $\mathbb{C}P^{2m}(4)$ satisfying

$$\mathbb{E}(f) < \left(\frac{1}{2(2+k)}\right) \int_{\Omega^n} \left(3l - \frac{\|h_\mu\|^2}{k}\right) f^2 dV. \tag{6}$$

Then, the following properties are satisfied:
(a) For the warped product submanifold Ω^n, there are no stable integral l-currents.
(b) The i integral homology groups of Ω^n with integer coefficients vanished; that is,

$$\mathbb{H}_l(\Omega^n, \mathbb{G}) = \mathbb{H}_k(\Omega^n, \mathbb{G}) = 0.$$

(c) The finite fundamental group $\pi_1(\Omega)$ is null, that is, $\pi_1(\Omega) = 0$. Moreover, Ω^n is simply connected warped product manifold.

Let Ω^n be an n-dimensional compact Riemannian manifold, and therefore, the Laplacian is a second-order quasilinear operator on Ω^n, given as

$$\Delta \varphi = -div(\nabla \varphi). \tag{7}$$

For such a Laplacian, we can found many applications in mathematics as well as in physics, and this is possible due to the eigenvalue problem of Δ. The corresponding Laplace eigenvalue equation is defined as follows: a real number λ is named eigenvalue if it is a non-vanishing function φ, which satisfies the following equation:

$$\Delta \varphi = \lambda \varphi, \quad \text{on } \Omega^n, \tag{8}$$

with appropriate boundary conditions. Considering a Riemannian manifold Ω^n with no boundary, the first nonzero eigenvalue of Δ, defined as λ_1, includes variational properties (cf. [26]):

$$\lambda_1 = \inf \left\{ \frac{\int_\Omega \|\nabla \varphi\|^2 dV}{\int_\Omega \|\varphi\|^2 dV} \mid \varphi \in W^{1,2}(\Omega^n) \setminus \{0\}, \int_\Omega \varphi dV = 0 \right\}. \tag{9}$$

Inspired by the above characterization, using the first non-zero eigenvalue of the Laplace operator and the maximum principle for the first non-zero eigenvalue λ_1, we deduce the following:

Theorem 4. Let $\Omega^n = N_T^l \times_f N_\phi^k$ be compact, oriented warped product pointwise semi-slant submanifolds of the complex projective space $\mathbb{C}P^{2m}(4)$; that is, f is a non-constant eigenfunction of the first non-zero eigenvalue λ_1. Assume that

$$\lambda_1 < \left(\frac{\int_{\Omega^n} \left(3l - \frac{\|h_\mu\|^2}{k}\right) f^2 dV}{(2 \csc^2 \phi + k) \int_{\Omega^n} f^2 dV} \right) \tag{10}$$

holds. Then the properties (a), (b), and (c) of Theorem 2 are satisfied.

Remark 2. Some important applications of this theory can be found for the singularity structure in liquid crystals, in the system in statistical mechanics with low dimensions, and physical phase transitions (see [27]). In addition, general relativity contains warped product manifolds as a model of space-times. There are two famous warped product spaces. One is the generalization of Robertson-Walker space-times, and the other is the standard static space-times [17,28–31]. General relativity depends heavily on the differential topological methods, especially in mathematical physics, and particularly regarding the way that the space-time homology is used in in quantum gravity [13,17]. On the other hand, the formulation of a theory which unifies quantum mechanics and the special theory of relativity, performed by Dirac nearly a century ago, required introduction of new mathematical and physical concepts which led to models that, on one hand, have been very successful in terms of the interpretation of physical reality but, on the other, still creates some challenges, both conceptual and computational. A central notion of relativistic quantum mechanics is a construct known as the Dirac operator. It may be defined as the result of factorization of a second-order differential operator in the Minkowski space. The eigenvalues of the Dirac operator on a curved spacetime are diffeomorphism-invariant functions of the geometry. They form an innite set of observables for general relativity. Some recent work suggests that they can be taken as variables for an invariant description of the gravitational field's dynamics. Because this paper is connected to both warped product manifold and homotopy-homology theory, its results can be used as physical applications.

2. Some Important Background

This part includes some notations and definitions that is important to the work relay essentially on [18,21,22]. Suppose $\mathbb{C}P^m$ is a m-dimensional complex projective space among the Fubini-Study metric g_{FS} with J being its almost complex structure. In the case where the Levi-Civita connection is defined using $\widetilde{\nabla}$, the Fubini-Study metric is Kähler, that is, $\widetilde{\nabla} J = 0$. A Kähler manifold $\widetilde{\Omega}^m$ for a positive constant sectional curvature $c = 4 > 0$ is named a complex projective space $\mathbb{C}P^m(4)$ and can be endowed with the Fubini-Study metric g_{FS}. Therefore, the curvature tensor $\widetilde{R}$ of $\mathbb{C}P^m(4)$ is given as:

$$\widetilde{R}(U_1, U_2, V_1, V_2) = g(U_1, V_2)g(U_2, V_1) - g(U_1, V_1)g(U_2, V_2) \\ + g(JU_1, V_2)g(JU_2, V_1) - g(JU_2, V_2)g(JU_1, V_1) \\ + 2g(U_1, JU_2)g(JV_1, V_2), \quad (11)$$

for all $U_1, U_2, V_1, V_2 \in \mathfrak{X}(CP^m(4))$. Assume that Ω^n is an isometrically immersed to an almost Hermitian manifold $\widetilde{\Omega}^m$ among the induced metric g. The Gauss equation of the submanifold Ω^n is determined by:

$$\widetilde{R}(U_1, U_2, V_1, V_2) = R(U_1, U_2, V_1, V_2) + g(h(U_1, V_1), h(U_2, V_2)) \\ - g(h(U_1, V_2), h(U_2, V_1)), \quad (12)$$

where $\widetilde{R}$ and R are curvature tensors at $\widetilde{M}^m$ and Ω^n, in the same order. The definition of mean curvature vector H of the orthonormal frame $\{e_1, e_2, \cdots e_n\}$ of the tangent space TM on Ω^n is given as

$$H = \frac{1}{n} trace(h) = \frac{1}{n} \sum_{i=1}^{n} h(e_A, e_A), \quad (13)$$

where $n = \dim \Omega$.

$$h_{AB}^r = g(h(e_A, e_B), e_r), \quad ||h||^2 = \sum_{A,B=1}^{n} g(h(e_A, e_B), h(e_A, e_B)). \quad (14)$$

The gradient positive function φ defined on Ω^n and its squared norm is written as:

$$\nabla \varphi = \sum_{i=1}^{n} e_i(\varphi) e_i, \quad \text{and} \quad ||\nabla \varphi||^2 = \sum_{i=1}^{n} ((\varphi) e_i)^2. \quad (15)$$

We will provide some short definitions of different classes of submanifold Ω^n according to J conserves all tangent spaces of Ω^n, such that

(i) Ω^n is *holomorphic* submanifold if $J(T_x\Omega) \subseteq T_x\Omega$ [22].
(ii) Ω^n is named *totally real* submanifold in the case where $J(T_x\Omega) \subseteq T_x^\perp \Omega$ [22].
(iii) Combining (i) and (ii) such that $T\Omega = \mathcal{D}^T \oplus \mathcal{D}^\perp$, then Ω^n is a CR-submanifold [22].

(iv) In the case where the angle $\phi(X)$ is enclosed by JX and the tangent space is $T_x\Omega$ for any vector field X of Ω^n that is not equal to zero, it is a real-valued function such that $\phi : \Omega \to \mathbb{R}$, then Ω^n is called a pointwise slant submanifold (more details in [24]). In the same paper, the authors provided a necessary and sufficient condition for Ω^n to be a pointwise slant $T^2X = -\cos^2\phi X$, where T is tangential $(1,1)$ tensor field [24].

(v) If the tangent space $T\Omega$ is introduced as a decomposition in the form of $T\Omega = \mathcal{D}^T \oplus \mathcal{D}^\phi$ for $J(\mathcal{D}^T) \subseteq \mathcal{D}^T$ and pointwise slant distribution $\mathcal{D}^\phi$, then Ω^n is classified as a pointwise semi-slant submanifold [21]. For some examples of pointwise semi-slant submanifolds in a Kähler manifold, and related problems, we recommend the Ref. [18,21].

Regarding the above study, we give some remarks as follows.

Remark 3. *If we consider a slant function $\phi : \Omega^n \to R$ that is globally constant on Ω^n and $\phi = \frac{\pi}{2}$, thus, Ω^n is named a CR-submanifold.*

Remark 4. *In the case where a slant function is $\phi : \Omega^n \to (0, \frac{\pi}{2})$, then Ω^n is called a proper pointwise semi-slant submanifold.*

Remark 5. *The normal bundle $T^\perp\Omega$ of Ω is expressed as $T^\perp\Omega = F\mathcal{D}^\phi \oplus \mu$ with respect to invariant subspace μ, that is, $J(\mu) \subseteq \mu$.*

2.1. Warped Product Submanifolds

Warped product manifolds $\Omega^n = N_1^l \times_f N_2^k$ were originally initiated by Bishop and O'Neill [28], where N_1^l and N_2^k are two Riemannian manifolds and their Riemannain metrics are g_1 and g_2 in the same order. f is also a smooth function defined on N_1^l. The warped product manifold $\Omega^n = N_1^l \times_f N_2^k$ is the manifold $N_1^l \times N_2^k$ furnished by the Riemannian metric $g = g_1 + f^2 g_2$, and the function f is named a warping function of Ω^n. The following important consequences of the warped product manifolds are given in [28,29]. For all $U_1, U_2 \in \mathfrak{X}(TN_1)$ and $V_1, V_2 \in \mathfrak{X}(TN_2)$, where we have

$$\nabla_{V_1} U_1 = \nabla_{U_1} V_1 = \frac{(U_1 f)}{f} V_1. \tag{16}$$

$$\mathcal{R}(U_1, V_1)U_2 = \frac{\mathcal{H}^f(U_1, V_1)}{f} U_2, \tag{17}$$

where $\mathcal{H}^f$ is a Hessian tensor of f. Furthermore, we have

$$g(\nabla \ln f, X) = X(\ln f). \tag{18}$$

2.2. The Non-Trivial Warped Product Pointwise Semi-Slant Submanifolds

Based on the pointwise semi-slant submanifold definition, it is possible to define the warped product pointwise semi-slant submanifolds of a Kähler manifold as follows:

$$(i)\ N_\phi^k \times_f N_T^l, \quad \text{and} \quad (ii)\ N_T^l \times_f N_\phi^k.$$

We will consider the second type because the first type of $N_\phi^k \times_f N_T^l$ is trivial (see Theorem 4.1 in [21]). Additionally for the non-trivial case $N_T^l \times_f N_\phi^k$ with examples, see the Ref. [21]. This warped product pointwise semi-slant submanifold is interesting because it is a generalized CR-warped product [22]. The proofs of the main results are ready to be introduced as follows.

3. Proof of the Main Results
3.1. Proof of Theorem 2

Let $\Omega^n = N_T^l \times_f N_\phi^k$ be an $n = l + k$-dimensional warped product pointwise semi-slant submanifold with $\dim N_T^l = l = 2A$ and $\dim N_\phi^k = k = 2B$, where N_ϕ^k and N_T^l are integral manifolds of $\mathcal{D}^\phi$ and $\mathcal{D}$, in the same order. Then, $\{e_1, e_2, \cdots e_A, e_{A+1} = Je_1, \cdots e_{2A} = Je_A\}$ and $\{e_{2A+1} = e_1^*, \cdots e_{2A+B} = e_B^*, e_{2A+B+1} = e_{B+1}^* = \sec \phi Pe_1^*, \cdots e_{l+k} = e_k^* = \sec \phi Pe_B^*\}$ will be orthonormal frames of TN_T and TN_ϕ, in the same order. Therefore, the orthonormal basis of $F\mathcal{D}^\phi$ and μ are $\{e_{n+1} = \bar{e}_1 = \csc \phi Fe_1^*, \cdots e_{n+B} = \bar{e}_B = \csc \phi Fe_1^*, e_{n+B+1} = \bar{e}_{B+1} = \csc \phi \sec \phi FPe_1^*, \cdots e_{n+2B} = \bar{e}_{2B} = \csc \phi \sec \phi FPe_B^*\}$ and $\{e_{n+2B+1}, \cdots e_{2m}\}$, respectively. Then, we arrange the terms

$$\sum_{A=1}^{l} \sum_{B=1}^{k} \left\{ 2\|h(e_A, e_B)\|^2 - g(h(e_B, e_B), h(e_A, e_A)) \right\}$$

$$= \sum_{r=n+1}^{2m} \sum_{A=1}^{l} \sum_{B=1}^{k} g(h(e_A, e_B^*), e_r)$$

$$+ \sum_{A=1}^{l} \sum_{B=1}^{k} \left\{ \|h(e_A, e_B)\|^2 - g(h(e_B, e_B), h(e_A, e_A)) \right\}.$$

Then, from the Gauss Equation (12), we have

$$\sum_{A=1}^{l} \sum_{B=1}^{k} \left\{ 2\|h(e_A, e_B)\|^2 - g(h(e_B, e_B), h(e_A, e_A)) \right\}$$

$$= \sum_{A=1}^{l} \sum_{B=1}^{k} g(R(e_A, e_B)e_A, e_B) \tag{19}$$

$$- \sum_{A=1}^{l} \sum_{B=1}^{k} g(\tilde{R}(e_A, e_B)e_A, e_B)$$

$$+ \sum_{r=n+1}^{2m} \sum_{A=1}^{l} \sum_{B=1}^{k} g(h(e_A, e_B^*), e_r)^2,$$

Using the orthonormal frames $\{e_i\}_{1 \leq A \leq p}$ as well as $\{e_B\}_{1 \leq B \leq q}$ of N_T^l and N_ϕ^k, respectively, in (17), we derive

$$R(e_A, e_B)e_A = \frac{e_B}{f} \mathcal{H}^f(e_A, e_A).$$

Summing up, with respect to the orthonormal frame $\{e_B\}_{1 \leq B \leq q}$ in addition to taking into account the adoption of the opposite of the usual sign convention for the Laplacian, one obtains:

$$\sum_{A=1}^{l} \sum_{B=1}^{k} g(R(e_A, e_B)e_A, e_B) = -\frac{k}{f} \sum_{A=1}^{l} g(\nabla_{e_A} \nabla f, e_A). \tag{20}$$

Thus, from Equations (19) and (20), we derive

$$\sum_{A=1}^{l}\sum_{B=1}^{k}\left\{2\|h(e_A,e_B)\|^2 - g\big(h(e_B,e_B), h(e_A,e_A)\big)\right\}$$
$$= \sum_{r=n+1}^{2m}\sum_{A=1}^{l}\sum_{B=1}^{k} g\big(h(e_A, e_B^*), e_r\big)^2 \qquad (21)$$
$$- \sum_{A=1}^{l}\sum_{B=1}^{k} g\big(\widetilde{R}(e_A,e_B)e_A, e_B\big)$$
$$- \frac{k}{f}\sum_{A=1}^{l}\sum_{B=1}^{k} g(\nabla_{e_A}\nabla f, e_A).$$

Firstly, the term Δf for Ω^n is computed, which is originally the Laplacian of f.

$$\Delta f = -\sum_{i=1}^{n} g(\nabla_{e_i}\mathrm{grad} f, e_i)$$
$$= -\sum_{A=1}^{l} g(\nabla_{e_A}\mathrm{grad} f, e_A) - \sum_{B=1}^{k} g(\nabla_{e_B}\mathrm{grad} f, e_B).$$

The previous equation will be rewritten using components of N_ϕ^k for an adapted orthonormal frame. One obtains:

$$\Delta f = -\sum_{A=1}^{l} g(\nabla_{e_A}\mathrm{grad} f, e_A) - \sum_{j=1}^{B} g(\nabla_{e_j}\mathrm{grad} f, e_j)$$
$$- \sec^2\phi \sum_{j=1}^{B} g(\nabla_{Te_j}\mathrm{grad} f, Te_j).$$

It is noted that ∇ is a Levi-Civita connection on Ω^n, and N_T^l is also totally geodesic in M^n. It leads to $\mathrm{grad} f \in \mathfrak{X}(TN_T)$, and then we have

$$\frac{\Delta f}{f} = -\frac{k}{f}\sum_{A=1}^{l} g(\nabla_{e_A}\mathrm{grad} f, e_A) - k\|\nabla(\ln f)\|^2.$$

It is clear that the next equation is satisfied

$$-\frac{1}{f}\sum_{A=1}^{l} g(\nabla_{e_A}\mathrm{grad} f, e_A) = \Delta(\ln f) + (k-1)\|\nabla \ln f\|^2. \qquad (22)$$

This result, combined with (21) yields

$$\sum_{A=1}^{l}\sum_{B=1}^{k}\left\{2\|h(e_A,e_B)\|^2 - g\big(h(e_B,e_B), h(e_A,e_A)\big)\right\}$$
$$= \sum_{r=n+1}^{2m}\sum_{A=1}^{l}\sum_{B=1}^{k} g\big(h(e_A, e_B^*), e_r\big)^2 \qquad (23)$$
$$- \sum_{A=1}^{l}\sum_{B=1}^{k} g\big(\widetilde{R}(e_A,e_B)e_A, e_B\big)$$
$$+ k\Delta(\ln f) + k(k-1)\|\nabla \ln f\|^2.$$

At this point, suppose $X = e_A$ and $Z = e_B$ for $1 \leq A \leq l$ and $1 \leq B \leq k$, in the same order. Thus, by the use of the bilinear form h definition according to an orthonormal basis, we can write

$$\sum_{r=n+1}^{2m} \sum_{A=1}^{l} \sum_{B=1}^{k} g(h(e_A, e_B^*), e_r)^2 = \sum_{r=n+1}^{n+2B} \sum_{A=1}^{l} \sum_{B=1}^{k} g(h(e_A, e_B^*), e_r) + \|h_\mu\|^2.$$

In the previous equation, the first term at the right-hand side is a FD^ϕ-component, while the second term is a μ invariant subspace. From the viewpoint of an adapted orthonormal basis, vector fields of N_T^l and N_ϕ^k are summed up over the vector fields of N_T^l and N_ϕ^k. Then, using Lemma 5.2 from [21] and (Equation (5.8) of Lemma 5.3 in [21]), we conclude that

$$\sum_{r=n+1}^{2m} \sum_{A=1}^{l} \sum_{B=1}^{k} g(h(e_A, e_B^*), e_r)^2 = 2(\cot^2 \phi + \csc^2 \phi) \sum_{A=1}^{l} \sum_{B=1}^{k} (e_A \ln f)^2 g(e_B^*, e_B^*)^2$$
$$+ 2(\cot^2 \phi + \csc^2 \phi) \sum_{A=1}^{l} \sum_{B=1}^{k} (Je_A \ln f)^2 g(e_B^*, e_B^*)^2$$
$$+ \|h_\mu\|^2.$$

Using the squared norm definition of the gradient function f (15) (ii), one obtains:

$$\sum_{r=n+1}^{2m} \sum_{A=1}^{l} \sum_{B=1}^{k} g(h(e_A, e_B^*), e_r)^2 = k(\cot^2 \phi + \csc^2 \phi) \|\nabla \ln f\|^2 + \|h_\mu\|^2. \tag{24}$$

From (23) and (24), we get:

$$\sum_{A=1}^{l} \sum_{B=1}^{k} \left\{ 2\|h(e_A, e_B)\|^2 - g(h(e_B, e_B), h(e_A, e_A)) \right\}$$
$$= k\Delta(\ln f) + k(k-1)\|\nabla(\ln f)\|^2 \tag{25}$$
$$+ k(1 + 2\cot^2 \phi)\|\nabla(\ln f)\|^2 + \|h_\mu\|^2$$
$$- \sum_{A=1}^{l} \sum_{B=1}^{k} g(\widetilde{R}(e_A, e_B)e_A, e_B).$$

For the symmetry of the curvature tensor R, the following relation holds:

$$\sum_{A=1}^{l} \sum_{B=1}^{k} g(\widetilde{R}(e_A, e_B)e_A, e_B) = \sum_{A=1}^{l} \sum_{B=1}^{k} \widetilde{R}(e_A, e_B, e_A, e_B). \tag{26}$$

Next, we remark that the curvature tensor Formula (11) for the complex projective space $\mathbb{C}P^{2m}(4)$ is easily given as

$$\sum_{A=1}^{l} \sum_{B=1}^{k} \widetilde{R}(e_A, e_B, e_A, e_B) = \sum_{A=1}^{l} \sum_{B=1}^{k} \Big\{ g(e_A, e_B)g(e_B, e_A) - g(e_A, e_A)g(e_B, e_B)$$
$$- g(Je_A, e_A)g(Je_B, e_B) \tag{27}$$
$$+ 3g(Je_A, e_B)g(Je_B, e_A) \Big\}.$$

As we know, if $e_A \in \mathfrak{X}(TN_T)$ and $e_B \in \mathfrak{X}(TN_\phi)$, then $g(e_A, e_B) = 0$, and $g(Je_A, e_A) = 0$ (resp, $g(Je_B, e_B) = 0$), using $Je_A \perp e_A(Je_B \perp e_B)$, respectively. Similarly, from

(Equation (2.6) in [21]), we derive that $g(Je_A, e_B) = g(Te_A + Fe_A, e_B) = 0$ for $Te_A \in \mathfrak{X}(TN_T)$ and $Fe_A \in \mathfrak{X}(FN_\phi)$. Thus, (27) implies that

$$\sum_{A=1}^{l}\sum_{B=1}^{k} \widetilde{R}(e_A, e_B, e_A, e_B) = -\sum_{A=1}^{l}\sum_{B=1}^{k} g(e_A, e_A)g(e_B, e_B) = -lk \qquad (28)$$

Therefore, using (26) and (28), we finally get

$$\sum_{A=1}^{l}\sum_{B=1}^{k}\left\{2\|h(e_A,e_B)\|^2 - g(h(e_B,e_B), h(e_A,e_A))\right\}$$
$$= k\Delta(\ln f) + k(k-1)\|\nabla(\ln f)\|^2 + \|h_\mu\|^2 \qquad (29)$$
$$+ k\left(\cot^2\phi + \csc^2\phi\right)\|\nabla(\ln f)\|^2 + lk.$$

Now, computing $\Delta \ln f$, we get:

$$\Delta(lnf) = -div(\nabla(lnf)) = -div\left(\frac{\nabla f}{f}\right)$$
$$= -g(\nabla(\tfrac{1}{f}), \nabla f) + \tfrac{1}{f}\Delta f \qquad (30)$$
$$= \tfrac{1}{f^2}\|\nabla f\|^2 + \tfrac{1}{f}\Delta f.$$

Then, from (29) and (30), we find that

$$\sum_{A=1}^{l}\sum_{B=1}^{k}\left\{2\|h(e_A,e_B)\|^2 - g(h(e_B,e_B), h(e_A,e_A))\right\}$$
$$= \frac{k\Delta f}{f} + \frac{k\|\nabla f\|^2}{f^2}\left(\cot^2\phi + \csc^2\phi + k\right) \qquad (31)$$
$$+ lk + \|h_\mu\|^2.$$

Let the pinching condition (2) be satisfied. Then, from (31), we get

$$\sum_{A=1}^{l}\sum_{B=1}^{k}\left\{2\|h(e_A,e_B)\|^2 - g(h(e_B,e_B), h(e_A,e_A))\right\} < 4lk.$$

It well-known that constant sectional curvature for the complex projective spaces $\mathbb{C}P^{2m}(4)$ is equal to $c = 4$. Then, the last equation is implied:

$$\sum_{A=1}^{l}\sum_{B=1}^{k}\left\{2\|h(e_A,e_B)\|^2 - g(h(e_B,e_B), h(e_A,e_A))\right\} < lkc. \qquad (32)$$

Therefore, using Theorem 1, we reached our promised results (a) and (b). For the third part, let us assume that $\pi_1(\Omega) \neq 0$. From the compactness of Ω^n, it follows from the classical theorem of Cartan and Hadamard that there is a minimal closed geodesic in any non-trivial homotopy class in $\pi_1(\Omega)$, which leads to a contradiction. Therefore, $\pi_1(\Omega) = 0$. This is the third part of the theorem. If the finite fundamental group is null of any Riemannian manifold, this Riemannian manifold is simply connected. As a result, Ω^n is simply connected.

3.2. Proof of Theorem 3

In the case where Ω^n is a compact Riemannian manifold with no boundary, $\partial \Omega^n = \emptyset$, thus using [32], the divergence property $\int_{\Omega^n} (\Delta f) dV = 0$. Using this fact, we get

$$0 = \int_{\Omega^n} \Delta \left(\frac{f^2}{2}\right) dV$$

$$= -\int_{\Omega^n} div\left(\nabla\left(\frac{f^2}{2}\right)\right) dV$$

$$= -\int_{\Omega^n} div(f \nabla f) dV = -\int_{\Omega^n} g(\nabla f, \nabla f) dV + \int_{\Omega^n} f \Delta f dV,$$

which implies that

$$\int_{\Omega^n} f \Delta f dV = \int_{\Omega^n} \|\nabla f\|^2 dV. \tag{33}$$

Using (3) with inequality (6), then it can be rewritten as:

$$\frac{1}{2} \int_{\Omega^n} \|\nabla f\|^2 dV < \left(\frac{1}{2(2\csc^2 \phi + k)}\right) \int_{\Omega^n} \left(3l - \frac{\|h_\mu\|^2}{k}\right) f^2 dV. \tag{34}$$

By using the trigonometric identities $1 + \cot^2 \phi = \csc^2 \phi$ and (33) in the above equation, we get

$$\int_{\Omega^n} f \Delta f dV + (\cot^2 \phi + \csc^2 \phi + k) \int_{\Omega^n} \|\nabla f\|^2 dV < \int_{\Omega^n} \left(3l - \frac{\|h_\mu\|^2}{k}\right) f^2 dV.$$

It is equivalent to the following:

$$f \Delta f + (\cot^2 \phi + \csc^2 \phi + k) \|\nabla f\|^2 < \left(3l - \frac{\|h_\mu\|^2}{k}\right) f^2. \tag{35}$$

Hence, using Theorem 3, we get the required results. This completes the proof of the Theorem.

3.3. Proof of Theorem 4

Assuming f is a non-constant warping function, by the use of the minimum principle on the first eigenvalue λ_1, one can obtain [26] (p. 186):

$$\lambda_1 \int_{\Omega^n} (f)^2 dV \leq \int_{\Omega^n} \|\nabla f\|^2 dV. \tag{36}$$

The equality holds if, and only if $\Delta f = \lambda_1 f$. On the other hand, if our assumption (10) holds, then using the equality in (36), we get

$$(2\csc^2 \phi + k) \int_{\Omega^n} \|\nabla f\|^2 dV < \int_{\Omega^n} \left(3l - \frac{\|h_\mu\|^2}{k}\right) f^2 dV.$$

Utilizing (33) and rearranging this with trignometric functions, we have

$$(\cot^2 \phi + \csc^2 \phi + k) \int_{\Omega^n} \|\nabla f\|^2 dV + \int_{\Omega^n} f \Delta f dV < \int_{\Omega^n} \left(3l - \frac{\|h_\mu\|^2}{k}\right) f^2 dV. \tag{37}$$

Hence, we get the inequality

$$(\cot^2 \phi + \csc^2 \phi + k) \|\nabla f\|^2 + f \Delta f < \left(3l - \frac{\|h_\mu\|^2}{k}\right) f^2.$$

Therefore, the assertion follows from Theorem 2. The proof is completed.

Hamiltonian at the point $x \in M^n$ for the local orthonormal frame, is given as (see [25]):

$$H(p,x) = \frac{1}{2}\sum_{i=1}^n p(e_i)^2. \tag{38}$$

Substituting $p = d\varphi$ into the previous equation, and since d is a differentiable operator, we use (15) to have:

$$H(d\varphi,x) = \frac{1}{2}\sum_{i=1}^n d\varphi(e_i)^2 = \frac{1}{2}\sum_{i=1}^n e_i(\varphi)^2 = \frac{1}{2}||\nabla\varphi||^2. \tag{39}$$

Using the previous equation leads to the next result from inequality (2), as the following:

Corollary 3. *Under the same assumption in Theorem 2, it satisfies the following inequality:*

$$H(df,x) < \frac{(3l - ||h_\mu||^2)f^2}{k(4\csc^2\phi + 2k)} - \frac{f\Delta f}{2}, \tag{40}$$

where $H(df,x)$ is the Hamiltonian of the warping function f, so no stable integral l-currents exist in Ω^n and $\mathbb{H}_l(\Omega^n, \mathbb{G}) = \mathbb{H}_k(\Omega^n, \mathbb{G}) = 0$.

Proof. Combining the Hamiltonian formula (39) and inequality (2), we have the result. □

3.4. Proof of the Corollarys 1 and 2

The proof of Corollarys 1 and 2 can be obtained directly from the Theorems 2 and 3 by substituting $\phi = \frac{\pi}{2}$ to derive a totally real submanifold from a pointwise slant submanifold.

Author Contributions: Writing and original draft, A.H.A.; funding acquisition, editing and draft, A.A.; review and editing, Y.L.; methodology, project administration, A.H.A.; P.L.-I.; formal analysis, resources, Y.L. All authors have read and agreed to the published version of the manuscript.

Funding: The authors would like to express their gratitude to Deanship of Scientific Research at King Khalid University, Saudi Arabia for providing funding research group under the research grant R. G. P. 2/74/42 and National Natural Science Foundation of China (Grant No. 12101168) and Zhejiang Provincial Natural Science Foundation of China (Grant No. LQ22A010014).

Institutional Review Board Statement: Not applicable.

Informed Consent Statement: Not applicable.

Data Availability Statement: There is no data use for this study.

Conflicts of Interest: The authors declare no conflict of interest.

References

1. Lawson, H.B.; Simons, J. On stable currents and their application to global problems in real and complex geometry. *Ann. Math.* **1973**, *98*, 427–450. [CrossRef]
2. Xin, Y.L. An application of integral currents to the vanishing theorems. *Sci. Sin. Ser. A* **1984**, *27*, 233–241.
3. Smale, S. Generalized Poincarẽ's conjecture in dimensions greater than four. *Ann. Math.* **1961**, *74*, 391–406. [CrossRef]
4. Leung, P.F. On the topology of a compact submanifold of a sphere with bounded second fundmental form. *Manuscripta Math.* **1993**, *79*, 183–185. [CrossRef]
5. Xu, H.W.; Gu, J.R. Geometric, topological and differentiable rigidity of submanifolds in space forms. *Geom. Funct. Anal.* **2013**, *23*, 1684. [CrossRef]
6. Fu, H.P.; Xu, H.W. Vanishing and topological sphere theorems for submanifolds of sphere. *Int. J. Math.* **2008**, *19*, 811–822. [CrossRef]
7. Lui, L.; Zhang, Q. Non-existence of stable currents in submanifolds of the Euclidean spaces. *J. Geom.* **2009**, *96*, 125–133.
8. Li, Y.L.; Liu, S.Y.; Wang, Z.G. Tangent developables and Darboux developables of framed curves. *Topol. Appl.* **2020**, 107526. [CrossRef]

9. Li, Y.L.; Wang, Z.G. Lightlike tangent developables in de Sitter 3-space. *J. Geom. Phys.* **2021**, *164*, 1–11. [CrossRef]
10. Li, Y.L.; Wang, Z.G.; Zhao, T.H. Geometric Algebra of Singular Ruled Surfaces. *Adv. Appl. Clifford Algebras.* **2021**, *31*, 1–19. [CrossRef]
11. Li, Y.L.; Zhu, Y.S.; Sun, Q.Y. Singularities and dualities of pedal curves in pseudo-hyperbolic and de Sitter space. *Int. J. Geom. Methods Mod. Phys.* **2021**, *18*, 1–31. [CrossRef]
12. Mofarreh, F.; Ali, A.; Othman, W.A.M. The normalized Ricci flow and homology in Lagrangian submanifolds of generalized complex space forms. *Int. J. Geom. Methods Mod. Phys.* **2020**, *17*, 2050094. [CrossRef]
13. Sahin, B.; Sahin, F. Homology of contact CR-warped product submanifolds of an odd-dimensional unit sphere. *Bull. Korean Math. Soc.* **2015**, *52*, 215–222. [CrossRef]
14. Sahin, F. On the topology of CR-warped product submanifolds. *Int. J. Geom. Methods Mod. Phys.* **2018**, *15*, 1850032. [CrossRef]
15. Sahin, F. Homology of submanifolds of six dimensional sphere. *J. Geom. Phys.* **2019**, *145*, 103471. [CrossRef]
16. Sahin, B.; Şahin, B. Homology of contact 3-CR-submanifolds of an almost 3-contact hypersurface. *Chaos Solitons Fractals* **2021**, *151*, 111267. [CrossRef]
17. Sjerve, D. Homology spheres which are covered by spheres. *J. Lond. Math. Soc.* **1973**, *6*, 333–336. [CrossRef]
18. Ali, A.; Mofarreh, F.; Ozel, C.; Othman, W.A.M. Homology of warped product submanifolds in the unit sphere and its applications. *Int. J. Geom. Methods Mod. Phys.* **2020**, *17*, 2050121. [CrossRef]
19. Ali, A.; Mofarreh, F.; Alluhaibi, N.; Laurian-Ioan, P. Null homology in warped product Lagrangian submanifolds of the nearly Kaehler $\mathbb{S}^6$ and its applications. *J. Geom. Phys.* **2020**, *158*, 103859. [CrossRef]
20. Ali, A.; Alkhaldi, A.H.; Laurian-Ioan, P. Stable currents and homology groups in a compact CR-warped product submanifold with negative constant sectional curvature. *J. Geom. Phys.* **2020**, *148*, 103566. [CrossRef]
21. Sahin, B. Warped product pointwise semi-slant submanifold of Kähler manifold. *Port. Math.* **2013**, *70*, 251–268. [CrossRef]
22. Chen, B.Y. Geometry of warped product CR-submanifold in Kähler manifolds I. *Monatsh. Math.* **2001**, *133*, 177–195 . [CrossRef]
23. Chen, B.Y. Geometry of warped product CR-submanifolds in Kähler manifolds II. *Monatsh. Mat.* **2001**, *134*, 103–119. [CrossRef]
24. Chen, B.Y.; Gray, O.J. Pointwise slant submanifolds in almost Hermitian manifolds. *Turk. J. Math.* **2012**, *36*, 630–640.
25. Calin, O.; Chang, D.C. *Geometric Mechanics on Riemannian Manifolds: Applications to Partial Differential Equations*; Springer Science & Business Media: New York, NY, USA, 2006.
26. Berger, M.; Gauduchon, P.; Mazet, E. *Le Spectre D'une Variétés Riemannienne*; Springer: Berlin, Germany, 1971.
27. Kenna, R. Homotopy in statistical physisc. *Condebs. Matter Phys.* **2006**, *9*, 283–304. [CrossRef]
28. Bishop, R.L.; O'Neil, B. Manifolds of negative curvature. *Trans. Am. Math. Soc.* **1969**, *145*, 1–9. [CrossRef]
29. O'Neil, B. *Semi-Riemannain Geometry with Applications to Relativity*; Academic Press: New York, NY, USA, 1983.
30. Surya, S. Causal set topology. *Theor. Comput. Sci.* **2008**, *405*, 188–197. [CrossRef]
31. Zhang, Z.X. Non-existence of stable currents in submanifolds of a product of two spheres. *Bull. Austral. Math. Soc.* **1991**, *44*, 325–336. [CrossRef]
32. Yano, K.; Kon, M. *CR-Submanifolds of Kählerian and Sasakian Manifolds*; Birkhauser: Boston, MA, USA, 1983.

Article

Vanishing Homology of Warped Product Submanifolds in Complex Space Forms and Applications

Ali H. Alkhaldi [1], Pişcoran Laurian-Ioan [2,*], Izhar Ahmad [3,4] and Akram Ali [1]

[1] Department of Mathematics, College of Science, King Khalid University, Abha 61413, Saudi Arabia
[2] Department of Mathematics and Computer Science Victoriei 76, North Center of Baia Mare Technical University of Cluj Napoca, 430122 Baia Mare, Romania
[3] Department of Mathematics, King Fahd University of Petroleum and Minerals, Dhahran 31261, Saudi Arabia
[4] Center for Intelligent Secure Systems, King Fahd University of Petroleum and Minerals, Dhahran 31261, Saudi Arabia
* Correspondence: laurian.piscoran@mi.utcluj.ro

Abstract: In this paper, we prove the nonexistence of stable integral currents in compact oriented warped product pointwise semi-slant submanifold M^n of a complex space form $\widetilde{M}(4\epsilon)$ under extrinsic conditions which involve the Laplacian, the squared norm gradient of the warped function, and pointwise slant functions. We show that i-the homology groups of M^n are vanished. As applications of homology groups, we derive new topological sphere theorems for warped product pointwise semi-slant submanifold M^n, in which M^n is homeomorphic to a sphere $\mathbb{S}^n$ if $n \geq 4$ and if $n = 3$, then M^3 is homotopic to a sphere $\mathbb{S}^3$ under the assumption of extrinsic conditions. Moreover, the same results are generalized for CR-warped product submanifolds.

Keywords: warped product submanifolds; complex space form; Homology groups; sphere theorem; stable currents; Dirichlet energy

MSC: 53C40; 53A20; 53C42; 53B25; 53Z05

1. Introduction and Main Results

A traditional topic in Riemannian geometry is to find the geometrical and topological structures of submanifolds; there has been much progress in this field. For instance, the rigidity theorem was proved by Berger [1] for an even-dimensional complete simply connected manifold M with sectional curvature $\frac{1}{4} \leq K_M \leq 1$. Further, Gauhmen [2] considered even $n = 2m$-dimensional submanifolds minimally immersed in the unit sphere $\mathbb{S}^{n+1}$ with a co-dimension equal to one, and showed that if $||h(u, u)||^2 < 1$ for any unit vector u of M^n where h is the second fundamental form M^n, then M^n is totally geodesic in $\mathbb{S}^{n+1}$. If $max_{u \in M}\{||h(u, u)||^2\} = 1$, then M^n is $\mathbb{S}^m(\frac{1}{2}) \times \mathbb{S}^m(\frac{1}{2})$ minimally embedded in $\mathbb{S}^{2m+1}$, as described. A very famous result in this respect was formulated by Poincare [3], who stated that every simply connected closed 3-manifold is homeomorphic to a 3-sphere. Smale [4] generalized the Poincare conjecture and proved that for a closed C^∞-manifold M^n which has the homotopic types of an n-dimensional sphere greater than five, the manifold M^n is homeomorphic to $\mathbb{S}^n$. The differentiable sphere theorem was proven by Brendle and Schoen [5] under Ricci flow. In recent years, much attention has been paid to the classification of geometric function theory, topological sphere theorems, and differentiable sphere theorems (see [6–11]). In the sequelae, the homology groups of a manifold are important topological invariants that provide algebraic information about the manifold. Federer-Fleming [7] showed that any non-trivial integral homology class in $\mathbb{H}_p(M, \mathbb{G}))$ corresponds to a stable current. Motivated by the work of Federer and Fleming [7], Lawson and Simon [9], and Xin [11] proved the nonexistence of stable integral currents in a submanifold M^n and vanishing homology groups of M^n with non-negative sectional curvature according to the following theorem.

Theorem 1 ([9,11]). *Let M^n be a compact n-dimensional submanifold isometrically immersed in the space form $\widetilde{M}(c)$ of curvature $c \geq 0$ with the second fundamental form h. Let l_1, l_2 be any positive integers such that $l_1 + l_2 = n$ and*

$$\sum_{\alpha=1}^{l_1}\sum_{\beta=l_1+1}^{n}\left\{2\|h(e_\alpha, e_\beta)\|^2 - g(h(e_\alpha, e_\alpha), h(e_\beta, e_\beta))\right\} < l_1 l_2 c, \qquad (1)$$

for any $x \in M^n$ and an orthonormal frame $\{e_i\}_{1 \leq i \leq n}$ of the tangent space TM^n. Then, there do not exist stable l_1-currents in M^n and

$$\mathbb{H}_{l_1}(M^n, \mathbb{G}) = \mathbb{H}_{n-l_1=l_2}(M^n, \mathbb{G}) = 0,$$

where $\mathbb{H}_i(M^n, \mathbb{G})$ stands for i-the homology group of M^n and $\mathbb{G}$ is a finite abelian group with integer coefficients.

Due to these previous studies on large scales, a particular case we consider here is that of warped product pointwise semi-slant submanifolds of complex space form where 4ϵ is represented as a constant sectional curvature. In this regard, our motivation comes from the study of Sahin [12], where he discussed the warped product pointwise semi-slant submanifolds in a Kaehler manifold and showed that a warped product pointwise semi-slant submanifold of type $N_T^{l_1} \times_f N_\theta^{l_2}$ is nontrivial when angle θ is treated as a slant function. Furthermore, it was shown in [12] that the warped product pointwise semi-slant submanifold $N_T^{l_1} \times_f N_\theta^{l_2}$ of a Kaehler manifold is a natural generalization of CR-warped products [13]. Inspired by this notion, we define the extrinsic condition to prove nonexistence-stable integral l_1-currents and vanishing homology groups in a warped product pointwise semi-slant submanifold of complex space forms $\widetilde{M}^m(4\epsilon)$. We use Theorem 1 on this basis to arrive at our first result.

Theorem 2. *Let $M^{l_1+l_2} = N_T^{l_1} \times_f N_\theta^{l_2}$ be a compact warped product pointwise semi-slant submanifold of a complex space form $\widetilde{M}^m(4\epsilon)$. If the following condition is satisfied*

$$\left(\csc^2\theta + \cot^2\theta + l_2\right)\|\nabla f\|^2 + f\Delta f + \frac{f^2}{l_2}\|h_\mu\|^2 < 3l_1\epsilon f^2, \qquad (2)$$

then there do not exist stable integral l_1-currents in $M^{l_1+l_\theta}$ and

$$\mathbb{H}_{l_1}(M^{l_1+l_2}, \mathbb{G}) = \mathbb{H}_{l_2}(M^{l_1+l_2}, \mathbb{G}) = 0,$$

where $\mathbb{H}_i(M^{l_1+l_2}, \mathbb{G})$ stands for i-the homology group of $M^{l_1+l_2}$ with integer coefficients, ∇f and Δf are the gradient and the Laplacian of the warped function f, respectively, and h_μ represents the components of the second fundamental form h in an invariant subspace μ.

Our next result is in accordance with Lemma 3.1 in [12], which states that the inner product of the second fundamental form of $N_T^{l_1}$ and F-components of $N_\theta^{l_1}$ is equal to zero. To be precise, we have the following result.

Theorem 3. *Let $M^{l_1+l_2} = N_T^{l_1} \times_f N_\theta^{l_2}$ be a compact warped product pointwise semi-slant submanifold of a complex space form $\widetilde{M}^m(4\epsilon)$. If the inequality*

$$\|\nabla f\|^2 < \left\{\frac{(4l_1 l_2 \epsilon - \|h_\mu\|^2)f^2}{2l_2\left(\csc^2\theta + \cot^2\theta\right)}\right\}, \qquad (3)$$

holds, then there do not exist stable integral l_1-currents in $M^{l_1+l_2}$ and

$$\mathbb{H}_{l_1}(M^{l_1+l_2}, \mathbb{G}) = \mathbb{H}_{l_2}(M^{l_1+l_2}, \mathbb{G}) = 0.$$

The notation is the same as in Theorem 2.

To apply Theorems 2 and 3 in [14], let the slant function θ become globally constant, setting $\theta = \frac{\pi}{2}$ in Theorems 2 and 3. Then, the pointwise slant submanifold $N_\theta^{l_1}$ is turned into a totally real submanifold $N_\perp^{l_2}$. Thus, a warped product pointwise semi-slant submanifold $M^{l_1+l_2} = N_T^{l_1} \times_f N_\theta^{l_2}$ becomes CR-warped products in a Kaehler manifold of type $M^n = N_T^{l_1} \times_f N_\perp^{l_2}$. Therefore, following to the motivation of Chen [13], we deduce the following result from Theorem 2 for the nonexistence of stable integral l_1-currents and vanishing homology in a CR-warped product submanifold of complex space forms $\widetilde{M}^m(4\epsilon)$.

Corollary 1. *Let $M^{l_1+l_2} = N_T^{l_1} \times_f N_\perp^{l_2}$ be a compact CR-warped product submanifold of complex space form $\widetilde{M}^{2m}(4\epsilon)$. If the following condition is satisfied*

$$(1+l_2)||\nabla f||^2 + f\Delta f + \frac{f^2}{l_2}||h_\mu||^2 < 3l_1\epsilon f^2, \tag{4}$$

then there do not exist stable integral l_1-currents in $M^{l_1+l_2}$ and $\mathbb{H}_{l_1}(M^{l_1+l_2}, \mathbb{G}) = \mathbb{H}_{l_2}(M^{l_1+l_2}, \mathbb{G}) = 0$.

As an immediate consequence of Theorem 3, we have

Corollary 2. *Let $M^{l_1+l_2} = N_T^{l_1} \times_f N_\perp^{l_2}$ be a compact CR-warped product submanifold of complex space form $\widetilde{M}^{2m}(4\epsilon)$ satisfying the following inequality*

$$||\nabla f||^2 < \left\{ \frac{(4l_1 l_2 \epsilon - ||h_\mu||^2)f^2}{2l_2} \right\}.$$

Then, there do not exist stable integral l_1-currents in $M^{l_1+l_2}$ and we have the trivial homology groups, i.e.,

$$\mathbb{H}_{l_1}(M^{l_1+l_2}, \mathbb{G}) = \mathbb{H}_{l_1}(M^{l_1+l_2}, \mathbb{G}) = 0.$$

Our next motivation comes from Calin [15] who studied geometric mechanics on Riemannian manifolds and defined a positive differentiable function φ ($\varphi \in \mathcal{F}(M^n)$) on a compact Riemannian manifold M^n. The *Dirichlet energy* of a function φ is defined in [15] (see p. 41) as follows:

$$\mathbb{E}(\varphi) = \frac{1}{2} \int_{M^n} ||\nabla \varphi||^2 dV \qquad 0 < E(\varphi) < \infty. \tag{5}$$

In view of the kinetic energy formula (5) for a compact oriented manifold without boundary along with Theorem 2, we arrive at the following result.

Theorem 4. *Let $M^{l_1+l_2} = N_T^{l_1} \times_f N_\perp^{l_2}$ be a compact warped product pointwise semi-slant submanifold of a complex space form $\widetilde{M}^{2m}(4\epsilon)$ without boundary. If the following condition is satisfied*

$$\mathbb{E}(f) < \left\{ \frac{\int_{M^n} \left(3l_1 l_2 \epsilon - ||h_\mu||^2 \right) f^2 dV}{2l_2(2\csc^2\theta + l_2)} \right\}, \tag{6}$$

where $\mathbb{E}(f)$ is the Dirichlet energy of the warping function f with respect to the volume element dV, then there do not exist stable integral l_1-currents in $M^{l_1+l_2}$ and $\mathbb{H}_{l_1}(M^{l_1+l_2},\mathbb{G})=\mathbb{H}_{l_2}(M^{l_1+l_2},\mathbb{G})=0$.

An important concept relates to the geometrical and topological properties on Riemannian manifolds when considering the pinched condition on its metric. It is interesting to investigate the curvature and topology of submanifolds in a Riemannian manifold and the usual sphere theorems in Riemannian geometry. For instance, using the nonexistence of stable currents on compact submanifolds, Lawson and Simon [9] obtained their striking sphere theorem, which proved that for an n-dimensional compact-oriented submanifold M^n in a unit sphere $\mathbb{S}^{n+k}$ with the second fundamental form bounded above by a constant which depends on the dimension n, then M^n is homeomorphic to a sphere $\mathbb{S}^n$ when $n \neq 3$ and M^3 are homotopic to a sphere $\mathbb{S}^3$.

Making use of Lawson and Simon [9], Leung [16] proved that for a compact connected oriented submanifold M^n in the unit sphere $\mathbb{S}^{n+k}$ such that $\|h(X,X)\|^2 < \frac{1}{3}$, when $n \neq 3$ and M^3 are homotopic to a sphere $\mathbb{S}^3$, then M^n is homeomorphic to a sphere $\mathbb{S}^n$. Recently, it has been shown in [17] that if the sectional curvature satisfies some pinching condition $K_M \geq \frac{l_1 \cdot \text{sign}(l_1-1)}{2(l_1+1)}$ for n-dimensional compact oriented minimal submanifold M in the unit sphere $\mathbb{S}^{n+l_1}$ with co-dimension l_1, then M is either a totally geodesic sphere, one of the Clifford minimal hyper-surfaces $\mathbb{S}^k(\frac{k}{n}) \times \mathbb{S}^{n-k}(\frac{n-k}{n})$ in $\mathbb{S}^{n+1}$ for $k=1,\ldots,n-1$, or a Veronese surface in $\mathbb{S}^4$. More recently, several results have been derived on topological and differentiable structures of submanifolds when imposing certain conditions on the second fundamental form, Ricci curvatures, and sectional curvatures in a series of articles [4,10,11,18–23] by different geometers. For the warped product structure, we refer to [20,24–30].

The second target of note is to establish topological sphere theorems from the viewpoint of warped product submanifold geometry with positive constant sectional curvature and pinching conditions in terms of the squared norm of the warping function and Laplacian of the warped function as extrinsic invariants. In this sense, we work with conditions on the extrinsic curvature (second fundamental form, warping function), which have the advantage of being invariant under rigid motions. Motivated by Lawson and Simon [9], (p. 441, Theorem 4), we consider a warped product pointwise semi-slant submanifold in a complex space form $\widetilde{M}^{2m}(4\epsilon)$ such that the constant holomorphic sectional curvature is 4ϵ, and state our main theorem of this paper.

Theorem 5. *Let $M^{l_1+l_2} = N_T^{l_1} \times_f N_\theta^{l_2}$ be a compact warped product pointwise semi-slant submanifold in a complex space form $\widetilde{M}^{2m}(4\epsilon)$ satisfying the condition (2). Then, $M^{l_1+l_2}$ is homeomorphic to sphere $\mathbb{S}^{l_1+l_2}$ when $l_1 + l_2 \geq 4$, while M^3 is homotopic to a sphere $\mathbb{S}^3$.*

Remark 1. *As a consequence of Theorem 5, we obtain the following sphere theorem for a compact CR-warped product submanifold in a complex space form $\widetilde{M}^{2m}(4\epsilon)$, thanks to Chen [13].*

Corollary 3. *Let $M^{l_1+l_2} = N_T^{l_1} \times_f N_\perp^{l_2}$ be a compact CR-warped product submanifold in a complex space form $\widetilde{M}^{2m}(4\epsilon)$ satisfying the pinching condition (4). Then, $M^{l_1+l_2}$ is homeomorphic to a sphere $\mathbb{S}^{l_1+l_2}$ when $l_1 + l_2 \geq 4$, and M^3 is homotopic to a sphere $\mathbb{S}^3$.*

Using Theorem 4 and 5, we can now obtain an important result.

Corollary 4. *Let $M^{p+q} = N_T^p \times_f N_\theta^q$ be a compact warped product pointwise semi-slant submanifold of complex space form $\widetilde{M}^{2m}(4\epsilon)$. If (6) is satisfied, then $M^{l_1+l_2}$ is homeomorphic to sphere $\mathbb{S}^{l_1+l_2}$ when $l_1 + l_2 \geq 4$ and M^3 is homotopic to a sphere $\mathbb{S}^3$.*

Remark 2. *The principle behind Cheng's eigenvalue comparison theorem (see [31]) forms the basis of the following finding. With the help of the first non-zero eigenvalue of the Laplacian operator, Cheng has demonstrated that if M is complete and isometric to the sphere of the standard unit then the following theorem can be inferred using the maximum principle for the first non-zero eigenvalue λ_1, provided that $Ric(M) \geq 1$ and $d(M) = \pi$.*

Theorem 6. *Let $M^{l_1+l_2} = N_T^{l_1} \times_f N_\theta^{l_2}$ be a compact warped product pointwise semi-slant submanifold of a complex space form $\tilde{M}^{2m}(4\epsilon)$ with f being a non-constant eigenfunction of the first non-zero eigenvalue λ_1 such that the following inequality is satisfied:*

$$\lambda_1 < \frac{3l_1 l_2 \epsilon - \|h_\mu\|}{l_1 (2 \csc^2 \theta + l_2)}. \tag{7}$$

Then, $M^{l_1+l_2}$ is homeomorphic to sphere $\mathbb{S}^{l_1+l_2}$ when $l_1 + l_2 \geq 4$ and M^3 is homotopic to a sphere $\mathbb{S}^3$ when $l_1 + l_2 = 3$.

Motivated by Bochner's formula [32], we arrive at the following result.

Theorem 7. *Let $M^{l_1+l_2} = N_T^{l_1} \times_f N_\theta^{l_2}$ be a compact warped product pointwise semi-slant submanifold of a complex space form $\tilde{M}^{2m}(4\epsilon)$ such that following inequality holds:*

$$\|\nabla^2 f\|^2 + Ric(\nabla f, \nabla f) > \left\{ \frac{(\|h_\mu\|^2 - 3l_1 l_2 \epsilon) f \Delta f}{(2 \csc^2 \theta + l_2)} \right\}, \tag{8}$$

where $\|\nabla^2 f\|^2$ denotes the Hessian form of the warping function f and Ric denotes the Ricci curvature along the base manifold $N_T^{l_1}$. Then, $M^{l_1+l_2}$ is homeomorphic to sphere $\mathbb{S}^{l_1+l_2}$ when $l_1 + l_2 \geq 4$ and M^3 is homotopic to a sphere $\mathbb{S}^3$ when $l_1 + l_2 = 3$.

2. Preliminaries

Let $M^{2m}(4\epsilon)$ be a complex space form with the complex dimension $\dim_{\mathbb{R}} M = 2m$. Then, the curvature tensor R of $M^{2m}(4\epsilon)$ with constant holomorphic sectional curvature 4ϵ is expressed as

$$R(X_2, Y_2)Z_2 = c \Big(g(X_2, Z_2)Y_2 - g(Y_2, Z_2)X_2 + g(X_2, JZ_2)JY_2$$
$$- g(Y_2, JZ_2)X_2 + 2g(X_2, JY_2)JZ_2 \Big). \tag{9}$$

The Gauss and Weingarten formulas for transforming submanifold M^n into an almost Hermitian manifold $\tilde{M}^{2m}$ are provided by

$$\tilde{\nabla}_{X_2} Y_2 = \nabla_{X_2} Y_2 + h(X_2, Y_2),$$
$$\tilde{\nabla}_{X_2} N = -A_N X_2 + \nabla^\perp_{X_2} N,$$

for each $X_2, Y_2 \in \mathfrak{X}(TM)$ and $N \in \mathfrak{X}(T^\perp M)$ such that the second fundamental form and the shape operator are denoted by h and A_N. They are connected as $g(h(U,V), N) = g(A_N U, V)$. Now, for any $X_2 \in \mathfrak{X}(M)$ and $N \in \mathfrak{X}(T^\perp M)$, we have

$$(i) \ JX_2 = TX_2 + FX_2, \quad (ii) \ JN = tN + fN, \tag{10}$$

where $TX_2(tN)$ and $FX_2(fN)$ are the tangential and normal components of $JX_2(JN)$, respectively.

The Gauss equation for a submanifold M^n is defined as

$$\tilde{R}(X_2, Y_2, Z_2, W_2) = R(X_2, Y_2, Z_2, W_2) + g(h(X_2, Z_2), h(Y_2, W_2)) \\ - g(h(X_2, W_2), h(Y_2, Z_2)), \quad (11)$$

for any $X_2, Y_2, Z_2, W_2 \in \mathfrak{X}(TM)$, where $\tilde{R}$ and R are the curvature tensors on $\tilde{M}^{2m}$ and M^n, respectively.

The norm of second fundamental form h for an orthonormal frame $\{e_1, e_2, \cdots e_n\}$ of the tangent space TM on M^n is defined by

$$h_{ij}^r = g(h(e_i, e_j), e_r), \quad ||h||^2 = \sum_{i,j=1}^{n} g(h(e_i, e_j), h(e_i, e_j)). \quad (12)$$

Let $\{e_1, \ldots, e_n\}$ be an local orthonormal frame of vector field M^n. Then, we have

$$\nabla \varphi = \sum_{i=1}^{n} e_i(\varphi) e_i.$$

and

$$||\nabla \varphi||^2 = \sum_{i=1}^{n} ((\varphi) e_i)^2, \quad (13)$$

where $\nabla \varphi$ and $||\nabla \varphi||^2$ are the gradient of function φ and its squared norm.

The following classifications can be provided as:
(i) If $J(T_x M) \subseteq T_x M$ for every $x \in M^n$, then M^n is a holomorphic submanifold.
(ii) If $J(T_x M) \subseteq T^\perp M$ for each $x \in M^n$, then M^n is a totally real submanifold.

There are four types of submanifolds of a Kaehler manifold, namely, the CR-submanifold, slant submanifold, semi-slant submanifold, pointwise slant submanifold, and pointwise semi-slant submanifold. The definitions and classifications of such submanifolds are discussed in [12,13]. Moreover, for examples of a pointwise semi-slant submanifold in a Kaehler manifold and related problems, we refer to [12]. It follows from Definition 3.1 in [12] that if we denote as l_1 and l_2 the dimensions of a complex distribution $\mathcal{D}^T$ and pointwise slant distribution $\mathcal{D}^\theta$ of a pointwise semi-slant submanifold in a Kaehler manifold $\tilde{M}^{2m}$, then the following remarks hold:

Remark 3. *M^n is invariant if $l_1 = 0$ and pointwise slant if $l_2 = 0$.*

Remark 4. *If we consider the slant function $\theta : M^n \to R$ as globally constant on M^n and $\theta = \frac{\pi}{2}$, then M^n is a CR-submanifold.*

Remark 5. *An invariant subspace μ under J of normal bundle $T^\perp M$, is defined as $T^\perp M = F\mathcal{D}^\theta \oplus \mu$.*

3. Warped Product Submanifolds

A product manifold of the type $M^n = N_1^{l_1} \times_f N_2^{l_2}$ is a warped product manifold if the metric is defined as $g = g_1 + f^2 g_2$, where $N_1^{l_1}$ and $N_2^{l_2}$ are two Riemannian manifolds and their Riemannian metrics are g_1 and g_2, respectively. It was discovered by Bishop and O'Neill [33] that the warping function f is a smooth function defined on base $N_1^{l_1}$. The following properties are a direct consequence of the warped product manifold $M^n = N_1^{l_1} \times_f N_2^{l_2}$:

(i) $\nabla_Z X = \nabla_X Z = \frac{(Xf)}{f} Z$,
(ii) $\nabla_Z W = \nabla'_Z W - \frac{g(Z,W)}{f} \nabla f$,

for any $X, Y \in \mathfrak{X}(TN_1)$ and $Z, W \in \mathfrak{X}(TN_2)$, where ∇ and ∇' denote the Levi-Civita connection on M^n and N_2, respectively.

The gradient ∇f of f is written as

$$g(\nabla \ln f, X_2) = X_2(\ln f). \tag{14}$$

The following relation is an interesting property of warped products:

$$\mathcal{R}(X_2, Z_2) Y_2 = \frac{\mathcal{H}^f(X_2, Z_2)}{f} Y_2, \tag{15}$$

where $\mathcal{H}^f$ is a Hessian tensor of f; the remarks below follow as a consequence.

Remark 6. *A warped product manifold $M^n = N_1^{l_1} \times_f N_2^{l_2}$ is said to be trivial or simply a Riemannian product manifold if the warping function f is a constant function along $N_1^{l_1}$.*

Remark 7. *If $M^n = N_1^{l_1} \times_f N_2^{l_2}$ is a warped product manifold, then $N_1^{l_1}$ is totally geodesic and $N_2^{l_2}$ is a totally umbilical submanifold of M^n, respectively.*

4. Non-Trivial Warped Product Pointwise Semi-Slant Submanifolds $N_T^{l_1} \times_f N_\theta^{l_2}$

It is well known that warped product submanifolds of types

$$(i) \ N_\theta^{l_2} \times_f N_T^{l_1}, \ \text{and} \ (ii) \ N_T^{l_1} \times_f N_\theta^{l_2},$$

are called warped product pointwise semi-slant submanifolds, which were discovered in [12]. They contain holomorphic and pointwise slant submanifolds of a Kähler manifold. The first case, with $M^n = N_\theta^{l_2} \times_f N_T^{l_1}$ in a Kähler manifold, is trivial. The second is non-trivial. Before proceeding to the second case, let us recall the following result [12].

Lemma 1. *Let $M^n = N_T^{l_1} \times_f N_\theta^{l_2}$ be a warped product pointwise semi-slant submanifold of a Kähler manifold $\widetilde{M}^m$. Then,*

$$g(h(X_2, Z_2), FTZ_2) = -(X_2 \ln f) \cos^2 \theta \|Z_2\|^2, \tag{16}$$

$$g(h(Z_2, JX_2), FZ_2) = (X_2 \ln f) \|Z_2\|^2, \tag{17}$$

for any $X_2, Y_2 \in \mathfrak{X}(TN_T)$ and $Z_2 \in \mathfrak{X}(TN_\theta)$.

5. Proof of Main Results

5.1. Proof of Theorem 2

The crucial point of this paper is to derive an upper bound for

$$\sum_{i=1}^{l_1} \sum_{j=l_1+1}^{n} \left\{ 2\|h(e_i, e_j)\|^2 - g(h(e_i, e_i), h(e_j, e_j)) \right\}$$

in terms of Δf and $\|\nabla f\|^2$.

Let $M = N_T^{l_1} \times_f N_\theta^{l_2}$ be an $n = l_1 + l_2$-dimensional warped product pointwise semi-slant submanifold with $\dim N_T^{l_1} = l_1 = 2\alpha$ and $\dim N_\theta^{l_2} = l_2 = 2\beta$, where $N_\theta^{l_1}$ and $N_T^{l_1}$ are integral manifolds of $\mathcal{D}^\theta$ and $\mathcal{D}$, respectively. Thus, we consider $\{e_1, e_2, \cdots e_\alpha, e_{\alpha+1} = Je_1, \cdots e_{2\alpha} = Je_\alpha\}$ and $\{e_{2\alpha+1} = e_1^*, \cdots e_{2\alpha+\beta} = e_\beta^*, e_{2\alpha+\beta+1} = e_{\beta+1}^* = \sec \theta P e_1^*, \cdots e_{l_1+l_2} = e_{l_2}^* = \sec \theta P e_\beta^*\}$ to be orthonormal frames of TN_T and TN_θ, respectively. Thus the orthonormal frames of the normal sub-bundles $F\mathcal{D}^\theta$ and μ are $\{e_{n+1} = \bar{e}_1 = \csc \theta F e_1^*, \cdots e_{n+\beta} =$

$\bar{e}_\beta = \csc\theta F e_1^*, e_{n+\beta+1} = \bar{e}_{\beta+1} = \csc\theta\sec\theta F P e_1^*, \cdots e_{n+2\beta} = \bar{e}_{2\beta} = \csc\theta\sec\theta F P e_\beta^*\}$ and $\{e_{n+2\beta+1}, \cdots e_{2m}\}$, respectively. Then, from the Gauss Equation (11), we have

$$\sum_{i=1}^{l_1}\sum_{j=1}^{l_2} g(R(e_i,e_j)e_i,e_j) = \sum_{i=1}^{l_1}\sum_{j=1}^{l_2} g(\widetilde{R}(e_i,e_j)e_i,e_j) + \|h(e_i,e_j)\|^2$$
$$- \sum_{i=1}^{l_1}\sum_{j=1}^{l_2} g(h(e_i,e_j),h(e_i,e_j)).$$

By adding the squared norm of the second fundamental terms in both side of the above equation, we obtain

$$\sum_{i=1}^{l_1}\sum_{j=1}^{l_2} g(R(e_i,e_j)e_i,e_j) + \|h(e_i,e_j)\|^2 = \sum_{i=1}^{l_1}\sum_{j=1}^{l_2} g(\widetilde{R}(e_i,e_j)e_i,e_j)$$
$$- \sum_{i=1}^{l_1}\sum_{j=1}^{l_2} g(h(e_j,e_j),h(e_i,e_i))$$
$$+ 2\|h(e_i,e_j)\|^2. \qquad (18)$$

Using the orthonormal frames $\{e_i\}_{1\le i\le l_1}$ and $\{e_j\}_{1\le j\le l_2}$ of $N_T^{l_1}$ and $N_\theta^{l_2}$, respectively, in (15), we derive

$$R(e_i,e_j)e_i = \frac{e_j}{f}\mathcal{H}^f(e_i,e_i).$$

Summing up with an orthonormal frame $\{e_j\}_{1\le j\le l_2}$ (here it should be pointed out that we have adopted the opposite sign from the usual sign convention for the Laplacian), then

$$\sum_{i=1}^{l_1}\sum_{j=1}^{l_2} g(R(e_i,e_j)e_i,e_j) = -\frac{l_2}{f}\sum_{i=1}^{l_1} g(\nabla_{e_i}\nabla f, e_i). \qquad (19)$$

Thus, from Equations (18) and (19), we can derive

$$\sum_{i=1}^{l_1}\sum_{j=1}^{l_2}\left\{2\|h(e_i,e_j)\|^2 - g(h(e_j,e_j),h(e_i,e_i))\right\} + \sum_{i=1}^{l_1}\sum_{j=1}^{l_2} g(\widetilde{R}(e_i,e_j)e_i,e_j)$$
$$= -\frac{l_2}{f}\sum_{i=1}^{l_1} g(\nabla_{e_i}\nabla f, e_i) + \sum_{i=1}^{l_1}\sum_{j=1}^{l_2}(h_{ij}^r)^2. \qquad (20)$$

First, we figure out the term Δf for M^n, which is the Laplacian of f.

$$\Delta f = -\sum_{i=1}^{n} g(\nabla_{e_i} \operatorname{grad} f, e_i)$$
$$= -\sum_{\alpha=1}^{l_1} g(\nabla_{e_\alpha}\operatorname{grad} f, e_\alpha) - \sum_{\beta=1}^{l_2} g(\nabla_{e_\beta}\operatorname{grad} f, e_\beta).$$

The above equation can be expressed as components of N_θ^q from adapted orthonormal framel in this way, we obtain

$$\Delta f = -\sum_{\alpha=1}^{l_1} g(\nabla_{e_\alpha} \operatorname{grad} f, e_\alpha) - \sum_{j=1}^{\beta} g(\nabla_{e_j} \operatorname{grad} f, e_j)$$
$$- \sec^2\theta \sum_{j=1}^{\beta} g(\nabla_{Te_j} \operatorname{grad} f, Te_j).$$

Benefiting from ∇ being a Levi-Civita connection on M^n, we derive

$$\Delta f = -\sum_{\alpha=1}^{l_1} g(\nabla_{e_\alpha} \operatorname{grad} f, e_\alpha) - \sum_{j=1}^{\beta} \left(e_j g(\operatorname{grad} f, e_j) - g(\nabla_{e_j} e_j, \operatorname{grad} f) \right).$$
$$- \sec^2\theta \sum_{j=1}^{\beta} \left(Te_j g(\operatorname{grad} f, Te_j) - g(\nabla_{Te_j} Te_j, \operatorname{grad} f) \right).$$

From the property of the gradient of function (14), we obtain

$$\Delta f = -\sum_{\alpha=1}^{l_1} g(\nabla_{e_\alpha} \operatorname{grad} f, e_\alpha) - \sum_{j=1}^{\beta} \left(e_j(e_j f) - (\nabla_{e_j} e_j f) \right)$$
$$- \sec^2\theta \sum_{j=1}^{\beta} \left(Te_j(Te_j(f)) - (\nabla_{Te_j} Te_j f) \right).$$

After computation, we have

$$\Delta f = -\sum_{\alpha=1}^{l_1} g(\nabla_{e_\alpha} \operatorname{grad} f, e_\alpha) - \sum_{j=1}^{\beta} \left(e_j \left(g(\operatorname{grad} f, e_j) \right) - g(\nabla_{e_j} e_j, \operatorname{grad} f) \right)$$
$$- \sec^2\theta \sum_{j=1}^{\beta} \left(Te_j \left(g(\operatorname{grad} f, Te_j) \right) - g(\nabla_{Te_j} Te_j, \operatorname{grad} f) \right).$$

Starting from the hypothesis of a warped product pointwise semi-slant submanifold, $N_T^{l_1}$ is totally geodesic in M^n. This implies that $\operatorname{grad} f \in \mathfrak{X}(TN_T)$, and from (i)–(ii) in Section 3, we obtain

$$\Delta f = -\frac{1}{f} \sum_{j=1}^{\beta} \left(g(e_j, e_j) \|\nabla f\|^2 + \sec^2\theta g(Te_j, Te_j) \|\nabla f\|^2 \right)$$
$$- \sum_{i=1}^{l_1} g(\nabla_{e_i} \operatorname{grad} f, e_i).$$

By multiplying the above equation by $\frac{1}{f}$, from (3.7) of Corollary 3.1 in [12] we obtain

$$\frac{\Delta f}{f} = -\frac{1}{f} \sum_{i=1}^{l_1} g(\nabla_{e_i} \operatorname{grad} f, e_i) - l_2 \|\nabla(\ln f)\|^2.$$

It is not difficult to check that

$$-\frac{1}{f} \sum_{i=1}^{l_1} g(\nabla_{e_i} \operatorname{grad} f, e_i) = \frac{\Delta f}{f} + l_2 \|\nabla \ln f\|^2.$$

This combines with (20) to yield

$$l_2^2||\nabla(\ln f)||^2 + \frac{l_2\Delta f}{f} + \sum_{\alpha=1}^{l_1}\sum_{\beta=1}^{l_2}(h_{\alpha\beta}^r)^2$$

$$= \sum_{i=1}^{l_1}\sum_{j=1}^{l_2}\left\{2||h(e_i,e_j)||^2 - g(h(e_j,e_j),h(e_i,e_i))\right\}$$

$$+ \sum_{i=1}^{l_1}\sum_{j=1}^{l_2}g(\widetilde{R}(e_i,e_j)e_i,e_j). \tag{21}$$

On taking $X = e_i$ and $Z = e_j$ for $1 \leq i \leq l_1$ and $1 \leq j \leq l_2$, respectively, we have

$$\sum_{r=n+1}^{2m}\sum_{i=1}^{l_1}\sum_{j=1}^{l_2}(h_{ij}^r)^2 = \sum_{r=n+1}^{n+2\beta}\sum_{i=1}^{l_1}\sum_{j=1}^{l_2}g(h(e_i,e_j^*),e_r)^2$$

$$+ \sum_{r=n+2\beta+1}^{2m}\sum_{i=1}^{l_1}\sum_{j=1}^{l_2}g(h(e_i,e_j^*),e_r)^2.$$

In the above equation, the first term on the right hand side is the $F\mathcal{D}^\theta$-component and the second term is the μ-component for the orthonormal frame for vector fields of $N_T^{l_1}$ and $N_\theta^{l_2}$. Summing over the vector fields of $N_T^{l_1}$ and $N_\theta^{l_2}$ and using (16) and (17) from Lemma 1 in the last equation, we are able to find that

$$\sum_{r=n+1}^{2m}\sum_{i=1}^{l_1}\sum_{j=1}^{l_2}(h_{ij}^r)^2 = 2\left(\csc^2\theta + \cot^2\theta\right)\sum_{i=1}^{\alpha}\sum_{j=1}^{\beta}(e_i\ln f)^2 g(e_j^*,e_j^*)^2$$

$$+ 2\left(\csc^2\theta + \cot^2\theta\right)\sum_{i=1}^{\alpha}\sum_{j=1}^{\beta}(Je_i\ln f)^2 g(e_j^*,e_j^*)^2$$

$$+ \sum_{r=n+2\beta+1}^{2m}\sum_{i=1}^{l_1}\sum_{j=1}^{l_2}g(h(e_i,e_j^*),e_r)^2.$$

From the adapted orthonormal frame for N_T, the last equation can then be expressed as follows:

$$\sum_{r=n+1}^{2m}\sum_{i=1}^{l_1}\sum_{j=1}^{l_2}(h_{ij}^r)^2 = 2\left(\csc^2\theta + \cot^2\theta\right)\sum_{i=1}^{l_1}(e_i(\ln f))^2 \sum_{j=1}^{l_2}g(e_j^*,e_j^*)^2$$

$$+ \sum_{r=n+2\beta+1}^{2m}\sum_{i=1}^{l_1}\sum_{j=1}^{l_2}g(h(e_i,e_j^*),e_r)^2.$$

Together with the definition of the squared norm of the gradient function f from (13), the above implies that

$$\sum_{r=n+1}^{2m}\sum_{i=1}^{l_1}\sum_{j=1}^{l_2}(h_{ij}^r)^2 = l_2\left(\csc^2\theta + \cot^2\theta\right)||\nabla\ln f||^2 + ||h_\mu||^2. \tag{22}$$

Following (21) and (22), we arrive at

$$\frac{l_2 \Delta f}{f} + l_2^2 ||\nabla(\ln f)||^2 + l_2(1 + 2\cot^2\theta)||\nabla(\ln f)||^2 + ||h_\mu||^2$$

$$= \sum_{i=1}^{l_1}\sum_{j=1}^{l_2} \left\{ 2||h(e_i, e_j)||^2 - g(h(e_j, e_j), h(e_i, e_i)) \right\}$$

$$+ \sum_{i=1}^{l_1}\sum_{j=1}^{l_2} g(\widetilde{R}(e_i, e_j)e_i, e_j).$$

Because we have the following relation for symmetry of the curvature tensor R,

$$\sum_{i=1}^{l_1}\sum_{j=1}^{l_2} g(\widetilde{R}(e_i, e_j)e_i, e_j) = \sum_{i=1}^{l_1}\sum_{j=1}^{l_2} \widetilde{R}(e_i, e_j, e_i, e_j). \tag{23}$$

Next, we use the curvature tensor from Formula (9) for the complex space form $\widetilde{M}^m(4\epsilon)$, which can be simply written as

$$\sum_{i=1}^{l_1}\sum_{j=1}^{l_2} \widetilde{R}(e_i, e_j, e_i, e_j) = \epsilon \sum_{i=1}^{l_1}\sum_{j=1}^{l_2} \Big\{ g(e_i, e_j)g(e_i, e_j) - g(e_i, e_i)g(e_j, e_j)$$

$$- g(Je_i, e_i)g(Je_j, e_j)$$

$$+ 3g(Je_i, e_j)g(Je_j, e_i) \Big\}. \tag{24}$$

As we know that $e_i \in \mathfrak{X}(TN_T)$ and $e_j \in \mathfrak{X}(TN_\theta)$, then $g(e_i, e_j) = 0$, and $g(Je_i, e_i) = 0 (resp, g(Je_j, e_i) = 0)$ by the fact that for $Je_i \perp e_i (Je_j \perp e_j)$, respectively. Similarly, from (10)i, we can derive that $g(Je_i, e_j) = g(Te_i + Fe_i, e_j) = 0$ for $Te_i \in \mathfrak{X}(TN_T)$ and $e_j \in \mathfrak{X}(TN_\theta)$; thus, (24) implies that

$$\sum_{i=1}^{l_1}\sum_{j=1}^{l_2} \widetilde{R}(e_i, e_j, e_i, e_j) = -\epsilon \sum_{i=1}^{l_1}\sum_{j=1}^{l_2} g(e_i, e_i)g(e_j, e_j).$$

After computation using the above equation, we can derive

$$\sum_{i=1}^{l_1}\sum_{j=1}^{l_2} \widetilde{R}(e_i, e_j, e_i, e_j) = -l_1 l_2 \epsilon, \tag{25}$$

Therefore, following (23) and (25), we finally obtain

$$\frac{l_2 \Delta f}{f} + l_2^2 ||\nabla(\ln f)||^2 + l_2(\csc^2\theta + \cot^2\theta)||\nabla(\ln f)||^2 + ||h_\mu||^2 + l_1 l_2 \epsilon$$

$$= \sum_{i=1}^{l_1}\sum_{j=1}^{l_2} \left\{ 2||h(e_i, e_j)||^2 - g(h(e_j, e_j), h(e_i, e_i)) \right\}. \tag{26}$$

If the pinching condition (2) is satisfied, then from (26) we have

$$\sum_{i=1}^{l_1}\sum_{j=1}^{l_2} \left\{ 2||h(e_i, e_j)||^2 - g(h(e_j, e_j), h(e_i, e_i)) \right\} < 4l_1 l_2 \epsilon$$

By applying Theorem 1 with $c = 4\epsilon > 0$, we obtain the following:

$$\sum_{i=1}^{l_1}\sum_{j=1}^{l_2}\left\{2||h(e_i,e_j)||^2 - g\big(h(e_j,e_j),h(e_i,e_i)\big)\right\} < l_1 l_2 c.$$

This completes the proof of Theorem 2, as the assertion follows from Theorem 1.

5.2. Proof of Theorem 4

If we consider M^n as the compact-oriented Riemannian manifold without boundary $\partial M^n = \emptyset$, then we are able to prove the strong result in terms of tthe *Dirichlet energy* and pointwise slant immersion as follows. Taking the integration along the volume element dV in (2), we obtain

$$\int_{M^n} (\csc^2\theta + \cot^2\theta + l_2)||\nabla f||^2 dV + \int_{M^n} f\Delta f \, dV$$
$$< \int_{M^n} \left(3 l_2 \epsilon - \frac{||h_\mu||^2}{l_2}\right) f^2 dV. \quad (27)$$

From the divergence theorem $\int_{M^n}(\Delta f)dV = 0$ in [34] without boundary. Using this fact, we can compute the following as

$$0 = \int_{M^n} \Delta\left(\frac{f^2}{2}\right) dV = -\int_{M^n} div\left(\nabla\left(\frac{f^2}{2}\right)\right) dV$$
$$= -\int_{M^n} div(f\nabla f) dV = -\int_{M^n} g(\nabla f, \nabla f) dV + \int_{M^n} f\Delta f \, dV$$

which implies that

$$\int_{M^n} f \Delta f \, dV = \int_{M^n} ||\nabla f||^2 dV. \quad (28)$$

The inequality (27) takes its new form by virtue of (28), that is,

$$2\int_{M^n} \big(\csc^2\theta ||\nabla f||^2\big) dV + l_2 \int_{M^n} ||\nabla f||^2 dV < \int_{M^n}\left(3 l_1 \epsilon - \frac{||h_\mu||^2}{l_2}\right) f^2 dV. \quad (29)$$

Using the Dirichlet energy from Formula (5) in the above equation, we have

$$2(2\csc^2\theta + l_2)\mathbb{E}(f) < \int_{M^n}\left(3 l_1 \epsilon - \frac{||h_\mu||^2}{l_2}\right) f^2 dV.$$

Thus, we obtain the required result (6). This completes the proof of the theorem.

5.3. Proof of Corollary 1 and 2

The proof of Corollary 1 and Corollary 3 arises directly from Theorems 2 and 5 by substituting $\theta = \frac{\pi}{2}$ to point out a totally real submanifold from a pointwise slant submanifold, which then provides the promised results.

5.4. Proof of Theorem 5

From Theorem 2, we can find that there do not exist stable integral l_1-currents in a warped product pointwise semi-slant submanifold M^n and that the homology groups are zero for all positive integers l_1, l_2 such that $n = l_1 + l_2 \neq 3$; that is, $\mathbb{H}_{l_1}(M^n,\mathbb{G}) = \mathbb{H}_{l_2}(M^n,\mathbb{G}) = 0$. Therefore, M^n is a homology sphere, and in addition is a homotopic sphere following the same arguments as in [19].

Therefore, applying the generalized *Poincarē conjecture* (Smale $n \geq 5$ [4], Freedman $n = 4$ [8]), we know that M^n is homotopic to the sphere $\mathbb{S}^n$ as an immediate consequence of Sjerve[10], implying that the fundamental group $\pi_1(M^n) = 0$ on M^n when applying the same arguments as above. This implies that $M^{l_1+l_2}$ is homeomorphic to the sphere $\mathbb{S}^{l_1+l_2}$. Similarly, it is not hard to check that M^3 is homotopic to a sphere $\mathbb{S}^3$ when $n = 3$ from [9,16]. This completes the proof of Theorem 5.

5.5. Proof of Theorem 6

From the minimum principle on the first eigenvalue λ_1, we can obtain the outcome from [32], p. 186. Let us assume that f is a non-constant warping function

$$\lambda_1 \int_{M^n} f^2 dV \leq \int_{M^n} \|\nabla f\|^2 dV. \tag{30}$$

where the equality holds if and only if $\Delta f = \lambda_1 f$. Integrating Equation (29) and Green's lemma, we have

$$(2\csc^2\theta + q)\int_{M^n} \|\nabla f\|^2 dV < \int_{M^n} \left(3l_1\epsilon - \frac{\|h_\mu\|^2}{l_2}\right) f^2 dV,$$

which implies that

$$\int_{M^n} \|\nabla f\|^2 dV < \frac{1}{(2\csc^2\theta + l_2)} \int_{M^n} \left(3l_1\epsilon - \frac{\|h_\mu\|^2}{l_2}\right) f^2 dV. \tag{31}$$

By virtue of (30) in (31), we can find that

$$\int_{M^n} \left\{ \lambda_1 - \frac{(3l_1 l_2 \epsilon - \|h_\mu\|)}{l_2(2\csc^2\theta + l_2)} \right\} f^2 dV < 0.$$

From this, we arrive at our result (7) by combining Theorems 2 and 5, which completes the proof.

Here, we remember the lemma below.

Lemma 2 ([12]). *Assume that $\widetilde{M}^{2m}$ is a Kaehler manifold and $M^{l_1+l_2} = N_T^{l_1} \times_f N_\theta^{l_2}$ is a warped product pointwise semi-slant submanifold of $\widetilde{M}^{2m}$. Then, we have*

$$g(h(X2, Y_2), FZ_2) = 0. \tag{32}$$

for any $X_2, Y_2 \in \mathfrak{X}(TN_T)$ *and* $Z_2, W_2 \in \mathfrak{X}(TN_\theta)$.

In view of Lemma 2, we can find our next result.

5.6. Proof of Theorem 3

We can write the following from (12) as follows:

$$\sum_{i=1}^{l_1}\sum_{j=1}^{l_2} \left\{ 2\|h(e_i,e_j)\|^2 - g(h(e_j,e_j),h(e_i,e_i)) \right\} = 2\sum_{i=1}^{l_1}\sum_{j=1}^{l_2} \|h(e_i,e_j)\|^2$$
$$- \sum_{i=1}^{l_1}\sum_{j=1}^{l_2} g(h(e_i,e_i),e_j)^2,$$

or equivalently as

$$\sum_{i=1}^{l_1}\sum_{j=1}^{l_2}\left\{2\|h(e_i,e_j)\|^2 - g(h(e_j,e_j),h(e_i,e_i))\right\}$$
$$= 2\sum_{i=1}^{l_1}\sum_{j=1}^{l_2}\|h(e_i,e_j)\|^2 - \sum_{i=1}^{l_1}\sum_{j=1}^{l_2}g(h(e_i,e_i).Fe_j^*)^2.$$

By virtue of (32), we have

$$\sum_{i=1}^{l_1}\sum_{j=1}^{l_2}\left\{2\|h(e_i,e_j)\|^2 - g(h(e_j,e_j),h(e_i,e_i))\right\} = 2\sum_{i=1}^{l_1}\sum_{j=1}^{l_2}\|h(e_i,e_j)\|^2.$$

Using Equation (22) on the right hand side of the above equation, we have

$$\sum_{i=1}^{l_1}\sum_{j=1}^{l_2}\left\{2\|h(e_i,e_j)\|^2 - g(h(e_j,e_j),h(e_i,e_i))\right\} = \frac{2l_2}{f^2}\left(\csc^2\theta + \cot^2\theta\right)\|\nabla f\|^2 + \|h_\mu\|^2. \quad (33)$$

If assumption (3) is satisfied, then the following inequality is implied by (33):

$$\sum_{i=1}^{l_1}\sum_{j=1}^{l_2}\left\{2\|h(e_i,e_j)\|^2 - g(h(e_j,e_j),h(e_i,e_i))\right\} < 4l_1l_2\epsilon. \quad (34)$$

Thus, the proof is complete from Theorem 1 and from (34).

Based on Theorem 3 and the similar proof of Theorem 5, we reach the following result.

Corollary 5. *Assume that $M^{l_1+l_2} = N_T^{l_1} \times_f N_\theta^{l_2}$ is a compact warped product pointwise semi-slant submanifold of a complex space form $\widetilde{M}^{2m}(4\epsilon)$ satisfying the following:*

$$\|\nabla f\|^2 < \left\{\frac{(4l_1l_2\epsilon - \|h_\mu\|^2)f^2}{2l_2\left(\csc^2\theta + \cot^2\theta\right)}\right\}.$$

Then, M^{p+q} is homeomorphic to a sphere $\mathbb{S}^{p+q}$ when $p+q \neq 3$, while M^3 is homotopic to a sphere $\mathbb{S}^3$.

5.7. Proof of Theorem 7

In this theorem, we replace our pinching condition (2) with the Hessian of the warping function and Ricci curvature by using the concept of the eigenvalue of the warped function. If f is a first eigenfunction of the Laplacian of M^n associated with the first eigenvalue λ_1, that is, $\Delta f = \lambda_1 f$, then we an recall Bochner's formula (see, e.g., [32]), which states that for a differentiable function f defined on a Riemannian manifold, the following relation holds:

$$\frac{1}{2}\Delta\|\nabla f\|^2 = \|\nabla^2 f\|^2 + Ric(\nabla f, \nabla f) + g(\nabla f, \nabla(\Delta f)).$$

By integrating the above equation with the aid of Stokes' theorem, we obtain

$$\int \|\nabla^2 f\|^2 dV + \int Ric(\nabla f, \nabla f)dV + \int g(\nabla f, \nabla(\Delta f))dV = 0.$$

Now, by using $\Delta f = \lambda_1 f$ and slightly rearranging the above equation, we derive

$$\int \|\nabla f\|^2 dV = -\frac{1}{\lambda_1}\left(\int \|\nabla^2 f\|^2 dV + \int Ric(\nabla f, \nabla f)dV\right). \quad (35)$$

On combing Equations (28) and (27), we obtain

$$(2\csc^2\theta + l_2)\int_{M^n} \|\nabla f\|^2 dV + \int_{M^n} \frac{f^2\|h_\mu\|^2}{l_2} dV < 3l_1\epsilon \int_{M^n} f^2 dV. \qquad (36)$$

Following from (35) and (36), we find that

$$\int_{M^n} \left(\frac{\|h_\mu\|^2}{l_2} - 3l_1\epsilon\right) f^2 dV < \frac{(2\csc^2\theta + l_2)}{\lambda_1} \int_{M^n} \left(\|\nabla^2 f\|^2 + Ric(\nabla f, \nabla f)\right) dV,$$

which implies that

$$\|\nabla^2 f\|^2 + Ric(\nabla f, \nabla f) > \left\{ \frac{(\|h_\mu\|^2 - 3l_1 l_2 \epsilon)\lambda_1 f^2}{(2\csc^2\theta + l_2)} \right\}. \qquad (37)$$

The proof follows from the above Equation (37) along with Theorem 2.

6. Consequences

It is well known that a complete simply-connected complex space form $\widetilde{M}^{2m}(4\epsilon)$ is holomorphicaly isometric to the complex Euclidean space $\mathbb{C}^m$, the complex projective m-space $\mathbb{C}P^m(4)$, and a complex hyperbolic m-space $\mathbb{C}H^m(-4)$ with $\epsilon = 0, 1$ & $\epsilon = -1$. Therefore, we define the following corollaries in consequence of our Theorem 2 and Theorem 5.

Corollary 6. Let $M^{l_1+l_2} = N_T^{l_1} \times_f N_\theta^{l_2}$ be a compact warped product pointwise semi-slant submanifold in a complex Euclidean space $\mathbb{C}^m$ satisfying the condition

$$\left(\csc^2\theta + \cot^2\theta + l_2\right)\|\nabla f\|^2 + f\Delta f + \frac{f^2}{l_2}\|h_\mu\|^2 < 0.$$

Then, there do not exist stable integral l_1-currents in $M^{l_1+l_2}$ and $\mathbb{H}_{l_1}(M^{l_1+l_2}, \mathbb{G}) = \mathbb{H}_{l_2}(M^{l_1+l_2}, \mathbb{G}) = 0$. Furthermore, $M^{l_1+l_2}$ is homeomorphic to a sphere $\mathbb{S}^{l_1+l_2}$ when $l_1 + l_2 \geq 4$, while M^3 is homotopic to a sphere $\mathbb{S}^3$.

Similarly, for the complex projective m-space $\mathbb{C}P^m(4)$ we have the following.

Corollary 7. Let $M^{l_1+l_2} = N_T^{l_1} \times_f N_\theta^{l_2}$ be a compact warped product pointwise semi-slant submanifold in a complex projective m-space $\mathbb{C}P^{2m}(4)$ satisfying the condition

$$\left(\csc^2\theta + \cot^2\theta + l_2\right)\|\nabla f\|^2 + f\Delta f < \frac{f^2}{l_2}(3l_1 l_2 - \|h_\mu\|^2).$$

Then, there do not exist stable integral l_1-currents in $M^{l_1+l_2}$ and $\mathbb{H}_{l_1}(M^{l_1+l_2}, \mathbb{G}) = \mathbb{H}_{l_2}(M^{l_1+l_2}, \mathbb{G}) = 0$. In addition, $M^{l_1+l_2}$ is homeomorphic to a sphere $\mathbb{S}^{l_1+l_2}$ when $l_1 + l_2 \geq 4$, while M^3 is homotopic to a sphere $\mathbb{S}^3$.

7. Conclusions

The presented study is significant in light of the extant literature thanks to the new pinching conditions presented in terms of pointwise slant functions and the Laplacian of the warped function. We have discussed the rigidity results and investigated several topological classifications. In addition, we have derived a number of extrinsic conditions involving relevant geometric quantities by analyzing the extent to which the topology of warped product submanifolds is affected by the conditions on the main intrinsic and main extrinsic curvature invariants. A number of topological sphere theorems have been investigated in refeence to the connection between warped product submanifolds and homotopic–

homologic theory. The contents of the present paper can be expected to attract researchers to the prospect of finding possible applications in various research areas of physics.

Author Contributions: Writing and original draft, A.H.A.; funding acquisition, editing and draft, A.A.; review and editing, I.A.; methodology, project administration, A.H.A.; formal analysis, resources, P.L.-I. All authors have read and agreed to the published version of the manuscript.

Funding: The authors would like to express their gratitude to Deanship of Scientific Research at King Khalid University, Saudi Arabia for providing funding to the research group under the research grant R.G.P. 2/199/43.

Acknowledgments: The authors are grateful to the referee for his/her valuable suggestions and critical comments which improve the quality and presentation of this paper in the present form.

Conflicts of Interest: The authors declare no conflict of interest.

References

1. Berger, M. Les variétés riemanniennes ($\frac{1}{4}$)-pincées. *Ann. Scuola Norm. Sup. Pisa Cl. Sei.* **1960**, *14*, 161–170.
2. Gauchman, H. Minimal submanifolds of sphere with bounded second fundamental form. *Trans. Am. Math. Soc.* **1993**, *79*, 779–791. [CrossRef]
3. Rauch, H.E. A contribution to differentail geometry in the large. *Ann. Math.* **1951**, *54*, 38–55. [CrossRef]
4. Smale, S. Generalized Poincarě's conjecture in dimensions greater than four. *Ann. Math.* **1961**, *74*, 391–406. [CrossRef]
5. Brendle, S.; Schoen, R. Curvature sphere theorem and Ricci flow. *Bull. Am. Math. Soc.* **2010** *48*, 1–32. [CrossRef]
6. Costa, E.; Ribeiro, E. Minimal volume invariants, topological sphere theorems and biorthogonal curvature on 4-manifolds. *arXiv* **2015**, arXiv:1504.06212v1.
7. Federer, H.; Fleming, W. Normal and integral currents. *Ann. Math.* **1960**, *72*, 458–520. [CrossRef]
8. Freedman, M. The topology of four-dimensional manifolds. *J. Diff. Geom.* **1982**, *17*, 357–453. [CrossRef]
9. Lawson, H.B.; Simons, J. On stable currents and their application to global problems in real and complex geometry. *Ann. Math.* **1973**, *98*, 427–450. [CrossRef]
10. Sjerve, D. Homology spheres which are covered by spheres. *J. Lond. Math. Soc.* **1973**, *6*, 333–336. [CrossRef]
11. Xin, Y.L. An application of integral currents to the vanishing theorems. *Sci. Sin. Ser. A* **1984**, *27*, 233–241.
12. Sahin, B. Warped product pointwise semi-slant submanifold of Kaehler manifold. *Port. Math.* **2013**, *70*, 251–268. [CrossRef]
13. Chen, B.Y. Geometry of warped product CR-submanifold in Kaehler manifolds I. *Monatsh. Math.* **2001**, *133*, 177–195. [CrossRef]
14. Chen, B.Y.; Gray, O.J. Pointwise slant submanifolds in almost Hermitian manifolds. *Turk. J. Math.* **2012**, *36*, 630–640. [CrossRef]
15. Calin, O.; Chang, D.C. *Geometric Mechanics on Riemannian Manifolds: Applications to Partial Differential Equations*; Springer Science & Business Media: Berlin, Germany, 2006.
16. Leung, P.F. On the topology of a compact submanifold of a sphere with bounded second fundamental form. *Manuscripta Math.* **1993**, *79*, 183–185. [CrossRef]
17. Gu, J.R.; Xu, H.W. On Yau rigidity theorem for minimal submanifolds in spheres. *Math. Res. Lett.* **2012**, *19*, 511–523. [CrossRef]
18. Fu, H.P.; Xu, H.W. Vanishing and topological sphere theorems for submanifolds of sphere. *Intern. J. Math.* **2008**, *19*, 811–822. [CrossRef]
19. Lui, L.; Zhang, Q. Non-existence of stable currents in submanifolds of the Euclidean spaces. *J. Geom.* **2009**, *96*, 125–133.
20. Sahin, F. On the topology of CR-warped product submanifolds. *Int. J. Geom. Methods Mod. Phys.* **2018**, *15*, 1850032. [CrossRef]
21. Vlachos, T. Homology vanishing theorems for submanifolds. *Proc. Am. Math. Soc.* **2007**, *135*, 2607–2617. [CrossRef]
22. Xu, H.W.; Zhao, E.T. Topological and differentiable sphere theorems for complete submanifolds. *Commun. Anal. Geom.* **2009**, *17*, 565–585. [CrossRef]
23. Xu, H.W.; Ye, F. Differentiable sphere theorems for submanifolds of positive *k*-th ricci curvature. *Manuscripta Math.* **2012**, *138*, 529–543. [CrossRef]
24. Ali, A.; Mofarreh, F.; Ozel, C.; Othman, W.A.M. Homology of warped product submanifolds in the unit sphere and its applications. *Int. J. Geom. Methods Mod. Phys.* **2020**, *17*, 2050121. [CrossRef]
25. Ali, A.; Mofarreh, F.; Alluhaibi, N.; Laurian-Ioan, P. Null homology in warped product Lagrangian submanifolds of the nearly Kaehler $\mathbb{S}^6$ and its applications. *J. Geom. Phys.* **2020**, *158*, 103859. [CrossRef]
26. Ali, A.; Alkhaldi, A.H.; Laurian-Ioan, P. Stable currents and homology groups in a compact CR-warped product submanifold with negative constant sectional curvature. *J. Geom. Phys.* **2020**, *148*, 103566. [CrossRef]
27. Sahin, F. Homology of submanifolds of six dimensional sphere. *J. Geom. Phys.* **2019**, *145*, 103471. [CrossRef]
28. Mofarreh, F.; Ali, A.; Alluhaibi, N.; Belova, O. Ricci curvature for warped product submanifolds of Sasakian space forms and Its Applications to differential equations. *J. Math.* **2021**, *2021*, 1207646. [CrossRef]
29. Sahin, B.; Şahin, F. Homology of contact CR-warped product submanifolds of an odd-dimensional unit sphere. *Bull. Korean Math. Soc.* **2015**, *52*, 215–222. [CrossRef]

30. Li, Y.; Alluhaibi, N.; Moarreh, F.; Ali, A.; Ozel, C. Homology groups in CR-warped products of complex space forms. *J. Math.* **2022**, *submitted*.
31. Cheng, S.Y. Eigenvalue comparison theorem and its geometric applications. *Math. Z.* **1975** *143*, 289–297. [CrossRef]
32. Berger, M.; Gauduchon, P.; Mazet, E. *Le Spectre d'une Variétés Riemannienne*; Springer: Berlin, Germany, 1971.
33. Bishop, R.L.; O'Neil, B. Manifolds of negative curvature. *Trans. Am. Math. Soc.* **1969**, *145*, 1–9. [CrossRef]
34. Yano, K.; Kon, M. *CR-Submanifolds of Kaehlerian and Sasakian Manifolds*; Birkhauser: Boston, MA, USA, 1983.

Article

Z-Symmetric Manifolds Admitting Schouten Tensor

Mohabbat Ali [1], Abdul Haseeb [2,*], Fatemah Mofarreh [3] and Mohd Vasiulla [1]

[1] Department of Applied Sciences & Humanities, Jamia Millia Islamia (Central University), New Delhi 110025, India
[2] Department of Mathematics, College of Science, Jazan University, Jazan 45142, Saudi Arabia
[3] Mathematical Science Department, Faculty of Science, Princess Nourah Bint Abdulrahman University, Riyadh 11546, Saudi Arabia
* Correspondence: malikhaseeb80@gmail.com or haseeb@jazanu.edu.sa

Abstract: The paper deals with the study of Z-symmetric manifolds $(ZS)_n$ admitting certain cases of Schouten tensor (specifically: Ricci-recurrent, cyclic parallel, Codazzi type and covariantly constant), and investigate some geometric and physical properties of the manifold. Moreover, we also study $(ZS)_4$ spacetimes admitting Codazzi type Schouten tensor. Finally, we construct an example of $(ZS)_4$ to verify our result.

Keywords: schouten tensor; Z-symmetric tensor; codazzi type tensor; Z symmetric spacetimes

MSC: 53C21; 53Z05

Citation: Ali, M.; Haseeb, A.; Mofarreh, F.; Vasiulla, M. Z-Symmetric Manifolds Admitting Schouten Tensor. *Mathematics* 2022, 10, 4293. https://doi.org/10.3390/math10224293

Academic Editor: Cristina-Elena Hretcanu

Received: 20 October 2022
Accepted: 15 November 2022
Published: 16 November 2022

Publisher's Note: MDPI stays neutral with regard to jurisdictional claims in published maps and institutional affiliations.

Copyright: © 2022 by the authors. Licensee MDPI, Basel, Switzerland. This article is an open access article distributed under the terms and conditions of the Creative Commons Attribution (CC BY) license (https://creativecommons.org/licenses/by/4.0/).

1. Introduction

Let the manifold (M^n, g) (dim $M = n \geq 3$) be connected and semi-Riemannian, and the endowed metric g is of signature $(s, n - s)$, $0 \leq s \leq n$. If $s = n$ or 0 (resp., $s = n - 1$ or 1), then (M^n, g) is a Riemannian (resp., Lorentzian) manifold. A Riemannian manifold is called locally symmetric [1] if $\nabla K = 0$, where K and ∇ appear for the Riemannian curvature tensor and the Levi-Civita connection, resectively. The class of Riemannian symmetric manifold is very natural generalization of the class of manifold of constant curvature. The notion of locally symmetric manifolds have been studied by many authors in several ways to a different extent such as conformally symmetric manifolds by Chaki and Gupta [2], recurrent manifolds by Walker [3], conformally recurrent manifolds by Adati and Miyazawa [4], pseudo symmetric manifolds by Chaki [5], weakly symmetric manifolds by Tamassy and Binh [6] etc.

The general relativity is the geometric theory of gravitation developed by Einstein. In this theory, the Einstein equations relate the geometry of spacetime to the distribution of matter within it [7]. As a consequence of the Einstein equations, the divergence of energy-momentum tensor $\mathcal{T}$ vanishes [8]. In 1966, the authors Chaki and Ray [9] proved that for a covariantly constant energy-momentum tensor, the general relativistic spacetime is Ricci-symmetric, that is, $\nabla \text{Ric} = 0$, where Ric denotes the Ricci tensor of the spacetime.

Approximately a decade ago, the notion of weakly Z-symmetric manifolds was introduced by Mantica and Molinari [10], this notion generalizes weakly Ricci-symmetric manifolds. During the last decade, Z-symmetric manifolds have been studied by various authors, for example, weakly cyclic Z-symmetric manifolds by De, Mantica and Suh [11], pseudo Z-symmetric Riemannian manifolds by Mantica and Suh [12], almost pseudo Z-symmetric manifolds by De and Pal [13], concircularly flat Z-symmetric manifold and Z-symmetric manifold with the projective curvature tensor by Zengin and Yavuz Tasci [14,15].

The symmetric endomorphism R corresponding to the Ricci tensor Ric of type $(0, 2)$ is defined through the relation

$$\text{Ric}(Y,V) = g(R(Y),V), \qquad (1)$$

for all vector fields Y and V.

In an (M^n, g), $(n > 2)$, a symmetric tensor of type $(0,2)$ is a generalized Z tensor if [12,16]

$$Z(Y,V) = \text{Ric}(Y,V) + \phi g(Y,V), \qquad (2)$$

where ϕ is an arbitrary scalar function.

From (2), we have

$$Z(Y,V) = Z(V,Y),$$

and

$$Z(Y,Q) = \text{Ric}(Y,Q) + \phi g(Y,Q).$$

Here the vector field Q is called the basic vector field of the manifold corresponding to the 1-form ϕ.

Contraction of (2) over Y and V gives the scalar $\tilde{Z}$ as follows:

$$\tilde{Z} = r + n\phi, \qquad (3)$$

where r is the scalar curvature. With the choice of $\phi = -\frac{1}{n}r$, we obtain the classical Z tensor. Here, the generalized Z tensor is referred as a Z tensor.

A Riemannian or a semi-Riemannian manifold (M^n, g), $(n > 2)$ is said to be weakly Z-symmetric [10] and denoted by $(WZS)_n$, if the generalized Z tensor satisfies the condition

$$(\nabla_U Z)(Y,V) = A(U)Z(Y,V) + B(Y)Z(U,V) + D(V)Z(Y,U), \qquad (4)$$

where A, B, D are 1-forms which are non-zero simultaneously. If $A = B = D = 0$, then the manifold reduces to a Z symmetric ($\nabla Z = 0$) manifold.

On an n-dimensional Riemannian (semi-Riemannian) manifold $(M^n, g), n \geq 3$, the Schouten tensor is defined by [17]

$$P(Y,V) = \frac{1}{n-2}\left[\text{Ric}(Y,V) - \frac{r}{2(n-1)}g(Y,V)\right]. \qquad (5)$$

By combining (2) and (5), we have

$$P(Y,V) = \frac{1}{n-2}\left[Z(Y,V) - \left\{\frac{r}{2(n-1)} + \phi\right\}g(Y,V)\right], \qquad (6)$$

where r is the scalar curvature and ϕ is a non-zero 1-form such that $g(Y,Q) = \phi(Y)$ for every vector field Y.

The Riemannian curvature tensor K decomposes as [18]

$$K = P \odot g + \mathcal{C},$$

where $\mathcal{C}, \odot$ and P represent the Weyl tensor of g, the Kulkarni-Nomizu product and the Schouten tensor, respectively. Since $\mathcal{C}$ is conformally invariant, therefore, to study the deformation of the conformal metric, we need a good understanding of the Schouten tensor [17,19].

The scalar $\tilde{P}$ is obtained by contracting (5) over Y and V as follows:

$$\tilde{P} = \frac{r}{2(n-1)}. \qquad (7)$$

An (M^n, g) is said to have Codazzi type Ricci tenor if its $Ric(\neq 0)$ of type $(0,2)$ satisfies [20,21]

$$(\nabla_U \text{Ric})(Y,V) = (\nabla_Y \text{Ric})(U,V). \qquad (8)$$

An (M^n, g) is said to have cyclic parallel Ricci tensor if its $\text{Ric}(\neq 0)$ of type $(0, 2)$ satisfies [20,22]

$$(\nabla_U \text{Ric})(Y, V) + (\nabla_Y \text{Ric})(U, V) + (\nabla_V \text{Ric})(Y, U) = 0. \tag{9}$$

An (M^n, g) is said to be Ricci-recurrent if its $\text{Ric}(\neq 0)$ of type $(0, 2)$ satisfies the following relation [23]

$$(\nabla_U \text{Ric})(Y, V) = \lambda(U) \text{Ric}(Y, V), \tag{10}$$

where λ is non-zero 1-form.

An (M^n, g) is said to be generalized Ricci-recurrent if the following relation holds [24,25]

$$(\nabla_U \text{Ric})(Y, V) = \lambda(U) \text{Ric}(Y, V) + \beta(U) g(Y, V), \tag{11}$$

where λ and β are two non-zero 1-forms of the manifold. If $\beta = 0$, then the generalized Ricci-recurrent manifold reduces to a Ricci-recurrent manifold.

The paper is presented as follows: After introduction in Section 2, we investigate the $(ZS)_n$ admitting certain cases of Schouten tensor and find out some interesting results on corresponding Z tensor. In Section 3, we study the $(ZS)_4$ spacetime admitting Schouten tensor and proved some remarkable results. In Section 4, we give an example to illustrate our result.

2. $(ZS)_n$ Admitting Schouten Tensor

In the current section, by using the concepts and definitions given in previous section, we will prove some results on $(ZS)_n$ admitting Schouten tensor satisfying certain curvature conditions. First we prove the following result:

Theorem 1. *If the Schouten tensor in a $(ZS)_n$ is Ricci-recurrent, then the corresponding Z tensor is generalized Ricci-recurrent.*

Proof. By taking the covariant derivative of (6) along U, we find

$$(\nabla_U P)(Y, V) = \frac{1}{n-2}\left[(\nabla_U Z)(Y, V) - \left\{\frac{(\nabla_U r)}{2(n-1)} + (\nabla_U \phi)\right\} g(Y, V)\right]. \tag{12}$$

Let the Schouten tensor be Ricci-recurrent, then by virtue of (10) we have

$$(\nabla_U P)(Y, V) = \lambda(U) P(Y, V), \tag{13}$$

which in view of (6) and (12) takes the form

$$(\nabla_U Z)(Y, V) - \left\{\frac{(\nabla_U r)}{2(n-1)} + (\nabla_U \phi)\right\} g(Y, V) \\ = \lambda(U)\left[Z(Y, V) - \left\{\frac{r}{2(n-1)} + \phi\right\} g(Y, V)\right]. \tag{14}$$

By using (7), (14) can be written as

$$(\nabla_U Z)(Y, V) \\ = \lambda(U) Z(Y, V) + \left[(\nabla_U \bar{P}) - \lambda(U)\bar{P} + (\nabla_U \phi) - \lambda(U)\phi\right] g(Y, V). \tag{15}$$

If we take $\left[(\nabla_U \bar{P}) - \lambda(U)\bar{P} + (\nabla_U \phi) - \lambda(U)\phi\right] = \beta(U)$, then (15) transforms to

$$(\nabla_U Z)(Y, V) = \lambda(U) Z(Y, V) + \beta(U) g(Y, V),$$

which shows that the Z-tensor is generalized Ricci-recurrent. □

Next we prove the following result:

Theorem 2. *If the Schouten tensor in a $(ZS)_n$ is cyclic parallel, then the scalar curvature of $(ZS)_n$ is constant.*

Proof. If the Schouten tensor in a $(ZS)_n$ is cyclic parallel. Then by virtue of (9), we have

$$(\nabla_U P)(Y,V) + (\nabla_Y P)(U,V) + (\nabla_V P)(U,Y) = 0. \tag{16}$$

The covariant differentiation of (5) over U leads to

$$(\nabla_U P)(Y,V) = \frac{1}{n-2}\left[(\nabla_U \mathrm{Ric})(Y,V) - \frac{(\nabla_U r)}{2(n-1)}g(Y,V)\right]. \tag{17}$$

In view of (17), (16) takes the form

$$\begin{aligned}&(\nabla_U \mathrm{Ric})(Y,V) - \frac{(\nabla_U r)}{2(n-1)}g(Y,V) + (\nabla_Y \mathrm{Ric})(U,V)\\&- \frac{(\nabla_Y r)}{2(n-1)}g(U,V) + (\nabla_V \mathrm{Ric})(U,Y) - \frac{(\nabla_V r)}{2(n-1)}g(U,Y) = 0.\end{aligned} \tag{18}$$

By contracting (18) over U and Y, we get

$$\nabla_V r = 0 \implies r = \text{constant}. \tag{19}$$

This implies that the scalar curvature r is constant. This completes the proof □

Now we prove the following:

Theorem 3. *If the Schouten tensor in a $(ZS)_n$ of constant scalar curvature is of Codazzi type, then the necessary and sufficient condition for the corresponding Z tensor to be Codazzi type is that the associated 1-form of the manifold is constant.*

Proof. We consider that the Schouten tensor in a $(ZS)_n$ is of Codazzi type. By interchanging V and U in (12) we have

$$(\nabla_V P)(Y,U) = \frac{1}{n-2}\left[(\nabla_V Z)(Y,U) - \left\{\frac{(\nabla_V r)}{2(n-1)} + (\nabla_V \phi)\right\}g(Y,U)\right]. \tag{20}$$

By using (12) and (20) in (8), we find

$$\begin{aligned}(\nabla_U Z)(Y,V) - (\nabla_V Z)(Y,U)\\- (\nabla_U \phi)g(Y,V) + (\nabla_V \phi)g(Y,U) = 0,\end{aligned} \tag{21}$$

r being constant.

Again, we assume that the Z tensor is of Codazzi type, then (21) reduces to

$$(\nabla_U \phi)g(Y,V) - (\nabla_V \phi)g(Y,U) = 0.$$

By contracting the foregoing equation over Y and V we infer

$$(\nabla_U \phi) = 0. \tag{22}$$

This implies that the 1-form ϕ is constant.

Conversely, if we assume that the 1-form ϕ is constant then from (21) it follows that the Z tensor is of Codazzi type. This completes the proof. □

Thus we have

Corollary 1. *In a $(ZS)_n$ of constant scalar curvature, if both the Z-symmetric and Schouten tensors are of Codazzi type, then the Z-symmetric tensor is of constant trace.*

Proof. By taking the covariant derivative of (3) along U, we find

$$(\nabla_U \tilde{Z}) = (\nabla_U r) + n(\nabla_U \phi). \tag{23}$$

Now we suppose that both the Z-symmetric and the Schouten tensors in a $(ZS)_n$ of constant scalar curvtaure tensor are of Codazzi type. Then in view of Theorem 3, (23) reduces to

$$(\nabla_U \tilde{Z}) = 0.$$

This implies that $\tilde{Z} = constant$. This completes the proof. □

Further, we prove the following:

Theorem 4. *If the Schouten tensor in a $(ZS)_n$ is covariantly constant, then the necessary and sufficient condition for the Z-symmetric tensor to be (i) covariantly constant, or (ii) Codazzi type is that ϕ is constant.*

Proof. We consider that the Schouten tensor in a $(ZS)_n$ is covariantly constant. Then from (5) it can be easily seen that r is constant. Thus (20) leads to

$$(\nabla_U Z)(Y, V) = (\nabla_U \phi) g(Y, V). \tag{24}$$

Since Z-symmetric tensor in $(ZS)_n$ is covariantly constant, then (24) reduces to

$$(\nabla_U \phi) = 0. \tag{25}$$

This implies that the 1-form ϕ is constant.

Conversely, if the 1-form ϕ of the manifold is constant then from (24), it follows that

$$(\nabla_U Z)(Y, V) = 0.$$

This implies that the Z tensor is covariantly constant.

By interchanging U and V in (24), we have

$$(\nabla_V Z)(Y, U) = (\nabla_V \phi) g(Y, U). \tag{26}$$

Now subtracting (26) from (25), we have

$$(\nabla_U Z)(Y, V) - (\nabla_V Z)(Y, U) = (\nabla_U \phi) g(Y, V) - (\nabla_V \phi) g(Y, U). \tag{27}$$

If the Z tensor is of Codazzi type, then from (27) it follows that

$$(\nabla_U \phi) g(Y, V) - (\nabla_V \phi) g(Y, U) = 0,$$

which on contracting over Y and V gives

$$(\nabla_U \phi) = 0. \tag{28}$$

Conversely, if the relation (28) holds, then from (27), we obtain

$$(\nabla_U Z)(Y, V) - (\nabla_V Z)(Y, U) = 0.$$

This shows that the Z tensor is of Codazzi type. □

3. $(ZS)_4$ Spacetimes Admitting Schouten Tensor

The energy-momentum tensor $\mathcal{T}$ of a perfect fluid spacetime is given by [8]:

$$T(Y,V) = (p+\sigma)\phi(Y)\phi(V) + pg(V,Y), \tag{29}$$

where p is the isotropic pressure of the fluid, σ is the energy denisty and ϕ is the non-zero 1-form such that

$$g(Y,\xi) = \phi(Y), \qquad g(\xi,\xi) = -1. \tag{30}$$

Here ξ being the unit timelike velocity vector field. For a perfect fluid spacetime the Einstein's field equation without cosmological constant is given by

$$\text{Ric}(Y,V) - \frac{r}{2}g(Y,V) = kT(Y,V), \tag{31}$$

where k as the gravitational constant.

By using (29), (31) turns to

$$\text{Ric}(Y,V) = k(\sigma+p)\phi(Y)\phi(V) + \left(\frac{r}{2}+kp\right)g(Y,V). \tag{32}$$

By contracting (32) over Y and V, we obtain

$$r = k(\sigma - 3p). \tag{33}$$

By using the relation (33) in (32), we have

$$\text{Ric}(Y,V) = k(\sigma+p)\phi(Y)\phi(V) + \frac{k}{2}(\sigma-p)g(Y,V). \tag{34}$$

Now combining (2) and (34), we finally obtain

$$Z(Y,V) = k(\sigma+p)\phi(Y)\phi(V) + \left(\phi + \frac{k}{2}(\sigma-p)\right). \tag{35}$$

Recently, spacetimes and its properties have been studied in several ways by various authors such as [16,26–34] and many others.

Now we prove the following:

Theorem 5. *Let a $(ZS)_4$ of constant scalar curvature tensor admit Codazzi type Schouten tensor. If the velocity vector $(\nabla_U \phi)$ associated with the 1-form ϕ is recurrent and the matter content is a perfect fluid whose velocity vector field is the basic vector field of $(ZS)_4$, then the matter contents of $(ZS)_4$ satisfy the vacuum-like equation of state.*

Proof. We consider that the Schouten tensor in $(ZS)_4$ of constant scalar curvature is of Codazzi type. Now by taking the covariant derivative of (33), we find

$$k[(\nabla_U \sigma) - 3(\nabla_U p)] = 0. \tag{36}$$

This implies that

$$(\nabla_U \sigma) = 3(\nabla_U p), \quad k \neq 0. \tag{37}$$

By the covariant differentiation of (35) along U, we arrive at

$$(\nabla_U Z)(Y,V) = k\left[(\nabla_U \sigma) + (\nabla_U p)\right]\phi(Y)\phi(V)$$
$$+ k(p+\sigma)\left[(\nabla_U \phi)(Y)\phi(V) + \phi(Y)(\nabla_U \phi)(V)\right] \tag{38}$$
$$+ \left[(\nabla_U \phi) - \frac{k}{2}\left\{(\nabla_U p) - (\nabla_U \sigma)\right\}\right]g(Y,V).$$

Now we consider that the velocity vector $\nabla_U \phi$ is recurrent, then from (37) and (38), we obtain

$$(\nabla_U Z)(Y,V) = 4k(\nabla_U p)\phi(Y)\phi(V) + 2k\lambda(U)(\sigma+p)\phi(Y)\phi(V)$$
$$+ \{(\nabla_U \phi) + k(\nabla_U p)\}g(Y,V). \tag{39}$$

On contracting (39) over Y and V, we lead to

$$(\nabla_U \tilde{Z}) = 4(\nabla_U \phi) - 2k\lambda(U)(\sigma+p). \tag{40}$$

Now taking the covariant derivative of (3) along U and comparing it with (40), we get

$$\lambda(U)(\sigma+p) = 0.$$

Since $\lambda(U)$ is non-vanishing, therefore, we find $\sigma + p = 0$, which leads to the statement of our theorem. □

Now we prove the following theorem:

Theorem 6. *Let $(ZS)_4$ of constant scalar curvature admit Codazzi type Schouten tensor. If the Z-symmetric tensor is covariantly constant and the matter content is a perfect fluid whose velocity vector field is the basic vector field, then both the isotropic pressure and the energy density are constant.*

Proof. We suppose that $(ZS)_4$ admits Codazzi type Schouten tensor and the Z tensor is covariantly constant. Then from (2) we find

$$(\nabla_U \text{Ric})(Y,V) + (\nabla_U \phi)g(Y,V) = 0,$$

which by contracting over Y and V, and considering r as constant gives

$$(\nabla_U \phi) = 0. \tag{41}$$

This shows that the 1-form ϕ is constant.

By virtue of (37) and (41) and the fact that Z-symmetric tensor is covariantly constant, the relation (38) reduces to

$$4k(\nabla_U p)\phi(Y)\phi(V) + k(\nabla_U p)g(Y,V) = 0,$$

which by taking $Y = V = \xi$ and using (30) leads to

$$\nabla_U p = 0,$$

i.e., the isotropic pressure p is constant. Thus from (37), we lead to $\nabla_U \sigma = 0$, i.e., the energy density is constant. This completes the proof. □

Now we have the following result:

Corollary 2. *Let a perfect fluid $(ZS)_4$ with constant scalar curvature admit Codazzi type Schouten tensor. If the Z tensor is covariantly constant and the velocity vector $(\nabla_U \phi)$ associated with the 1-form ϕ is recurrent, then the spacetime reduces to an Einstein space.*

Proof. We suppose that in $(ZS)_4$, the Z tensor is covariantly constant and the Schouten tensor is of Codazzi type. Then in view of Theorems 5 and 6, from (34), we get

$$\text{Ric}(Y,V) = \frac{k}{2}(\sigma - p)g(Y,V), \tag{42}$$

which by contracting over Y and V gives

$$r = 2k(\sigma - p). \tag{43}$$

On comparing (42) and (43), we obtain

$$\text{Ric}(Y, V) = \frac{r}{4}g(Y, V). \tag{44}$$

This shows that our spacetime is an Einstein space. □

4. Example

In this section, we construct an example of Z-symmetric manifold admitting Schouten tensor on the real number space $\mathbb{R}^4$. First we calculate the components of K, Ric, Z-symmetric tensor and P. Then we verify Theorem 4(i).
Define a semi-Riemannian metric on $\mathbb{R}^4$ by

$$ds^2 = -(dx^1)^2 + e^{x^1}[(dx^2)^2 + (dx^3)^2 + (dx^4)^2]. \tag{45}$$

The non-vanishing components of the Christoffel symbols are given by

$$\Gamma^1_{22} = \Gamma^1_{33} = \Gamma^1_{44} = \frac{1}{2}e^{x^1}, \quad \Gamma^2_{12} = \Gamma^3_{13} = \Gamma^4_{14} = \frac{1}{2}. \tag{46}$$

The curvature tensor and the Ricci tensor are obtained as follows:

$$K_{1221} = K_{1331} = K_{1441} = -\frac{1}{4}e^{x^1}, \quad K_{2332} = K_{2442} = K_{3443} = -\frac{1}{4}e^{2x^1}, \tag{47}$$

$$R_{11} = -\frac{1}{2}, \quad R_{22} = R_{33} = R_{44} = -\frac{1}{4}e^{x^1},$$

and the components enlisted by the symmetry properties. Thus we can easily show that $r = -\frac{1}{4}$. The non-vanishing components of the Z tensor and the Schouten tensor are as follows:

$$Z_{11} = -\frac{1}{2} - \phi, \quad Z_{22} = Z_{33} = Z_{44} = e^{x^1}(-\frac{1}{4} + \phi), \tag{48}$$

$$P_{11} = -\frac{13}{48}, \quad P_{22} = P_{33} = P_{44} = -\frac{5}{48}e^{x^1}.$$

In view of the above relations, the non-zero components of the covariant derivatives of the Z tensor are obatined as follows:

$$Z_{11,i} = -\phi_i, \quad Z_{22,i} = Z_{33,i} = Z_{44,i} = \phi_i e^{x^1}, \quad \text{for} \quad i = 1, 2, 3, 4, \tag{49}$$

and the components can be easily obtained from (49) by the symmetric properties where "," denotes for the covariant differentiation with respect to the metric tensor g. Hence the manifold under the consideration has covariantly constant Schouten tensor.

If Z-symmetric tensor is covariantly constant, then

$$Z_{11,i} = Z_{22,i} = Z_{33,i} = Z_{44,i} = 0. \tag{50}$$

Thus from (49), we obtain

$$\phi_{,i} = 0 \quad \text{for} \quad i = 1, 2, 3, 4. \tag{51}$$

This verifies Theorem 4 (i).

5. Discussion

The importance of spaces with constant curvature is well understood in cosmology. The simplest cosmological model of the universe is obtained by assuming that the universe is isotropic and homogeneous. This is called the cosmological principle. Isotropy means that all spatial directions are equivalent, whereas homogeneity means that no place in the universe can be distinguished from another. In terms of Riemannian geometry it asserts that the three dimensional position space is a space of maximal symmetry [35], that is, a space of constant curvature whose curvature depends upon time. The cosmological solution of Einstein's equations which contain a three dimensional spacelike surface of a constant curvature are the Robertson-Walker metrics, while four dimensional space of constant curvature is the de Sitter model of the universe [35,36].

The current research is focused on Z-symmetric manifold admitting Schouten tensor with certain investigations in general relativity by the coordinate free method of differential geometry. In this way the spacetime of general relativity is treated as a connected four-dimensional semi-Riemannian manifold $(ZS)_4$ with Lorentz metric g with signature $(-,+,+,+)$. The geometry of the Lorentz manifold begins with the study of the causal character of vectors of the manifold. It is due to this causality that the Lorentz manifold becomes a convenient choice for the study of general relativity. The general theory of relativity, which is a field theory of gravitation, is described by the Einstein's field equations. The Einstein's equations [8] imply that the energy-momentum tensor is of vanishing divergence; and in this direction the authors in [9] showed that for a covariantly constant energy-momentum tensor, the general relativistic spacetime is Ricci symmetric ($\nabla \text{Ric} = 0$).

As a generalization of Ricci symmetric manifold many authors such as [10–13,16,37] studied Z-symmetric manifolds in several ways to a different extent. Motivated by above studies and concepts, we tried to study Z-symmetric manifolds admitting certain types of Schouten tensors, namely, Ricci-recurrent, cyclic parallel, Codazzi type and covariantly constant; and also Z-symmetric spacetime admitting Codazzi type Schouten tensor to prove the some results. In the future, we plan to focus on studying different kinds of curvature tensors on the generalized cases of Z-symmetric manifold. Many problems related to this study are still unresolved, and we hope that the readers of the present paper can do a good amount of work on the subject.

Author Contributions: Conceptualization, M.A., A.H. and M.V.; methodology, M.A., A.H. and F.M.; investigation, M.A., F.M. and M.V.; writing—original draft preparation, A.H., F.M. and M.V.; writing—review and editing, M.A., A.H. and M.V. All authors have read and agreed to the published version of the manuscript.

Funding: The author, Fatemah Mofarreh, expresses her gratitude to Princess Nourah bint Abdulrahman University Researchers Supporting Project number (PNURSP2022R27), Princess Nourah bint Abdulrahman University, Riyadh, Saudi Arabia.

Institutional Review Board Statement: Not applicable.

Informed Consent Statement: Not applicable.

Data Availability Statement: Not applicable.

Acknowledgments: The authors are thankful to the editor and anonymous referees for the constructive comments given to improve the quality of the paper. The third author, Fatemah Mofarreh, expresses her gratitude to Princess Nourah bint Abdulrahman University Researchers Supporting Project number (PNURSP2022R27), Princess Nourah bint Abdulrahman University, Riyadh, Saudi Arabia.

Conflicts of Interest: The authors declare no conflict of interest.

References

1. Cartan, E. Sur une classe remarquable d'espaces de Riemannian. *Bull. Soc. Math. Fr.* **1926**, *54*, 214–264. [CrossRef]
2. Chaki, M.C.; Gupta, B. On conformally symmetric spaces. *Indian J. Math.* **1963**, *5*, 113–122.

3. Walker, A.G. On Ruse's spaces of recurrent curvature. *Proc. Lond. Math. Soc.* **1951**, *52*, 36–64. [CrossRef]
4. Adati, T.; Miyazawa, T. On a Riemannian space with recurrent conformal curvature. *Tensor* **1967**, *18*, 348–354.
5. Chaki, M.C. On pseudo symmetric manifolds. *Ann. Stiint. Univ. Alexandru Ioan I Cuza Iasi* **1987**, *33*, 53–58.
6. Tamassy, L.; Binh, T.Q. On weak symmetries of Einstein and Sasakian manifolds. *Tensor* **1993**, *53*, 140–148.
7. Einstein, A. The Foundation of the General Theory of Relativity. *Ann. Der Phys.* **1916**, *354*, 769–822. [CrossRef]
8. O'Neill, B. *Semi-Riemannian Geometry with Application to the Relativity*; Academic Press: New York, NY, USA; London, UK, 1983.
9. Chaki, M.C.; Ray, S. Spacetimes with covariant constant energy momentum tensor. *Int. J. Theor. Phys.* **1996**, *35*, 1027–1032. [CrossRef]
10. Mantica, C.A.; Molinari, L.G. Weakly Z-symmetric manifols. *Acta Math. Hung.* **2012**, *135*, 80–96. [CrossRef]
11. De, U.C.; Mantica, C.A.; Suh, Y.J. On weakly cyclic Z-symmetric manifolds. *Acta Math. Hung.* **2015**, *146*, 153–167. [CrossRef]
12. Mantica, C.A.; Suh, Y.J. Pseudo Z-symmetric Riemannian manifolds with harmonic curvature tensors. *Int. J. Geom. Methods Mod. Phys.* **2012**, *9*, 1250004. [CrossRef]
13. De, U.C.; Pal, P. On almost pseudo-Z-symmetric manifolds. *Acta Univ. Palack. Olomuc Fac. Rerum. Natur. Math.* **2014**, *53*, 25–43.
14. Yavuz Tascia, A.; Zengin, F.Ö. Concircularly flat Z-symmetric manifolds. *Ann. Alexandru Ioan Cuza-Univ.-Math.* **2019**, *65*, 241–250.
15. Yavuz Tascia, A.; Zengin, F.Ö. On Z-symmetric manifold admitting projective curvature tensor. *Int. Elec. J. Geom.* **2022**, *15*, 39–46. [CrossRef]
16. Mantica, C.A.; Suh, Y.J. Pseudo Z-symmetric spacetimes. *J. Math. Phys.* **2014**, *55*, 042502. [CrossRef]
17. Guan, P.; Viaclovsky, J.; Wang, G. Some properties of the Schouten tensor and applications to conformal geometry. *Trans. Am. Math. Soc.* **2003**, *355*, 925–933. [CrossRef]
18. Besse, A.L. *Einstein Manifolds*; Springer: Berlin/Heidelberg, Germany; New York, NY, USA, 1987.
19. Ali, M.; Vasiulla, M. Almost pseudo Ricci symmetric manifold admitting Schouten tensor. *J. Dyn. Syst. Geom. Theor.* **2021**, *19*, 217–225. [CrossRef]
20. Gray, A. Einstein-like manifolds which are not Einstein. *Geom. Dedicata* **1978**, *7*, 259–280. [CrossRef]
21. Haseeb, A.; De, U.C. η-Ricci solitons in ϵ-Kenmotsu manifolds. *J. Geom.* **2019**, *110*, 34. [CrossRef]
22. Haseeb, A.; Bilal, M.; Chaubey, S.K.; Khan, M.N.I. Geometry of Indefinite Kenmotsu Manifolds as $*$-η-Ricci-Yamabe Solitons. *Axioms* **2022**, *11*, 461. [CrossRef]
23. Patterson, E.M. Some theorems on Ricci-recurrent spaces. *J. Lond. Math. Soc.* **1952**, *27*, 287–295. [CrossRef]
24. Chaubey, S.K.; Suh, Y.J. Generalized Ricci recurrent spacetimes and GRW spacetimes. *Int. J. Geom. Methods Mod. Phys.* **2021**, *18*, 2150209. [CrossRef]
25. De, U.C.; Guha, N.; Kamilya, D. On generalized Ricci-recurrent manifolds. *Tensor* **1995**, *56*, 312–317.
26. Ahsan, Z.; Siddiqui, S.A. Concircular curvature tensor and fluid spacetimes. *Int. J. Theor. Phys.* **2009**, *48*, 32023212. [CrossRef]
27. Chattopadhyay, K.; Bhunia, N.; Bhattacharyya, A. On Ricci-symmetric mixed generalized quasi Einstein spacetime. *Bull. Cal. Math. Soc.* **2018**, *110*, 513–524.
28. Chaubey, S.K. Characterization of perfect fluid spacetimes admitting gradient η-Ricci and gradient Einstein solitons. *J. Geom. Phys.* **2021**, *162*, 104069. [CrossRef]
29. Chaubey, S.K.; Suh, Y.J. Characterizations of Lorentzian manifolds. *J. Math. Phys.* **2022**, *63*, 062501. [CrossRef]
30. De, U.C.; Ghosh, G.C. On weakly Ricci symmetric spacetime manifolds. *Rad. Mat.* **2004**, *13*, 93–101.
31. De, U.C.; Velimirovic, L. Spacetimes with semi-symmetric energy-momentum tensor. *Int. J. Theor. Phys.* **2015**, *54*, 1779–1783. [CrossRef]
32. Li, Y.; Haseeb, A.; Ali, M. LP-Kenmotsu manifolds admitting η-Ricci solitons and spacetime. *J. Math.* **2022**, *2022*, 6605127. [CrossRef]
33. Vasiulla, M.; Haseeb, A.; Mofarreh, F.; Ali, M. Application of mixed generalized quasi-Einstein spacetimes in general relativity. *Mathematics* **2022**, *10*, 3749. [CrossRef]
34. Zengin, F.Ö. M-projectively flat spacetimes. *Math. Rep.* **2012**, *4*, 363–370.
35. Stephani, H. *General Relativity: An Introduction to the Theory of Gravitational Field*; Cambridge University Press: New York, NY, USA, 1982.
36. Narlikar, J.V. *General Relativity and Gravitation*; The Macmillan Co. of India: New Delhi, India, 1978.
37. De, U.C.; Mantica, C.A.; Molinari, L.G.; Suh, Y.J. On weakly cyclic Z-symmetric spacetimes. *Acta Math. Hungar.* **2016**, *149*, 462–477. [CrossRef]

Article

The ∗-Ricci Operator on Hopf Real Hypersurfaces in the Complex Quadric

Rongsheng Ma [1] and Donghe Pei [2],*

[1] School of Science, Yanshan University, Qinhuangdao 066004, China
[2] School of Mathematics and Statistics, Northeast Normal University, Changchun 130024, China
* Correspondence: peidh340@nenu.edu.cn

Abstract: We study the ∗-Ricci operator on Hopf real hypersurfaces in the complex quadric. We prove that for Hopf real hypersurfaces in the complex quadric, the ∗-Ricci tensor is symmetric if and only if the unit normal vector field is singular. In the following, we obtain that if the ∗-Ricci tensor of Hopf real hypersurfaces in the complex quadric is symmetric, then the ∗-Ricci operator is both Reeb-flow-invariant and Reeb-parallel. As the correspondence to the semi-symmetric Ricci tensor, we give a classification of real hypersurfaces in the complex quadric with the semi-symmetric ∗-Ricci tensor.

Keywords: Reeb-flow-invariant ∗-Ricci operator; Reeb-parallel ∗-Ricci operator; semi-symmetric ∗-Ricci tensor; singular-unit normal vector field

MSC: 53C40; 53C55

Citation: Ma, R.; Pei, D. The ∗-Ricci Operator on Hopf Real Hypersurfaces in the Complex Quadric. *Mathematics* 2023, 11, 90. https://doi.org/10.3390/math11010090

Academic Editor: Cristina–Elena Hretcanu

Received: 15 November 2022
Accepted: 21 December 2022
Published: 26 December 2022

Copyright: © 2022 by the authors. Licensee MDPI, Basel, Switzerland. This article is an open access article distributed under the terms and conditions of the Creative Commons Attribution (CC BY) license (https://creativecommons.org/licenses/by/4.0/).

1. Introduction

There are many Hermitian symmetric spaces of rank 2. For example, complex two-plane Grassmannians and complex hyperbolic two-plane Grassmannians, which are denoted by $G_2(\mathbb{C}^{m+2}) = SU_{m+2}/S(U_2 U_m)$ and $G_2^*(\mathbb{C}^{m+2}) = SU_{m,2}/S(U_2 U_m)$, respectively. They are Hermitian symmetric spaces and quaternionic Kähler symmetric spaces equipped with the Kähler structure J and quaternionic Kähler structure $\mathfrak{J}$.

The complex quadric $Q^m = SO_{m+2}/SO_m SO_2$ is another kind of compact Hermitian symmetric space different from the above ones. For $m \geq 2$, the maximal sectional curvature of Q^m is equal to 4 (see [1,2]). It is the complex hypersurface in complex projective space $\mathbb{C}P^{m+1}$ [3], and it is also a kind of real Grassmannian manifold with rank 2 [4]. So, we know that apart from the Kähler structure J, there is another distinguished geometric structure, namely, a parallel rank two vector field bundle $\mathfrak{A}$ that contains an S^1-bundle of real structures, that is, complex conjugations A on the tangent spaces of Q^m. The complex conjugation A and the Kähler structure J anti-commute with each other, that is, $AJ = -JA$.

The Kähler manifold is the subject of symplectic geometry. Contact geometry appears as the odd dimensional counterpart of symplectic geometry, in which the almost-contact manifold corresponds to the almost complex manifold. Mathematicians are interested in submanifolds or hypersurfaces with some certain structure or curvature properties (see [5–11]). The real hypersurface M in the complex quadric Q^m is naturally an almost contact metric manifold. Many mathematicians have investigated it from various aspects. For example, some classifications of M related to the parallel Ricci tensor and Reeb-parallel Ricci tensor were obtained in Suh [12,13]. Moreover, Suh studied the real hypersurface M with the commuting Ricci tensor and the Ricci soliton in [14,15]. In [16], Suh and his partner Pérez gave the classification of the real hypersurface M in Q^m with the killing shape operator, and in [17], Pérez obtained some results when the structure vector field of the almost contact structure of M was of the Jacobi type.

The real hypersurface M is a Hopf hypersurface when the integral curves of the Reeb vector field ξ are geodesic. Moreover, the integral curves of ξ are geodesic if and only if ξ is a principal curvature vector of M everywhere, that is,

$$S\xi = \alpha\xi,$$

where S is the shape operator of M, and α is Reeb function. The classification of the Hopf hypersurface M in Q^m with some other geometric properties can be found in [12].

The unit normal vector field N of the real hypersurface M in Q^m has a great impact on the geometric properties of the hypersurface M. Usually, N can be put into two classes: N is $\mathfrak{A}$-principal or $\mathfrak{A}$-isotropic. In [18], Berndt and Suh proved that if M has isometric Reeb flow, then N is $\mathfrak{A}$-isotropic, and it is locally congruent to a tube over a totally geodesic $\mathbb{C}P^k$ in Q^{2k}. When M is in contact with the $\mathfrak{A}$-principal unit normal vector field N, then the classification of M can be found in [19].

In differential geometry, the Ricci tensor Ric is very significant to the nature of a manifold. For example, in [12] Suh proved that there was no Hopf real hypersurface with a parallel Ricci tensor in the complex quadric Q^m, $m \geq 4$. Moreover, in [20], Lee, Suh, and Woo showed that there were not any Hopf real hypersurfaces in the complex quadric Q^m with the semi-symmetric Ricci tensor and the $\mathfrak{A}$-principal unit normal vector field and gave the classification when the unit normal vector field was $\mathfrak{A}$-isotropic. In [21], Suh classified the the real hypersurface in the complex quadric Q^m with the Reeb-invarient Ricci tensor, and some classification about the Reeb-parallel Ricci tensor could be found in [13]. In [22], we obtained several properties on Lorentzian generalized Sasakian space-forms, which are related to the Ricci tensor.

Apart from the Ricci tensor, there is another important curvature tensor for the almost-contact manifold, that is, the $*$-Ricci tensor Ric*. The notion of the $*$-Ricci tensor was introduced by Tachibana in [23], and Hamada extended this notion to almost-contact manifolds in [24]. Its definition is similar to the Ricci tensor, but its properties are different from the Ricci tensor. For instance, it may be not symmetric since it is related to the structure tensor ϕ. If the $*$-Ricci tensor is symmetric, we can directly investigate it. Many authors has investigated the $*$-Ricci soliton, which replaced Ricci tensor with the $*$-Ricci tensor in the Ricci soliton (see [25,26]). In [27], we gave the classification of the trans-Sasakian three-manifolds with the Reeb invariant $*$-Ricci opertator. In [28], we gave the notion of the semi-symmetric $*$-Ricci tensor and investigated the properties of it on the (κ, μ)-contact manifold.

In the present paper, we study the real hypersurface M in Q^m with the Reeb invariant and the Reeb-parallel $*$-Ricci operator. We also investigate the Hopf real hypersurfaces with the semi-symmetric $*$-Ricci tensor.

Generally, the conditions of the Reeb invariant $*$-Ricci operator and the Reeb-parallel $*$-Ricci operator are not the same since the Reeb invariant $*$-Ricci operator is defined by $L_\xi Q^* = 0$ and the Reeb-parallel $*$-Ricci operator is $\nabla_\xi Q^* = 0$; in other words, one is a Lie derivative and the other is a connection derivative. However, we can see from the following theorem that they are the same for the Hopf real hypersurface in the complex quadric with the singular-unit normal vector field.

Theorem 1. *Let M be a Hopf real hypersurface in the complex quadric Q^m, $m \geq 3$, with the $\mathfrak{A}$-principal or $\mathfrak{A}$-isotropic unit normal vector field N; then,*

$$L_\xi Q^* = \nabla_\xi Q^* = 0,$$

where Q^* is the $*$-Ricci operator, ξ is Reeb vector field, L is Lie derivative, and ∇ is Riemannian connection of M. That is, the $*$-Ricci operator on a Hopf real hypersurface in the complex quadric Q^m, $m \geq 3$, with a singular-unit normal vector field that is both Reeb-flow-invariant and Reeb-parallel.

Aa an analogue to the notion of the semi-symmetric Ricci tensor, we consider the notion of the semi-symmetric $*$-Ricci tensor defined by

$$0 = (R(X,Y)\text{Ric}^*)(Z,W) = -\text{Ric}^*(R(X,Y)Z,W) - \text{Ric}^*(Z,R(X,Y)W),$$

for any vector field X, Y, Z, and W on the manifold. It has been proved that there are no Hopf hypersurfaces in the complex quadric with the semi-symmetric Ricci tensor and the $\mathfrak{A}$-principal unit normal vector field in [20]. For the $*$-Ricci tensor, we draw the conclusion that:

Theorem 2. *Hopf real hypersurfaces with the semi-symmetric $*$-Ricci tensor and $\mathfrak{A}$-principal unit normal vector field do not exist in the complex quadric Q^m, $m \geq 3$.*

2. Some General Equations and Key Lemmas

As we have mentioned above, the complex quadric Q^m is the complex hypersurface in the complex projective space $\mathbb{C}P^{m+1}$. If $z_0, \ldots, z_{m+1}$ are the homogeneous coordinates of $\mathbb{C}P^{m+1}$, then Q^m is the image of the equation $z_0^2 + \ldots + z_{m+1}^2 = 0$. Now, we denote the Kähler structure of $\mathbb{C}P^{m+1}$ by $(J, \bar{g})$, where $\bar{g}$ is the Fubini–Study metric on $\mathbb{C}P^{m+1}$, which has constant holomorphic sectional curvature 4. We know that the complex hypersurface of a Kähler manifold has an induced Kähler structure; in other words, it is a Kähler manifold. Then, the complex quadric Q^m has a canonical induced Kähler structure (J, g), where g is the Riemannian metric on Q^m induced from the Fubini–Study metric $\bar{g}$. Now, we explain why Q^m is $SO_{m+2}/SO_m SO_2$. Firstly, it is known that the complex projective space $\mathbb{C}P^{m+1} = SU_{m+2}/S(U_{m+1}U_1)$ because it is a Hermitian symmetric space of the special unitary group SU_{m+2}. As the subgroup of SU_{m+2}, SO_{m+2} acts on $\mathbb{C}P^{m+1}$ with cohomogeneity one. If the orbit of SO_{m+2} contains the fixed point of the action of the stabilizer $S(U_{m+1}U_1)$, namely, $o = [0, \ldots, 0, 1] \in \mathbb{C}P^{m+1}$, then this orbit is a totally geodesic real projective space $\mathbb{R}P^{m+1} \subset \mathbb{C}P^{m+1}$. The complex quadric $Q^m = SO_{m+2}/SO_m SO_2$ is just the second singular orbit of this action. It also gives the geometric interpretation of why Q^m is the Grassmann manifold $G_2^+(\mathbb{R}^{m+2})$ of oriented 2-planes in $\mathbb{R}^{m+2}$. In this paper, we focus on the condition of $m \geq 3$ because Q^1 is just S^1 and Q^2 is $S^1 \times S^1$.

Let us denote the unit normal vector field of Q^m by $\bar{N}$, and $A_{\bar{N}}$ is the shape operator of Q^m respect to $\bar{N}$. $A_{\bar{N}}$ is anti-commuting with the Kähler structure J, and it is involution. Then, the shape operator $A_{\bar{N}}$ is one of the complex conjugations A restricted to TQ^m. In some sense, we can consider the set of all shape operators of Q^m as the complex conjugations on TQ^m. Then, the tangent space of Q^m can be decomposed as

$$TQ^m = V(A_{\bar{N}}) \oplus JV(A_{\bar{N}}),$$

where $V(A_{\bar{N}})$ and $JV(A_{\bar{N}})$ are the $(+1)$-eigenspace and (-1)-eigenspace, respectively. So, $A_{\bar{N}}$ defines a real structure, and since the real codimension of Q^m in $\mathbb{C}P^{m+1}$ is 2, there is an S^1-subbundle $\mathfrak{A}$ of the endomorphism bundle $\text{End}(TQ^m)$ consisting of complex conjugations.

In terms of the complex conjugations $A \in \mathfrak{A}$ and the Kähler structure J, we obtain the curvature tensor $\bar{R}$ of Q^m from the Gauss equation for $Q^m \subset \mathbb{C}P^{m+1}$

$$\begin{aligned}\bar{R}(X,Y)Z &= g(Y,Z)X - g(X,Z)Y + g(JY,Z)JX - g(JX,Z)JY - 2g(JX,Y)JZ \\ &+ g(AY,Z)AX - g(AX,Z)AY + g(JAY,Z)JAX - g(JAX,Z)JAY.\end{aligned}$$

A nonzero vector field $Z \in TQ^m$ is singular if it is $\mathfrak{A}$-principal or $\mathfrak{A}$-isotropic. For these two types of singular vector fields, we have

1. If there is a conjugation $A \in \mathfrak{A}$ so that $Z \in V(A)$, then Z is $\mathfrak{A}$-principal.
2. If there is a conjugation $A \in \mathfrak{A}$ and two orthonormal vector fields $X, Y \in V(A)$ so that $Z/\|Z\| = (X + JY)/\sqrt{2}$, then Z is $\mathfrak{A}$-isotropic.

Let M be the real hypersurface of Q^m and (ϕ, ξ, η, g) be its induced almost contact structure. Then, we have the following basic equations [29]:

$$\phi\xi = 0, \quad \eta \circ \phi = 0,$$
$$\phi^2 X = -X + \eta(X)\xi, \quad \eta(\xi) = 1,$$
$$\eta(X) = g(\xi, X),$$
$$g(\phi X, \phi Y) = g(X, Y) - \eta(X)\eta(Y),$$

where ϕ is the structure tensor, ξ is Reeb vector field, and η is the dual 1-form of ξ, for any vector fields X and Y. Moreover, $\xi = -JN$ where J is the Kähler structure of Q^m and N is the unit normal vector field of M. The structure tensor ϕ and the Kähler structure J are related by

$$JX = \phi X + \eta(X)N.$$

Thus, ϕ and J coincide with each other when restricted to the kernel of η.

For any complex conjugation $A \in \mathfrak{A}$, we can choose two orthonormal vectors $Z_1, Z_2 \in V(A)$, such that

$$\begin{aligned} N &= \cos(t)Z_1 + \sin(t)JZ_2, \\ AN &= \cos(t)Z_1 - \sin(t)JZ_2, \\ \xi &= \sin(t)Z_2 - \cos(t)JZ_1, \\ A\xi &= \sin(t)Z_2 + \cos(t)JZ_1, \end{aligned}$$

where $0 \leq t \leq \frac{\pi}{4}$ (see [12]). The $\mathfrak{A}$-principal unit normal vector field N corresponds to the value $t = 0$; thus, we have $g(AN, N) = -g(\xi, A\xi) = 1$, $g(N, AY) = g(AN, Y) = 0$. The $\mathfrak{A}$-isotropic unit normal vector field N corresponds to the value $t = \frac{\pi}{4}$, so we have $g(AN, N) = g(\xi, A\xi) = 0$. Thus, $AN \in TM$.

In particular, we see that $A\xi$ is always the tangent on M (because it holds

$$\begin{aligned} g(A\xi, N) &= g(\sin(t)Z_2 + \cos(t)JZ_1, \cos(t)Z_1 + \sin(t)JZ_2) \\ &= \sin(t)\cos(t)g(Z_2, Z_1) + \sin2(t)g(Z_2, JZ_2) \\ &\quad + \cos2(t)g(JZ_1, Z_1) + \cos(t)\sin(t)g(JZ_1, JZ_2) \\ &= 0, \end{aligned}$$

for two orthonormal vectors $Z_1z, Z_2 \in V(A)$). So, from this and the property of $JA = -AJ$, we obtain

$$AN = AJ\xi = -JA\xi = -\phi A\xi - g(A\xi, \xi)N.$$

In fact, on a real hypersurface M in the complex quadric Q^m, for any vector field X on M, we can put

$$AX = BX + g(AX, N)N = BX + \rho(X)N,$$

here, BX denotes the tangential part of AX and 1-form ρ is given by

$$\begin{aligned} \rho(X) &= g(X, AN) = g(AX, N) \\ &= g(X, -\phi A\xi - g(A\xi, \xi)N) \\ &= -g(X, \phi A\xi), \end{aligned}$$

so

$$\begin{aligned} JAX &= JBX + g(X, AN)JN \\ &= JBX - g(X, \phi A\xi)JN \\ &= JBX + g(X, \phi A\xi)\xi \\ &= \phi BX + \eta(BX)N + g(X, \phi A\xi)\xi \\ &= \phi BX + \eta(BX)N - \rho(X)\xi, \end{aligned}$$

and

$$(JAX)^T = \phi BX - \rho(X)\xi,$$

where $(\cdots)^T$ denotes the tangential component of the vector $(\cdots)$ in Q^m.

Denote the induced Riemannian connection and the shape operator on M by ∇, S, respectively. Then, the Gauss–Weingarten equations are

$$\bar{\nabla}_X Y = \nabla_X Y + g(SX, Y)N, \quad \bar{\nabla}_X N = -SX,$$

where $\bar{\nabla}$ is the Riemannian connection on Q^m with respect to $\bar{g}$. Moreover, we have the following two equations:

$$(\nabla_X \phi)Y = \eta(Y)SX - g(SX, Y)\xi, \quad \nabla_X \xi = \phi SX.$$

Additionally, from the Gauss–Weingarten equation, in terms of the Kähler structure J and the complex conjugation $A \in \mathfrak{A}$, the curvature tensor R of M induced from $\bar{R}$ of Q^m is

$$\begin{aligned}
R(X,Y)Z &= g(Y,Z)X - g(X,Z)Y + g(\phi Y, Z)\phi X - g(\phi X, Z)\phi Y - 2g(\phi X, Y)\phi Z \\
&\quad + g(AY, Z)(AX)^T - g(AX, Z)(AY)^T + g(JAY, Z)(JAX)^T \\
&\quad - g(JAX, Z)(JAY)^T + g(SY, Z)SX - g(SX, Z)SY \\
&= g(Y,Z)X - g(X,Z)Y + g(\phi Y, Z)\phi X - g(\phi X, Z)\phi Y - 2g(\phi X, Y)\phi Z \\
&\quad + g(BY, Z)BX - g(BX, Z)BY \\
&\quad + g(\phi BY, Z)\phi BX - g(\phi BY, Z)\rho(X)\xi - \rho(Y)\eta(Z)\phi BX \\
&\quad - g(\phi BX, Z)\phi BY + g(\phi BY, Z)\rho(Y)\xi + \rho(X)\eta(Z)\phi BY \\
&\quad + g(SY, Z)SX - g(SX, Z)SY.
\end{aligned}$$

For an almost contact metric manifold, the $*$-Ricci tensor Ric^* is (see [24,25])

$$\mathrm{Ric}^*(X,Y) = \frac{1}{2} \mathrm{trace}\{Z \to R(X, \phi Y)\phi Z\}.$$

So, we can calculate the $*$-Ricci tensor Ric^* of M

$$\begin{aligned}
\mathrm{Ric}^*(X,Y) &= \frac{1}{2} \sum_{i=1}^{2m-1} g(R(X, \phi Y)\phi e_i, e_i) \\
&= \frac{1}{2}\{g(\phi X, \phi Y) + g(\phi X, \phi Y) + g(\phi X, \phi Y) \\
&\quad + g(\phi X, \phi Y) + 4(m-1)g(\phi X, \phi Y) - g(\phi B\phi Y, BX) \\
&\quad + g(\phi BX, B\phi Y) - g(\phi^2 B\phi Y, \phi BX) + g(\phi^2 B\phi Y, \xi)\rho(X) \\
&\quad + g(\phi^2 B\phi X, \phi B\phi Y) + g(\phi^2 BX, \xi)\rho(\phi Y) \\
&\quad - g(SX, \phi S\phi Y) + g(\phi SX, S\phi Y)\} \\
&= 2mg(\phi X, \phi Y) + 2g(\phi BX, B\phi Y) + g(\phi SX, S\phi Y),
\end{aligned}$$

where $\{e_i\}$ is a local orthonormal basis of M.

Generally, Ric^* is not symmetric because it has an asymmetric part $g(\phi BX, B\phi Y)$ and $g(\phi SX, S\phi Y)$. So, it is not a geometric invariant. The asymmetric $*$-Ricci tensor is just a tensor on a manifold; it makes little sense of geometry or physics. Hence, when we investigate the $*$-Ricci tensor, we only focus on the symmetric $*$-Ricci tensor or the symmetric part of the $*$-Ricci tensor. The following theorem tells us when the $*$-Ricci tensor is symmetric on a Hopf hypersurface in the complex quadric.

Theorem 3. *Let M be a Hopf hypersurface in the complex quadric Q^m, $m \geq 3$. Then, the $*$-Ricci tensor Ric^* of M is symmetric if and only if the unit normal vector field N of M is singular, that is, N is either $\mathfrak{A}$-principal or $\mathfrak{A}$-isotropic.*

In particular, if N is $\mathfrak{A}$-principal, then

$$\mathrm{Ric}^*(X,Y) = 2(m-1)g(\phi X, \phi Y) - g((\phi S)^2 X, Y),$$

if N is $\mathfrak{A}$-isotropic, then

$$\text{Ric}^*(X,Y) = 2(m-1)g(\phi X, \phi Y) - g((\phi S)^2 X, Y)$$
$$+ 2g(X, A\xi)g(Y, A\xi) + 2g(X, AN)g(Y, AN),$$

for any vector fields X, Y on M.

Proof. In [25], it has been proved that if M is Hopf, then $(\phi S)^2 = (S\phi)^2$. So, we have

$$g(\phi SX, S\phi Y) = -g((\phi S)^2 X, Y) = -g((S\phi)^2 X, Y) = g(\phi SY, S\phi X).$$

Now, we calculate $g(\phi BX, B\phi Y)$:

$$\begin{aligned}
g(\phi BX, B\phi Y) &= g(JBX - \eta(BX)N, B\phi Y) = g(JBX, B\phi Y) \\
&= g(JBX, A\phi Y - g(A\phi Y, N)N) \\
&= -g(BX, JA\phi Y - g(A\phi Y, N)JN) \\
&= -g(AX - g(AX, N)N, JA\phi Y - g(A\phi Y, N)JN) \\
&= -g(AX, JA\phi Y) + g(A\phi Y, N)g(AX, JN) + g(AX, N)g(N, JA\phi Y) \\
&= g(X, \phi^2 Y) + g(JY, AN)g(AX, JN) - \eta(Y)g(N, AN)g(AX, JN) \\
&\quad + g(X, AN)g(Y, AN) \\
&= g(X, \phi^2 Y) + g(Y, A\xi)g(X, A\xi) + \eta(Y)g(N, AN)g(X, A\xi) \\
&\quad + g(X, AN)g(Y, AN).
\end{aligned}$$

First, we assume the ∗-Ricci tensor is symmetric, that is, $\text{Ric}^*(X, Y) = \text{Ric}^*(Y, X)$. From the above equation, there must be

$$\eta(Y)g(N, AN)g(X, A\xi) = \eta(X)g(N, AN)g(Y, A\xi),$$

If $g(N, AN) = 0$, that is, N is $\mathfrak{A}$-isotropic. If $g(N, AN) \neq 0$, putting $X = \xi, Y = A\xi$, we have $g(A\xi, \xi)^2 = \eta(\xi)g(A\xi, A\xi) = 1$. We know

$$\begin{aligned}
g(A\xi, \xi) &= g(\sin(t)Z_2 + \cos(t)JZ_1, \sin(t)Z_2 - \cos(t)JZ_1) \\
&= -\cos(2t),
\end{aligned}$$

where $0 \leq t \leq \frac{\pi}{4}$. According to these facts, $g(A\xi, \xi) = -1$, that is, $t = 0$. It implies that the normal vector field N is $\mathfrak{A}$-principal.

Conversely, if N is $\mathfrak{A}$-principal, from $g(AN, N) = -g(\xi, A\xi) = 1$, $g(N, AY) = g(AN, Y) = 0$, we have

$$\begin{aligned}
\text{Ric}^*(X, Y) &= 2mg(\phi X, \phi Y) + 2g(\phi BX, B\phi Y) + g(\phi SX, S\phi Y) \\
&= 2mg(\phi X, \phi Y) + 2g(X, \phi^2 Y) + g(X, \xi)g(Y, \xi) - \eta(Y)g(X, \xi) \\
&\quad + g(\phi SX, S\phi Y) \\
&= 2(m-1)g(\phi X, \phi Y) - g((\phi S)^2 X, Y).
\end{aligned}$$

If N is $\mathfrak{A}$-isotropic, from $g(AN, N) = g(\xi, A\xi) = 0$, we have

$$\begin{aligned}
\text{Ric}^*(X, Y) &= 2mg(\phi X, \phi Y) + 2g(\phi BX, B\phi Y) + g(\phi SX, S\phi Y) \\
&= 2mg(\phi X, \phi Y) + 2(g(X, \phi^2 Y) + g(Y, A\xi)g(X, A\xi) \\
&\quad + g(X, AN)g(Y, AN)) + g(\phi SX, S\phi Y) \\
&= 2(m-1)g(\phi X, \phi Y) - g((\phi S)^2 X, Y) \\
&\quad + 2g(X, A\xi)g(Y, A\xi) + 2g(X, AN)g(Y, AN),
\end{aligned}$$

From the above two equations, we know that when the condition of N is singular, the ∗-Ricci tensor is symmetric. □

When the ∗-Ricci tensor is symmetric, we can define the ∗-Ricci operator by

$$\text{Ric}^*(X, Y) = g(Q^* X, Y).$$

The following are some important theorems that will be used in the proof of our main theorems.

Theorem 4 ([30]). *Let M be a real hypersurface in the complex quadric Q^m, $M \geq 3$, with $\mathfrak{A}$-principal normal vector field N. Then,*
(a) $A\phi X = -\phi A X$,
(b) $A\phi S X = -\phi S X$,
(c) $ASX = SX - 2g(SX, \xi)\xi$ and $SAX = SX - 2\eta(X)S\xi$,
for any $X \in TM$.

In particular, if M is Hopf, then we obtain $ASX = SAX$ for any tangent vector field X on M.

Theorem 5 ([12]). *Let M be a Hopf real hypersurface in the complex quadric Q^m, $M \geq 3$. Then, M has an $\mathfrak{A}$-principal singular normal vector field N if and only if M is a contact real hypersurface with constant mean curvature and non-vanishing Reeb function in Q^m.*

Moreover, for a contact manifold, we have

Theorem 6 ([29]). *Let M be a hypersurface of a Kähler manifold, (ϕ, ξ, η, g) its induced almost contact metric structure, and S its shape operator. Then, (ϕ, ξ, η, g) is a contact metric structure if and only if $S\phi + \phi S = -2\phi$.*

Theorem 7 ([31]). *Let M be a Hopf hypersurface in the complex quadric Q^m with the singular unite normal vector field; then, the Reeb function α is the constant function.*

3. Proof of Theorem 1 with $\mathfrak{A}$-Principal unit Normal VECTOR field

Firstly, let us calculate the derivative and Lie derivative of Q^* along ξ. Now

$$L_\xi(g(Q^*X, Y)) = \xi(g(X, Y)) = \nabla_\xi(g(Q^*X, Y)).$$

So, we have

$$(L_\xi g)(Q^*X, Y) + g((L_\xi Q^*)X, Y) + g(Q^*(L_\xi X), Y) + g(Q^*X, L_\xi Y) \\ = g((\nabla_\xi Q^*)X, Y) + g(Q^*(\nabla_\xi X), Y) + g(Q^*X, \nabla_\xi Y). \quad (1)$$

From $\nabla_X \xi = \phi S X$, we have

$$\begin{aligned}(L_\xi g)(X, Y) &= g(\nabla_X \xi, Y) + g(X, \nabla_Y \xi) \\ &= g(\phi S X, Y) + g(X, \phi S Y) \\ &= g((\phi S - S\phi)X, Y).\end{aligned}$$

Then, Equation (1) becomes

$$\begin{aligned}&g((\nabla_\xi Q^*)X, Y) + g(Q^*(\nabla_\xi X), Y) + g(Q^*X, \nabla_\xi Y) \\ =\, &g((\phi S - S\phi)Q^*X, Y) + g((L_\xi Q^*)X, Y) \\ &+ g(Q^*(\nabla_\xi X - \nabla_X \xi), Y) + g(Q^*X, \nabla_\xi Y - \nabla_Y \xi).\end{aligned}$$

From the above equation, we have

$$\begin{aligned}g((L_\xi Q^*)X, Y) &= g((\nabla_\xi Q^*)X, Y) - g(\phi S Q^* X, Y) + g(Q^*\phi S X, Y) \\ &= g((\nabla_\xi Q^*)X, Y) + g(Q^*X, S\phi Y) + g(Q^*\phi S X, Y)\end{aligned} \quad (2)$$

In this section, we assume the real hypersurface M in Q^m is Hopf and the unit normal vector field is $\mathfrak{A}$-principal. From Theorem 3, we have

$$\begin{aligned}
g((L_\xi Q^*)X,Y) &= g((\nabla_\xi Q^*)X,Y) + g(Q^*X, S\phi Y) + g(Q^*\phi SX, Y)\\
&= g((\nabla_\xi Q^*)X,Y)\\
&\quad + 2(m-1)g(\phi X, \phi S\phi Y) - g((\phi S)^2 X, S\phi Y)\\
&\quad + 2(m-1)g(\phi^2 SX, \phi Y) - g((\phi S)^2 \phi SX, Y)\\
&= g((\nabla_\xi Q^*)X,Y),
\end{aligned}$$

we have $(L_\xi Q^*)X = (\nabla_\xi Q^*)X$.

Now, we prove that when N is $\mathfrak{A}$-principal, then $(L_\xi Q^*)X = (\nabla_\xi Q^*)X = 0$. The Codazzi equation (see [12]) is

$$\begin{aligned}
g((\nabla_X S)Y - (\nabla_Y S)X, Z) &= \eta(X)g(\phi Y, Z) - \eta(Y)g(\phi X, Z) - 2\eta(Z)g(\phi X, Y)\\
&\quad + g(X, AN)g(AY, Z) - g(Y, AN)g(AX, Z)\\
&\quad + g(X, A\xi)g(JAY, Z) - g(Y, A\xi)g(JAX, Z). \quad (3)
\end{aligned}$$

Putting $X = \xi$ in (3) and in considerationation of $g(AN,N) = -g(\xi, A\xi) = 1$, we have

$$g((\nabla_\xi S)Y - (\nabla_Y S)\xi, Z) = g(\phi Y, Z) - g(JAY, Z). \quad (4)$$

Since M is Hopf, $S\xi = \alpha\xi$ and α are constant from Lemma 7,

$$(\nabla_Y S)\xi = \nabla_Y(S\xi) - S(\nabla_Y \xi) = \alpha \nabla_Y \xi - S\phi SY = \alpha\phi SY - S\phi SY. \quad (5)$$

From Equations (4) and (5), we have

$$\begin{aligned}
g((\nabla_\xi S)Y, Z) &= g(\phi Y, Z) - g(JAY, Z) + g((\nabla_Y S)\xi, Z)\\
&= g(\phi Y, Z) - g(JAY, Z) + g(\alpha\phi SY - S\phi SY, Z). \quad (6)
\end{aligned}$$

In [12], Suh proved that for a Hopf hypersurface M in Q^m, the following equation:

$$\begin{aligned}
0 &= 2g(S\phi SY, Z) - \alpha g((\phi S + S\phi)Y, Z) - 2g(\phi Y, Z)\\
&\quad + 2g(Y, AN)g(Z, A\xi) - 2g(Z, AN)g(Y, A\xi)\\
&\quad + 2g(\xi, A\xi)\{g(Z, AN)\eta(Y) - g(Y, AN)\eta(Z)\}, \quad (7)
\end{aligned}$$

holds for all vector fields Y, Z on M. From Equations (6) and (7), in consideration of $g(X, AN) = 0$, we have

$$\begin{aligned}
g((\nabla_\xi S)Y, Z) &= -g(JAY, Z) + \alpha g(\phi SY, Z) - \frac{\alpha}{2}g((\phi S + S\phi)Y, Z)\\
&= g(AJY, Z) + \frac{\alpha}{2}g((\phi S - S\phi)Y, Z). \quad (8)
\end{aligned}$$

When the unit normal vector field N is $\mathfrak{A}$-principal, we have that the $*$-Ricci tensor Ric* on M is

$$g(Q^*Y, Z) = \text{Ric}^*(Y, Z) = 2(m-1)g(\phi Y, \phi Z) - g((\phi S)^2 Y, Z),$$

from Theorem 3. Applying ∇_ξ to both side of this equation, we have

$$g((\nabla_\xi Q^*)Y, Z) = g((\nabla_\xi S)\phi SY, \phi Z) - g((\nabla_\xi S)Y, \phi S\phi Z), \quad (9)$$

by $(\nabla_\xi \phi)Y = \eta(Y)S\xi - g(S\xi, Y)\xi = 0$. Putting Equation (8) in Equation (9), we have

$$\begin{aligned}
g((\nabla_\zeta Q^*)Y, Z) &= g(AJ\phi SY, \phi Z) + \frac{\alpha}{2}g((\phi S - S\phi)\phi SY, \phi Z) \\
&\quad - g(AJY, \phi S\phi Z) - \frac{\alpha}{2}g((\phi S - S\phi)Y, \phi S\phi Z) \\
&= g(AJ\phi SY, \phi Z) + g(JAY, \phi S\phi Z) \\
&= g(\phi^2 SY, A\phi Z) - g(AY, \phi^2 S\phi Z) \\
&= -g(SY, A\phi Z) + g(AY, S\phi Z) \\
&= g((\phi AS - \phi SA)Y, Z),
\end{aligned} \qquad (10)$$

by $JX = \phi X + \eta(X)N$ and $A\zeta = -\zeta$ if N is $\mathfrak{A}$-principal.

From Lemma 4 and Equation (10), we have

$$g((\nabla_\zeta Q^*)Y, Z) = g((\phi AS - \phi SA)Y, Z) = 0.$$

That is

$$(\nabla_\zeta Q^*)X = 0.$$

4. Proof of Theorem 1 with $\mathfrak{A}$-Isotropic unit Normal Vector Field

In this section, we assume the real hypersurface M in Q^m is Hopf and the unit normal vector field is $\mathfrak{A}$-isotropic. We have $g(AN, N) = g(\zeta, A\zeta) = 0$ and $AN \in TM$.

In [12], the authors have proved that for a Hopf hypersurface M in Q^m, $m \geq 3$, with $\mathfrak{A}$-isotropic unit normal vector field N, the following two equations are satisfied:

$$SAN = 0, \quad \text{and} \quad SA\zeta = 0.$$

Thus, we have

$$\begin{aligned}
g(X, AN)g(S\phi Y, AN) &= g(X, AN)g(\phi Y, SAN) = 0, \\
g(X, A\zeta)g(S\phi Y, A\zeta) &= g(X, A\zeta)g(\phi Y, SA\zeta) = 0, \\
g(Y, AN)g(\phi SX, AN) &= g(Y, AN)g(AN, JSX - \eta(SX)N) \\
&= g(Y, AN)g(AJN, SX) \\
&= -g(Y, AN)g(SA\zeta, X) = 0 \\
g(Y, A\zeta)g(\phi SX, A\zeta) &= g(Y, A\zeta)g(A\zeta, JSX - \eta(SX)N) \\
&= -g(Y, A\zeta)g(JA\zeta, SX) \\
&= g(Y, A\zeta)g(AJ\zeta, SX) \\
&= g(Y, A\zeta)g(SAN, X) = 0.
\end{aligned}$$

Then, from Equation (2) and Theorem 3, we have

$$\begin{aligned}
g((L_\zeta Q^*)X, Y) &= g((\nabla_\zeta Q^*)X, Y) + g(Q^*X, S\phi Y) + g(Q^*\phi SX, Y) \\
&= g((\nabla_\zeta Q^*)X, Y) \\
&\quad + 2(m-1)g(\phi X, \phi S\phi Y) - g((\phi S)^2 X, S\phi Y) \\
&\quad + g(X, A\zeta)g(S\phi Y, A\zeta) + g(X, AN)g(S\phi Y, AN) \\
&\quad + 2(m-1)g(\phi^2 SX, \phi Y) - g((\phi S)^2 \phi SX, Y) \\
&\quad + g(Y, A\zeta)g(\phi SX, A\zeta) + g(Y, AN)g(\phi SX, AN) \\
&= g((\nabla_\zeta Q^*)X, Y),
\end{aligned}$$

we obtain $(L_\zeta Q^*)X = (\nabla_\zeta Q^*)X$. From

$$\begin{aligned}
g(Q^*X, Y) &= 2(m-1)g(\phi X, \phi Y) - g((\phi S)^2 X, Y) \\
&\quad + 2g(X, A\zeta)g(Y, A\zeta) + 2g(X, AN)g(Y, AN),
\end{aligned}$$

we can calculate that

$$\begin{aligned}g((\nabla_\xi Q^*)X,Y) &= 2g(\nabla_\xi(AN),X)g(AN,Y)+2g(\nabla_\xi(AN),Y)g(AN,X)\\&+2g(\nabla_\xi(A\xi),X)g(A\xi,Y)+2g(\nabla_\xi(A\xi),Y)g(A\xi,X)\\&-g(\phi(\nabla_\xi S)\phi SX,Y)-g(\phi S\phi(\nabla_\xi S)X,Y),\end{aligned} \qquad (11)$$

by $AN \in TM$ and $(\nabla_\xi \phi)X = 0$.

In the following, we give the proof of

$$g(\phi(\nabla_\xi S)\phi SX,Y)+g(\phi S\phi(\nabla_\xi S)X,Y)=0. \qquad (12)$$

From Equation (7) and $g(\xi, A\xi) = 0$, we have

$$\begin{aligned}0 &= 2g(S\phi SX,Y) - \alpha g((\phi S + S\phi)X,Y) - 2g(\phi X,Y)\\&+2g(X,AN)g(Y,A\xi)-2g(Y,AN)g(X,A\xi).\end{aligned}$$

Then, we have

$$S\phi SX = \frac{1}{2}\alpha(\phi S + S\phi)X + \phi X - g(X,AN)A\xi + g(X,A\xi)AN. \qquad (13)$$

From $\phi AN = JAN = A\xi$ and $\phi A\xi = JA\xi = -AN$, we have

$$\begin{aligned}S\phi SX + \phi S\phi S\phi X &= \frac{1}{2}\alpha(\phi S + S\phi)X + \phi X - g(X,AN)A\xi + g(X,A\xi)AN\\&\quad \frac{1}{2}\alpha\phi(\phi S + S\phi)\phi X + \phi^3 X - g(\phi X, AN)\phi A\xi\\&\quad +g(\phi X, A\xi)\phi AN\\&= 0\end{aligned} \qquad (14)$$

Putting $X = \xi$ in Codazzi Equation (3) and in consideration of

$$g(AN,N) = g(\xi, A\xi) = 0,$$

we have

$$g((\nabla_\xi S)Y - (\nabla_Y S)\xi, Z) = g(\phi Y, Z) - g(Y,AN)g(A\xi, Z) - g(Y, A\xi)g(JA\xi, Z),$$

thus,

$$\begin{aligned}g((\nabla_\xi S)Y,Z) &= g(\phi Y,Z) - g(Y,AN)g(A\xi,Z)\\&-g(Y,A\xi)g(JA\xi,Z)+g(\alpha\phi SY - S\phi SY,Z),\end{aligned}$$

by Equation (5). So, we have

$$(\nabla_\xi S)Y = \phi Y - g(Y,AN)A\xi + g(Y,A\xi)AN + \alpha\phi SY - S\phi SY. \qquad (15)$$

Then, from Equations (13) and (15), we have

$$(\nabla_\xi S)Y = \alpha\phi SY - \frac{1}{2}\alpha(\phi S + S\phi)Y = \frac{\alpha}{2}(\phi S - S\phi)Y.$$

From Equation (14), we have

$$\begin{aligned}g(\phi(\nabla_\xi S)\phi SX,Y) &+ g(\phi S\phi(\nabla_\xi S)X,Y)\\&= \frac{\alpha}{2}g(\phi(\phi S - S\phi)\phi SX,Y) + \frac{\alpha}{2}g(\phi S\phi(\phi S - S\phi)X,Y)\\&= 0.\end{aligned}$$

Thus, we prove Equation (12).

The derivative of AN and $A\xi$ is

$$\begin{aligned}
\nabla_X(AN) &= \bar{\nabla}_X(AN) - g(SX, AN)N \\
&= (\bar{\nabla}_X A)N + A(\bar{\nabla}_X N) \\
&= q(X)JAN - ASX \\
&= q(X)A\xi - ASX, \\
\nabla_X(A\xi) &= \bar{\nabla}_X(A\xi) - g(SX, A\xi)N \\
&= (\bar{\nabla}_X A)\xi + A(\bar{\nabla}_X \xi) \\
&= (\bar{\nabla}_X A)\xi + A(\bar{\nabla}_X(-JN)) \\
&= q(X)JA\xi - A((\bar{\nabla}_X J)N + J(\bar{\nabla}_X N)) \\
&= q(X)JA\xi + AJSX \\
&= q(X)JA\xi - JASX,
\end{aligned}$$

by $(\bar{\nabla}_U A)V = q(U)JAV$ for all $U, V \in TQ^m$, so $\nabla_\xi(AN) = q(\xi)A\xi - \alpha A\xi$ and $\nabla_\xi(A\xi) = q(\xi)JA\xi - \alpha JA\xi$, to obtain Equation (11), we have

$$\begin{aligned}
g((\nabla_\xi Q^*)X, Y) &= 2g(q(\xi)A\xi - \alpha A\xi, X)g(AN, Y) \\
&\quad + 2g(q(\xi)A\xi - \alpha A\xi, Y)g(AN, X) \\
&\quad + 2g(q(\xi)JA\xi - \alpha JA\xi, X)g(A\xi, Y) \\
&\quad + 2g(q(\xi)JA\xi - \alpha JA\xi, Y)g(A\xi, X) \\
&= 2(q(\xi) - \alpha)(g(A\xi, X)g(AN, Y) + g(A\xi, Y)g(AN, X)) \\
&\quad + 2(q(\xi) - \alpha)(g(JA\xi, X)g(A\xi, Y) + g(JA\xi, Y)g(A\xi, X)) \\
&= 0
\end{aligned}$$

So, there must be $(\nabla_\xi Q^*)X = 0$. So $(L_\xi Q^*)X = (\nabla_\xi Q^*)X = 0$.

5. Proof of Theorem 2

First, we assume that the $*$-Ricci tensor of the Hopf real hypersurface M^{2m-1} of the complex quadric Q^m is semi-symmetric, that is,

$$0 = (R(X, Y)\mathrm{Ric}^*)(Z, W) = -\mathrm{Ric}^*(R(X, Y)Z, W) - \mathrm{Ric}^*(Z, R(X, Y)W).$$

Putting $W = Y = \xi$ and from the fact that

$$\mathrm{Ric}^*(R(X, \xi)Z, \xi) = 0,$$

and

$$\begin{aligned}
R(X, \xi)\xi &= X - \eta(X)\xi + g(A\xi, \xi)(AX)^T - g(AX, \xi)(A\xi)^T \\
&\quad + g(JA\xi, \xi)(JAX)^T - g(JAX, \xi)(JA\xi)^T \\
&\quad + \alpha SX - \alpha^2 \eta(X)\xi,
\end{aligned}$$

since the unit normal vector filed N is $\mathfrak{A}$-principal, we have $AN = N$ and $A\xi = -\xi$, $(AX)^T = BX = AX$; then, the above equation becomes

$$\begin{aligned}
R(X, \xi)\xi &= X - \eta(X)\xi - BX - \eta(X)\xi + \alpha SX - \alpha^2 \eta(X)\xi \\
&= X - 2\eta(X)\xi - AX + \alpha SX - \alpha^2 \eta(X)\xi.
\end{aligned}$$

Then, from Theorem 3, we have

$$\begin{aligned}
0 &= \text{Ric}^*(R(X,\xi)\xi, Z) \\
&= 2(m-1)g(\phi R(X,\xi)\xi, \phi Z) - g((\phi S)^2 R(X,\xi)\xi, Z) \\
&= 2(m-1)g(\phi X - \phi AX + \alpha \phi SX, \phi Z) \\
&\quad - g((\phi S)^2 X - (\phi S)^2 AX + \alpha(\phi S)^2 SX, Z) \\
&= 2(m-1)g(AX - X - \alpha SX, \phi^2 Z) \\
&\quad - g((X - AX + \alpha SX, (\phi S)^2 Z) \\
&= g(AX - X - \alpha SX, 2(m-1)\phi^2 Z + (\phi S)^2 Z)
\end{aligned} \quad (16)$$

where we have used the fact that $(\phi S)^2 = (S\phi)^2$ since M is Hopf.

By replacing X with AX in Equation (16) and from Lemma 4, we have

$$\begin{aligned}
0 &= \text{Ric}^*(R(AX,\xi)\xi, Z) \\
&= g(A^2 X - AX - \alpha SAX, 2(m-1)\phi^2 Z + (\phi S)^2 Z), \\
&= g(X - AX - \alpha SX + 2\alpha^2 \eta(X)\xi, 2(m-1)\phi^2 Z + (\phi S)^2 Z), \\
&= g(X - AX - \alpha SX, 2(m-1)\phi^2 Z + (\phi S)^2 Z).
\end{aligned} \quad (17)$$

From Equations (16) and (17), we have

$$0 = \alpha g(SX, 2(m-1)\phi^2 Z + (\phi S)^2 Z).$$

By replacing Z by ϕZ in the above equation, we have

$$\begin{aligned}
0 &= \alpha g(SX, 2(m-1)\phi^3 Z + (\phi S)^2 \phi Z) \\
&= \alpha g(SX, -2(m-1)\phi Z + \phi^2 S\phi SZ) \\
&= \alpha g(SX, -2(m-1)\phi Z - S\phi SZ) \\
&= \alpha g(X, -2(m-1)S\phi Z - S^2 \phi SZ).
\end{aligned}$$

So, we have

$$2(m-1)S\phi Z + S^2 \phi SZ = 0, \quad (18)$$

since α is a nonzero constant from Lemma 5 and the arbitrariness of vector field X.

Applying A to both sides of Equation (18), and the fact that $A\phi SZ = -\phi SZ$, $ASZ = SAZ$ from Lemma 4, we have

$$\begin{aligned}
0 &= 2(m-1)AS\phi Z + AS^2 \phi SZ \\
&= 2(m-1)AS\phi Z + S^2 A\phi SZ \\
&= 2(m-1)AS\phi Z - S^2 \phi SZ
\end{aligned} \quad (19)$$

From Equations (18) and (19), we have

$$AS\phi Z + S\phi Z = 0. \quad (20)$$

From Lemma 4, we have

$$AS\phi Z = S\phi Z - 2g(S\phi Z, \xi)\xi = S\phi Z,$$

to obatain Equation (20), we have

$$S\phi Z = 0.$$

From Lemmas 5 and 6, we know the Hopf hypersurface M is in contact and $S\phi Z + \phi SZ = -2\phi Z$. So,

$$\phi SZ = -2\phi Z.$$

Then, we will have

$$0 = (S\phi)^2 Z = (\phi S)^2 Z = 4\phi^2 Z.$$

That is, $\phi^2 = 0$, which cannot happen. Thus, we complete the proof of Theorem 2.

6. Conclusions

In our paper, we study the Hopf real hypersurface M in the complex quadric Q^m, $m \geq 3$, with some certain $*$-Ricci operator properties. We give the necessary and sufficient condition that the $*$-Ricci tensor on the Hopf real hypersurface in the complex quadric is symetric. We know that the $*$-Ricci operator on the Hopf real hypersurface M with the singular-unit normal vector field N is Reeb-invariant and Reeb-parallel. Moreover, we prove that the $*$-Ricci tensor on the Hopf real hypersurface M in the complex quadric with the $\mathfrak{A}$-principal unit normal vector field cannot be semi-symmetric.

Author Contributions: Writing—original draft preparation, R.M.; writing—review and editing, D.P.; and funding acquisition, D.P. and R.M. All authors have read and agreed to the published version of the manuscript.

Funding: The first author is funded by Yanshan University Basic Innovation Scientific Research Cultivation Project (Youth Project). The second author is funded by the National Natural Science Foundation of China grant number 11671070.

Data Availability Statement: Not applicable.

Acknowledgments: The authors wish to express their sincere thanks to the referees.

Conflicts of Interest: The authors declare no conflict of interest.

References

1. Klein, S. Totally geodesic submanifolds of the complex quadric. *Differ. Geom. Appl.* **2008**, *26*, 79–96. [CrossRef]
2. Reckziegel, H. On the geometry of the complex quadric. In *Geometry and Topology of Submanifolds VIII*; World Scientific Publishing: Brussels, Belgium, 1995; Nordfjordeid, Norway, 1995; River Edge, NJ, USA, 1996; pp. 302–315.
3. Smyth, B. Differential geometry of complex hypersurfaces. *Ann. Math.* **1967**, *85*, 246–266. [CrossRef]
4. Kobayashi, S.; Nomizu, K. *Foundations of Differential Geometry*; Wiley Classics Library; John Wiley & Sons, Inc.: New York, NY, USA, 1996; Volume II; pp. xvi+468. Reprint of the 1969 original, A Wiley-Interscience Publication.
5. Crasmareanu, M.; Hreţcanu, C.E.; Munteanu, M.I. Golden- and product-shaped hypersurfaces in real space forms. *Int. J. Geom. Methods Mod. Phys.* **2013**, *10*, 1320006. [CrossRef]
6. Li, Y.; Abdel-Salam, A.; Saad, M.K. Primitivoids of curves in Minkowski plane. *AIMS Math* **2023**, *2023*, 2386–2406. [CrossRef]
7. Li, Y.; Eren, K.; Ayvacı, K.H.; Ersoy, S. The developable surfaces with pointwise 1-type Gauss map of Frenet type framed base curves in Euclidean 3-space. *AIMS Math* **2023**, *2023*, 2226–2239. [CrossRef]
8. Li, Y.; Eren, K.; Ayvacı, K.H.; Ersoy, S. Simultaneous characterizations of partner ruled surfaces using Flc frame. *AIMS Math* **2022**, *7*, 20213–20229. [CrossRef]
9. Li, Y.; Prasad, R.; Haseeb, A.; Kumar, S.; Kumar, S. A study of Clairaut semi-invariant Riemannian maps from cosymplectic manifolds. *Axioms* **2022**, *11*, 503. [CrossRef]
10. Li, Y.; Nazra, S.H.; Abdel-Baky, R.A. Singularity properties of Timelike sweeping surface in Minkowski 3-space. *Symmetry* **2022**, *14*, 1996. [CrossRef]
11. Li, Y.; Alkhaldi, A.H.; Ali, A.; Laurian-Ioan, P. On the Topology of Warped Product Pointwise Semi-Slant Submanifolds with Positive Curvature. *Mathematics* **2021**, *9*, 3156. [CrossRef]
12. Lee, H.; Suh, Y.J. A new classification on parallel Ricci tensor for real hypersurfaces in the complex quadric. *P. Roy. Soc. Edinb. A* **2020**, *151*, 1846–1868. [CrossRef]
13. Suh, Y.J. Real hypersurfaces in the complex quadric with Reeb parallel Ricci tensor. *J. Geom. Anal.* **2019**, *29*, 3248–3269. [CrossRef]
14. Suh, Y.J. Pseudo-anti commuting Ricci tensor and Ricci soliton real hypersurfaces in the complex quadric. *J. Math. Pures Appl.* **2017**, *107*, 429–450. [CrossRef]
15. Suh, Y.J.; Hwang, D.H. Real hypersurfaces in the complex quadric with commuting Ricci tensor. *Sci. China Math.* **2016**, *59*, 2185–2198. [CrossRef]
16. Pérez, J.D.D.; Jeong, I.; Ko, J.; Suh, Y.J. Real hypersurfaces with Killing shape operator in the complex quadric. *Mediterr. J. Math.* **2018**, *15*, 15. [CrossRef]

17. Pérez, J.D.D. On the structure vector field of a real hypersurface in complex quadric. *Open Math.* **2018**, *16*, 185–189. [CrossRef]
18. Berndt, J.; Suh, Y.J. Real hypersurfaces with isometric Reeb flow in complex quadrics. *Internat. J. Math.* **2013**, *24*, 1350050. [CrossRef]
19. Berndt, J.; Suh, Y.J. Contact hypersurfaces in Kähler manifolds. *Proc. Amer. Math. Soc.* **2015**, *143*, 2637–2649. [CrossRef]
20. Lee, H.; Suh, Y.J.; Woo, C. A classification of Ricci semi-symmetric real hypersurfaces in the complex quadric. *J. Geom. Phys.* **2021**, *164*, 104177. [CrossRef]
21. Suh, Y.J.; Hwang, D.H.; Woo, C. Real hypersurfaces in the complex quadric with Reeb invariant Ricci tensor. *J. Geom. Phys.* **2017**, *120*, 96–105. [CrossRef]
22. Ma, R.; Pei, D. Some curvature properties on Lorentzian generalized Sasakian-space-forms. *Adv. Math. Phys.* **2019**, *2019*, 5136758. [CrossRef]
23. Tachibana, S.i. On almost-analytic vectors in certain almost-Hermitian manifolds. *Tohoku Math. J.* **1959**, *11*, 351–363. [CrossRef]
24. Hamada, T. Real hypersurfaces of complex space forms in terms of Ricci $*$-tensor. *Tokyo J. Math.* **2002**, *25*, 473–483. [CrossRef]
25. Chen, X. Real hypersurfaces of complex quadric in terms of star-Ricci tensor. *Tokyo J. Math.* **2018**, *41*, 587–601. [CrossRef]
26. Ghosh, A.; Patra, D.S. $*$-Ricci soliton within the frame-work of Sasakian and (κ, μ)-contact manifold. *Int. J. Geom. Methods Mod. Phys.* **2018**, *15*, 1850120. [CrossRef]
27. Ma, R.; Pei, D. Reeb-flow-invariant $*$-Ricci operators on trans-Sasakian three-manifolds. *Math. Slovaca* **2021**, *71*, 749–756. [CrossRef]
28. Ma, R.; Pei, D. $*$-Ricci tensor on (κ, μ)-contact manifolds. *AIMS Math.* **2022**, *7*, 11519–11528. [CrossRef]
29. Blair, D.E. Riemannian Geometry of Contact and Symplectic Manifolds. In *Progress in Mathematics*, 2nd ed.; Birkhäuser Boston, Ltd.: Boston, MA, USA, 2010; Volume 203; pp. xvi+343. [CrossRef]
30. Lee, H.; Suh, Y.J. A new classification of real hypersurfaces with Reeb parallel structure Jacobi operator in the complex quadric. *J. Korean Math. Soc.* **2021**, *58*, 895–920. [CrossRef]
31. Suh, Y.J. Real hypersurfaces in the complex quadric with Reeb parallel shape operator. *Internat. J. Math.* **2014**, *25*, 1450059. [CrossRef]

Disclaimer/Publisher's Note: The statements, opinions and data contained in all publications are solely those of the individual author(s) and contributor(s) and not of MDPI and/or the editor(s). MDPI and/or the editor(s) disclaim responsibility for any injury to people or property resulting from any ideas, methods, instructions or products referred to in the content.

Article

First Natural Connection on Riemannian Π-Manifolds

Hristo Manev

Department of Medical Physics and Biophysics, Faculty of Pharmacy, Medical University of Plovdiv, 15A Vasil Aprilov Blvd., 4002 Plovdiv, Bulgaria; hristo.manev@mu-plovdiv.bg; Tel.: +359-887-440-560

Abstract: A natural connection with torsion is defined, and it is called the first natural connection on the Riemannian Π-manifold. Relations between the introduced connection and the Levi–Civita connection are obtained. Additionally, relations between their respective curvature tensors, torsion tensors, Ricci tensors, and scalar curvatures in the main classes of a classification of Riemannian Π-manifolds are presented. An explicit example of dimension five is provided.

Keywords: first natural connection; affine connection; natural connection; Riemannian Π-manifolds

MSC: 53C25; 53D15; 53C50; 53B05; 53D35; 70G45

Citation: Manev, H. First Natural Connection on Riemannian Π-Manifolds. *Mathematics* **2023**, *11*, 1146. https://doi.org/10.3390/math11051146

Academic Editor: Cristina-Elena Hretcanu

Received: 30 January 2023
Revised: 21 February 2023
Accepted: 24 February 2023
Published: 25 February 2023

Copyright: © 2023 by the authors. Licensee MDPI, Basel, Switzerland. This article is an open access article distributed under the terms and conditions of the Creative Commons Attribution (CC BY) license (https://creativecommons.org/licenses/by/4.0/).

1. Introduction

In the present work, we study the differential geometry of the almost paracontact, almost paracomplex Riemannian manifolds, called briefly Riemannian Π-manifolds [1,2]. The considered odd dimensional manifolds have a traceless induced almost product structure on the paracontact distribution, and the restriction on the paracontact distribution of the almost paracontact structure is an almost paracomplex structure. The start of the investigation of the Riemannian Π-manifolds is given in [1] by the name almost paracontact Riemannian manifolds of type (n,n). After that, their study continues in a series of works (e.g., [2–5]).

In [1], M. Manev and M. Staikova presented a classification of the Riemannian Π-manifolds with respect to the fundamental tensor F, which contains eleven basic classes. We consider four of these eleven basic classes, the so-called main classes, in which F is expressed explicitly by the metrics and the Lee forms.

In differential geometry of manifolds with additional tensor structures, those affine connections play an important role, which is to preserve the structure tensors and the metric, known also as natural connections (e.g., [6–15]). We define a non-symmetric natural connection, and we call it the first natural connection on a Riemannian Π-manifold. We obtain relations between the introduced connection and the Levi–Civita connection, as well as studying some of its curvature characteristics in the main classes.

The paper is structured as follows. After this introductory Section 1, in Section 2, we recall some preliminary background facts about the considered geometry. In the next Section 3, we define the concept of natural connection on the Riemannian Π-manifold, and we prove the necessary and sufficient condition for the affine connection to be natural. Section 4 is devoted to the first natural connection on the Riemannian Π-manifold and its relations to the Levi–Civita connection. Moreover, in this section, we prove assertions for relations between these two connections and their respective curvature tensors, torsion tensors, Ricci tensors, and scalar curvatures. In the final Section 5, we support the results with an explicit example of dimension five.

2. Riemannian Π-Manifolds

Let $(\mathcal{M}, \phi, \xi, \eta, g)$ be a Riemannian Π-manifold, where $\mathcal{M}$ is $(2n+1)$-dimensional differentiable manifold, equipped with a Riemannian metric g and a Riemannian Π-structure

(ϕ, ξ, η). This structure consists of a (1,1)-tensor field ϕ, a Reeb vector field ξ and its dual 1-form η. The following basic identities and their immediately derived properties are valid:

$$\begin{array}{cccc} \phi\xi = 0, & \phi^2 = I - \eta \otimes \xi, & \eta \circ \phi = 0, & \eta(\xi) = 1, \\ \operatorname{tr}\phi = 0, & g(\phi x, \phi y) = g(x,y) - \eta(x)\eta(y), & & \end{array} \qquad (1)$$

$$\begin{array}{cc} g(\phi x, y) = g(x, \phi y), & g(x, \xi) = \eta(x), \\ g(\xi, \xi) = 1, & \eta(\nabla_x \xi) = 0, \end{array} \qquad (2)$$

where I and ∇ denote the identity transformation on TM and the Levi–Civita connection of g, respectively ([2,16]). Here and further, x, y, z, and w stand for arbitrary differentiable vector fields on M or tangent vectors at a point of M.

The associated metric $\tilde{g}$ of g on (M, ϕ, ξ, η, g) is defined by $\tilde{g}(x,y) = g(x, \phi y) + \eta(x)\eta(y)$. It is an indefinite metric of signature $(n+1, n)$, and it is compatible with the manifold in the same way as g. In further investigations, we use the following notations:

$$g^*(x,y) = g(x, \phi y), \qquad g^{**}(x,y) = g(\phi x, \phi y). \qquad (3)$$

Using ξ and η on an arbitrary Riemannian Π-manifold (M, ϕ, ξ, η, g), we consider two complementary distributions of TM—the horizontal distribution $\mathcal{H} = \ker(\eta)$ and the vertical distribution $\mathcal{V} = \operatorname{span}(\xi)$. They are mutually orthogonal with respect to the both metrics g and $\tilde{g}$, i.e.,

$$\mathcal{H} \oplus \mathcal{V} = TM, \qquad \mathcal{H} \perp \mathcal{V}, \qquad \mathcal{H} \cap \mathcal{V} = \{o\}, \qquad (4)$$

where o stands for the zero vector field on M. In this way, the respective horizontal and vertical projectors are determined by $\mathrm{h}: TM \mapsto \mathcal{H}$ and $\mathrm{v}: TM \mapsto \mathcal{V}$.

An arbitrary vector field x has corresponding projections x^{h} and x^{v} such that

$$x = x^{\mathrm{h}} + x^{\mathrm{v}}, \qquad (5)$$

where

$$x^{\mathrm{h}} = \phi^2 x, \qquad x^{\mathrm{v}} = \eta(x)\xi \qquad (6)$$

are the so-called horizontal and vertical component of x, respectively.

Let us denote by ∇ the Levi–Civita connection of g. The following tensor field F of type $(0,3)$ plays an important role in the geometry of the Riemannian Π-manifolds [1]:

$$F(x,y,z) = g((\nabla_x \phi)y, z). \qquad (7)$$

From (1) and (7), the following general properties of F are obtained [1]:

$$\begin{array}{l} F(x,y,z) = F(x,z,y) = -F(x, \phi y, \phi z) + \eta(y)F(x, \xi, z) + \eta(z)F(x, y, \xi), \\ F(x,y,\phi z) = -F(x, \phi y, z) + \eta(z)F(x, \phi y, \xi) + \eta(y)F(x, \phi z, \xi), \\ F(x, \phi y, \phi z) = -F(x, \phi^2 y, \phi^2 z), \\ F(x, \phi y, \phi^2 z) = -F(x, \phi^2 y, \phi z). \end{array} \qquad (8)$$

Lemma 1 ([2]). *The following identities are valid:*
(1) $(\nabla_x \eta)(y) = g(\nabla_x \xi, y)$;
(2) $\eta(\nabla_x \xi) = 0$;
(3) $F(x, \phi y, \xi) = -(\nabla_x \eta)(y)$.

The 1-forms associated with F, known as Lee forms, are defined by

$$\theta = g^{ij} F(e_i, e_j, \cdot), \qquad \theta^* = g^{ij} F(e_i, \phi e_j, \cdot), \qquad \omega = F(\xi, \xi, \cdot),$$

where (g^{ij}) is the inverse matrix of (g_{ij}) of g with respect to a basis $\{\xi; e_i\}$ of $T_p\mathcal{M}$ ($i = 1, 2, \ldots, 2n$; $p \in \mathcal{M}$). Using (8), the following relations for the Lee forms are obtained [1]:

$$\omega(\xi) = 0, \qquad \theta^* \circ \phi = -\theta \circ \phi^2, \qquad \theta^* \circ \phi^2 = \theta \circ \phi. \tag{9}$$

In [1], M. Manev and M. Staikova presented a classification of Riemannian Π-manifolds with respect to the fundamental tensor F, which contains eleven basic classes denoted by $\mathcal{F}_1, \mathcal{F}_2, \ldots, \mathcal{F}_{11}$. The intersection of the basic classes is the special class $\mathcal{F}_0$ determined by the condition $F = 0$. Let us remark that the main objects of our consideration are the so-called main classes of the considered manifolds among the basic eleven. These are the classes $\mathcal{F}_1, \mathcal{F}_4, \mathcal{F}_5, \mathcal{F}_{11}$ in which the fundamental tensor F is expressed explicitly by the metrics and the Lee forms. The characteristic conditions of these classes are [1,2]

$$\begin{aligned}
\mathcal{F}_1: \quad & F(x,y,z) = \frac{1}{2n}\{g(\phi x, \phi y)\theta(\phi^2 z) + g(\phi x, \phi z)\theta(\phi^2 y) \\
& \qquad\qquad - g(x, \phi y)\theta(\phi z) - g(x, \phi z)\theta(\phi y)\}; \\
\mathcal{F}_4: \quad & F(x,y,z) = \frac{\theta(\xi)}{2n}\{g(\phi x, \phi y)\eta(z) + g(\phi x, \phi z)\eta(y)\}; \\
\mathcal{F}_5: \quad & F(x,y,z) = \frac{\theta^*(\xi)}{2n}\{g(x, \phi y)\eta(z) + g(x, \phi z)\eta(y)\}; \\
\mathcal{F}_{11}: \quad & F(x,y,z) = \eta(x)\{\eta(y)\omega(z) + \eta(z)\omega(y)\}.
\end{aligned} \tag{10}$$

The (1,2)-tensors N and $\widehat{N}$ defined by

$$\begin{aligned}
N(x,y) &= (\nabla_{\phi x}\phi)y - \phi(\nabla_x\phi)y - (\nabla_x\eta)(y)\xi \\
&\quad - (\nabla_{\phi y}\phi)x + \phi(\nabla_y\phi)x + (\nabla_y\eta)(x)\xi, \\
\widehat{N}(x,y) &= (\nabla_{\phi x}\phi)y - \phi(\nabla_x\phi)y - (\nabla_x\eta)(y)\xi \\
&\quad + (\nabla_{\phi y}\phi)x - \phi(\nabla_y\phi)x - (\nabla_y\eta)(x)\xi
\end{aligned}$$

are called the Nijenhuis tensor and associated Nijenhuis tensor, respectively, for the Π-structure on $\mathcal{M}$ [2].

It can be immediately established that we have an antisymmetric tensor N and a symmetric $\widehat{N}$, i.e.,

$$N(x,y) = -N(y,x), \qquad \widehat{N}(x,y) = \widehat{N}(y,x). \tag{11}$$

The corresponding (0,3)-tensors of N and $\widehat{N}$ on $(\mathcal{M}, \phi, \xi, \eta, g)$ are denoted by the same letter and are expressed by means of F through the equalities [2]

$$\begin{aligned}
N(x,y,z) &= g(N(x,y), z) \\
&= F(\phi x, y, z) - F(\phi y, x, z) - F(x, y, \phi z) + F(y, x, \phi z) \\
&\quad + \eta(z)\{F(x, \phi y, \xi) - F(y, \phi x, \xi)\}, \\
\widehat{N}(x,y,z) &= g\big(\widehat{N}(x,y), z\big) \\
&= F(\phi x, y, z) + F(\phi y, x, z) - F(x, y, \phi z) - F(y, x, \phi z) \\
&\quad + \eta(z)\{F(x, \phi y, \xi) + F(y, \phi x, \xi)\}.
\end{aligned}$$

On the other hand, the fundamental tensor F of a Riemannian Π-manifold can be expressed only by the pair of tensors N and $\widehat{N}$ as follows [2]:

$$F(x,y,z) = \frac{1}{4}\{N(\phi x,y,z) + N(\phi x,z,y) + \widehat{N}(\phi x,y,z) + \widehat{N}(\phi x,z,y)\} \\ - \frac{1}{2}\eta(x)\{N(\xi,y,\phi z) + \widehat{N}(\xi,y,\phi z) + \eta(z)\widehat{N}(\xi,\xi,\phi y)\}. \tag{12}$$

Let R denote the curvature tensor of type $(1,3)$ for the Levi–Civita connection ∇ generated by the metric g on $(\mathcal{M}, \phi, \xi, \eta, g)$, i.e.,

$$R(x,y)z = \nabla_x \nabla_y z - \nabla_y \nabla_x z - \nabla_{[x,y]} z. \tag{13}$$

Let us denote the corresponding curvature $(0,4)$-tensor by the same letter and let us define it by the following equality:

$$R(x,y,z,w) = g(R(x,y)z,w). \tag{14}$$

The following known basic properties hold for R:

$$R(x,y,z,w) = -R(y,x,z,w) = -R(x,y,w,z), \tag{15}$$

$$R(x,y,z,w) + R(y,z,x,w) + R(z,x,y,w) = 0. \tag{16}$$

For R, we define Ricci tensor ρ of type $(0,2)$ as follows:

$$\rho(x,y) = g^{ij} R(e_i, x, y, e_j), \tag{17}$$

and scalar curvature τ as the trace of ρ through

$$\tau = g^{ij}\rho(e_i, e_j). \tag{18}$$

The associated quantities ρ^* and τ^* corresponding to ρ and τ are determined by the following equalities:

$$\rho^*(x,y) = g^{ij} R(e_i, x, y, \phi e_j), \qquad \tau^* = g^{ij}\rho^*(e_i, e_j). \tag{19}$$

The notation $S \owedge P$ stands for the Kulkarni–Nomizu product of two tensors S and P of type $(0,2)$, defined as follows:

$$(S \owedge P)(x,y,z,w) = S(x,z)P(y,w) - S(y,z)P(x,w) \\ + S(y,w)P(x,z) - S(x,w)P(y,z). \tag{20}$$

It is easy to see that $S \owedge P$ possesses the basic properties (15) and (16) of R just when S and P are symmetric tensors.

Let T denote the torsion tensor of an arbitrary affine connection D, i.e.,

$$T(x,y) = D_x y - D_y x - [x,y]. \tag{21}$$

Let us remark that D is symmetric if and only if its torsion tensor T is zero.

Let us denote by the same letter the corresponding $(0,3)$-tensor with respect to the metric g, i.e.,

$$T(x,y,z) = g(T(x,y),z). \tag{22}$$

Torsion forms t, t^* and $\hat{t}$ of T we call the associated 1-forms of T defined by

$$t(x) = g^{ij} T(x, e_i, e_j), \qquad t^*(x) = g^{ij} T(x, e_i, \phi e_j), \qquad \hat{t}(x) = T(x, \xi, \xi) \tag{23}$$

with respect to a basis $\{\xi; e_i\}$ of $T_p\mathcal{M}$ ($i = 1, 2, \ldots, 2n; p \in \mathcal{M}$). Obviously, the identity $\hat{t}(\xi) = 0$ holds.

3. Natural Connection on Riemannian Π-Manifolds

Let us consider an arbitrary Riemannian Π-manifold $(\mathcal{M}, \phi, \xi, \eta, g)$.

Definition 1. *An affine connection D on a Riemannian Π-manifold $(\mathcal{M}, \phi, \xi, \eta, g)$ is called a natural connection for the Riemannian Π-structure (ϕ, ξ, η, g) if this structure is parallel with respect to D, i.e.,*
$$D\phi = D\xi = D\eta = Dg = 0.$$

It is easily verified, as a consequence, that the associated metric $\tilde{g}$ is also parallel with respect to the natural connection D on $(\mathcal{M}, \phi, \xi, \eta, g)$, i.e., $D\tilde{g} = 0$.

Therefore, D on a Riemannian Π-manifold $(\mathcal{M}, \phi, \xi, \eta, g) \notin \mathcal{F}_0$ plays the same role as ∇ on $(\mathcal{M}, \phi, \xi, \eta, g) \in \mathcal{F}_0$. Obviously, D and ∇ coincide when $(\mathcal{M}, \phi, \xi, \eta, g) \in \mathcal{F}_0$.

Let Q denote the difference of D and ∇ which we call the potential of D with respect to ∇. Then we have
$$D_x y = \nabla_x y + Q(x, y). \tag{24}$$

Moreover, by the same letter, we denote the corresponding $(0,3)$-tensor field of Q with respect to g, i.e.,
$$Q(x, y, z) = g(Q(x, y), z). \tag{25}$$

Proposition 1. *An affine connection D is a natural connection on the Riemannian Π-manifold if and only if the following properties hold:*
$$Q(x, y, \phi z) - Q(x, \phi y, z) = F(x, y, z), \tag{26}$$
$$Q(x, y, z) = -Q(x, z, y). \tag{27}$$

Proof. Using (24) and (25), we obtain the following relations:
$$g(D_x \phi y, z) = g(\nabla_x \phi y, z) + Q(x, \phi y, z),$$
$$g(D_x y, \phi z) = g(\nabla_x y, \phi z) + Q(x, y, \phi z).$$

We form the difference of the last two equalities and directly obtain the identity
$$g((D_x \phi) y, z) = F(x, y, z) + Q(x, \phi y, z) - Q(x, y, \phi z).$$

Then the condition $D\phi = 0$ is equivalent to (26).
We obtain, sequentially,
$$(D_x g)(y, z) = g(\nabla_x y, z) + g(y, \nabla_x z) - g(D_x y, z) - g(y, D_x z)$$
$$= -Q(x, y, z) - Q(x, z, y).$$

Therefore, the condition $Dg = 0$ holds if and only if (27) holds.
From (24), we obtain
$$g(D_x \xi, z) = g(\nabla_x \xi, z) + g(Q(x, \xi), z) = g(\nabla_x \xi, z) + Q(x, \xi, z). \tag{28}$$

After that, from Lemma 1 and (8), we derive the following relation:
$$g(\nabla_x \xi, z) = -F(x, \xi, \phi z).$$

Substituting the latter result into (28), we obtain
$$g(D_x \xi, z) = -F(x, \xi, \phi z) + Q(x, \xi, z),$$

i.e., the condition $D\xi = 0$ is equivalent to the following relation

$$-F(x, \xi, \phi z) + Q(x, \xi, z) = 0,$$

which is a consequence of (26).

Since the relation $\eta(\cdot) = g(\cdot, \xi)$ holds, then, using $Dg = 0$, we obtain that $D\xi = 0$ is valid if and only if $D\eta = 0$. □

Theorem 1. *An affine connection D is natural on a Riemannian Π-manifold if and only if*

$$D\phi = Dg = 0.$$

Proof. In the proof of the preceding statement, we showed that the condition $D\phi = 0$ is equivalent to (26) and $Dg = 0$ holds if and only if (27) holds. In this way, according to Proposition 1, we complete the proof. □

4. First Natural Connection on Riemannian Π-Manifolds

Let $\dot{D}$ denote an affine connection on $(\mathcal{M}, \phi, \xi, \eta, g)$ defined by

$$\dot{D}_x y = \nabla_x y - \frac{1}{2}\{(\nabla_x \phi)\phi y - (\nabla_x \eta)y \cdot \xi\} - \eta(y)\nabla_x \xi. \tag{29}$$

Therefore, the potential $\dot{Q}$ of $\dot{D}$ with respect to ∇ is defined by

$$\dot{Q}(x, y) = -\frac{1}{2}\{(\nabla_x \phi)\phi y - (\nabla_x \eta)y \cdot \xi\} - \eta(y)\nabla_x \xi. \tag{30}$$

Using (1), (7) and (8), we verify that $\dot{D}\phi = \dot{D}g = 0$. Therefore, according to Theorem 1, $\dot{D}$ is a natural connection.

Definition 2. *The natural connection $\dot{D}$, defined by (29), is called first natural connection on a Riemannian Π-manifold $(\mathcal{M}, \phi, \xi, \eta, g)$.*

Obviously, $\dot{D}$ and ∇ coincide only on a manifold of class $\mathcal{F}_0$. Therefore, ∇ is a first natural connection when $(\mathcal{M}, \phi, \xi, \eta, g) \in \mathcal{F}_0$.

Let us remark that the restriction of $\dot{D}$ on the paracontact distribution $\mathcal{H}$ of $(\mathcal{M}, \phi, \xi, \eta, g)$ is another studied natural connection (called P-connection) on the corresponding Riemannian manifold equipped with an almost product structure (see [9]).

Theorem 2. *Let $(\mathcal{M}, \phi, \xi, \eta, g)$ be a $(2n + 1)$-dimensional Riemannian Π-manifold belonging to the main classes $\mathcal{F}_i$ ($i = 1, 4, 5, 11$). Then, the first natural connection $\dot{D}$ is determined by*

1. *If $(\mathcal{M}, \phi, \xi, \eta, g) \in \mathcal{F}_1$, then*

$$\dot{D}_x y = \nabla_x y - \frac{1}{4n}\left\{\theta(\phi y)\phi^2 x - \theta(\phi^2 y)\phi x + g(x, \phi y)\phi^2 \theta^\sharp - g(\phi x, \phi y)\phi \theta^\sharp\right\},$$

where $\theta(\cdot) = g(\theta^\sharp, \cdot)$;

2. *If $(\mathcal{M}, \phi, \xi, \eta, g) \in \mathcal{F}_4$, then*

$$\dot{D}_x y = \nabla_x y - \frac{1}{2n}\theta(\xi)\{g(x, \phi y)\xi - \eta(y)\phi x\};$$

3. *If $(\mathcal{M}, \phi, \xi, \eta, g) \in \mathcal{F}_5$, then*

$$\dot{D}_x y = \nabla_x y - \frac{1}{2n}\theta^*(\xi)\{g(\phi x, \phi y)\xi - \eta(y)\phi^2 x\};$$

4. If $(\mathcal{M}, \phi, \xi, \eta, g) \in \mathcal{F}_{11}$, then

$$\dot{D}_x y = \nabla_x y - \eta(x)\left\{\omega(\phi y)\xi - \eta(y)\phi\omega^\sharp\right\},$$

where $\omega(\cdot) = g(\omega^\sharp, \cdot)$.

Proof. We present the proof of the theorem in the first considered case, i.e., $(\mathcal{M}, \phi, \xi, \eta, g) \in \mathcal{F}_1$.

The potential $\dot{Q}$ has the following form given in (30):

$$\dot{Q}(x,y) = -\frac{1}{2}\left\{(\nabla_x \phi)\phi y - (\nabla_x \eta)y \cdot \xi\right\} - \eta(y)\nabla_x \xi.$$

Using (7), Lemma 1 and the analogous definitions of (24) and (25) for $\dot{Q}$,

$$\dot{D}_x y = \nabla_x y + \dot{Q}(x,y), \tag{31}$$

$$\dot{Q}(x,y,z) = g(\dot{Q}(x,y), z), \tag{32}$$

we obtain the corresponding form of $\dot{Q}$ as a tensor of type $(0,3)$

$$\dot{Q}(x,y,z) = -\frac{1}{2}\left\{F(x, \phi y, z) + \eta(z)F(x, \phi y, \xi)\right\} + \eta(y)F(x, \phi z, \xi).$$

Applying the definition condition of F in $\mathcal{F}_1$ from (10)

$$F(x,y,z) = \frac{1}{2n}\left\{g(\phi x, \phi y)\theta(\phi^2 z) + g(\phi x, \phi z)\theta(\phi^2 y)\right.$$
$$\left. - g(x, \phi y)\theta(\phi z) - g(x, \phi z)\theta(\phi y)\right\} \tag{33}$$

in the latter formula and using (1) and (2), we obtain

$$\dot{Q}(x,y,z) = -\frac{1}{4n}\left\{g(\phi x, \phi^2 y)\theta(\phi^2 z) - g(x, \phi^2 y)\theta(\phi z)\right.$$
$$\left. + g(\phi x, \phi z)\theta(\phi y) - g(x, \phi z)\theta(\phi^2 y)\right\}. \tag{34}$$

From the latter equality and (32), we obtain

$$\dot{Q}(x,y) = -\frac{1}{4n}\left\{\theta(\phi y)\phi^2 x - \theta(\phi^2 y)\phi x + g(x, \phi y)\phi^2 \theta^\sharp - g(\phi x, \phi y)\phi\theta^\sharp\right\}, \tag{35}$$

where $\theta(\cdot) = g(\theta^\sharp, \cdot)$.

Thus, we establish the truthfulness of the first statement in the theorem, considering (31). The other cases are proved in a similar way. □

Let $\dot{T}$ denote the torsion tensor of $\dot{D}$, i.e., according to (21), we have

$$\dot{T}(x,y) = \dot{D}_x y - \dot{D}_y x - [x,y].$$

Then, using (29), we obtain

$$\dot{T}(x,y) = -\frac{1}{2}\left\{(\nabla_x \phi)\phi y - (\nabla_y \phi)\phi x - d\eta(x,y)\xi\right\} + \eta(x)\nabla_y \xi - \eta(y)\nabla_x \xi. \tag{36}$$

Let us remark that $\dot{D}$ is not a symmetric connection since obviously $\dot{T}$ is nonzero.

The corresponding $(0,3)$-tensor with respect to g is determined as follows:

$$\dot{T}(x,y,z) = g(\dot{T}(x,y),z). \tag{37}$$

Then, by (36), (7) and Lemma 1, we obtain

$$\begin{aligned}\dot{T}(x,y,z) = &-\frac{1}{2}\{F(x,\phi y,z) - F(y,\phi x,z)\} \\ &-\frac{1}{2}\eta(z)\{F(x,\phi y,\xi) - F(y,\phi x,\xi)\} \\ &+ \eta(y)F(x,\phi z,\xi) - \eta(x)F(y,\phi z,\xi).\end{aligned} \tag{38}$$

We apply (12) in (38). Thus, taking into account (11), we obtain the form of the torsion of the first natural connection with respect to N and $\widehat{N}$:

$$\begin{aligned}\dot{T}(x,y,z) = &-\frac{1}{8}\{2N(\phi x,\phi y,z) + N(\phi x,z,\phi y) - N(\phi y,z,\phi x) \\ &+ \widehat{N}(\phi x,z,\phi y) - \widehat{N}(\phi y,z,\phi x)\} \\ &+ \frac{1}{4}\eta(x)\{2N(\xi,\phi y,\phi z) - N(\phi y,\phi z,\xi) \\ &+ 2\eta(z)\widehat{N}(\xi,\xi,\phi^2 y) - \widehat{N}(\phi y,\phi z,\xi)\} \\ &- \frac{1}{4}\eta(y)\{2N(\xi,\phi x,\phi z) - N(\phi x,\phi z,\xi) \\ &+ 2\eta(z)\widehat{N}(\xi,\xi,\phi^2 x) - \widehat{N}(\phi x,\phi z,\xi)\} \\ &- \frac{1}{8}\eta(z)\{2N(\phi x,\phi y,\xi) + N(\phi x,\xi,\phi y) - N(\phi y,\xi,\phi x) \\ &+ \widehat{N}(\phi x,\xi,\phi y) - \widehat{N}(\phi y,\xi,\phi x)\}.\end{aligned} \tag{39}$$

We use (39) and the decomposition in (4)–(6) to obtain the following form of $\dot{T}$ regarding the pair N and $\widehat{N}$ with respect to the horizontal and the vertical components of the vector fields:

$$\begin{aligned}\dot{T}(x,y,z) = &-\frac{1}{8}\{\mathfrak{S}\,N(x^h,y^h,z^h) + N(x^h,y^h,z^h) \\ &+ \widehat{N}(y^h,z^h,x^h) - \widehat{N}(z^h,x^h,y^h)\} \\ &-\frac{1}{4}\{2N(x^h,y^h,z^v) + N(y^h,z^v,x^h) + N(z^v,x^h,y^h) \\ &+ 2N(x^v,y^h,z^h) + N(y^h,z^h,x^v) + 2N(x^h,y^v,z^h) \\ &+ N(z^h,x^h,y^v) + 2\widehat{N}(y^h,z^h,x^v) - \widehat{N}(z^v,x^h,y^h) \\ &- \widehat{N}(z^h,x^h,y^v) - 2\widehat{N}(z^v,x^v,y^h) + 2\widehat{N}(y^v,z^v,x^h)\},\end{aligned}$$

where $\mathfrak{S}$ stands for the cyclic sum by the three arguments.

Theorem 3. *Let $(\mathcal{M},\phi,\xi,\eta,g)$ be a $(2n+1)$-dimensional Riemannian Π-manifold belonging to the main classes $\mathcal{F}_i$ ($i=1,4,5,11$). Then, the torsion tensor $\dot{T}$ of the first natural connection $\dot{D}$ has the form*

1. *If $(\mathcal{M},\phi,\xi,\eta,g) \in \mathcal{F}_1$, then*

$$\dot{T}(x,y) = -\frac{1}{4n}\{\theta(\phi y)\phi^2 x - \theta(\phi x)\phi^2 y + \theta(\phi^2 x)\phi y - \theta(\phi^2 y)\phi x\};$$

2. If $(\mathcal{M}, \phi, \xi, \eta, g) \in \mathcal{F}_4$, then

$$\dot{T}(x,y) = \frac{1}{2n}\theta(\xi)\{\eta(y)\phi x - \eta(x)\phi y\};$$

3. If $(\mathcal{M}, \phi, \xi, \eta, g) \in \mathcal{F}_5$, then

$$\dot{T}(x,y) = \frac{1}{2n}\theta^*(\xi)\{\eta(y)\phi^2 x - \eta(x)\phi^2 y\};$$

4. If $(\mathcal{M}, \phi, \xi, \eta, g) \in \mathcal{F}_{11}$, then

$$\dot{T}(x,y) = \{\eta(y)\omega(\phi x) - \eta(x)\omega(\phi y)\}\xi.$$

Proof. We present the proof of the theorem in the first considered case, i.e., $(\mathcal{M}, \phi, \xi, \eta, g) \in \mathcal{F}_1$.

We apply (33) in (38) and taking into account (1) and (2), we obtain

$$\dot{T}(x,y,z) = -\frac{1}{4n}\{g(\phi x, \phi z)\theta(\phi y) - g(\phi y, \phi z)\theta(\phi x)$$
$$-g(x, \phi z)\theta(\phi^2 y) + g(y, \phi z)\theta(\phi^2 x)\}.$$

The form of $\dot{T}$ in case 1 follows from the last expression and (37).

Thus, we establish the truthfulness of the first statement in the theorem. The other cases are proved in a similar way. □

Similarly to (23), we define torsion forms $\dot{t}$, $\dot{t}^*$ and $\widehat{\dot{t}}$ for $\dot{T}$ with respect to a basis $\{\xi; e_i\}$ of $T_p\mathcal{M}$ ($i = 1, 2, \ldots, 2n; p \in \mathcal{M}$):

$$\dot{t}(x) = g^{ij}\dot{T}(x, e_i, e_j), \qquad \dot{t}^*(x) = g^{ij}\dot{T}(x, e_i, \phi e_j), \qquad \widehat{\dot{t}}(x) = \dot{T}(x, \xi, \xi). \tag{40}$$

Using (38), (40) and $\eta(e_i) = 0$ ($i = 1, \ldots, 2n$), we obtain

$$\dot{t}(x) = -\frac{1}{2}g^{ij}\{F(x, \phi_i^m e_m, e_j) - F(e_i, \phi x, e_j) + 2\eta(x)F(e_i, \phi_j^m e_m, \xi)\}.$$

On the one hand, by (1) and the identities $\phi_i^k \phi_j^s g^{ij} = g^{ks} - \xi^k \xi^s$ and $\eta(e_i) = 0$ ($i = 1, \ldots, 2n$), for the first addend of the last equality, we obtain

$$g^{ij}F(x, \phi_i^s e_s, e_j) = g^{ij}F(x, \phi_i^s e_s, \phi_j^m \phi_m^l e_l) = \phi_i^s \phi_j^l g^{ij} F(x, e_s, \phi_l^m e_m)$$
$$= g^{sl}F(x, e_s, \phi_l^m e_m) - \xi^s \xi^l F(x, e_s, \phi_l^m e_m) = g^{ij}F(x, e_i, \phi_j^l e_l).$$

On the other hand, from (8), we have for it

$$g^{ij}F(x, \phi_i^s e_s, e_j) = -g^{ij}F(x, \phi_i^m \phi_m^s e_s, \phi_j^l e_l) = -g^{ij}F(x, e_i, \phi_j^l e_l).$$

Therefore, $g^{ij}F(x, \phi_i^s e_s, e_j) = g^{ij}F(x, e_i, \phi_j^l e_l) = 0$.

Thus, according to (23), we obtain the following formula:

$$\dot{t}(x) = \frac{1}{2}\theta(\phi x) - \theta^*(\xi)\eta(x). \tag{41}$$

By an analogous approach, we calculate the form of $\overset{*}{t}$ and $\widehat{t}$ as follows:

$$\overset{*}{t}(x) = \frac{1}{2}\theta^*(\phi x) - \theta(\xi)\eta(x), \qquad (42)$$
$$\widehat{t}(x) = \omega(\phi x).$$

Taking into account (9), (41) and (42), we obtain the following relations between the torsion forms t, $\overset{*}{t}$ and the Lee forms θ, θ^*:

$$\overset{*}{t} \circ \phi = t \circ \phi^2,$$
$$2t \circ \phi = \theta \circ \phi^2, \qquad 2t \circ \phi^2 = \theta \circ \phi, \qquad (43)$$
$$2\overset{*}{t} \circ \phi = \theta^* \circ \phi^2, \qquad 2\overset{*}{t} \circ \phi^2 = \theta^* \circ \phi.$$

Corollary 3. *Let $(\mathcal{M}, \phi, \xi, \eta, g)$ be a $(2n+1)$-dimensional Riemannian Π-manifold belonging to the main classes $\mathcal{F}_i$ $(i = 1, 4, 5, 11)$. Then the torsion tensor $\dot{T}$ of the first natural connection $\dot{D}$ is expressed by its torsion forms t, $\overset{*}{t}$ and $\widehat{t}$ as follows:*

$$\mathcal{F}_1: \quad \dot{T}(x,y) = -\frac{1}{2n}\{t(\phi^2 y)\phi^2 x - t(\phi^2 x)\phi^2 y + t(\phi x)\phi y - t(\phi y)\phi x\};$$
$$\mathcal{F}_4: \quad \dot{T}(x,y) = -\frac{1}{2n}\overset{*}{t}(\xi)\{\eta(y)\phi x - \eta(x)\phi y\};$$
$$\mathcal{F}_5: \quad \dot{T}(x,y) = -\frac{1}{2n}t(\xi)\{\eta(y)\phi^2 x - \eta(x)\phi^2 y\};$$
$$\mathcal{F}_{11}: \quad \dot{T}(x,y) = \left\{\eta(y)\widehat{t}(x) - \eta(x)\widehat{t}(y)\right\}\xi.$$

Proof. We obtain the expression of $\dot{T}$ using its form from Theorem 3 and the relations (43) between the torsion forms and the Lee forms. □

Let $\dot{R}$ denote the curvature tensor for the first natural connection $\dot{D}$. Similarly to the definitions (13) and (14) of R regarding ∇, we define $\dot{R}$ as a tensor of type $(1,3)$ and $(0,4)$ for $\dot{D}$, respectively, by

$$\dot{R}(x,y)z = \dot{D}_x \dot{D}_y z - \dot{D}_y \dot{D}_x z - \dot{D}_{[x,y]} z, \qquad (44)$$

$$\dot{R}(x,y,z,w) = g(\dot{R}(x,y)z, w). \qquad (45)$$

Theorem 4. *Let $(\mathcal{M}, \phi, \xi, \eta, g)$ be a $(2n+1)$-dimensional Riemannian Π-manifold belonging to the main classes $\mathcal{F}_i$ $(i = 1, 4, 5, 11)$. Then, the curvature tensor $\dot{R}$ of the first natural connection $\dot{D}$ has the form*

1. *If $(\mathcal{M}, \phi, \xi, \eta, g) \in \mathcal{F}_1$, then*

$$\dot{R}(x,y,z,w) = R(x,y,z,w)$$
$$+ \frac{1}{4n}\{(g^* \oslash S_1 - g^{**} \oslash S_2)(x,y,z,w)$$
$$- \theta(\phi\theta^\sharp)(g^* \oslash g^{**})(x,y,z,w)$$
$$- \theta(\phi^2\theta^\sharp)(g \oslash g^{**} + g^* \oslash \tilde{g} - \tilde{g} \oslash g)(x,y,z,w)\},$$

where

$$S_1(x,y) = (\nabla_x(\theta \circ \phi^2))(y) + \frac{1}{4n}\{\theta(\phi x)\theta(\phi^2 y) + \theta(\phi^2 x)\theta(\phi y)\},$$
$$S_2(x,y) = (\nabla_x(\theta \circ \phi))(y) + \frac{1}{4n}\{\theta(\phi^2 x)\theta(\phi^2 y) + \theta(\phi x)\theta(\phi y)\};$$

2. If $(\mathcal{M}, \phi, \xi, \eta, g) \in \mathcal{F}_4$, then

$$\dot{R}(x,y,z,w) = R(x,y,z,w)$$
$$+ \frac{1}{2n}\{x(\theta(\xi))\{(\eta \otimes \eta) \oslash g^*\}(\xi,y,z,w)$$
$$-y(\theta(\xi))\{(\eta \otimes \eta) \oslash g^*\}(\xi,x,z,w)\}$$
$$- \frac{1}{8n^2}(\theta(\xi))^2\{2(\eta \otimes \eta) \oslash g - g^* \oslash g^*\}(x,y,z,w);$$

3. If $(\mathcal{M}, \phi, \xi, \eta, g) \in \mathcal{F}_5$, then

$$\dot{R}(x,y,z,w) = R(x,y,z,w)$$
$$+ \frac{1}{4n}\{x(\theta^*(\xi))\{g \oslash g\}(\xi,y,z,w)$$
$$-y(\theta^*(\xi))\{g \oslash g\}(\xi,x,z,w)\}$$
$$+ \frac{1}{8n^2}(\theta^*(\xi))^2\{g \oslash g\}(x,y,z,w);$$

4. If $(\mathcal{M}, \phi, \xi, \eta, g) \in \mathcal{F}_{11}$, then

$$\dot{R}(x,y,z,w) = R(x,y,z,w)$$
$$-\{(\eta \otimes \eta) \oslash S_3\}(x,y,z,w),$$

where

$$S_3(x,y) = (\nabla_x \omega)(\phi y) + \omega(\phi x)\omega(\phi y).$$

Proof. We present the proof of the theorem in the first considered case, i.e., $(\mathcal{M}, \phi, \xi, \eta, g) \in \mathcal{F}_1$.

Using (44) and (45) together with (31), (32) and the analogous relation of (27) for $\dot{Q}$, we obtain the following form of $\dot{R}$ for an arbitrary Riemannian Π-manifold $(\mathcal{M}, \phi, \xi, \eta, g)$:

$$\dot{R}(x,y,z,w) = R(x,y,z,w) + (\nabla_x \dot{Q})(y,z,w) - (\nabla_y \dot{Q})(x,z,w) \qquad (46)$$
$$+ g(\dot{Q}(x,z), \dot{Q}(y,w)) - g(\dot{Q}(y,z), \dot{Q}(x,w)).$$

Taking into account (7), (8) and (34), we obtain

$$(\nabla_x \dot{Q})(y,z,w) = -\frac{1}{4n}\{x(\theta(\phi^2 w))g(y,\phi z) + x(\theta(\phi z))g(\phi y, \phi w)$$
$$-x(\theta(\phi w))g(\phi y, \phi z) - x(\theta(\phi^2 z))g(y, \phi w)$$
$$+\theta(\phi^2 w)F(x,y,z) - \theta(\phi^2 z)F(x,y,w)$$
$$-\theta(\phi w)\{F(x,y,\phi z) + F(x,z,\phi y)\} \qquad (47)$$
$$+\theta(\phi z)\{F(x,y,\phi w) + F(x,w,\phi y)\}$$
$$-\theta(\phi^2 \nabla_x w)g(y,\phi z) + \theta(\phi \nabla_x w)g(\phi y, \phi z)$$
$$+\theta(\phi^2 \nabla_x z)g(y,\phi w) - \theta(\phi \nabla_x z)g(\phi y, \phi w)\}.$$

Then, using (35), we obtain

$$g(\dot{Q}(x,z), \dot{Q}(y,w))$$
$$= -\frac{1}{16n^2} \Big\{ \theta(\phi z) \left[\theta(\phi w) g(\phi x, \phi y) - \theta(\phi^2 w) g(\phi x, y) \right.$$
$$\left. + \theta(\phi^2 x) g(y, \phi w) - \theta(\phi x) g(\phi y, \phi w) \right]$$
$$- \theta(\phi^2 z) \left[\theta(\phi w) g(x, \phi y) - \theta(\phi^2 w) g(\phi x, \phi y) \right.$$
$$\left. + \theta(\phi x) g(y, \phi w) - \theta(\phi^2 x) g(\phi y, \phi w) \right] \quad (48)$$
$$+ g(x, \phi z) \left[\theta(\phi^2 y) \theta(\phi w) - \theta(\phi y) \theta(\phi^2 w) \right.$$
$$\left. + \theta(\phi^2 \theta^\sharp) g(y, \phi w) - \theta(\phi \theta^\sharp) g(\phi y, \phi w) \right]$$
$$- g(\phi x, \phi z) \left[\theta(\phi y) \theta(\phi w) - \theta(\phi^2 y) \theta(\phi^2 w) \right.$$
$$\left. + \theta(\phi \theta^\sharp) g(y, \phi w) - \theta(\phi^2 \theta^\sharp) g(\phi y, \phi w) \right] \Big\}.$$

Applying (47) and (48) into (46) and using (1) and (2) as well as the notations (3) and (20), we obtain the form of $\dot{R}$ presented in the theorem.

Thus, we establish the truthfulness of the first statement in the theorem. The other cases are proved in a similar way. □

Similarly to the definitions (17)–(19) for ρ, τ, ρ^* and τ^* regarding R, we define the corresponding ones with respect to $\dot{R}$ as follows:

$$\dot{\rho}(x,y) = g^{ij} \dot{R}(e_i, x, y, e_j), \qquad \dot{\tau} = g^{ij} \dot{\rho}(e_i, e_j),$$
$$\dot{\rho}^*(x,y) = g^{ij} \dot{R}(e_i, x, y, \phi e_j), \qquad \dot{\tau}^* = g^{ij} \dot{\rho}^*(e_i, e_j).$$

Corollary 4. *Let $(\mathcal{M}, \phi, \xi, \eta, g)$ be a $(2n+1)$-dimensional Riemannian Π-manifold belonging to the main classes $\mathcal{F}_i$ ($i = 1, 4, 5, 11$). Then the following relations for the Ricci tensors and the scalar curvatures with respect to $\dot{D}$ and ∇ hold:*

1. *If $(\mathcal{M}, \phi, \xi, \eta, g) \in \mathcal{F}_1$, then*

$$\dot{\rho}(y,z) = \rho(y,z)$$
$$+ \frac{1}{2} \Big\{ (\nabla_y (\theta \circ \phi))(z) + \frac{1}{4n} \{ \theta(\phi^2 y) \theta(\phi^2 z) + \theta(\phi y) \theta(\phi z) \} \Big\}$$
$$- \frac{1}{4n} \Big\{ \Big(\operatorname{div}(\theta \circ \phi^2) - \frac{4n^2 - 4n - 1}{2n} \theta(\phi \theta^\sharp) $$
$$+ 2(n-1) \theta(\phi^2 \theta^\sharp) \Big) g(y, \phi z)$$
$$- \Big(\operatorname{div}(\theta \circ \phi) + \frac{8n^2 - 8n + 1}{2n} \theta(\phi^2 \theta^\sharp) \Big) g(\phi y, \phi z) \Big\},$$

$$\dot{\rho}^*(y,z) = \rho^*(y,z)$$
$$- \frac{1}{2} \Big\{ (\nabla_y (\theta \circ \phi^2))(z) + \frac{1}{4n} \{ \theta(\phi y) \theta(\phi^2 z) + \theta(\phi^2 y) \theta(\phi z) \} \Big\}$$
$$+ \frac{1}{4n} \Big\{ \Big(\operatorname{div}^*(\theta \circ \phi) + \frac{(2n-1)^2}{2n} \theta(\phi \theta^\sharp)$$
$$- 2(n-1) \theta(\phi^2 \theta^\sharp) \Big) g(\phi y, \phi z)$$
$$- \Big(\operatorname{div}^*(\theta \circ \phi^2) - \frac{8n^2 - 8n - 1}{2n} \theta(\phi^2 \theta^\sharp) \Big) g(y, \phi z) \Big\},$$

$$\dot{\tau} = \tau + \mathrm{div}(\theta \circ \phi) + \frac{(2n-1)^2}{2n}\theta(\phi^2\theta^\sharp),$$
$$\dot{\tau}^* = \tau^* + (n-1)\theta(\phi\theta^\sharp) - \frac{2n-3}{2}\theta(\phi^2\theta^\sharp),$$

where $\mathrm{div}(\theta) = g^{ij}(\nabla_{e_i}\theta)(e_j)$, $\mathrm{div}^*(\theta) = g^{ij}(\nabla_{e_i}\theta)(\phi e_j)$;

2. If $(\mathcal{M}, \phi, \xi, \eta, g) \in \mathcal{F}_4$, then

$$\dot{\rho}(y,z) = \rho(y,z)$$
$$- \frac{1}{2n}\{\xi(\theta(\xi))g(y,\phi z) - \phi y(\theta(\xi))\eta(z)\}$$
$$+ \frac{1}{2n^2}(\theta(\xi))^2\{g(y,z) + (n-1)\eta(y)\eta(z)\},$$
$$\dot{\rho}^*(y,z) = \rho^*(y,z)$$
$$+ \frac{1}{2n}\{\phi^2 y(\theta(\xi)) - 2n\,y(\theta(\xi))\}\eta(z)$$
$$- \frac{2n-1}{4n^2}(\theta(\xi))^2 g(y,\phi z),$$
$$\dot{\tau} = \tau + \frac{1}{2n}(\theta(\xi))^2,$$
$$\dot{\tau}^* = \tau^* - \xi(\theta(\xi));$$

3. If $(\mathcal{M}, \phi, \xi, \eta, g) \in \mathcal{F}_5$, then

$$\dot{\rho}(y,z) = \rho(y,z)$$
$$- \frac{1}{2n}\{\xi(\theta^*(\xi))g(y,z) + (2n-1)\,y(\theta^*(\xi))\eta(z)\}$$
$$- \frac{1}{2n}(\theta^*(\xi))^2 g(y,z),$$

$$\dot{\rho}^*(y,z) = \rho^*(y,z)$$
$$- \frac{1}{2n}\{\phi y(\theta^*(\xi))\eta(z)\} + \frac{1}{4n^2}(\theta^*(\xi))^2 g(y,\phi z),$$
$$\dot{\tau} = \tau - 2\xi(\theta^*(\xi)) - \frac{2n+1}{2n}(\theta^*(\xi))^2,$$
$$\dot{\tau}^* = \tau^*;$$

4. If $(\mathcal{M}, \phi, \xi, \eta, g) \in \mathcal{F}_{11}$, then

$$\dot{\rho}(y,z) = \rho(y,z)$$
$$+ (\nabla_y \omega)(\phi z) + \omega(\phi y)\omega(\phi z)$$
$$+ \{\mathrm{div}^*(\omega) + \omega(\phi^2\omega^\sharp)\}\eta(y)\eta(z),$$
$$\dot{\rho}^*(y,z) = \rho^*(y,z)$$
$$+ \{\mathrm{div}(\omega) + \omega(\phi\omega^\sharp)\}\eta(y)\eta(z),$$
$$\dot{\tau} = \tau + 2\{\mathrm{div}^*(\omega) + \omega(\phi^2\omega^\sharp)\},$$
$$\dot{\tau}^* = \tau^* + \{\mathrm{div}(\omega) + \omega(\phi\omega^\sharp)\},$$

where $\mathrm{div}(\omega) = g^{ij}(\nabla_{e_i}\omega)(e_j)$, $\mathrm{div}^*(\omega) = g^{ij}(\nabla_{e_i}\omega)(\phi e_j)$;

Proof. We present the proof of the theorem in the first considered case, i.e., $(\mathcal{M}, \phi, \xi, \eta, g) \in \mathcal{F}_1$.

Using (1) and (2), we easily compute $\dot{\rho}$ as the trace of $\dot{R}(x,y,z,w)$, given in Theorem 4 (1), by g^{ij} for $x = e_i$ and $w = e_j$.

Similarly, we calculate the trace of $\dot{R}(x,y,z,w)$ by g^{ij} for $x = e_i$ and $w = \phi e_j$, and we obtain the form of $\dot{\rho}^*$, again taking into account (1) and (2).

Finally, the values of $\dot{\tau}$ and $\dot{\tau}^*$ are obtained by calculating the traces of $\dot{\rho}(y,z)$ and $\dot{\rho}^*(y,z)$ by g^{ij} for $y = e_i$ and $z = e_j$.

Thus, we establish the truthfulness of the first statement in the corollary. The other cases are proved in a similar way. □

5. Example

In this section, we consider a known example of a Riemannian Π-manifold of dimension five, recalling some obtained results for it and presenting new ones related to the studied theory.

The authors of [2] studied the so-called paracontact almost paracomplex Riemannian manifolds, which are Riemannian Π-manifolds having the property $2g(x, \phi y) = (\nabla_x \eta)(y) + (\nabla_y \eta)(x)$.

According to the classification of the considered manifolds from [1], we denote by $\mathcal{F}_4'$ a subclass of $\mathcal{F}_4$, which is defined by the condition $\theta(\xi) = -2n$. It is important to note that $\mathcal{F}_4'$ and $\mathcal{F}_0$ are subclasses of $\mathcal{F}_4$ but without common elements.

A paracontact almost paracomplex Riemannian manifold having the additional condition $\phi x = \nabla_x \xi$ is called a para-Sasakian paracomplex Riemannian manifold, and it belongs to the class $\mathcal{F}_4'$ [2].

In [3], the same class of manifolds is obtained by a cone construction of a paraholomorphic paracomplex Riemannian manifold. There, they are called para-Sasaki-like paracontact paracomplex Riemannian manifolds.

Let us consider a Lie group $\mathcal{G}$ of dimension 5 (i.e., $n = 2$) which has a basis of left-invariant vector fields $\{e_0, \ldots, e_4\}$ and the corresponding Lie algebra is defined for $\lambda, \mu \in \mathbb{R}$ by the following commutators:

$$[e_0, e_1] = \lambda e_2 - e_3 + \mu e_4, \quad [e_0, e_2] = -\lambda e_1 - \mu e_3 - e_4, \quad (49)$$
$$[e_0, e_3] = -e_1 + \mu e_2 + \lambda e_4, \quad [e_0, e_4] = -\mu e_1 - e_2 - \lambda e_3.$$

The defined Lie group $\mathcal{G}$ is equipped with an invariant Riemannian Π-structure (ϕ, ξ, η, g) as follows:

$$\xi = e_0, \quad \phi e_1 = e_3, \quad \phi e_2 = e_4, \quad \phi e_3 = e_1, \quad \phi e_4 = e_2,$$
$$\eta(e_1) = \eta(e_2) = \eta(e_3) = \eta(e_4) = 0, \quad \eta(e_0) = 1, \quad (50)$$
$$g(e_0, e_0) = g(e_1, e_1) = g(e_2, e_2) = g(e_3, e_3) = g(e_4, e_4) = 1,$$
$$g(e_i, e_j) = 0, \quad i, j \in \{0, 1, \ldots, 4\}, \; i \neq j.$$

It is proved that the constructed manifold $(\mathcal{G}, \phi, \xi, \eta, g)$ is a para-Sasaki-like paracontact paracomplex Riemannian manifold, i.e., $(\mathcal{G}, \phi, \xi, \eta, g) \in \mathcal{F}_4$ [3].

Using (49), (50) and the well-known Koszul equality regarding g and ∇, we calculate the components of the Levi–Civita connection, and the nonzero ones of them are the following:

$$\nabla_{e_0} e_1 = \lambda e_2 + \mu e_4, \quad \nabla_{e_1} e_0 = e_3,$$
$$\nabla_{e_0} e_2 = -\lambda e_1 - \mu e_3, \quad \nabla_{e_2} e_0 = e_4,$$
$$\nabla_{e_0} e_3 = \mu e_2 + \lambda e_4, \quad \nabla_{e_3} e_0 = e_1, \quad (51)$$
$$\nabla_{e_0} e_4 = -\mu e_1 - \lambda e_3, \quad \nabla_{e_4} e_0 = e_2,$$
$$\nabla_{e_1} e_3 = \nabla_{e_2} e_4 = \nabla_{e_3} e_1 = \nabla_{e_4} e_2 = -e_0.$$

Taking into account (49)–(51), we calculate the components $R\_ijkl = R(e\_i, e\_j, e\_k, e\_l)$, $\rho_{ij} = \rho(e_i, e_j)$ and $\rho^*_{ij} = \rho^*(e_i, e_j)$ as well as the values of τ and τ^*. The nonzero ones of them are determined by the following equalities and their well-known symmetries and antisymmetries:

$$R_{0101} = R_{0202} = R_{0303} = R_{0404} = R_{1331} = R_{2442} = R_{1234} = R_{1432} = 1,$$
$$\rho_{00} = -4, \qquad \rho^*_{13} = \rho^*_{24} = -3, \qquad \tau = -4. \tag{52}$$

Let us consider the first natural connection $\dot{D}$ on $(\mathcal{G}, \phi, \xi, \eta, g)$ defined by (29). Then, by the relation between $\dot{D}$ and ∇ in the case of $\mathcal{F}_4$ from Theorem 2, and using (51), we obtain the components of $\dot{D}$. The nonzero ones of them are the following:

$$\dot{D}_{e_0} e_1 = \lambda e_2 + \mu e_4, \qquad \dot{D}_{e_0} e_2 = -\lambda e_1 - \mu e_3,$$
$$\dot{D}_{e_0} e_3 = \mu e_2 + \lambda e_4, \qquad \dot{D}_{e_0} e_4 = -\mu e_1 - \lambda e_3. \tag{53}$$

Proposition 2. *The Riemannian Π-manifold $(\mathcal{G}, \phi, \xi, \eta, g)$ has a flat first natural connection $\dot{D}$, i.e., $\dot{R} = 0$.*

Proof. Using (44) and (53), we establish that the components of $\dot{R}$ vanish. Thus, we prove the assertion. □

Corollary 4. *The Riemannian Π-manifold $(\mathcal{G}, \phi, \xi, \eta, g)$ is Ricci flat and scalar flat with respect to the first natural connection $\dot{D}$, i.e., $\dot{\rho} = 0$ and $\dot{\tau} = 0$.*

Proof. The truthfulness of the corollary is obvious bearing in mind Proposition 2. □

Taking into account (20), (50) and (52), Proposition 2 and Corollary 4, the presented example confirms the statements in Theorem 4 and Corollary 4.

By virtue of (36), (37), (50) and (51), we calculate the components $\dot{T}_{ijk} = \dot{T}(e\_i, e\_j, e\_k)$. The nonzero ones of them are determined by the following equalities and their well-known antisymmetries:

$$\dot{T}_{013} = \dot{T}_{031} = \dot{T}_{024} = \dot{T}_{042} = 1. \tag{54}$$

Then, using (40) and (54), we calculate $\dot{t}$, $\dot{t}^*$, and $\widehat{\dot{t}}$. The only nonzero one of them is

$$\dot{t}^*(e_0) = 4. \tag{55}$$

The obtained results in (54) and (55) regarding the torsion properties of the studied example confirm the assertion made in Corollary 3 in the case of the class $\mathcal{F}_4$.

6. Conclusions

In the present work, we defined a non-symmetric natural connection and called it the first natural connection on a Riemannian Π-manifold. The most significant results obtained in this work are as follows. We introduced the notion of a natural connection on the Riemannian Π-manifolds and proved the necessary and sufficient conditions for an affine connection to be natural on them. We defined the first natural connection $\dot{D}$ by an explicit expression and obtained relations between $\dot{D}$ and the Levi–Civita connection ∇ in the main classes of the studied manifolds, as well as determining the relations between their respective curvature tensors, torsion tensors, Ricci tensors, and scalar curvatures. Finally, we supported the results with an explicit five-dimensional example.

Funding: This research received no external funding.

Data Availability Statement: Data are contained within the article.

Conflicts of Interest: The author declares no conflict of interest.

References

1. Manev, M.; Staikova, M. On almost paracontact Riemannian manifolds of type (n,n). *J. Geom.* **2001**, *72*, 108–114. [CrossRef]
2. Manev, M.; Tavkova, V. On the almost paracontact almost paracomplex Riemannian manifolds. *Facta Univ. Ser. Math. Inform.* **2018**, *33*, 637–657.
3. Ivanov, S.; Manev, H.; Manev, M. Para-Sasaki-like Riemannian manifolds and new Einstein metrics. *Rev. Real Acad. Cienc. Exactas Fis. Nat. Ser. A Mat.* **2021**, *115*, 112. [CrossRef]
4. Manev, H.; Manev, M. Pair of associated Schouten-van Kampen connections adapted to an almost paracontact almost paracomplex Riemannian structure. *Mathematics* **2021**, *9*, 736. [CrossRef]
5. Manev, H.; Manev, M. Para-Ricci-like solitons on Riemannian manifolds with almost paracontact structure and almost paracomplex structure. *Mathematics* **2021**, *9*, 1704. [CrossRef]
6. Kobayashi, S.; Nomizu, K. *Foundations of Differential Geometry*; Wiley-Interscience: Hoboken, NJ, USA, 1963; Volume I.
7. Alexiev, V.; Ganchev, G. Canonical connection on a conformal almost contact metric manifolds. *Annu. Sofia Univ. St. Kliment Ohridski Fac. Math. Inform.* **1987**, *81*, 29–38.
8. Ganchev, G.; Mihova, V. Canonical connection and the canonical conformal group on an almost complex manifold with B-metric. *Annu. Sofia Univ. St. Kliment Ohridski Fac. Math. Inform.* **1987**, *81*, 195–206.
9. Mekerov, D. P-connection on Riemannian almost product manifolds. *Comptes Rendus Acad. Bulg. Des Sci.-En.* **2009**, *62*, 1363–1370.
10. Manev, M.; Gribachev, K. Conformally invariant tensors on almost contact manifolds with B-metric. *Serdica Mathe J.* **1994**, *20*, 133–147.
11. Staikova, M.; Gribachev, K. Canonical connections and their conformal invariants on Riemannian P-manifolds. *Serdica Math. J.* **1992**, *18*, 150–161.
12. Slovak, J. On natural connections on Riemannian manifolds. *Comment. Math. Univ. Carol.* **1989**, *30*, 389–393.
13. Munoz Masque, J.; Valdes, A. Characterizing the Blaschke connection. *Differ. Geom. Appl.* **1999**, *11*, 237–243. [CrossRef]
14. Blaga, A.; Crasmareanu, M. Special connections in almost paracontact metric geometry. *Bull. Iran. Math. Soc.* **2015**, *41*, 1345–1353.
15. Blaga, A.; Nannicini, A. On the geometry of metallic pseudo-Riemannian structures. *Riv. Mat. Della Univ. Parma* **2020**, *11*, 69–87.
16. Satō, I. On a structure similar to the almost contact structure. *Tensor* **1976**, *30*, 219–224.

Disclaimer/Publisher's Note: The statements, opinions and data contained in all publications are solely those of the individual author(s) and contributor(s) and not of MDPI and/or the editor(s). MDPI and/or the editor(s) disclaim responsibility for any injury to people or property resulting from any ideas, methods, instructions or products referred to in the content.

Article

On Nearly Sasakian and Nearly Kähler Statistical Manifolds

Siraj Uddin [1,*], Esmaeil Peyghan [2], Leila Nourmohammadifar [2] and Rawan Bossly [1,3]

[1] Department of Mathematics, Faculty of Science, King Abdulaziz University, Jeddah 21589, Saudi Arabia; rboslly@stu.kau.edu.sa

[2] Department of Mathematics, Faculty of Science, Arak University, Arak 38156-8-8349, Iran; e-peyghan@araku.ac.ir (E.P.); l.nourmohammadi@gmail.com (L.N.)

[3] Department of Mathematics, College of Science, Jazan University, Jazan 82817, Saudi Arabia

* Correspondence: sshehabaldeen@kau.edu.sa

Abstract: In this paper, we introduce the notions of nearly Sasakian and nearly Kähler statistical structures with a non-trivial example. The conditions for a real hypersurface in a nearly Kähler statistical manifold to admit a nearly Sasakian statistical structure are given. We also study invariant and anti-invariant statistical submanifolds of nearly Sasakian statistical manifolds. Finally, some conditions under which such a submanifold of a nearly Sasakian statistical manifold is itself a nearly Sasakian statistical manifold are given.

Keywords: information geometry; nearly Kähler statistical manifold; nearly Sasakian statistical manifold

MSC: 62B11; 53D15; 60D05

1. Introduction

Information geometry, as a well-known theory in geometry, is a gadget used to peruse spaces including of probability measures. At present, this interdisciplinary field, as a combination of differential geometry and statistics, plays an impressive role in various sciences. For instance, a manifold learning theory in a hypothetic space consisting of models is developed in [1]. The semi-Riemannian metric of this hypothesis space, which is uniquely derived, relies on the information geometry of the probability distributions. In [2], Amari also presented the geometrical and statistical ideas used to investigate neural networks, including invisible units or unobservable variables. To see more applications of this geometry in other sciences, refer to [3,4].

Suppose that ζ is an open subset of $\mathbb{R}^n$, and χ is a sample space with parameters $\xi = (\xi^1, \cdots, \xi^n)$. A statistical model S is the set of probability density functions defined by

$$S = \{ p(y;\xi) : \int_\chi p(y;\xi)dy = 1, \ p(y;\xi) > 0, \ \xi \in \zeta \subseteq \mathbb{R}^n \}.$$

The Fisher information matrix $g(\xi) = [g_{ls}(\xi)]$ on S is given as

$$g_{ls}(\xi) := \int_\chi \partial_l \ell_\xi \partial_s \ell_\xi p(y;\xi) dy = E_p[\partial_l \ell_\xi \partial_s \ell_\xi], \tag{1}$$

where $E_p[\ell]$ is the expectation of $\ell(y)$ with respect to $p(y;\xi)$, $\ell_\xi = \ell(y;\xi) := \log p(y;\xi)$ and $\partial_l := \frac{\partial}{\partial \xi^l}$. The space S, together with the information matrices, is a statistical manifold. In 1920, Fisher was the first to offer (1) as a mathematical purpose of information (see [5]). It is observed that (S,g) is a Riemannian manifold if all components of g are converging to real numbers and g is positive-definite. Therefore, g is called a Fisher metric on S. Using g, an affine connection ∇ with respect to $p(y;\xi)$ is described by

$$\Gamma_{ls,k} = g(\nabla_{\partial_l} \partial_s, \partial_k) := E_p[(\partial_l \partial_s \ell_\xi) \partial_k \ell_\xi]. \tag{2}$$

Citation: Uddin, S.; Peyghan, E.; Nourmohammadifar, L.; Bossly, R. On Nearly Sasakian and Nearly Kähler Statistical Manifolds. *Mathematics* **2023**, *11*, 2644. https://doi.org/10.3390/math11122644

Academic Editor: Cristina-Elena Hretcanu

Received: 17 May 2023
Revised: 5 June 2023
Accepted: 8 June 2023
Published: 9 June 2023

Copyright: © 2023 by the authors. Licensee MDPI, Basel, Switzerland. This article is an open access article distributed under the terms and conditions of the Creative Commons Attribution (CC BY) license (https://creativecommons.org/licenses/by/4.0/).

Nearly Kähler structures on Riemannian manifolds were specified by Gray [6] to describe a special class of almost Hermitian structures in every even dimension. As an odd-dimensional peer of nearly Kähler manifolds, nearly Sasakian manifolds were introduced by Blair, Yano and Showers in [7]. They showed that a normal nearly Sasakian structure is Sasakian and a hypersurface of a nearly Kähler structure is nearly Sasakian if and only if it is quasi-umbilical with the (almost) contact form. In particular, S^5 properly imbedded in S^6 inherits a nearly Sasakian structure which is not Sasakian.

A statistical manifold can be considered as an expanse of a Riemannian manifold such that the compatibility of the Riemannian metric is developed to a general condition. By applying this opinion in geometry, we create a convenient nearly Sasakian structure on statistical structures and define a nearly Sasakian statistical manifold.

The purpose of this paper is to present nearly Sasakian and nearly Kähler structures on statistical manifolds and show the relation between two geometric notions. To achieve this goal, the notions and attributes of statistical manifolds are obtained in Section 2. In Section 3, we describe a nearly Sasakian structure on statistical manifolds and present some of their properties. In Section 4, we investigate nearly Kähler structures on statistical manifolds. In this context, the conditions needed for a real hypersurface in a nearly Kähler statistical manifold to admit a nearly Sasakian statistical structure are provided. Section 5 is devoted to studying (anti-)invariant statistical submanifolds of nearly Sasakian statistical manifolds. Some conditions under which an invariant submanifold of a nearly Sasakian statistical manifold is itself a nearly Sasakian statistical manifold are given at the end.

2. Preliminaries

For an n-dimensional manifold N, consider (U, x^i), $i = 1, \ldots, n$, as a local chart of the point $x \in U$. Considering the coordinates (x^i) on N, we have the local field $\frac{\partial}{\partial x^i}|_p$ as frames on $T_p N$.

An affine connection ∇ is called *Codazzi connection* if the Codazzi equations satisfy:

$$(\nabla_{X_1} g)(X_2, X_3) = (\nabla_{X_2} g)(X_1, X_3), \quad (= (\nabla_{X_3} g)(X_1, X_2)), \tag{3}$$

for any $X_1, X_2, X_3 \in \Gamma(TN)$ where

$$(\nabla_{X_1} g)(X_2, X_3) = X_1 g(X_2, X_3) - g(\nabla_{X_1} X_2, X_3) - g(X_2, \nabla_{X_1} X_3). \tag{4}$$

The triplet (N, g, ∇) is also called a *statistical manifold* if the Codazzi connection ∇ is a statistical connection, i.e., a torsion-free Codazzi connection. Moreover, the affine connection ∇^* as a (dual) *conjugate connection* of ∇ with respect to g is determined by

$$X_1 g(X_2, X_3) = g(\nabla_{X_1} X_2, X_3) + g(X_2, \nabla^*_{X_1} X_3). \tag{5}$$

Considering ∇^g as the Levi–Civita connection on N, one can see $\nabla^g = \frac{1}{2}(\nabla + \nabla^*)$ and

$$\nabla^* g = -\nabla g.$$

Thus, (N, g, ∇^*) forms a statistical manifold. In particular, the torsion-free Codazzi connection ∇ reduces to the Levi–Civita connection ∇^g if $\nabla g = 0$.

A $(1,2)$-tensor field K on a statistical manifold (N, g, ∇) is described by

$$K_{X_1} X_2 = \nabla_{X_1} X_2 - \nabla^g_{X_1} X_2, \tag{6}$$

from (2) and (3), we have

$$K = \nabla^g - \nabla^* = \frac{1}{2}(\nabla - \nabla^*). \tag{7}$$

Hence, it follows that K satisfies

$$K_{X_1}X_2 = K_{X_2}X_1, \quad g(K_{X_3}X_2, X_1) = g(X_2, K_{X_3}X_1). \tag{8}$$

The curvature tensor $\mathcal{R}^\nabla$ of a torsion-free linear connection ∇ is described by

$$\mathcal{R}^\nabla(X_1, X_2) = \nabla_{X_1}\nabla_{X_2} - \nabla_{X_2}\nabla_{X_1} - \nabla_{[X_1, X_2]}, \tag{9}$$

for any $X_1, X_2 \in \Gamma(TN)$. On a statistical structure (∇, g), denote the curvature tensor of ∇ as $\mathcal{R}^\nabla$ or $\mathcal{R}$ for short, and denote $\mathcal{R}^{\nabla^*}$ as $\mathcal{R}^*$ in a similar argument. It is obvious that

$$\mathcal{R}(X_1, X_2) = -\mathcal{R}(X_2, X_1), \tag{10}$$
$$\mathcal{R}^*(X_1, X_2) = -\mathcal{R}^*(X_2, X_1). \tag{11}$$

Moreover, setting $\mathcal{R}(X_1, X_2, X_3, X_4) = g(\mathcal{R}(X_1, X_2)X_3, X_4)$, we can see that

$$\mathcal{R}(X_1, X_2, X_3, X_4) = -\mathcal{R}^*(X_1, X_2, X_4, X_3), \tag{12}$$
$$\mathcal{R}(X_1, X_2)X_3 + \mathcal{R}(X_2, X_3)X_1 + \mathcal{R}(X_3, X_1)X_2 = 0, \tag{13}$$
$$\mathcal{R}^*(X_1, X_2)X_3 + \mathcal{R}^*(X_2, X_3)X_1 + \mathcal{R}^*(X_3, X_1)X_2 = 0. \tag{14}$$

The statistical curvature tensor field $\mathcal{S}$ of the statistical structure (∇, g) is given by

$$\mathcal{S}(X_1, X_2)X_3 = \frac{1}{2}\{\mathcal{R}(X_1, X_2)X_3 + \mathcal{R}^*(X_1, X_2)X_3\}. \tag{15}$$

using the definition of $\mathcal{R}$, it follows that

$$\mathcal{S}(X_1, X_2, X_3, X_4) = -\mathcal{S}(X_2, X_1, X_3, X_4),$$
$$\mathcal{S}(X_1, X_2, X_3, X_4) = -\mathcal{S}(X_1, X_2, X_4, X_3),$$
$$\mathcal{S}(X_1, X_2, X_3, X_4) = \mathcal{S}(X_3, X_4, X_1, X_2),$$

where $\mathcal{S}(X_1, X_2, X_3, X_4) = g(\mathcal{S}(X_1, X_2)X_3, X_4)$.

The Lie derivative with respect to a metric tensor g in a statistical manifold (N, g, ∇), for any $X_1, X_2, v \in \Gamma(TN)$ is given by

$$(\mathcal{L}_v g)(X_1, X_2) = g(\nabla^g_{X_1}v, X_2) + g(X_1, \nabla^g_{X_2}v)$$
$$= g(\nabla_{X_1}v, X_2) - g(K_{X_1}v, X_2) + g(X_1, \nabla_{X_2}v) - g(X_1, K_{X_2}v).$$

The vector field v is said to be the Killing vector field or infinitesimal isometry if $\mathcal{L}_v g = 0$. Hence, using the above equation and (8), it follows that

$$g(\nabla_{X_1}v, X_2) + g(X_1, \nabla_{X_2}v) = 2g(K_{X_1}v, X_2). \tag{16}$$

Similarly, (7) implies

$$g(\nabla^*_{X_1}v, X_2) + g(X_1, \nabla^*_{X_2}v) = -2g(K_{X_1}v, X_2).$$

The curvature tensor $\mathcal{R}^g$ of a Riemannian manifold (N, g) admitting a Killing vector field v satisfies the following

$$\mathcal{R}^g(X_1, v)X_2 = \nabla^g_{X_1}\nabla^g_{X_2}v - \nabla^g_{\nabla^g_{X_1}X_2}v, \tag{17}$$

for any $X_1, X_2, v \in \Gamma(TN)$ [8].

3. Nearly Sasakian Statistical Manifolds

An almost contact manifold is a $(2n+1)$-dimensional differentiable manifold N equipped with an almost contact structure $(\mathcal{F}, v, u)$ where $\mathcal{F}$ is a tensor field of type $(1,1)$, v a vector field and u a 1-form, such that

$$\mathcal{F}^2 = -I + u \otimes v, \quad \mathcal{F}v = 0, \quad u(v) = 1. \tag{18}$$

Additionally, N will be called an almost contact metric manifold if it admits a pseudo-Riemannian metric g with the following condition

$$g(\mathcal{F}X_1, \mathcal{F}X_2) = g(X_1, X_2) - u(X_1)u(X_2), \quad \forall X_1, X_2 \in \Gamma(TN). \tag{19}$$

Moreover, as in the almost contact case, (19) yields $u = g(.,v)$ and $g(.,\mathcal{F}) = -g(\mathcal{F},.)$.

Theorem 1. *The statistical curvature tensor field $\mathcal{S}$ of a statistical manifold (N, g, ∇) with an almost contact metric structure $(\mathcal{F}, v, u, g)$, such that the vector field v is Killing, which satisfies the equation*

$$2\mathcal{S}(X_1, v)X_2 = \nabla_{X_1}\nabla_{X_2}v - \nabla_{\nabla_{X_1}X_2}v + \nabla^*_{X_1}\nabla^*_{X_2}v - \nabla^*_{\nabla^*_{X_1}X_2}v,$$

for any $X_1, X_2 \in \Gamma(TN)$.

Proof. According to (10), (12) and (14), we can write

$$\begin{aligned}\mathcal{R}^*(X_2, X_3, X_1, v) &= -\mathcal{R}^*(X_3, X_1, X_2, v) - \mathcal{R}^*(X_1, X_2, X_3, v) \\ &= \mathcal{R}(X_3, X_1, v, X_2) + \mathcal{R}(X_1, X_2, v, X_3) \\ &= -\mathcal{R}(X_1, X_3, v, X_2) - \mathcal{R}(X_2, X_1, v, X_3).\end{aligned}$$

Applying (9) to the above equation, we find

$$\begin{aligned}\mathcal{R}^*(X_2, X_3, X_1, v) =& g(-\nabla_{X_1}\nabla_{X_3}v + \nabla_{X_3}\nabla_{X_1}v + \nabla_{[X_1, X_3]}v, X_2) \\ &+ g(-\nabla_{X_2}\nabla_{X_1}v + \nabla_{X_1}\nabla_{X_2}v + \nabla_{[X_2, X_1]}v, X_3).\end{aligned} \tag{20}$$

Since v is Killing, by differentiating

$$g(\nabla_{X_2}v, X_3) + g(X_2, \nabla_{X_3}v) = 2g(K_{X_2}v, X_3),$$

with respect to X_1, we obtain

$$\begin{aligned}2X_1 g(K_{X_3}X_2 v) =& (\nabla_{X_1}g)(\nabla_{X_3}v, X_2) + g(\nabla_{X_1}\nabla_{X_3}v, X_2) \\ &+ g(\nabla_{X_3}v, \nabla_{X_1}X_2) + (\nabla_{X_1}g)(\nabla_{X_2}v, X_3) \\ &+ g(\nabla_{X_1}\nabla_{X_2}v, X_3) + g(\nabla_{X_2}v, \nabla_{X_1}X_3).\end{aligned}$$

Setting the last equation in (20), it follows that

$$\begin{aligned}\mathcal{R}^*(X_2, X_3, X_1, v) =& 2g(\nabla_{X_1}\nabla_{X_2}v, X_3) - 2g(\nabla_{\nabla_{X_1}X_2}v, X_3) + 2(\nabla_{X_1}g)(\nabla_{X_3}v, X_2) \\ &+ 2g(K_{X_3}v, \nabla_{X_1}X_2) - 2X_1 g(K_{X_3}X_2, v) - 2g(K_{X_1}v, [X_3, X_2]) \\ &+ 2X_3 g(K_{X_1}X_2, v) + 2g(K_{X_2}v, [X_1, X_3]) - 2X_2 g(K_{X_1}X_3, v) \\ &+ 2g(K_{X_3}v, \nabla_{X_2}X_1) + \mathcal{R}(X_2, X_3, v, X_1).\end{aligned}$$

As $(\nabla_{X_1}g)(\nabla_{X_3}v, X_2) = -2g(K_{X_1}\nabla_{X_3}v, X_2)$, and using (12) in the above equation, we can obtain

$$\begin{aligned}\mathcal{R}(X_2, X_3, v, X_1) = &-g(\nabla_{X_1}\nabla_{X_2}v, X_3) + g(\nabla_{\nabla_{X_1}X_2}v, X_3) + 2g(K_{X_1}X_2, \nabla_{X_3}v) \\ &- g(K_{X_3}v, \nabla_{X_1}X_2) - g(K_{X_2}v, [X_1, X_3]) + X_1 g(K_{X_3}X_2, v) \\ &+ g(K_{X_1}v, [X_3, X_2]) - X_3 g(K_{X_1}X_2, v) + X_2 g(K_{X_1}X_3, v) \\ &- g(K_{X_3}v, \nabla_{X_2}X_1).\end{aligned}$$

Similarly, we find

$$\begin{aligned}\mathcal{R}^*(X_2, X_3, v, X_1) = &-g(\nabla^*_{X_1}\nabla^*_{X_2}v, X_3) + g(\nabla^*_{\nabla^*_{X_1}X_2}v, X_3) - 2g(K_{X_1}X_2, \nabla^*_{X_3}v) \\ &+ g(K_{X_3}v, \nabla^*_{X_1}X_2) + g(K_{X_2}v, [X_1, X_3]) - X_1 g(K_{X_3}X_2, v) \\ &- g(K_{X_1}v, [X_3, X_2]) + X_3 g(K_{X_1}X_2, v) - X_2 g(K_{X_1}X_3, v) \\ &+ g(K_{X_3}v, \nabla^*_{X_2}X_1).\end{aligned}$$

Adding the previous relations and using (7) and (15), we obtain the following assertion. □

A nearly Sasakian manifold is an almost contact metric manifold $(N, \mathcal{F}, v, u, g)$ if

$$(\nabla^g_{X_1}\mathcal{F})X_2 + (\nabla^g_{X_2}\mathcal{F})X_1 = -2g(X_1, X_2)v + u(X_1)X_2 + u(X_2)X_1, \tag{21}$$

for any $X_1, X_2 \in \Gamma(TN)$ [7]. In such manifolds, the vector field v is Killing. Moreover, a tensor field h of type $(1,1)$ is determined by

$$\nabla^g_{X_1}v = \mathcal{F}X_1 + hX_1. \tag{22}$$

The last equation immediately shows that h is skew-symmetric and

$$h \circ \mathcal{F} = -\mathcal{F} \circ h, \quad hv = 0, \quad u \circ h = 0,$$

and

$$\nabla^g_v h = \nabla^g_v \mathcal{F} = \mathcal{F} \circ h = \frac{1}{3}\pounds_v \mathcal{F}.$$

Moreover, Olszak proved the following formulas in [9]:

$$\begin{aligned}\mathcal{R}^g(\mathcal{F}X_1, X_2, X_3, X_4) &+ \mathcal{R}^g(X_1, \mathcal{F}X_2, X_3, X_4) + \mathcal{R}^g(X_1, X_2, \mathcal{F}X_3, X_4) \\ &+ \mathcal{R}^g(X_1, X_2, X_3, \mathcal{F}X_4) = 0,\end{aligned} \tag{23}$$

$$\begin{aligned}\mathcal{R}^g(\mathcal{F}X_1, \mathcal{F}X_2, \mathcal{F}X_3, \mathcal{F}X_4) &= \mathcal{R}^g(X_1, X_2, X_3, X_4) - \mathcal{R}^g(v, X_2, X_3, X_4)u(X_1) \\ &+ \mathcal{R}^g(v, X_1, X_3, X_4)u(X_2),\end{aligned} \tag{24}$$

$$\mathcal{R}^g(v, X_1)X_2 = g(X_1 - h^2 X_1, X_2)v - u(X_2)(X_1 - h^2 X_1), \tag{25}$$

$$\mathcal{R}^g(\mathcal{F}X_1, \mathcal{F}X_2)v = 0, \tag{26}$$

for any $X_1, X_2, X_3, X_4 \in \Gamma(TN)$.

Lemma 1. *For a manifold N with a statistical structure (∇, g), and an almost contact metric structure $(\mathcal{F}, v, u, g)$, the following holds*

$$\begin{aligned}\nabla_{X_1}\mathcal{F}X_2 - \mathcal{F}\nabla^*_{X_1}X_2 + \nabla_{X_2}\mathcal{F}X_1 - \mathcal{F}\nabla^*_{X_2}X_1 = &(\nabla^g_{X_1}\mathcal{F})X_2 + (\nabla^g_{X_2}\mathcal{F})X_1 \\ &+ K_{X_1}\mathcal{F}X_2 + K_{X_2}\mathcal{F}X_1 + 2\mathcal{F}K_{X_1}X_2,\end{aligned}$$

for any $X_1, X_2 \in \Gamma(TN)$.

Proof. (6) and (7) imply

$$\nabla_{X_1}\mathcal{F}X_2 - \mathcal{F}\nabla^*_{X_1}X_2 + \nabla_{X_2}\mathcal{F}X_1 - \mathcal{F}\nabla^*_{X_2}X_1 = \nabla^g_{X_1}\mathcal{F}X_2 + K_{X_1}\mathcal{F}X_2 - \mathcal{F}\nabla^g_{X_1}X_2$$
$$+ \mathcal{F}K_{X_1}X_2 + \nabla^g_{X_2}\mathcal{F}X_1 + K_{X_2}\mathcal{F}X_1$$
$$- \mathcal{F}\nabla^g_{X_2}X_1 + \mathcal{F}K_{X_2}X_1$$
$$= (\nabla^g_{X_1}\mathcal{F})X_2 + (\nabla^g_{X_2}\mathcal{F})X_1 + K_{X_1}\mathcal{F}X_2$$
$$+ K_{X_2}\mathcal{F}X_1 + 2\mathcal{F}K_{X_1}X_2.$$

Hence, the proof is complete. □

Definition 1. *A nearly Sasakian statistical structure on N is a quintuple* $(\nabla, g, \mathcal{F}, v, u)$ *consisting of a statistical structure* (∇, g) *and a nearly Sasakian structure* $(g, \mathcal{F}, v, u)$, *satisfying*

$$K_{X_1}\mathcal{F}X_2 + K_{X_2}\mathcal{F}X_1 = -2\mathcal{F}K_{X_1}X_2, \quad (27)$$

for any $X_1, X_2 \in \Gamma(TN)$.

A nearly Sasakian statistical manifold is a manifold that admits a nearly Sasakian statistical structure.

Remark 1. *A multiple* $(N, \nabla^*, g, \mathcal{F}, v, u)$ *is also a nearly Sasakian statistical manifold if* $(N, \nabla, g, \mathcal{F}, v, u)$ *is a nearly Sasakian statistical manifold. In this case, from Lemma 1 and Definition 1, we have*

$$\nabla^*_{X_1}\mathcal{F}X_2 - \mathcal{F}\nabla_{X_1}X_2 + \nabla^*_{X_2}\mathcal{F}X_1 - \mathcal{F}\nabla_{X_2}X_1 = (\nabla^g_{X_1}\mathcal{F})X_2 + (\nabla^g_{X_2}\mathcal{F})X_1,$$

for any $X_1, X_2 \in \Gamma(TN)$.

Theorem 2. *If* (N, ∇, g) *is a statistical manifold, and* $(g, \mathcal{F}, v)$ *an almost contact metric structure on N; then,* $(\nabla, g, \mathcal{F}, v)$ *is a nearly Sasakian statistical structure on N if and only if the following formulas hold:*

$$\nabla_{X_1}\mathcal{F}X_2 - \mathcal{F}\nabla^*_{X_1}X_2 + \nabla_{X_2}\mathcal{F}X_1 - \mathcal{F}\nabla^*_{X_2}X_1 = u(X_1)X_2 + u(X_2)X_1 - 2g(X_1, X_2)v, \quad (28)$$
$$\nabla^*_{X_1}\mathcal{F}X_2 - \mathcal{F}\nabla_{X_1}X_2 + \nabla^*_{X_2}\mathcal{F}X_1 - \mathcal{F}\nabla_{X_2}X_1 = u(X_1)X_2 + u(X_2)X_1 - 2g(X_1, X_2)v, \quad (29)$$

for any $X_1, X_2 \in \Gamma(TN)$.

Proof. Let $(N, \nabla, g, \mathcal{F}, v)$ be a nearly Sasakian statistical manifold. Applying (21), Lemma 1 and Definition 1, we get (28). Additionally, (29) follows from Remark 1. Conversely, using (7) and subtracting the relations (28) and (29), we can obtain (27). □

Example 1. *Let us consider the three-dimensional unite sphere* S^3 *in the complex two-dimensional space* $\mathbb{C}^2$. *As* S^3 *is isomorphic to the Lie group* $SU(2)$, *set* $\{e_1, e_2, e_3\}$ *as the basis of the Lie algebra* $\mathfrak{su}(2)$ *of* $SU(2)$ *obtained by*

$$e_1 = \frac{\sqrt{2}}{2}\begin{pmatrix} i & 0 \\ 0 & i \end{pmatrix}, \quad e_2 = \frac{\sqrt{2}}{2}\begin{pmatrix} 0 & 1 \\ -1 & 0 \end{pmatrix}, \quad e_3 = \frac{1}{2}\begin{pmatrix} 0 & i \\ i & 0 \end{pmatrix}.$$

Therefore, the Lie bracket is described by

$$[e_1, e_2] = 2e_3, \quad [e_2, e_3] = e_1, \quad [e_1, e_3] = -e_2.$$

The Riemannian metric g on S^3 *is defined by the following*

$$g(e_1,e_2) = g(e_1,e_3) = g(e_2,e_3) = 0, \quad g(e_1,e_1) = g(e_2,e_2) = g(e_3,e_3) = 1.$$

Assume that $v = e_3$ and u is the 1-form described by $u(X_1) = g(X_1,v)$ for any $X_1 \in \Gamma(TS^3)$. Considering $\mathcal{F}$ as a $(1,1)$-tensor field determined by $\mathcal{F}(e_1) = -e_2, \mathcal{F}(e_2) = e_1$ and $\mathcal{F}(v) = 0$; the above equations imply that $(S^3, \mathcal{F}, v, u, g)$ is an almost contact metric manifold. Using Koszul's formula, it follows that $\nabla^g_{e_i} e_j = 0, i, j = 1, 2, 3$, except

$$\nabla^g_{e_1} e_2 = v = -\nabla^g_{e_2} e_1, \quad \nabla^g_{e_1} v = -e_2, \quad \nabla^g_{e_2} v = e_1.$$

According to the above equations, we can see that

$$(\nabla^g_{e_i}\mathcal{F})e_j + (\nabla^g_{e_j}\mathcal{F})e_i = 0 = -2g(e_i,e_j)v + u(e_i)e_j + u(e_j)e_i, \quad i,j = 1,2,3,$$

unless

$$(\nabla^g_{e_1}\mathcal{F})e_1 + (\nabla^g_{e_1}\mathcal{F})e_1 = -2v = -2g(e_1,e_1)v + u(e_1)e_1 + u(e_1)e_1,$$
$$(\nabla^g_{e_1}\mathcal{F})v + (\nabla^g_{v}\mathcal{F})e_1 = e_1 = -2g(e_1,v)v + u(e_1)v + u(v)e_1,$$
$$(\nabla^g_{e_2}\mathcal{F})e_2 + (\nabla^g_{e_2}\mathcal{F})e_2 = -2v = -2g(e_2,e_2)v + u(e_2)e_2 + u(e_2)e_2,$$
$$(\nabla^g_{e_2}\mathcal{F})e_3 + (\nabla^g_{e_3}\mathcal{F})e_2 = e_2 = -2g(e_2,e_3)v + u(e_2)e_3 + u(e_3)e_2,$$

which gives $(g, \mathcal{F}, v, u)$, a nearly Sasakian structure on S^3. By setting

$$K(e_1,e_1) = e_1, \quad K(e_1,e_2) = K(e_2,e_1) = -e_2, \quad K(e_2,e_2) = -e_1,$$

while the other cases are zero, one see that K satisfies (8). From (6), it follows that

$$\nabla_{e_1} e_1 = e_1, \ \nabla_{e_1} e_2 = e_3 - e_2, \ \nabla_{e_1} e_3 = -e_2, \ \nabla_{e_2} e_1 = -e_2 - e_3, \ \nabla_{e_2} e_2 = -e_1, \ \nabla_{e_2} e_3 = e_1.$$

Therefore, we can obtain $(\nabla_{e_i} g)(e_j, e_k) = 0, i, j, k = 1, 2, 3$, except

$$(\nabla_{e_1} g)(e_1, e_1) = -2, \quad (\nabla_{e_1} g)(e_2, e_2) = (\nabla_{e_2} g)(e_1, e_2) = (\nabla_{e_2} g)(e_2, e_1) = 2.$$

Hence, (∇, g) is a statistical structure on S^3. Moreover, the equations

$$K_{e_1}\mathcal{F}(e_1) + K_{e_1}\mathcal{F}(e_1) = 2e_2 = -2\mathcal{F}K_{e_1}e_1,$$
$$K_{e_1}\mathcal{F}(e_2) + K_{e_2}\mathcal{F}(e_1) = 2e_1 = -2\mathcal{F}K_{e_1}e_2,$$
$$K_{e_2}\mathcal{F}(e_2) + K_{e_2}\mathcal{F}(e_2) = -2e_2 = -2\mathcal{F}K_{e_2}e_2,$$

hold. Therefore, $(S^3, \nabla, g, \mathcal{F}, v, u)$ is a nearly Sasakian statistical manifold.

Proposition 1. *For a nearly Sasakian statistical manifold $(N, \nabla, g, \mathcal{F}, v, u)$, the following conditions hold:*

(i) $\mathcal{F}K_v v = 0,$
(ii) $\mathcal{F}K_{\mathcal{F}X_1} v = 0,$
(iii) $K_v X_1 = u(X_1) K_v v,$
(iv) $\nabla_{X_1} v = \nabla^g_{X_1} v + u(X_1) K_v v,$
(v) $\nabla^*_{X_1} v = \nabla^g_{X_1} v - u(X_1) K_v v,$

for any $X_1 \in \Gamma(TN)$.

Proof. Setting $X_1 = X_2 = v$ in (27), it follows (i). For $X_2 = v$ in (27), we have

$$K_{\mathcal{F}X_1}v = -2\mathcal{F}K_{X_1}v. \tag{30}$$

Putting $X_1 = \mathcal{F}X_1$ in the last equation and using (18), we can obtain

$$K_{X_1}v = u(X_1)K_v v + 2\mathcal{F}K_{\mathcal{F}X_1}v. \tag{31}$$

Applying $\mathcal{F}$ yields

$$\mathcal{F}K_{X_1}v = -2K_{\mathcal{F}X_1}v + 2u(K_{\mathcal{F}X_1}v)v.$$

(30) and the last equation imply that

$$3K_{\mathcal{F}X_1}v = 4u(K_{\mathcal{F}X_1}v)v,$$

which gives us $\mathcal{F}K_{\mathcal{F}X_1}v = 0$, so (ii) holds. This and (31) yield (iii). From (6), (7) and (iii), we have (iv) and (v). □

Corollary 1. *A nearly Sasakian statistical manifold satisfies the following*

$$u(X_2)K_{X_1}K_v v = u(X_1)K_{X_2}K_v v = u(K_{X_1}X_2)K_v v,$$

for any $X_1, X_2 \in \Gamma(TN)$.

Proof. (6) and (30) imply

$$-\mathcal{F}^2(\nabla_{X_1}v - \nabla^g_{X_1}v) = 0,$$

which gives us

$$\nabla_{X_1}v = \nabla^g_{X_1}v + g(\nabla_{X_1}v, v)v.$$

Similarly,

$$\nabla^*_{X_1}v = \nabla^g_{X_1}v + g(\nabla^*_{X_1}v, v)v.$$

Then, subtracting the above two equations yields

$$K_{X_1}v = g(\nabla_{X_1}v, v)v,$$

which gives us $K_v v = g(\nabla_v v, v)v$. Thus, we obtain

$$u(X_2)K_{X_1}K_v v = u(X_2)g(\nabla_v v, v)K_{X_1}v = u(X_1)u(X_2)g(\nabla_v v, v)K_v v = u(X_1)K_{X_2}K_v v.$$

Moreover, (iii) implies

$$u(K_{X_1}X_2)K_v v = g(K_{X_1}X_2, v)K_v v = g(K_{X_1}v, X_2)K_v v = u(X_1)u(X_2)g(\nabla_v v, v)K_v v.$$

Therefore, the assertion follows. □

Corollary 2. *In a nearly Sasakian statistical manifold N, let* $X_1 \in \Gamma(TN)$ *and* $X_1 \perp v$. *Then,*
1. $K_{X_1}v = 0$,
2. $\nabla_{X_1}v = \nabla^*_{X_1}v = \nabla^g_{X_1}v$.

Proposition 2. *On a nearly Sasakian statistical manifold, the following holds*

$$g(\nabla_{X_1}v, X_2) + g(\nabla_{X_2}v, X_1) = 2u(X_1)u(X_2)g(K_v v, v),$$

for any $X_1, X_2 \in \Gamma(TN)$.

Proof. Since v is a Killing vector field in a nearly Sasakian manifold (see [7]); hence, we have

$$g(\nabla^g_{X_1} v, X_2) + g(\nabla^g_{X_2} v, X_1) = 0.$$

Setting (6) in the above equation, we have the following assertion. □

Lemma 2. *Let* $(N, \nabla, g, \mathcal{F}, v)$ *be a nearly Sasakian statistical manifold. Then, the statistical curvature tensor field satisfies*

$$\mathcal{S}(v, X_1) X_2 = g(X_1 - h^2 X_1, X_2) v - u(X_2)(X_1 - h^2 X_1),$$

for any $X_1, X_2 \in \Gamma(TN)$.

Proof. According to (6), (7) and Theorem 1, we can write

$$\nabla_{X_1} \nabla_{X_2} v - \nabla_{\nabla_{X_1} X_2} v = \nabla_{X_1} \nabla^g_{X_2} v + \nabla_{X_1} (u(X_2) K_v v) - \nabla^g_{\nabla_{X_1} X_2} v - u(\nabla_{X_1} X_2) K_v v$$
$$= K_{X_1} \nabla^g_{X_2} v + \nabla^g_{X_1} \nabla^g_{X_2} v + (\nabla_{X_1} u) X_2 K_v v$$
$$+ u(X_2)(K_{X_1} K_v v + \nabla^g_{X_1} K_v v) - \nabla^g_{\nabla^g_{X_1} X_2} v - \nabla^g_{K_{X_1} X_2} v.$$

Applying (17) in the above equation, we have

$$\nabla_{X_1} \nabla_{X_2} v - \nabla_{\nabla_{X_1} X_2} v = \mathcal{R}^g(X_1, v) X_2 + K_{X_1} \nabla^g_{X_2} v + (\nabla_{X_1} u) X_2 K_v v$$
$$+ u(X_2)(K_{X_1} K_v v + \nabla^g_{X_1} K_v v) - \nabla^g_{K_{X_1} X_2} v.$$

We can similarly conclude that

$$\nabla^*_{X_1} \nabla^*_{X_2} v - \nabla^*_{\nabla^*_{X_1} X_2} v = \mathcal{R}^g(X_1, v) X_2 - K_{X_1} \nabla^g_{X_2} v - (\nabla^*_{X_1} u) X_2 K_v v$$
$$+ u(X_2)(K_{X_1} K_v v - \nabla^g_{X_1} K_v v) + \nabla^g_{K_{X_1} X_2} v.$$

The above two equations imply

$$\nabla_{X_1} \nabla_{X_2} v - \nabla_{\nabla_{X_1} X_2} v + \nabla^*_{X_1} \nabla^*_{X_2} v - \nabla^*_{\nabla^*_{X_1} X_2} v$$
$$= 2\mathcal{R}^g(X_1, v) X_2 - 2u(K_{X_1} X_2) K_v v + 2u(X_2) K_{X_1} K_v v,$$

from this and Theorem 1, we have

$$\mathcal{S}(X_1, v) X_2 = \mathcal{R}^g(X_1, v) X_2 - u(K_{X_1} X_2) K_v v + u(X_2) K_{X_1} K_v v. \quad (32)$$

Thus, the assertion follows from (25), (32) and Corollary 1. □

Corollary 3. *On a nearly Sasakian statistical manifold N, the following holds*

$$\mathcal{S}(X_1, X_2) v = g(-X_1 + h^2 X_1, X_2) v + u(X_2)(X_1 - h^2 X_1) \quad (33)$$
$$+ g(X_2 - h^2 X_2, X_1) v - u(X_1)(X_2 - h^2 X_2),$$
$$\mathcal{S}(\mathcal{F} X_1, \mathcal{F} X_2) v = 0, \quad (34)$$

for any $X_1, X_2 \in \Gamma(TN)$.

Proof. We have

$$\mathcal{S}(X_1, X_2) v = -\mathcal{S}(v, X_1) X_2 - \mathcal{S}(X_2, v) X_1.$$

Applying Lemma 2 in the last equation, it follows that (33). To prove (34), using $X_1 = \mathcal{F}X_1$ and $X_2 = \mathcal{F}X_2$ in the above equation and using the skew-symmetric property of h, we can obtain

$$\mathcal{S}(\mathcal{F}X_1, \mathcal{F}X_2)v = g(-\mathcal{F}X_1 + h^2\mathcal{F}X_1, \mathcal{F}X_2)v + g(\mathcal{F}X_2 - h^2\mathcal{F}X_2, \mathcal{F}X_1)v = 0.$$

□

Proposition 3. *The statistical curvature tensor field S of a nearly Sasakian statistical manifold N satisfies the following*

$$\mathcal{S}(\mathcal{F}X_1, X_2, X_3, X_4) + \mathcal{S}(X_1, \mathcal{F}X_2, X_3, X_4) + \mathcal{S}(X_1, X_2, \mathcal{F}X_3, X_4) + \mathcal{S}(X_1, X_2, X_3, \mathcal{F}X_4) = 0, \tag{35}$$

$$\mathcal{S}(\mathcal{F}X_1, \mathcal{F}X_2, \mathcal{F}X_3, \mathcal{F}X_4) = \mathcal{S}(X_1, X_2, X_3, X_4) + u(X_2)\mathcal{R}^g(v, X_1, X_3, X_4) - u(X_1)\mathcal{R}^g(v, X_2, X_3, X_4), \tag{36}$$

for any $X_1, X_2, X_3, X_4 \in \Gamma(TN)$.

Proof. Applying (7) in (15), it follows that

$$\mathcal{S}(X_1, X_2)X_3 = \mathcal{R}^g(X_1, X_2)X_3 + [K_{X_1}, K_{X_2}]X_3. \tag{37}$$

Thus, using (23) and (37), we can write

$$\mathcal{S}(\mathcal{F}X_1, X_2, X_3, X_4) + \mathcal{S}(X_1, \mathcal{F}X_2, X_3, X_4) + \mathcal{S}(X_1, X_2, \mathcal{F}X_3, X_4) + \mathcal{S}(X_1, X_2, X_3, \mathcal{F}X_4)$$
$$= g(K_{\mathcal{F}X_1}K_{X_2}X_3 - K_{X_2}K_{\mathcal{F}X_1}X_3 + K_{X_1}K_{\mathcal{F}X_2}X_3 - K_{\mathcal{F}X_2}K_{X_1}X_3 + K_{X_1}K_{X_2}\mathcal{F}X_3 - K_{X_2}K_{X_1}\mathcal{F}X_3, X_4)$$
$$+ g(K_{X_1}K_{X_2}X_3 - K_{X_2}K_{X_1}X_3, \mathcal{F}X_4). \tag{38}$$

On the other hand, (27) implies

$$g(K_{X_1}\mathcal{F}X_2 + K_{X_2}\mathcal{F}X_1, X_3) = 2g(K_{X_1}X_2, \mathcal{F}X_3),$$

which gives us

$$g(K_{\mathcal{F}X_1}K_{X_2}X_3 - K_{X_2}K_{\mathcal{F}X_1}X_3 + K_{X_1}K_{\mathcal{F}X_2}X_3 - K_{\mathcal{F}X_2}K_{X_1}X_3 + K_{X_1}K_{X_2}\mathcal{F}X_3$$
$$- K_{X_2}K_{X_1}\mathcal{F}X_3, X_4) + g(K_{X_1}K_{X_2}X_3 - K_{X_2}K_{X_1}X_3, \mathcal{F}X_4)$$
$$= 2g(K_{X_2}X_3, \mathcal{F}K_{X_1}X_4) - 2g(K_{X_1}X_3, \mathcal{F}K_{X_2}X_4) + 2g(\mathcal{F}K_{X_2}X_3, K_{X_1}X_4)$$
$$- 2g(\mathcal{F}K_{X_1}X_3, K_{X_2}X_4)$$
$$= 0.$$

Using the above equation in (38), we obtain (35). Considering $X_1 = \mathcal{F}X_1$ in (35) and using (18), it follows that

$$-\mathcal{S}(X_1, X_2, X_3, X_4) + u(X_1)\mathcal{S}(v, X_2, X_3, X_4) + \mathcal{S}(\mathcal{F}X_1, \mathcal{F}X_2, X_3, X_4) + \mathcal{S}(\mathcal{F}X_1, X_2, \mathcal{F}X_3, X_4) + \mathcal{S}(\mathcal{F}X_1, X_2, X_3, \mathcal{F}X_4) = 0. \tag{39}$$

Similarly, setting $X_2 = \mathcal{F}X_2$, $X_3 = \mathcal{F}X_3$ and $X_4 = \mathcal{F}X_4$, respectively, we have

$$\mathcal{S}(\mathcal{F}X_1, \mathcal{F}X_2, X_3, X_4) - \mathcal{S}(X_1, X_2, X_3, X_4) + u(X_2)\mathcal{S}(X_1, v, X_3, X_4) + \mathcal{S}(X_1, \mathcal{F}X_2, \mathcal{F}X_3, X_4) + \mathcal{S}(X_1, \mathcal{F}X_2, X_3, \mathcal{F}X_4) = 0, \tag{40}$$

$$\mathcal{S}(\mathcal{F}X_1, X_2, \mathcal{F}X_3, X_4) + \mathcal{S}(X_1, \mathcal{F}X_2, \mathcal{F}X_3, X_4) - \mathcal{S}(X_1, X_2, X_3, X_4)$$
$$+ u(X_3)\mathcal{S}(X_1, X_2, v, X_4) + \mathcal{S}(X_1, X_2, \mathcal{F}X_3, \mathcal{F}X_4) = 0, \quad (41)$$

and

$$\mathcal{S}(\mathcal{F}X_1, X_2, X_3, \mathcal{F}X_4) + \mathcal{S}(X_1, \mathcal{F}X_2, X_3, \mathcal{F}X_4) + \mathcal{S}(X_1, X_2, \mathcal{F}X_3, \mathcal{F}X_4)$$
$$- \mathcal{S}(X_1, X_2, X_3, X_4) + u(X_4)\mathcal{S}(X_1, X_2, X_3, v) = 0. \quad (42)$$

By adding (39) and (40), and subtracting the expression obtained from (41) and (42), we obtain

$$2\mathcal{S}(\mathcal{F}X_1, \mathcal{F}X_2, X_3, X_4) - 2\mathcal{S}(X_1, X_2, \mathcal{F}X_3, \mathcal{F}X_4) + u(X_1)\mathcal{S}(v, X_2, X_3, X_4)$$
$$+ u(X_2)\mathcal{S}(X_1, v, X_3, X_4) - u(X_3)\mathcal{S}(X_1, X_2, v, X_4) - u(X_4)\mathcal{S}(X_1, X_2, X_3, v) = 0.$$

Replacing X_1 and X_2 by $\mathcal{F}X_1$ and $\mathcal{F}X_2$, we can rewrite the last equation as

$$2\mathcal{S}(\mathcal{F}^2X_1, \mathcal{F}^2X_2, X_3, X_4) - 2\mathcal{S}(\mathcal{F}X_1, \mathcal{F}X_2, \mathcal{F}X_3, \mathcal{F}X_4)$$
$$- u(X_3)\mathcal{S}(\mathcal{F}X_1, \mathcal{F}X_2, v, X_4) - u(X_4)\mathcal{S}(\mathcal{F}X_1, \mathcal{F}X_2, X_3, v) = 0.$$

Applying (34) in the above equation, we obtain

$$\mathcal{S}(\mathcal{F}^2X_1, \mathcal{F}^2X_2, X_3, X_4) = \mathcal{S}(\mathcal{F}X_1, \mathcal{F}X_2, \mathcal{F}X_3, \mathcal{F}X_4).$$

On the other hand, using (18), it can be seen that

$$\mathcal{S}(\mathcal{F}^2X_1, \mathcal{F}^2X_2, X_3, X_4) = \mathcal{S}(X_1, X_2, X_3, X_4) - u(X_2)\mathcal{S}(X_1, v, X_3, X_4)$$
$$- u(X_1)\mathcal{S}(v, X_2, X_3, X_4).$$

According to Corollary 1 and (32), we have

$$\mathcal{R}^g(v, X_1, X_3, X_4) = \mathcal{R}^g(X_3, X_4, v, X_1) = \mathcal{S}(X_3, X_4, v, X_1) = \mathcal{S}(v, X_1, X_3, X_4).$$

The above three equations imply (36). □

Corollary 4. *The tensor field K in a nearly Sasakian statistical manifold, N, satisfies the relation*

$$\mathcal{F}[K_{\mathcal{F}X_2}, K_{\mathcal{F}X_1}]\mathcal{F} = [K_{X_1}, K_{X_2}],$$

for any $X_1, X_2 \in \Gamma(TN)$.

Proof. Using (24) and (37), we obtain

$$\mathcal{S}(\mathcal{F}X_1, \mathcal{F}X_2, \mathcal{F}X_3, \mathcal{F}X_4) - \mathcal{S}(X_1, X_2, X_3, X_4) - u(X_2)\mathcal{R}^g(v, X_1, X_3, X_4)$$
$$+ u(X_1)\mathcal{R}^g(v, X_2, X_3, X_4)$$
$$= g(K_{\mathcal{F}X_1}K_{\mathcal{F}X_2}\mathcal{F}X_3 - K_{\mathcal{F}X_2}K_{\mathcal{F}X_1}\mathcal{F}X_3, \mathcal{F}X_4) - g(K_{X_1}K_{X_2}X_3 - K_{X_2}K_{X_1}X_3, X_4)$$
$$= g(\mathcal{F}[K_{\mathcal{F}X_2}, K_{\mathcal{F}X_1}]\mathcal{F}X_3 - [K_{X_1}, K_{X_2}]X_3, X_4).$$

Comparing this with relation (36) yields the following assertion. □

A statistical manifold is called *conjugate symmetric* if the curvature tensors of the connections ∇ and ∇^*, are equal, i.e.,

$$\mathcal{R}(X_1, X_2)X_3 = \mathcal{R}^*(X_1, X_2)X_3,$$

for all $X_1, X_2, X_3 \in \Gamma(TN)$.

Corollary 5. *Let $(N, \nabla, g, \mathcal{F}, v)$ be a conjugate symmetric nearly Sasakian statistical manifold. Then, the following holds*

$$\mathcal{R}(\mathcal{F}X_1, \mathcal{F}X_2, \mathcal{F}X_3, \mathcal{F}X_4) - \mathcal{R}(X_1, X_2, X_3, X_4)$$
$$= u(X_2)\mathcal{R}(X_3, X_4, v, X_1) - u(X_1)\mathcal{R}(X_3, X_4, v, X_2),$$
$$\mathcal{R}(X_1, X_2)v = \mathcal{R}^g(X_1, X_2)v,$$
$$\mathcal{R}(\mathcal{F}X_1, \mathcal{F}X_2)v = 0,$$

for any $X_1, X_2, X_3, X_4 \in \Gamma(TN)$.

4. Hypersurfaces in Nearly Kähler Statistical Manifolds

Let $\tilde{N}$ be a smooth manifold. A pair $(\tilde{g}, J)$ is said to be an almost Hermitian structure on $\tilde{N}$ if

$$J^2 = -Id, \quad \tilde{g}(JX_1, JX_2) = \tilde{g}(X_1, X_2),$$

for any $X_1, X_2 \in \Gamma(T\tilde{N})$. Let $\tilde{\nabla}^g$ denote the Riemannian connection of $\tilde{g}$. Then, J is Killing if and only if

$$(\tilde{\nabla}^g_{X_1} J)X_2 + (\tilde{\nabla}^g_{X_2} J)X_1 = 0.$$

In this case, the pair $(\tilde{g}, \tilde{J})$ is called a nearly Kähler structure and if J is integrable, the structure is Kählerian [7].

Lemma 3. *Let $(\tilde{\nabla}, \tilde{g})$ be a statistical structure, and $(\tilde{g}, J)$ a nearly Kähler structure on $\tilde{N}$. We have the following formula:*

$$\tilde{\nabla}_{X_1} JX_2 - J\tilde{\nabla}^*_{X_1} X_2 + \tilde{\nabla}_{X_2} JX_1 - J\tilde{\nabla}^*_{X_2} X_1 = \tilde{K}_{X_1} JX_2 + \tilde{K}_{X_2} JX_1 + 2J\tilde{K}_{X_1} X_2,$$

for any $X_1, X_2 \in \Gamma(T\tilde{N})$, where $\tilde{K}$ is given as (8) for $(\tilde{\nabla}, \tilde{g})$.

Remark 2. *A multiple $(\tilde{N}, \tilde{\nabla}^*, \tilde{g}, J)$ is also a nearly Kähler statistical manifold if $(\tilde{N}, \tilde{\nabla}, \tilde{g}, J)$ is a nearly Kähler statistical manifold. In this case, from the above lemma, we have*

$$\tilde{\nabla}^*_{X_1} JX_2 - J\tilde{\nabla}_{X_1} X_2 + \tilde{\nabla}^*_{X_2} JX_1 - J\tilde{\nabla}_{X_2} X_1 = -(\tilde{K}_{X_1} JX_2 + \tilde{K}_{X_2} JX_1 + 2J\tilde{K}_{X_1} X_2),$$

for any $X_1, X_2 \in \Gamma(T\tilde{N})$.

Definition 2. *A nearly Kähler statistical structure on $\tilde{N}$ is a triple $(\tilde{\nabla}, \tilde{g}, J)$, where $(\tilde{\nabla}, \tilde{g})$ is a statistical structure, $(\tilde{g}, J)$ is a nearly Kähler structure on $\tilde{N}$ and the following equality is satisfied*

$$\tilde{K}_{X_1} JX_2 + \tilde{K}_{X_2} JX_1 = -2J\tilde{K}_{X_1} X_2,$$

for any $X_1, X_2 \in \Gamma(T\tilde{N})$.

Let N be a hypersurface of a statistical manifold $(\tilde{N}, \tilde{g}, \tilde{\nabla}, \tilde{\nabla}^*)$. Considering $\mathbf{n}$ and g as a unit normal vector field and the induced metric on N, respectively, the following relations hold

$$\tilde{\nabla}_{X_1} X_2 = \nabla_{X_1} X_2 + h(X_1, X_2)\mathbf{n}, \quad \tilde{\nabla}_{X_1} \mathbf{n} = -AX_1 + \tau(X_1)\mathbf{n}, \quad (43)$$
$$\tilde{\nabla}^*_{X_1} X_2 = \nabla^*_{X_1} X_2 + h^*(X_1, X_2)\mathbf{n}, \quad \tilde{\nabla}^*_{X_1} \mathbf{n} = -A^*X_1 + \tau^*(X_1)\mathbf{n}, \quad (44)$$

for any $X_1, X_2 \in \Gamma(TN)$. It follows that

$$g(AX_1, X_2) = \mathbf{h}^*(X_1, X_2), \quad g(A^*X_1, X_2) = \mathbf{h}(X_1, X_2), \quad \tau(X_1) + \tau^*(X_1) = 0. \quad (45)$$

Furthermore, the second fundamental form $\mathbf{h}^g$ is related to the Levi–Civita connections $\tilde{\nabla}^g$ and ∇^g by

$$\tilde{\nabla}^g_{X_1} X_2 = \nabla^g_{X_1} X_2 + \mathbf{h}^g(X_1, X_2)\mathbf{n}, \quad \tilde{\nabla}^g_{X_1} \mathbf{n} = -A^g X_1,$$

where $g(A^g X_1, X_2) = \mathbf{h}^g(X_1, X_2)$.

Remark 3. *Let $(\tilde{N}, \tilde{g}, J)$ be a nearly Kähler manifold, and N be a hypersurface with a unit normal vector field $\mathbf{n}$. Let g be the induced metric on N, and consider v, u and $\mathcal{F}$ as a vector field, a 1-form and a tensor of type $(1,1)$ on N, respectively, such that*

$$v = -J\mathbf{n}, \quad (46)$$
$$JX_1 = \mathcal{F}X_1 + u(X_1)\mathbf{n}, \quad (47)$$

for any $X_1 \in \Gamma(TN)$. Then, $(g, \mathcal{F}, v)$ is an almost contact metric structure on N [7].

Lemma 4. *Let $(\tilde{N}, \tilde{\nabla}, \tilde{g}, J)$ be a nearly Kähler statistical manifold. If $(N, g, \mathcal{F}, v)$ is a hypersurface with the induced almost contact metric structure as in Remark 2, and (∇, g) is the induced statistical structure on N as in 42, then the following holds*

(i) $\mathcal{F}Av = 0$,
(ii) $g(AX_1, v) = u(Av)u(X_1)$,
(iii) $AX_1 = \nabla_v \mathcal{F}X_1 - \mathcal{F}\nabla^*_v X_1 - \mathcal{F}\nabla^*_{X_1} v + u(X_1)Av$,
(iv) $\tau(X_1) = g(\nabla^*_{X_1} v, v) - g(X_1, \nabla_v v) - u(X_1)\tau(v)$,
(v) $\nabla_{X_1} \mathcal{F}X_2 - \mathcal{F}\nabla^*_{X_1} X_2 + \nabla_{X_2} \mathcal{F}X_1 - \mathcal{F}\nabla^*_{X_2} X_1 = -2g(AX_1, X_2)v + u(X_2)AX_1$
$\qquad + u(X_1)AX_2$,
(vi) $g(\nabla_{X_1} v, X_2) + g(\nabla_{X_2} v, X_1) = g(\mathcal{F}A^* X_1, X_2) + g(\mathcal{F}A^* X_2, X_1) - u(X_1)\tau(X_2)$
$\qquad - u(X_2)\tau(X_1)$,

for any $X_1, X_2 \in \Gamma(TN)$. For the induced statistical structure (∇^*, g) on N, we have

$(i)^*$ $\mathcal{F}A^*v = 0$,
$(ii)^*$ $g(A^*X_1, v) = u(A^*v)u(X_1)$,
$(iii)^*$ $A^*X_1 = \nabla^*_v \mathcal{F}X_1 - \mathcal{F}\nabla_v X_1 - \mathcal{F}\nabla_{X_1} v + u(X_1)A^*v$,
$(iv)^*$ $\tau^*(X_1) = g(\nabla_{X_1} v, v) - g(X_1, \nabla^*_v v) - u(X_1)\tau^*(v)$,
$(v)^*$ $\nabla^*_{X_1} \mathcal{F}X_2 - \mathcal{F}\nabla_{X_1} X_2 + \nabla^*_{X_2} \mathcal{F}X_1 - \mathcal{F}\nabla_{X_2} X_1 = -2g(A^*X_1, X_2)v + u(X_2)A^*X_1$
$\qquad + u(X_1)A^*X_2$,
$(vi)^*$ $g(\nabla^*_{X_1} v, X_2) + g(\nabla^*_{X_2} v, X_1) = g(\mathcal{F}AX_1, X_2) + g(\mathcal{F}AX_2, X_1) - u(X_1)\tau^*(X_2)$
$\qquad - u(X_2)\tau^*(X_1)$.

Proof. According to Definition 2 and (46), we can write

$$0 = \tilde{\nabla}_{X_1} Jv - \tilde{\nabla}_{X_1} \mathbf{n} = J\tilde{\nabla}^*_{X_1} v - \tilde{\nabla}_v JX_1 + J\tilde{\nabla}^*_v X_1 - \tilde{\nabla}_{X_1} \mathbf{n}.$$

Applying (43), (44) and (47) in the above equation, we have

$$
\begin{aligned}
0 &= J(\nabla^*_{X_1}v + g(AX_1,v)\mathbf{n}) - \tilde{\nabla}_v(\mathcal{F}X_1 + u(X_1)\mathbf{n}) + J(\nabla^*_v X_1 + g(Av,X_1)\mathbf{n}) \\
&\quad + AX_1 - \tau(X_1)\mathbf{n} \\
&= \mathcal{F}(\nabla^*_{X_1}v) - g(AX_1,v)v - \nabla_v\mathcal{F}(X_1) + u(X_1)Av + \mathcal{F}(\nabla^*_v X_1) - g(Av,X_1)v + AX_1 \\
&\quad + \{u(\nabla^*_{X_1}v) - g(A^*v, \mathcal{F}X_1) - v(u(X_1)) - u(X_1)\tau(v) + u(\nabla^*_v X_1) - \tau(X_1)\}\mathbf{n}.
\end{aligned} \quad (48)
$$

The vanishing tangential part yields

$$AX_1 = \nabla_v \mathcal{F}X_1 - \mathcal{F}\nabla^*_v X_1 - \mathcal{F}\nabla^*_{X_1}v + 2g(AX_1,v)v - u(X_1)Av. \quad (49)$$

Setting $X_1 = v$ in the above equation, it follows that

$$Av = u(Av)v, \quad (50)$$

hence, $\mathcal{F}Av = 0$ and implies (i), from which (ii) follows because $0 = g(\mathcal{F}Av, \mathcal{F}X_1) = g(Av, X_1) - u(Av)u(X_1)$. From (49) and (50) we have (iii). Vanishing vertical part in (48), and using $(i)^*$ and

$$v(u(X_1)) = g(\nabla^*_v X_1, v) + g(X_1, \nabla_v v),$$

we obtain (iv). As

$$\tilde{\nabla}_{X_1} J X_2 - J\tilde{\nabla}^*_{X_1} X_2 + \tilde{\nabla}_{X_2} J X_1 - J\tilde{\nabla}^*_{X_2} X_1 = 0;$$

thus, (43), (44), (46) and (47) imply

$$
\begin{aligned}
&\nabla_{X_1}\mathcal{F}X_2 - u(X_2)AX_1 - \mathcal{F}(\nabla^*_{X_1}X_2) + g(AX_1,X_2)v + \nabla_{X_2}\mathcal{F}X_1 - u(X_1)AX_2 - \mathcal{F}(\nabla^*_{X_2}X_1) \\
&+ g(AX_2,X_1)v + \{g(A^*X_1, \mathcal{F}X_2) + g(\nabla_{X_1}v, X_2) + u(X_2)\tau(X_1) + g(A^*X_2, \mathcal{F}X_1) \\
&+ g(X_1, \nabla_{X_2}v) + u(X_1)\tau(X_2)\}\mathbf{n} = 0.
\end{aligned}
$$

From the above equation, (v) and (vi) follow. In a similar fashion, we have $(i)^*$–$(vi)^*$. □

Theorem 3. *Let $(\tilde{N}, \tilde{\nabla}, \tilde{g}, J)$ be a nearly Kähler statistical manifold and $(N, \nabla, g, \mathcal{F}, v)$ be an almost contact metric statistical hypersurface in $\tilde{N}$ given by (43), (44), (46) and (47). Then, $(N, \nabla, g, \mathcal{F}, v)$ is a nearly Sasakian statistical manifold if and only if*

$$AX_1 = X_1 + u(X_1)(Av - v), \quad (51)$$
$$A^*X_1 = X_1 + u(X_1)(A^*v - v), \quad (52)$$

for any $X_1 \in \Gamma(TN)$.

Proof. Let $(\nabla, g, \mathcal{F}, v)$ be a nearly Sasakian statistical structure on N. According to Definition 1, we have

$$\nabla_{X_1}\mathcal{F}X_2 - \mathcal{F}\nabla^*_{X_1}X_2 + \nabla_{X_2}\mathcal{F}X_1 - \mathcal{F}\nabla^*_{X_2}X_1 = -2g(X_1,X_2)v + u(X_1)X_2 + u(X_2)X_1,$$

which gives us

$$\nabla_v \mathcal{F}X_1 - \mathcal{F}\nabla^*_{X_1}v - \mathcal{F}\nabla^*_v X_1 = -u(X_1)v + X_1.$$

Placing the last equation in part (iii) of Lemma 4, we obtain (51). Similarly, we can prove (52). Conversely, let the shape operators satisfy (51). Part (v) of Lemma 4 yields

$$\nabla_{X_1}\mathcal{F}X_2 - \mathcal{F}\nabla^*_{X_1}X_2 + \nabla_{X_2}\mathcal{F}X_1 - \mathcal{F}\nabla^*_{X_2}X_1 = -2g(X_1 + u(X_1)(Av - v), X_2)v$$
$$+ u(X_2)(X_1 + u(X_1)(Av - v))$$
$$+ u(X_1)(X_2 + u(X_2)(Av - v))$$
$$= -2g(X_1, X_2)v + u(X_1)X_2 + u(X_2)X_1.$$

In the same way, (v)* and (52) imply

$$\nabla^*_{X_1}\mathcal{F}X_2 - \mathcal{F}\nabla_{X_1}X_2 + \nabla^*_{X_2}\mathcal{F}X_1 - \mathcal{F}\nabla_{X_2}X_1 = -2g(X_1, X_2)v + u(X_1)X_2 + u(X_2)X_1.$$

According to the above equations and Theorem 2, the proof is completed. □

5. Submanifolds of Nearly Sasakian Statistical Manifolds

Let N be a n-dimensional submanifold of an almost contact metric statistical manifold $(\tilde{N}, \tilde{\nabla}, g, \tilde{\mathcal{F}}, \tilde{v}, \tilde{u})$. We denote the induced metric on N by g. For all $U_1 \in \Gamma(TN)$ and $\zeta \in \Gamma(T^\perp N)$, we put $\tilde{\mathcal{F}}U_1 = \mathcal{F}U_1 + \overline{\mathcal{F}}U_1$ and $\tilde{\mathcal{F}}\zeta = \mathcal{F}\zeta + \overline{\mathcal{F}}\zeta$, where $\mathcal{F}U_1, \mathcal{F}\zeta \in \Gamma(TN)$ and $\overline{\mathcal{F}}U_1, \overline{\mathcal{F}}\zeta \in \Gamma(T^\perp N)$. If $\tilde{\mathcal{F}}(T_pN) \subset T_pN$ and $\tilde{\mathcal{F}}(T_pN) \subset T_p^\perp N$ for any $p \in N$, then N is called $\tilde{\mathcal{F}}$-invariant and $\tilde{\mathcal{F}}$-anti-invariant, respectively.

Proposition 4 ([10]). *Any $\tilde{\mathcal{F}}$-invariant submanifold N embedded in an almost contact metric manifold $(\tilde{N}, \tilde{\nabla}, g, \tilde{\mathcal{F}}, \tilde{v}, \tilde{u})$ in such a way that the vector field $\tilde{v}$ is always tangent to N, induces an almost contact metric structure $(g, \mathcal{F}, v, u)$.*

For any $U_1, U_2 \in \Gamma(TN)$, the corresponding Gauss formulas are given by

$$\tilde{\nabla}_{U_1}U_2 = \nabla_{U_1}U_2 + \mathbf{h}(U_1, U_2), \qquad \tilde{\nabla}^*_{U_1}U_2 = \nabla^*_{U_1}U_2 + \mathbf{h}^*(U_1, U_2). \tag{53}$$

It is proved that (∇, g) and (∇^*, g) are statistical structures on N, and $\mathbf{h}$ and $\mathbf{h}^*$ are symmetric and bilinear. The mean curvature vector field with respect to $\tilde{\nabla}$ is described by

$$H = \frac{1}{m}trace(\mathbf{h}).$$

The submanifold N is a $\tilde{\nabla}$ totally umbilical submanifold if $\mathbf{h}(U_1, U_2) = g(U_1, U_2)H$ for all $U_1, U_2 \in \Gamma(TN)$. The submanifold N is called $\tilde{\nabla}$-autoparallel if $\mathbf{h}(U_1, U_2) = 0$ for any $U_1, U_2 \in \Gamma(TN)$. The submanifold N is said to be dual-autoparallel if it is both $\tilde{\nabla}$- and $\tilde{\nabla}^*$-autoparallel, i.e., $\mathbf{h}(U_1, U_2) = \mathbf{h}^*(U_1, U_2) = 0$ for any $U_1, U_2 \in \Gamma(TN)$. If $\mathbf{h}^g(U_1, U_2) = 0$ for any $U_1, U_2 \in \Gamma(TN)$, the submanifold N is called totally geodesic. Moreover, the submanifold N is called $\tilde{\nabla}$-minimal ($\tilde{\nabla}^*$-minimal) if $H = 0$ ($H^* = 0$).

For any $U_1 \in \Gamma(TN)$ and $\zeta \in \Gamma(T^\perp N)$, the Weingarten formulas are

$$\tilde{\nabla}_{U_1}\zeta = -A_\zeta U_1 + D_{U_1}\zeta, \qquad \tilde{\nabla}^*_{X_1}\zeta = -A^*_\zeta U_1 + D^*_{U_1}\zeta, \tag{54}$$

where D and D^* are the normal connections on $\Gamma(T^\perp N)$ and the tensor fields $\mathbf{h}$, $\mathbf{h}^*$, A and A^*, satisfy

$$g(A_\zeta U_1, U_2) = g(\mathbf{h}^*(U_1, U_2), \zeta), \qquad g(A^*_\zeta U_1, U_2) = g(\mathbf{h}(U_1, U_2), \zeta).$$

The Levi–Civita connections ∇^g and $\tilde{\nabla}^g$ are associated with the second fundamental form $\mathbf{h}^g$ by

$$\tilde{\nabla}^g_{U_1}U_2 = \nabla^g_{U_1}U_2 + \mathbf{h}^g(U_1, U_2), \qquad \tilde{\nabla}^g_{U_1}\zeta = -A^g_\zeta U_1 + D^g_{U_1}\zeta, \tag{55}$$

where $g(A^g_\zeta U_1, U_2) = g(\mathbf{h}^g(U_1, U_2), \zeta)$.

On a statistical submanifold (N, ∇, g) of a statistical manifold $(\tilde{N}, \tilde{\nabla}, g)$, for any tangent vector fields $U_1, U_2 \in \Gamma(TN)$, we consider the difference tensor K on N as

$$2K_{U_1}U_2 = \nabla_{U_1}U_2 - \nabla^*_{U_1}U_2. \tag{56}$$

From (7), (53) and the above equation, it follows that

$$2\tilde{K}_{U_1}U_2 = 2K_{U_1}U_2 + \mathbf{h}(U_1, U_2) - \mathbf{h}^*(U_1, U_2). \tag{57}$$

More precisely, for the tangential part and the normal part, we have

$$(\tilde{K}_{U_1}U_2)^\top = K_{U_1}U_2, \quad (\tilde{K}_{U_1}U_2)^\perp = \frac{1}{2}(\mathbf{h}(U_1, U_2) - \mathbf{h}^*(U_1, U_2)),$$

respectively. Similarly, for $U_1 \in \Gamma(TN)$ and $\zeta \in \Gamma(T^\perp N)$ we have

$$\tilde{K}_{U_1}\zeta = (\tilde{K}_{U_1}\zeta)^\top + (\tilde{K}_{U_1}\zeta)^\perp,$$

where

$$(\tilde{K}_{U_1}\zeta)^\top = \frac{1}{2}(A^*_\zeta U_1 - A_\zeta U_1), \quad (\tilde{K}_{U_1}\zeta)^\perp = \frac{1}{2}(D_{U_1}\zeta - D^*_{U_1}\zeta).$$

Now, suppose that (N, g) is a submanifold of a nearly Sasakian statistical manifold $(\tilde{N}, \tilde{\nabla}, g, \tilde{\mathcal{F}}, \tilde{v})$. As a tensor field, $\tilde{h}$ of type $(1,1)$ on $\tilde{N}$ is described by $\tilde{\nabla}^g \tilde{v} = \tilde{\mathcal{F}} + \tilde{h}$; we can set $\tilde{h}U_1 = hU_1 + \overline{h}U_1$ and $\tilde{h}\zeta = h\zeta + \overline{h}\zeta$ where $hU_1, h\zeta \in \Gamma(TN)$ and $\overline{h}U_1, \overline{h}\zeta \in \Gamma(T^\perp N)$ for any $U_1 \in \Gamma(TN)$ and $\zeta \in \Gamma(T^\perp N)$. Furthermore, if $\tilde{h}(T_pN) \subset T_pN$ and $\tilde{h}(T_pN) \subset T_p^\perp N$, then N is called $\tilde{h}$-invariant and $\tilde{h}$-anti-invariant, respectively.

Proposition 5. *Let N be a submanifold of a nearly Sasakian statistical manifold $(\tilde{N}, \tilde{\nabla}, g, \tilde{\mathcal{F}}, \tilde{v}, \tilde{u})$, where the vector field $\tilde{v}$ is normal to N. Then,*

$$g(\tilde{\mathcal{F}}U_1, U_2) = g(U_1, \tilde{h}U_2), \quad \forall U_1, U_2 \in \Gamma(TN). \tag{58}$$

Moreover,
(i) N is a $\tilde{h}$-anti-invariant submanifold if and only if N is a $\tilde{\mathcal{F}}$-anti-invariant submanifold.
(ii) If $\tilde{h} = 0$, then N is a $\tilde{\mathcal{F}}$-anti-invariant submanifold.
(iii) If N is a $\tilde{h}$-invariant and $\tilde{\mathcal{F}}$-invariant submanifold, then $hU_1 = -\mathcal{F}U_1$, for any $U_1 \in \Gamma(TN)$.

Proof. Using (22) and Proposition 1 for any $U_1, U_2 \in \Gamma(TN)$, we can write

$$g(\tilde{\mathcal{F}}U_1 + \tilde{h}U_1, U_2) = g(\tilde{\nabla}^g_{U_1}\tilde{v}, U_2) = g(\tilde{\nabla}_{U_1}\tilde{v}, U_2).$$

(54) and the above equation imply

$$g(\tilde{\mathcal{F}}U_1 + \tilde{h}U_1, U_2) = g(-A_{\tilde{v}}U_1 + D_{U_1}\tilde{v}, U_2) = -g(A_{\tilde{v}}U_1, U_2) = -g(\tilde{v}, \mathbf{h}^*(U_1, U_2)).$$

As $\mathbf{h}^*$ is symmetric and the operators $\tilde{h}$ and g are skew-symmetric, the above equation yields

$$g(\tilde{\mathcal{F}}U_1 + \tilde{h}U_1, U_2) = g(\tilde{\mathcal{F}}U_2 + \tilde{h}U_2, U_1) = -g(\tilde{\mathcal{F}}U_1 + \tilde{h}U_1, U_2).$$

Hence, $g(\tilde{\mathcal{F}}U_1 + \tilde{h}U_1, U_2) = 0$, which gives (58). If N is a $\tilde{h}$-anti-invariant submanifold, we have $g(U_1, \tilde{h}U_2) = 0$. Thus, (i) follows from (58). Similarly, we have (ii) and (iii). □

Lemma 5. *Let (N, ∇, g) be a $\tilde{\mathcal{F}}$-anti-invariant statistical submanifold of a nearly Sasakian statistical manifold $(\tilde{N}, \tilde{\nabla}, g, \tilde{\mathcal{F}}, \tilde{v}, \tilde{u})$ such that the structure $(\mathcal{F}, v, u)$ on N is given by Proposition 4.*

(i) If $\tilde{v}$ is tangent to N, then

$$\nabla_{U_1} v = u(U_1)K_v v = -\nabla^*_{U_1} v, \; \mathbf{h}(U_1, v) = \overline{\mathcal{F}}U_1 + \overline{h}U_1 = \mathbf{h}^*(U_1, v), \; \forall U_1 \in \Gamma(TN).$$

(ii) If $\tilde{v}$ is normal to N, then

$$A_{\tilde{v}} = 0 = A^*_{\tilde{v}}, \quad D_{U_1}\tilde{v} = \overline{\mathcal{F}}U_1 + \overline{h}U_1 = D^*_{U_1}\tilde{v}, \qquad \forall U_1 \in \Gamma(TN).$$

Proof. Applying (22), (53) and Proposition 1, and using $\tilde{K}_v v = K_v v = g(\nabla_v v, v)v$, we have

$$\overline{\mathcal{F}}U_1 + \overline{h}U_1 + u(U_1)K_v v = \tilde{\nabla}^g_{U_1} v + u(U_1)K_v v = \tilde{\nabla}_{U_1} v = \nabla_{U_1} v + \mathbf{h}(U_1, v).$$

Thus, the normal part is $\mathbf{h}(U_1, v) = \overline{\mathcal{F}}U_1 + \overline{h}U_1$ and the tangential part is $\nabla_{U_1} v = u(U_1)K_v v$. Similarly, we can obtain their dual parts. Hence, (i) holds. If $\tilde{v}$ is normal to N, from (22) and (54), it follows that

$$\overline{\mathcal{F}}U_1 + \overline{h}U_1 = \tilde{\nabla}^g_{U_1}\tilde{v} = \tilde{\nabla}_{U_1}\tilde{v} = -A_{\tilde{v}}U_1 + D_{U_1}\tilde{v}.$$

Considering the normal and tangential components of the last equation, we obtain (ii). Since $\tilde{\nabla}_{U_1} v = \tilde{\nabla}^g_{U_1} v = \tilde{\nabla}^*_{U_1} v$, we have the dual part of the assertion. □

Lemma 6. *Let (N, ∇, g) be a $\tilde{\mathcal{F}}$-invariant and $\tilde{h}$-invariant statistical submanifold of a nearly Sasakian statistical manifold $(\tilde{N}, \tilde{\nabla}, g, \tilde{\mathcal{F}}, \tilde{v}, \tilde{u})$. Then, for any $U_1 \in \Gamma(TN)$, if*
(i) *$\tilde{v}$ is tangent to N, then*

$$\nabla_{U_1} v = \mathcal{F}U_1 + hU_1 + u(U_1)K_v v, \quad \nabla^*_{U_1} v = \mathcal{F}U_1 + hU_1 - u(U_1)K_v v,$$
$$\mathbf{h}(U_1, v) = 0 = \mathbf{h}^*(U_1, v).$$

(ii) *$\tilde{v}$ is normal to N, then*

$$A_{\tilde{v}}U_1 = -\mathcal{F}U_1 - hU_1 = A^*_{\tilde{v}}U_1, \quad D\tilde{v} = 0 = D^*\tilde{v}.$$

Proof. The relations are proved using the method applied to the proof of Lemma 5. □

Theorem 4. *On a nearly Sasakian statistical manifold $(\tilde{N}, \tilde{\nabla}, g, \tilde{\mathcal{F}}, \tilde{v}, \tilde{u})$, if N is a $\tilde{\mathcal{F}}$-anti-invariant $\tilde{\nabla}$ totally umbilical statistical submanifold of $\tilde{N}$ and $\tilde{v}$ is tangent to N, then N is $\tilde{\nabla}$-minimal in $\tilde{N}$.*

Proof. According to Lemma 5, $\mathbf{h}(v, v) = 0$. As N is a totally umbilical submanifold, it follows that

$$0 = \mathbf{h}(v, v) = g(v, v)H = H,$$

which gives us the assertion. □

Theorem 5. *Let N be a $\tilde{\mathcal{F}}$-invariant submanifold of a nearly Sasakian statistical manifold $(\tilde{N}, \tilde{\nabla}, g, \tilde{\mathcal{F}}, \tilde{v}, \tilde{u})$, where the vector field $\tilde{v}$ is tangent to N. If*

$$\mathbf{h}^g(U_1, \mathcal{F}U_2) = \tilde{\mathcal{F}}\mathbf{h}^g(U_1, U_2), \tag{59}$$
$$\mathbf{h}(U_1, \mathcal{F}U_2) - \mathbf{h}^*(U_1, \mathcal{F}U_2) = \tilde{\mathcal{F}}\mathbf{h}^*(U_1, U_2) - \tilde{\mathcal{F}}\mathbf{h}(U_1, U_2), \tag{60}$$

for all $U_1, U_2 \in \Gamma(TN)$, then $(\nabla, g, \mathcal{F}, v, u)$ forms a nearly Sasakian statistical structure on N.

Proof. According to Proposition 4, N induces the almost contact metric structure $(g, \mathcal{F}, v, u)$. Furthermore, (53) shows that (∇, g) is a statistical structure on N. By applying (55), we can write

$$\tilde{\nabla}^g_{U_1}\tilde{\mathcal{F}}U_2 = \nabla^g_{U_1}\mathcal{F}U_2 + \mathbf{h}^g(U_1,\mathcal{F}U_2)$$
$$= (\nabla^g_{U_1}\mathcal{F})U_2 + \mathcal{F}\nabla^g_{U_1}U_2 + \mathbf{h}^g(U_1,\mathcal{F}U_2).$$

As $\mathbf{h}^g$ is symmetric, from (59), we have $\mathbf{h}^g(\mathcal{F}U_1,U_2) = \mathbf{h}^g(U_1,\mathcal{F}U_2)$. Hence, the above equation implies

$$\tilde{\nabla}^g_{U_1}\tilde{\mathcal{F}}U_2 + \tilde{\nabla}^g_{U_2}\tilde{\mathcal{F}}U_1 = (\nabla^g_{U_1}\mathcal{F})U_2 + (\nabla^g_{U_2}\mathcal{F})U_1 + \mathcal{F}\nabla^g_{U_1}U_2 + \mathcal{F}\nabla^g_{U_2}U_1 + 2\mathbf{h}^g(U_1,\mathcal{F}U_2).$$

On the other hand, since $\tilde{N}$ has a nearly Sasakian structure, we have

$$\tilde{\nabla}^g_{U_1}\tilde{\mathcal{F}}U_2 + \tilde{\nabla}^g_{U_2}\tilde{\mathcal{F}}U_1$$
$$= (\tilde{\nabla}^g_{U_1}\tilde{\mathcal{F}})U_2 + (\tilde{\nabla}^g_{U_2}\tilde{\mathcal{F}})U_1 + \tilde{\mathcal{F}}(\tilde{\nabla}^g_{U_1}U_2 + \tilde{\nabla}^g_{U_2}U_1)$$
$$= (\tilde{\nabla}^g_{U_1}\tilde{\mathcal{F}})U_2 + (\tilde{\nabla}^g_{U_2}\tilde{\mathcal{F}})U_1 + \tilde{\mathcal{F}}(\nabla^g_{U_1}U_2 + \nabla^g_{U_2}U_1 + 2\mathbf{h}^g(U_1,U_2))$$
$$= -2g(U_1,U_2)v + u(U_1)U_2 + u(U_2)U_1 + \tilde{\mathcal{F}}(\nabla^g_{U_1}U_2 + \nabla^g_{U_2}U + 2\mathbf{h}^g(U,U_2))$$
$$= -2g(U_1,U_2)v + u(U_1)U_2 + u(U_2)U_1 + \mathcal{F}\nabla^g_{U_1}U_2 + \mathcal{F}\nabla^g_{U_2}U_1 + 2\tilde{\mathcal{F}}\mathbf{h}^g(U_1,U_2).$$

(59) and the above two equations yield

$$(\nabla^g_{U_1}\mathcal{F})U_2 + (\nabla^g_{U_2}\mathcal{F})U_1 = -2g(U_1,U_2)v + u(U_1)U_2 + u(U_2)U_1.$$

Thus, $(N,\nabla^g,g,\mathcal{F},v,u)$ is a nearly Sasakian manifold. For the nearly Sasakian statistical manifold $\tilde{N}$, using (27), we have

$$\tilde{K}_{U_1}\mathcal{F}U_2 + \tilde{K}_{U_2}\mathcal{F}U_1 = -2\tilde{\mathcal{F}}\tilde{K}_{U_1}U_2,$$

for any $U_1,U_2 \in \Gamma(TN)$. Applying (57) in the last equation, it follows

$$K_{U_1}\mathcal{F}U_2 + \frac{1}{2}(\mathbf{h}(U_1,\mathcal{F}U_2) - \mathbf{h}^*(U_1,\mathcal{F}U_2)) + K_{U_2}\mathcal{F}U_1 + \frac{1}{2}(\mathbf{h}(U_2,\mathcal{F}U_1) - \mathbf{h}^*(U_2,\mathcal{F}U_1))$$
$$= -2\mathcal{F}K_{U_1}U_2 + \tilde{\mathcal{F}}\mathbf{h}^*(U_1,U_2) - \tilde{\mathcal{F}}\mathbf{h}(U_1,U_2).$$

From the above equation and (60), we obtain

$$K_{U_1}\mathcal{F}U_2 + K_{U_2}\mathcal{F}U_1 = -2\mathcal{F}K_{U_1}U_2.$$

Therefore, $(N,\nabla^g,g,\mathcal{F},v,u)$ is a nearly Sasakian statistical manifold. Hence, the proof is completed. □

Proposition 6. *Let N be a $\tilde{\mathcal{F}}$-invariant and $\tilde{h}$-invariant statistical submanifold of a nearly Sasakian statistical manifold $(\tilde{N},\tilde{\nabla},g,\tilde{\mathcal{F}},\tilde{v},\tilde{u})$, such that $\tilde{v}$ is tangent to N. Then,*

$$(\tilde{\nabla}_{U_1}\mathbf{h})(U_2,v) = (\tilde{\nabla}^*_{U_1}\mathbf{h})(U_2,v) = (\tilde{\nabla}^g_{U_1}\mathbf{h})(U_2,v) = -\mathbf{h}(U_2,\mathcal{F}U_1 + hU_1),$$

and

$$(\tilde{\nabla}_{U_1}\mathbf{h}^*)(U_2,v) = (\tilde{\nabla}^*_{U_1}\mathbf{h}^*)(U_2,v) = (\tilde{\nabla}^g_{U_1}\mathbf{h}^*)(U_2,v) = -\mathbf{h}^*(U_2,\mathcal{F}U_1 + hU_1),$$

for any $U_1,U_2 \in \Gamma(TN)$.

Proof. We have

$$(\tilde{\nabla}_{U_1}\mathbf{h})(U_2,v) = \tilde{\nabla}_{U_1}\mathbf{h}(U_2,v) - \mathbf{h}(\tilde{\nabla}_{U_1}U_2,v) - \mathbf{h}(U_2,\tilde{\nabla}_{U_1}v),$$

for any $U_1, U_2 \in \Gamma(TN)$. According to Proposition 1, part (i) of Lemma 6 and the above equation, we have

$$(\tilde{\nabla}_{U_1}\mathbf{h})(U_2, v) = -\mathbf{h}(U_2, \tilde{\nabla}_{U_1}v) = -\mathbf{h}(U_2, \mathcal{F}U_1 + hU_1 + u(U_1)K_v v) = -\mathbf{h}(U_2, \mathcal{F}U_1 + hU_1).$$

Similarly, other parts are obtained. □

Corollary 6. *Let N be a $\tilde{\mathcal{F}}$-invariant and $\tilde{h}$-invariant statistical submanifold of a nearly Sasakian statistical manifold $(\tilde{N}, \tilde{\nabla}, g, \tilde{\mathcal{F}}, \tilde{v}, \tilde{u})$. If $\tilde{v}$ is tangent to N, then the following conditions are equivalent*
(i) $\mathbf{h}$ and $\mathbf{h}^*$ are parallel with respect to the connection $\tilde{\nabla}$;
(ii) N is dual-autoparallel.

Author Contributions: Writing—original draft, S.U., E.P. and L.N.; Writing—review and editing, R.B. All authors have read and agreed to the published version of the manuscript.

Funding: This research work was funded by Institutional Fund Projects under grant no. (IFPIP: 1184-130-1443). The authors gratefully acknowledge the technical and financial support provided by the Ministry of Education and King Abdulaziz University, DSR, Jeddah, Saudi Arabia.

Data Availability Statement: Not applicable.

Conflicts of Interest: The authors declare no conflict of interest.

References

1. Sun, K.; Marchand-Maillet, S. An information geometry of statistical manifold learning. In Proceedings of the 31st International Conference on Machine Learning (ICML-14), Beijing, China, 21–26 June 2014; pp. 1–9.
2. Amari, S. Information geometry of the EM and em algorithms for neural networks. *Neural Netw.* **1995**, *8*, 1379–1408. [CrossRef]
3. Belkin, M.; Niyogi, P.; Sindhwani, V. Manifold regularization: A geometric framework for learning from labeled and unlabeled examples. *J. Mach. Learn. Res.* **2006**, *7*, 2399–2434.
4. Caticha, A. Geometry from information geometry. *arXiv* **2015**, arxiv:1512.09076v1.
5. Fisher, R.A. On the mathematical foundations of theoretical statistics. *Philos. Trans. R. Soc. Lond.* **1922**, *222*, 309–368.
6. Gray, A. Nearly Kähler manifolds. *J. Differ. Geom.* **1970**, *4*, 283–309. [CrossRef]
7. Blair, D.E.; Showers, D.K.; Yano, K. Nearly Sasakian structures. *Kodai Math. Semin. Rep.* **1976**, *27*, 175–180. [CrossRef]
8. Blair, D.E. *Riemannian Geometry of Contact and Symplectic Manifolds*; Birkhäuser: Basel, Switzerland, 2002.
9. Olszak, Z. Nearly Sasakian manifolds. *Tensor* **1979**, *33*, 277–286.
10. Yano, K.; Ishihara, S. Invariant submanifolds of almost contact manifolds. *Kōdai Math. Semin. Rep.* **1969**, *21*, 350–364. [CrossRef]

Disclaimer/Publisher's Note: The statements, opinions and data contained in all publications are solely those of the individual author(s) and contributor(s) and not of MDPI and/or the editor(s). MDPI and/or the editor(s) disclaim responsibility for any injury to people or property resulting from any ideas, methods, instructions or products referred to in the content.

Article

The (α, p)-Golden Metric Manifolds and Their Submanifolds

Cristina E. Hretcanu [1,*,†] and Mircea Crasmareanu [2,†]

[1] Faculty of Food Engineernig, University Stefan cel Mare, 720229 Suceava, Romania
[2] Faculty of Mathematics, University "Al. I. Cuza", 700506 Iasi, Romania; mcrasm@uaic.ro
* Correspondence: cristina.hretcanu@fia.usv.ro
† These authors contributed equally to this work.

Abstract: The notion of a golden structure was introduced 15 years ago by the present authors and has been a constant interest of several geometers. Now, we propose a new generalization apart from that called the metallic structure, which is also considered by the authors. By adding a compatible Riemannian metric, we focus on the study of the structure induced on submanifolds in this setting and its properties. Also, to illustrate our results, some suitable examples of this type of manifold are presented.

Keywords: almost product structure; almost complex structure; $\Phi_{\alpha,p}$ structure; Riemannian manifold; submanifold

MSC: 53B20; 53B25; 53C42; 53C15

1. Introduction

The *real metallic number*, denoted by $\sigma_{p,q} := \frac{p + \sqrt{p^2 + 4q}}{2}$, is the positive solution of the equation $x^2 - px - q = 0$, where p and q are positive integers and $p^2 + 4q > 0$ [1]. These $\sigma_{p,q}$ numbers are members of the *metallic means family*, defined by V.W. de Spinadel in [2,3], which appear as a natural generalization of the golden number $\phi = \frac{1 + \sqrt{5}}{2}$. Moreover, A.P. Stakhov gave some new generalizations of the golden section and Fibonacci numbers and developed a scientific principle called the Generalized Principle of the Golden Section in [4,5].

The golden and metallic structures are particular cases of polynomial structures on a manifold which were generally defined by S. I. Goldberg, K. Yano and N. C. Petridis in [6,7].

If $\overline{M}$ is a smooth manifold, then an endomorphism J of the tangent bundle $T\overline{M}$ is called a *metallic structure* on $\overline{M}$ if it satisfies $J^2 = pJ + qId$, where Id stands for the identity (or Kronecker) endomorphism and p and q are positive integers [1]. Moreover, the pair $(\overline{M}, J)$ is called an *almost metallic manifold*. In particular, for $p = q = 1$, the metallic structure J becomes a *golden structure* as defined in [8].

The complex version of the above numbers (namely the *complex metallic numbers*), $\sigma^c_{p,q} = \frac{p + \sqrt{p^2 - 6q}}{2}$, appears as a solution to the equation $x^2 - px + \frac{3}{2}q = 0$, where p and q are now real numbers satisfying the conditions $q \geq 0$ and $p^2 < 6q$. Moreover, an almost complex metallic structure is defined as an endomorphism J_M which satisfies the relation $J_M^2 - pJ_M + \frac{3}{2}qId = 0$ [9]. For $p = q = 1$, the almost complex metallic structure becomes a *complex golden structure*.

F. Etayo et al. defined in [10] the *α-metallic numbers* of the form $\frac{p + \sqrt{\alpha(p^2 + 4q)}}{2}$, where p and q are positive integers which satisfy $p^2 + 4q > 0$ and $\alpha \in \{1, -1\}$. Moreover, they introduced the α-metallic metric manifolds using the α-metallic structure, defined by the identity

$$\varphi^2 = p\varphi + \frac{p^2(\alpha - 1) + 4q\alpha}{4} Id. \tag{1}$$

Some similar manifolds, such as holomorphic golden Norden–Hessian manifolds [11], almost golden Riemannian manifolds [12,13] and α-golden metric manifolds [14], have been studied.

The geometry of submanifolds in Riemannian manifolds was widely studied by many geometers. The properties of the submanifolds in golden Riemannian manifolds were studied in [15]. By generalizing the geometry of the golden Riemannian manifods, we presented in [1,16] the properties of the submanifolds in metallic Riemannian manifolds. The properties of the submanifolds in almost complex metallic manifolds were studied in [17].

The aim of the present paper is to propose a new generalization of the golden structure called the *almost (α, p)-golden structure* and to investigate the geometry of a Riemannian manifold endowed by this structure. This manifold is a natural generalization of the golden Riemannian manifold, presented in [8] and of almost Hermitian golden manifold, studied in [18].

In Section 2, we consider several frameworks in which almost product and almost complex structures are treated in our language of the (α, p)-golden structure. These two structures can be unified under the notion of the α-structure, denoted by J_α, which was defined and studied in [10,19].

In Section 3, we study the properties of a Riemannian manifold endowed by a $\Phi_{\alpha,p}$ structure and a compatible Riemannian metric g, called an *almost (α, p)-golden Riemannian manifold*.

In Section 4, we obtain a characterization of the structure induced on a submanifold by the almost (α, p)-golden structure. Finally, we find the necessary and sufficient conditions of a submanifold in an almost (α, p)-golden Riemannian manifold to be an invariant submanifold.

2. The Almost (α, p)-Golden Structure

In order to state the main results of this paper, we need some definitions and notations.

Let us consider the (α, p)-golden means family, which contains the (α, p)-golden numbers obtained as the solutions of the equation

$$x^2 - px - \frac{5\alpha - 1}{4}p^2 = 0, \tag{2}$$

where $\alpha \in \{-1, 1\}$ and p is a real nonzero number. The (α, p)-golden numbers have the form

$$\varphi_{\alpha,p} = p\frac{1 + \sqrt{5\alpha}}{2}, \quad \overline{\varphi}_{\alpha,p} = p\frac{1 - \sqrt{5\alpha}}{2}. \tag{3}$$

Using these numbers, we define a new structure on a smooth manifold $\overline{M}$ (of even dimensions) which generalizes both the almost golden structure and the almost complex golden structure.

An endomorphism J_1 of the tangent bundle $T\overline{M}$, such as $J_1^2 = Id$, is called an *almost product structure*, where Id is the identity or Kronecker endomorphism. Moreover, the pair $(\overline{M}, J_1)$ is called an *almost product manifold*.

An endomorphism J_{-1} of the tangent bundle $T\overline{M}$ is called an *almost complex structure* on $\overline{M}$ if it satisfies $J_{-1}^2 = -Id$, and $(\overline{M}, J_{-1})$ is called an *almost complex manifold*. In this case, the dimension of $\overline{M}$ is even (e.g., $2m$).

Definition 1. *An endomorphism J_α of the tangent bundle $T\overline{M}$ is called an α-structure on $\overline{M}$ if it satisfies the equality*

$$J_\alpha^2 = \alpha \cdot Id, \tag{4}$$

on the even dimensional manifold $\overline{M}$, where $\alpha \in \{-1,1\}$ [19].

Using the Equation (1), for $q = p^2$, we obtain the following definition:

Definition 2. *An endomorphism $\Phi_{\alpha,p}$ of the tangent bundle $T\overline{M}$ is called an almost (α, p)-golden structure on $\overline{M}$ if it satisfies the equality*

$$\Phi_{\alpha,p}^2 = p\Phi_{\alpha,p} + \frac{5\alpha - 1}{4}p^2 \cdot Id, \tag{5}$$

where p is a nonzero real number and $\alpha \in \{-1,1\}$. The pair $(\overline{M}, \Phi_{\alpha,p})$ is called an almost (α, p)-golden manifold.

In particular, the $\Phi_{\alpha,1}$ structure is named an α-golden structure, and it was studied in [14].

Remark 1. *The eigenvalues of the almost (α, p)-golden structure $\Phi_{\alpha,p}$ are $\varphi_{\alpha,p}$ and $\overline{\varphi}_{\alpha,p} = p - \varphi_{\alpha,p}$, given in Equation (3).*

In particular, for $\alpha = 1$, we obtain $\varphi_{1,p} = p\frac{1+\sqrt{5}}{2} = p\phi$ as a zero of the polynomial $X^2 - pX - p^2$, and we remark that $\varphi_{1,p}$ is a member of the metallic numbers family, where $q = p^2$ and ϕ is the golden number.

For $\alpha = -1$, we obtain $\varphi_{-1,p} = p\frac{1+i\sqrt{5}}{2} = p\phi_c$ as a zero of the polynomial $X^2 - pX + \frac{3}{2}p^2$, and $\varphi_{-1,p}$ is a member of the complex metallic numbers family, where $q = p^2$ and ϕ_c is the complex golden number.

Moreover, if $(\alpha, p) = (1,1)$, then one obtains the *golden structure* determined by an endomorphism Φ with $\Phi^2 = \Phi + Id$, as studied in [8]. The same structure was studied in [12], using the name of the *almost golden structure*. In this case, $(\overline{M}, \Phi)$ is called the *almost golden manifold*.

If $(\alpha, p) = (-1,1)$, then one obtains the *almost complex golden structure* determined by an endomorphism Φ_c, which verifies $\Phi_c^2 = \Phi_c + \frac{3}{2}Id$. In this case, $(\overline{M}, \Phi_c)$ is called the *almost complex golden manifold*, as studied in [11,18].

An important remark is that (α, p)-golden structures appear in pairs. In particular, if $\Phi_{\alpha,p}$ is an (α, p)-golden structure, then $\overline{\Phi}_{\alpha,p} = pId - \Phi_{\alpha,p}$ is also an (α, p)-golden structure. Thus is the case for the almost product structures (J_1 and $-J_1$) and for the almost complex structures (J_{-1} and $-J_{-1}$).

We point out that the almost (α, p)-golden structure $\Phi_{\alpha,p}$ and the α-structure J_α are closely related. Thus, we obtain the correspondence $\Phi_{\alpha,p} \longleftrightarrow J_\alpha$, and we have

$$\overline{\Phi}_{\alpha,p} = pId - \Phi_{\alpha,p} \longleftrightarrow \overline{J}_\alpha = -J_\alpha,$$

where $\Phi_{\alpha,p} =: \Phi_{\alpha,p}^+$, $\overline{\Phi}_{\alpha,p} =: \Phi_{\alpha,p}^-$, $J_\alpha =: J_\alpha^+$ and $\overline{J}_\alpha =: J_\alpha^-$.

Proposition 1. *Every α-structure J_α on $\overline{M}$ defines two almost (α, p)-golden structures, given by the equality*

$$\Phi_{\alpha,p}^\pm = \frac{p}{2}(Id \pm \sqrt{5}J_\alpha); \tag{6}$$

Conversely, two α-structures can be associated to a given almost (α, p)-golden structure as follows:

$$J_\alpha^\pm = \pm\frac{2}{p\sqrt{5}}\left(\Phi_{\alpha,p} - \frac{p}{2}Id\right). \tag{7}$$

Proof. First of all, we seek the real numbers a and b such that $\Phi_{\alpha,p} = aId + bJ_\alpha$. Considering $\Phi_{\alpha,p}^2$, from the identities (4) and (5), we obtain $a = \frac{p}{2}$ and $b = \pm\frac{\sqrt{5}p}{2}$, which implies identity (6). Moreover, $\Phi_{\alpha,p}^{\pm}$ verifies the identity (5).

On the other hand, if $\Phi_{\alpha,p}^{\pm}$ verifies identity (6), then we obtain that $J_\alpha^{\pm}$ verifies identities (4) and (7). Conversely, if $J_\alpha^{\pm}$ verifies identity (7), then $\Phi_{\alpha,p}^{\pm}$ verifies the identity (6). □

Example 1. *(i) An almost product structure J_1 induces two almost $(1,p)$-golden structures:*

$$\Phi_{1,p}^{\pm} = p\frac{Id \pm \sqrt{5}J_1}{2}; \tag{8}$$

(ii) An almost complex structure J_{-1} induces two almost $(-1,p)$-golden structures:

$$\Phi_{-1,p}^{\pm} = p\frac{Id \pm \sqrt{5}J_{-1}}{2}. \tag{9}$$

A straightforward computation using the Equations (5) and (6) gives us the following property:

Proposition 2. *An (α,p)-golden structure $\Phi_{\alpha,p}$ is an isomorphism on the tangent space of the manifold $T_x\overline{M}$ for every $x \in \overline{M}$. It follows that $\Phi_{\alpha,p}$ is invertible, and its inverse is a structure given by the equality*

$$\Phi_{\alpha,p}^{-1} = \frac{4}{p^2(5\alpha-1)}\Phi_{\alpha,p} - \frac{4}{p(5\alpha-1)}Id. \tag{10}$$

Lemma 1. *A fixed α-structure J_α yields two complementary projectors P and Q, given by*

$$P = \frac{1}{2}(Id + \sqrt{\alpha}J_\alpha), \quad Q = \frac{1}{2}(Id - \sqrt{\alpha}J_\alpha). \tag{11}$$

Then, we can easily see that

$$P + Q = Id, \quad P^2 = P, \quad Q^2 = Q, \quad PQ = QP = 0, \tag{12}$$

and

$$\sqrt{\alpha}J_\alpha = P - Q. \tag{13}$$

Taking into account the identities (11) and (12), one has the following remark:

Remark 2. *The operators P and Q are orthogonal complementary projection operators and define the complementary distributions $\mathcal{D}_1$ and $\mathcal{D}_2$, where $\mathcal{D}_1$ contains the eigenvectors corresponding to the eigenvalue $\sqrt{\alpha}$ and $\mathcal{D}_2$ contains the eigenvectors corresponding to the eigenvalue $-\sqrt{\alpha}$.*

If the multiplicity of the eigenvalue $\sqrt{\alpha}$ (or $-\sqrt{\alpha}$) is a (or b), where $a + b = \dim(\overline{M}) = 2m$, then the dimension of $\mathcal{D}_1$ is a, while the dimension of $\mathcal{D}_2$ is b.

Conversely, if there exist in $\overline{M}$ two complementary distributions $\mathcal{D}_1$ and $\mathcal{D}_2$ of dimensions $a \geq 1$ and $b \geq 1$, respectively, where $a + b = \dim(\overline{M}) = 2m$, then we can define an α structure J_α on $\overline{M}$, which verifies identity (13).

A straightforward computation using the identities (7), (11) and (12) gives us the following property:

Proposition 3. *The projection operators $P_{\alpha,p}$ and $Q_{\alpha,p}$ on the almost (α,p)-golden manifold $(\overline{M}, \Phi_{\alpha,p})$ have the form*

$$P_{\alpha,p} = \frac{\sqrt{5\alpha}}{5p} \cdot \Phi_{\alpha,p} + \frac{5 - \sqrt{5\alpha}}{10}Id, \quad Q_{\alpha,p} = -\frac{\sqrt{5\alpha}}{5p} \cdot \Phi_{\alpha,p} + \frac{5 + \sqrt{5\alpha}}{10}Id \tag{14}$$

which verifies

$$P_{\alpha,p} + Q_{\alpha,p} = Id, \quad P_{\alpha,p}^2 = P_{\alpha,p}; \quad Q_{\alpha,p}^2 = Q_{\alpha,p}, \quad P_{\alpha,p} \cdot Q_{\alpha,p} = Q_{\alpha,p} \cdot P_{\alpha,p} = 0 \quad (15)$$

and

$$\Phi_{\alpha,p} = \frac{p\alpha\sqrt{5\alpha}}{2}(P_{\alpha,p} - Q_{\alpha,p}) - \frac{p}{2} Id. \quad (16)$$

Remark 3. *The operators $P_{\alpha,p}$ and $Q_{\alpha,p}$ given in the identities (14) are orthogonal complementary projection operators and define the complementary distributions $\mathcal{D}_1$ and $\mathcal{D}_2$ on $\overline{M}$, which contain the eigenvectors of $\Phi_{\alpha,p}$, corresponding to the eigenvalues $\varphi_{\alpha,p}$ and $\overline{\varphi}_{\alpha,p} = p - \varphi_{\alpha,p}$, respectively.*

3. Almost (α, p)-Golden Riemannian Geometry

Let $\overline{M}$ be an even dimensional manifold endowed with an α-structure J_α. We fix a Riemannian metric $\overline{g}$ such that

$$\overline{g}(J_\alpha X, Y) = \alpha \overline{g}(X, J_\alpha Y), \quad (17)$$

which is equivalent to

$$\overline{g}(J_\alpha X, J_\alpha Y) = \overline{g}(X, Y), \quad (18)$$

for any vector fields $X, Y \in \Gamma(T\overline{M})$, where $\Gamma(T\overline{M})$ is the set of smooth sections of $T\overline{M}$.

Definition 3. *The Riemannian metric $\overline{g}$, defined on an even dimensional manifold $\overline{M}$ and endowed with an α-structure J_α which verifies the equivalent identities (17) and (18), is called a metric (α, J_α)-compatible.*

Thus, by using the identities (7) and (17), we obtain that the Riemannian metric $\overline{g}$ verifies the identity

$$\overline{g}(\Phi_{\alpha,p} X, Y) - \alpha \overline{g}(X, \Phi_{\alpha,p} Y) = \frac{p}{2}(1-\alpha)\overline{g}(X, Y), \quad (19)$$

for any $X, Y \in \Gamma(T\overline{M})$.

Moreover, from identities (7) and (18), we remark that $\overline{g}$ and $(\Phi_{\alpha,p})$ are related by

$$\overline{g}(\Phi_{\alpha,p} X, \Phi_{\alpha,p} Y) = \frac{p}{2}\left(\overline{g}(\Phi_{\alpha,p} X, Y) + \overline{g}(X, \Phi_{\alpha,p} Y)\right) + p^2 \overline{g}(X, Y), \quad (20)$$

for any $X, Y \in \Gamma(T\overline{M})$.

Definition 4. *An almost (α, p)-golden Riemannian manifold is a triple $(\overline{M}, \Phi_{\alpha,p}, \overline{g})$, where $\overline{M}$ is an even dimensional manifold, $\Phi_{\alpha,p}$ is an almost (α, p)-golden structure and $\overline{g}$ is a Riemannian metric which verifies identities (19) and (20).*

Remark 4. *For $\alpha = 1$ in the identities (19) and (20), we obtain*

$$\overline{g}(\Phi_{1,p} X, Y) = \overline{g}(X, \Phi_{1,p} Y)), \quad (21)$$

which is equivalent to

$$\overline{g}(\Phi_{1,p} X, \Phi_{1,p} Y) = p\overline{g}(\Phi_{1,p} X, Y) + p^2 \overline{g}(X, Y), \quad (22)$$

and the triple $(\overline{M}, \Phi_{1,p}, \overline{g})$ is a particular case of an almost metallic Riemannian manifold, which was studied in [1,16].

Remark 5. For $\alpha = -1$ in the identities (19) and (20), we have

$$\overline{g}(\Phi_{-1,p}X, Y) + \overline{g}(X, \Phi_{-1,p}Y) = p\overline{g}(X, Y), \tag{23}$$

which is equivalent to

$$\overline{g}(\Phi_{-1,p}X, \Phi_{-1,p}Y) = \frac{3}{2}p^2\overline{g}(X, Y), \tag{24}$$

and the triple $(\overline{M}, \Phi_{-1,p}, \overline{g})$ is a particular case of an almost complex metallic Riemannian manifold, which was studied in [9].

Proposition 4. If $(\overline{M}, \Phi_{\alpha,p}, \overline{g})$ is an almost (α, p)-golden Riemannian manifold of dimmension $2m$, then the trace of the $\Phi_{\alpha,p}$ structure satisfies

$$trace(\Phi_{\alpha,p}^2) = p \cdot trace(\Phi_{\alpha,p}) + \frac{5\alpha - 1}{2}mp^2. \tag{25}$$

Proof. If we denote a local orthonormal basis of $T\overline{M}$ by $\{E_1, E_2, \ldots, E_{2m}\}$, then from the identity (5), we obtain

$$\overline{g}(\Phi_{\alpha,p}^2 E_i, E_i) = p\overline{g}(\Phi_{\alpha,p} E_i, E_i) + \frac{5\alpha - 1}{4}p^2\overline{g}(E_i, E_i),$$

and by summing this equality for $i \in \{1, \ldots 2m\}$, we obtain the claimed relation. $\square$

Example 2. Using $\varphi_{\alpha,p}$ and $\overline{\varphi}_{\alpha,p}$, defined in Equation (3), let us consider the endomorphism $\Phi_{\alpha,p}: \mathbb{R}^{2m} \to \mathbb{R}^{2m}$, given by

$$\Phi_{\alpha,p}(X^i, Y^i) := (\varphi_{\alpha,p}X^1, \ldots, \varphi_{\alpha,p}X^m, \overline{\varphi}_{\alpha,p}Y^1, \ldots, \overline{\varphi}_{\alpha,p}Y^m), \tag{26}$$

where $(X^i, Y^i) := (X^1, \ldots, X^m, Y^1, \ldots, Y^m)$ and $i \in \{1, \ldots, m\}$.

Using identities (2) and (26), a straightforward computation yields

$$\Phi_{\alpha,p}^2(X^i, Y^i) := (\varphi_{\alpha,p}^2 X^i, \overline{\varphi}_{\alpha,p}^2 Y^i) = (p\varphi_{\alpha,p}X^i + \frac{5\alpha - 1}{4}p^2 X^i, p\overline{\varphi}_{\alpha,p}Y^i + \frac{5\alpha - 1}{4}p^2 Y^i).$$

Thus, we obtain

$$\Phi_{\alpha,p}^2(X^i, Y^i) = p(\varphi_{\alpha,p}X^i, \overline{\varphi}_{\alpha,p}Y^i) + \frac{5\alpha - 1}{4}p^2(X^i, Y^i) = p\Phi_{\alpha,p}(X^i, Y^i) + \frac{5\alpha - 1}{4}p^2(X^i, Y^i)$$

and hence $\Phi_{\alpha,p}$ verifies Equation (5).

Let us consider the structure J_α associated with $\Phi_{\alpha,p}$ by identities (6) and (7):

$$J_\alpha(X^i, Y^i) := (X^1, \ldots, X^m, \alpha Y^1, \ldots, \alpha Y^m).$$

Using the identity (17), we remark that the Euclidean metric $\overline{g} := \langle , \rangle$ on $\mathbb{R}^{2m}$ verifies

$$\overline{g}(J_\alpha Z, Z') = \alpha \Sigma_{i=1}^m (X^i X'^i + Y^i Y'^i) = \alpha \overline{g}(Z, J_\alpha Z'),$$

for any $Z := (X^1, \ldots, X^m, Y^1, \ldots, Y^m), Z' = (X'^1, \ldots, X'^m, Y'^1, \ldots, Y'^m) \in \Gamma(\mathbb{R}^{2m})$. Thus, it is (α, J_α)-compatible. Using the identity (7), we obtain

$$\overline{g}(\Phi_{\alpha,p}Z, \Phi_{\alpha,p}Z') = \frac{p}{2}(\overline{g}(\Phi_{\alpha,p}Z, Z') + \overline{g}(Z, \Phi_{\alpha,p}Z')) + p^2\overline{g}(Z, Z').$$

Therefore, $\overline{g}$ verifies the identity (20), which implies that $(\mathbb{R}^{2m}, \Phi_{\alpha,p}, \overline{g})$ is an almost (α, p)-golden Riemannian manifold.

Definition 5. *If ∇ is the Levi-Civita connection on $(\overline{M}, \overline{g})$, then the covariant derivative ∇J_α is a tensor field of the type $(1, 2)$, defined by*

$$(\nabla_X J_\alpha)Y := \nabla_X J_\alpha Y - J_\alpha \nabla_X Y, \tag{27}$$

for any $X, Y \in \Gamma(T\overline{M})$.

Hence, from the identity (6), we obtain

$$(\nabla_X \Phi_{\alpha,p})Y = \frac{p\sqrt{5}}{2}(\nabla_X J_\alpha)Y. \tag{28}$$

Let us consider now the Nijenhuis tensor field of J_α. Using a similar approach to that in [19] (Definition 2.8 and Proposition 2.9), we obtain

$$N_{J_\alpha}(X, Y) = J_\alpha^2[X, Y] + [J_\alpha X, J_\alpha Y] - J_\alpha[J_\alpha X, Y] - J_\alpha[X, J_\alpha Y], \tag{29}$$

for any $X, Y \in \Gamma(T\overline{M})$, which is equivalent to

$$N_{J_\alpha}(X, Y) = (\nabla_{J_\alpha X} J_\alpha)Y - (\nabla_{J_\alpha Y} J_\alpha)X + (\nabla_X J_\alpha)J_\alpha Y - (\nabla_Y J_\alpha)J_\alpha X. \tag{30}$$

The Nijenhuis tensor field corresponding to the (α, p)-golden structure $\Phi := \Phi_{\alpha,p}$ is given by the equality

$$N_\Phi(X, Y) := \Phi^2[X, Y] + [\Phi X, \Phi Y] - \Phi[\Phi X, Y] - \Phi[X, \Phi Y]. \tag{31}$$

Thus, from the identity (31), we obtain

$$N_\Phi(X, Y) = (\nabla_{\Phi X} \Phi)Y - (\nabla_{\Phi Y} \Phi)X - \Phi(\nabla_X \Phi)Y + \Phi(\nabla_Y \Phi)X, \tag{32}$$

for any $X, Y \in \Gamma(T\overline{M})$. Moreover, from identities (28), (30) and (32), we obtain

$$N_\Phi(X, Y) = \frac{5p^2}{4} N_{J_\alpha}(X, Y). \tag{33}$$

Recall that a structure J on a differentiable manifold is *integrable* if the Nijenhuis tensor field N_J corresponding to the structure J vanishes identically (i.e., $N_J = 0$). We point out that necessary and sufficient conditions for the integrability of a polynomial structure whose characteristic polynomial has only simple roots were given in [20].

For an *integrable almost (α, p)-golden structure* (i.e., $N_{\Phi_{\alpha,p}} = 0$), we drop the adjective "almost" and then simply call it an (α, p)-*golden structure*. From Equation (6), it is found that $\Phi_{\alpha,p}$ is integrable if and only if the associated almost α structure J_α is integrable. The distribution $\mathcal{D}_1$ is integrable if $Q_{\alpha,p}[P_{\alpha,p}X, P_{\alpha,p}Y] = 0$ and also analogous, the distribution $\mathcal{D}_2$ is integrable if $P_{\alpha,p}[Q_{\alpha,p}X, Q_{\alpha,p}Y] = 0$, for any $X, Y \in \Gamma(T\overline{M})$.

Let us consider now the second fundamental form Ω, which is a 2-form on $(\overline{M}, J_\alpha, \overline{g})$, where J_α is an α structure defined in Equation (4) and the metric $\overline{g}$ is (α, J_α)-compatible. The 2-form Ω is defined as follows:

$$\Omega(X, Y) := \overline{g}(J_\alpha X, Y), \tag{34}$$

for any $X, Y \in \Gamma(T\overline{M})$. From Equaitons (17) and (34), we obtain the following property:

Proposition 5. *If $\overline{M}$ is a Riemannian manifold endowed by an α structure J_α and the metric $\overline{g}$, which is (α, J_α)-compatible, then for any $X, Y \in \Gamma(T\overline{M})$, we have*

$$\Omega(X, Y) = \alpha \Omega(Y, X). \tag{35}$$

By using the correspondence between $\Phi_{\alpha,p}$ and J_α given in the identities (6) and (7), we obtain the following Lemma:

Lemma 2. *If $(\overline{M}, \Phi_{\alpha,p}, \overline{g})$ is an almost (α, p)-golden Riemannian manifold, then*

$$\Omega(X, Y) = \pm \frac{2}{p\sqrt{5}} [\overline{g}(\Phi_{\alpha,p} X, Y) - \frac{p}{2}\overline{g}(X, Y)], \tag{36}$$

$$\Omega(\Phi_{\alpha,p} X, Y) = \frac{p}{2}\Omega(X, Y) + \frac{p\alpha\sqrt{5}}{2}\overline{g}(X, Y), \tag{37}$$

for any $X, Y \in \Gamma(T\overline{M})$.

Hence, by inverting $X \leftrightarrow Y$ in Equation (37), we obtain

$$\Omega(\Phi_{\alpha,p} Y, X) = \frac{p}{2}\Omega(Y, X) + \frac{p\alpha\sqrt{5}}{2}\overline{g}(X, Y). \tag{38}$$

Using the identity (35) in the equality (38) and multiplying by $\alpha = \pm 1$, we obtain

$$\Omega(X, \Phi_{\alpha,p} Y) = \frac{p}{2}\Omega(X, Y) + \frac{p\sqrt{5}}{2}\overline{g}(X, Y). \tag{39}$$

Proposition 6. *Let $(\overline{M}, \Phi_{\alpha,p}, \overline{g})$ be an almost (α, p)-golden Riemannian manifold. Then, we have*

$$\Omega(\Phi_{\alpha,p} X, Y) - \Omega(X, \Phi_{\alpha,p} Y) = \frac{p(\alpha - 1)\sqrt{5}}{2}\overline{g}(X, Y), \tag{40}$$

$$\Omega(\Phi_{\alpha,p} X, Y) + \Omega(X, \Phi_{\alpha,p} Y) = p\Omega(X, Y) + \frac{p(\alpha + 1)\sqrt{5}}{2}\overline{g}(X, Y), \tag{41}$$

for any $X, Y \in \Gamma(T\overline{M})$.

Remark 6. *Let $(\overline{M}, \Phi_{\alpha,p}, \overline{g})$ be an almost (α, p)-golden Riemannian manifold. In particular, for any $X, Y \in \Gamma(T\overline{M})$, we have the following:*
(1) For $\alpha = 1$, we have

$$\Omega(\Phi_{1,p} X, Y) = \Omega(X, \Phi_{1,p} Y) = \frac{p}{2}\Omega(X, Y) + \frac{p\sqrt{5}}{2}\overline{g}(X, Y) \tag{42}$$

(2) For $\alpha = -1$, we have

$$\Omega(\Phi_{-1,p} X, Y) + \Omega(X, \Phi_{-1,p} Y) = p\Omega(Y, X). \tag{43}$$

Lemma 3. *Let $\overline{M}$ be a Riemannian manifold endowed with an α structure J_α and the metric $\overline{g}$, which is (α, J_α)-compatible. Then, for any $X, Y, Z \in \Gamma(T\overline{M})$, we obtain*

$$\overline{g}((\nabla_X J_\alpha)Y, Z) = \alpha \overline{g}(Y, (\nabla_X J_\alpha)Z). \tag{44}$$

Also, from Equations (28) and (44), we obtain the following:

Proposition 7. *If $(\overline{M}, \Phi_{\alpha,p}, \overline{g})$ is an almost (α, p)-golden Riemannian manifold, then for any $X, Y, Z \in \Gamma(T\overline{M})$, the structure $\Phi_{\alpha,p}$ satisfies*

$$\overline{g}((\nabla_X \Phi_{\alpha,p})Y, Z) = \alpha \overline{g}(Y, (\nabla_X \Phi_{\alpha,p})Z). \tag{45}$$

4. Submanifolds in the Almost (α, p)-Golden Riemannian Manifold

In this section, we assume that M is a $2n$-dimensional submanifold isometrically immersed in a $2m$-dimensional almost (α, p)-golden Riemannian manifold $(\overline{M}, \Phi_{\alpha,p}, \overline{g})$. We study some properties of the submanifold M in the almost (α, p)-golden Riemannian geometry regarding the structure induced by the given $\Phi_{\alpha,p}$ structure.

We shall denote with $\Gamma(TM)$ the set of smooth sections of TM. Let us denote with $T_x M$ (and with $T_x^\perp M$) the tangent space (and the normal space) of M in a given point $x \in M$. For any $x \in \overline{M}$, we have the direct sum decomposition:

$$T_x \overline{M} = T_x M \oplus T_x^\perp M.$$

If g is the induced Riemannian metric on M, then it is given by $g(X, Y) = \overline{g}(i_* X, i_* Y)$ for any $X, Y \in \Gamma(TM)$, where i_* is the differential of the immersion $i : M \to \overline{M}$. We shall assume that all of the immersions are injective. In the rest of the paper, we shall denote with X the vector field $i_* X$ for any $X \in \Gamma(TM)$ in order to simplify the notations.

From Equations (17) and (18), we remark that the induced metric on the submanifold M verifies the following equalities:

$$(i) \; g(J_\alpha X, Y) = \alpha g(X, J_\alpha Y), \quad (ii) \; g(J_\alpha X, J_\alpha Y) = g(X, Y), \tag{46}$$

for any $X, Y \in \Gamma(TM)$.

The decomposition into the tangential and normal parts of $\Phi_{\alpha,p} X$ and $\Phi_{\alpha,p} V$ for any $X \in \Gamma(TM)$ and $U \in \Gamma(T^\perp M)$ is given by

$$(i) \; \Phi_{\alpha,p} X = \mathcal{T} X + \mathcal{N} X, \quad (ii) \; \Phi_{\alpha,p} U = \mathfrak{t} U + \mathfrak{n} U, \tag{47}$$

where $\mathcal{T} : \Gamma(TM) \to \Gamma(TM)$, $\mathcal{N} : \Gamma(TM) \to \Gamma(T^\perp M)$, $\mathfrak{t} : \Gamma(T^\perp M) \to \Gamma(TM)$ and $\mathfrak{n} : \Gamma(T^\perp M) \to \Gamma(T^\perp M)$.

In the next considerations, we denote with $\overline{\nabla}$ and ∇ the Levi-Civita connections on $(\overline{M}, \overline{g})$ and on the submanifold (M, g), respectively.

The Gauss and Weingarten formulas are given by the respective equalities

$$(i) \; \overline{\nabla}_X Y = \nabla_X Y + h(X, Y), \quad (ii) \; \overline{\nabla}_X U = -A_U X + \nabla_X^\perp U, \tag{48}$$

for any tangent vector fields $X, Y \in \Gamma(TM)$ and any normal vector field $U \in \Gamma(T^\perp M)$, where h is the second fundamental form and A_U is the shape operator of M with respect to U, while $\nabla^\perp$ is the normal connection to the normal bundle $\Gamma(T^\perp M)$. Furthermore, the second fundamental form h and the shape operator A_U are related as follows:

$$\overline{g}(h(X, Y), U) = \overline{g}(A_U X, Y), \tag{49}$$

for any $X, Y \in \Gamma(TM)$ and $U \in \Gamma(T^\perp M)$.

For the α structure J_α, the decompositions into tangential and normal parts of $J_\alpha X$ and $J_\alpha U$ for any $X \in \Gamma(TM)$ and $U \in \Gamma(T^\perp M)$ are given by the respective formulas

$$(i) \; J_\alpha X = fX + \omega X, \quad (ii) \; J_\alpha U = BU + CU, \tag{50}$$

where $f : \Gamma(TM) \to \Gamma(TM)$, $fX := (J_\alpha X)^T$, $\omega : \Gamma(TM) \to \Gamma(T^\perp M)$, $\omega X := (J_\alpha X)^\perp$, $B : \Gamma(T^\perp M) \to \Gamma(TM)$, $BU := (J_\alpha U)^T$ and $C : \Gamma(T^\perp M) \to \Gamma(T^\perp M)$, $CU := (V)^{J_\alpha \perp}$.

Direct calculus shows that the maps f, ω, B and C satisfy the following identity:

$$(i) \; \overline{g}(fX, Y) = \alpha \overline{g}(X, fY), \quad (ii) \; \overline{g}(CU, V) = \alpha \overline{g}(U, CV) \tag{51}$$

$$\overline{g}(\omega X, V) = \alpha \overline{g}(X, BV), \tag{52}$$

for any $X, Y \in \Gamma(TM)$ and $U, V \in \Gamma(T^\perp M)$. Using Equation (47), we obtain the following lemma:

Lemma 4. *Let $(\overline{M}, \overline{g})$ be a Riemannian manifold endowed with an α structure J_α, and let $\Phi_{\alpha,p}$ be the almost (α, p)-golden structure related by J_α through the relationships in Equation (6). Thus, we obtain*

$$(i)\ \mathcal{T}X = \frac{p}{2}X \pm \frac{\sqrt{5\alpha}}{2}fX, \quad (ii)\ \mathcal{N}X = \pm\frac{\sqrt{5\alpha}}{2}\omega X \tag{53}$$

$$(i)\ \mathfrak{t}V = \pm\frac{\sqrt{5\alpha}}{2}BV, \quad (ii)\ \mathfrak{n}V = \frac{p}{2}V \pm \frac{\sqrt{5\alpha}}{2}CV, \tag{54}$$

for any $X \in \Gamma(TM)$ and $V \in \Gamma(T^\perp M)$.

Now, by using Equations (53) and (54) in the Equations (51) and (52), respectively, we obtain the following property:

Proposition 8. *Let $(\overline{M}, \overline{g})$ be a Riemannian manifold endowed with an almost (α, p)-golden structure. Thus, for any $X, Y \in \Gamma(TM)$, the maps $\mathcal{T}$ and $\mathfrak{n}$ satisfy*

$$\overline{g}(\mathcal{T}X, Y) = \alpha\overline{g}(X, \mathcal{T}Y) + \frac{p(1-\alpha)}{2}g(X, Y), \tag{55}$$

$$\overline{g}(\mathfrak{n}U, V) = \alpha\overline{g}(U, \mathfrak{n}V) + \frac{p(1-\alpha)}{2}g(U, V). \tag{56}$$

Moreover, for any $U, V \in \Gamma(T^\perp M)$, $\mathcal{N}$ and $\mathfrak{t}$ satisfy

$$\overline{g}(\mathcal{N}X, U) = \alpha\overline{g}(X, \mathfrak{t}U). \tag{57}$$

Definition 6. *The covariant derivatives of the tangential and normal parts of $\Phi_{\alpha,p}X$ (and $\Phi_{\alpha,p}V$) are given by*

$$(i)\ (\nabla_X \mathcal{T})Y = \nabla_X \mathcal{T}Y - \mathcal{T}(\nabla_X Y), \quad (ii)\ (\overline{\nabla}_X \mathcal{N})Y = \nabla^\perp_X \mathcal{N}Y - \mathcal{N}(\nabla_X Y), \tag{58}$$

$$(i)\ (\nabla_X \mathfrak{t})U = \nabla_X \mathfrak{t}U - \mathfrak{t}(\nabla^\perp_X U), \quad (ii)\ (\overline{\nabla}_X \mathfrak{n})U = \nabla^\perp_X \mathfrak{n}U - \mathfrak{n}(\nabla^\perp_X U), \tag{59}$$

for any $X, Y \in \Gamma(TM)$ and $U \in \Gamma(T^\perp M)$.

Remark 7. *Let M be an isometrically immersed submanifold of a Riemannian manifold $(\overline{M}, \overline{g})$ endowed by a J_α structure and a $\Phi_{(\alpha,p)}$-golden structure. Then, for any $X, Y, Z \in \Gamma(TM)$, we obtain*

$$(i)\ \overline{g}((\nabla_X f)Y, Z) = \alpha\overline{g}(Y, (\nabla_X f)Z), \quad (ii)\ \overline{g}((\nabla_X \mathcal{T})Y, Z) = \alpha\overline{g}(Y, (\nabla_X \mathcal{T})Z). \tag{60}$$

The identities (60) result from Equations (51)(i) and (53)(i).

Let M a submanifold of co-dimension $2r$ in $\overline{M}$. We fix a local orthonormal basis $\{N_1, ..., N_{2r}\}$ of the normal space $T_x^\perp M$ for any $x \in \overline{M}$. Hereafter, we assume that the indices i, j and k run over the range $\{1, ..., 2r\}$.

Let $\Phi_{\alpha,p} := \Phi$ be the almost (α, p)-golden structure. Then, we obtain the decomposition

$$(i)\ \Phi X = \mathcal{T}X + \sum_{i=1}^{2r} u_i(X)N_i, \quad (ii)\ \Phi N_i = \xi_i + \sum_{j=1}^{2r} \mathcal{A}_{ij} N_j, \tag{61}$$

for any $X \in T_x M$, where ξ_i represents the vector fields on M, u_i represents the 1-forms on M and $\mathcal{A} := (\mathcal{A}_{ij})_{2r}$ is a $2r \times 2r$ matrix of smooth real functions on M.

Moreover, from Equations (47) and (61), we remark that

$$\mathcal{N}X = \sum_{i=1}^{2r} u_i(X) N_i, \tag{62}$$

for any $X \in T_x M$ and

$$(i)\ \mathfrak{t}N_i = \xi_i, \quad (ii)\ \mathfrak{n}N_i = \sum_{k=1}^{2r} \mathcal{A}_{ik} N_k. \tag{63}$$

Therefore, we find the structure $\Sigma = (\mathcal{T}, g, u_i, \xi_i, \mathcal{A})$ on the submanifold M through $\Phi_{\alpha,p}$, and we shall obtain a characterization of the structure induced on a submanifold M by the almost (α, p)-golden structure in a similar manner to that in Theorem 3.1. from [15].

Theorem 1. *The structure $\Sigma = (\mathcal{T}, g, u_i, \xi_i, \mathcal{A})$ induced on the submanifold M by the almost (α, p)-golden structure $\Phi_{\alpha,p}$ on $\overline{M}$ satisfies the following equalities:*

$$\mathcal{T}^2 X = p \mathcal{T} X + \frac{5\alpha - 1}{4} p^2 X - \sum_{i=1}^{2r} u_i(X) \xi_i, \tag{64}$$

$$\mathcal{A}_{ij} = \alpha \mathcal{A}_{ji} + \frac{p(1-\alpha)}{2} \delta_{ij}, \tag{65}$$

$$u_i(X) = \alpha g(X, \xi_i), \tag{66}$$

$$\mathcal{T} \xi_i = p \xi_i - \sum_{j=1}^{2r} \mathcal{A}_{ij} \xi_j, \tag{67}$$

$$u_j(\xi_i) = \frac{5\alpha - 1}{4} p^2 \delta_{ij} + p \mathcal{A}_{ij} - \sum_{k=1}^{2r} \mathcal{A}_{ik} \mathcal{A}_{kj}, \tag{68}$$

for any $X \in \Gamma(TM)$, where $\mathcal{T}$ is a $(1,1)$-tensor field on M, ξ_i represents the tangent vector fields on M, u_i represents the 1-form M and the matrix $\mathcal{A}$ is determined by its entries $\mathcal{A}_{ij}$, which are real functions on M (for any $i, j \in \{1, \ldots, 2r\}$).

Proof. Using $\Phi_{\alpha,p} := \Phi$ in the identity (47)(i) and (5), we obtain $p \Phi X + \frac{5\alpha-1}{4} p^2 \cdot X = \Phi \mathcal{T} X + \Phi \mathcal{N} X$. Moreover, using identities (47)(i) and (61)(i), we obtain

$$p \mathcal{T} X + p \sum_{i=1}^{2r} u_i(X) N_i + \frac{5\alpha - 1}{4} p^2 \cdot X = \mathcal{T}^2 X + \mathcal{N} \mathcal{T} X + \sum_{i=1}^{2r} u_i(X) \Phi N_i \tag{69}$$

By using the identity (62) and equalizing the tangential part of the identity (69), we obtain equality (64).

Now, using the identity (56), we obtain

$$\overline{g}(\mathfrak{n} N_i, N_j) = \alpha \overline{g}(N_i, \mathfrak{n} N_j) + \frac{p(1-\alpha)}{2} g(N_i, N_j)$$

and from the equality (63)(ii), we obtain the identity (65).

From the identity (57), we obtain $\overline{g}(\mathcal{N} X, N_j) = \alpha \overline{g}(X, \mathfrak{t} N_j)$ and by using identities (62) and (63)(i), we obtain the equality (66).

From the Equation (5), we obtain $\Phi^2 N_i = p \Phi N_i + \frac{5\alpha-1}{4} p^2 \cdot N_i$ and from the identity (61)(ii), we obtain

$$\Phi(\xi_i + \sum_{j=1}^{2r} \mathcal{A}_{ij} N_j) = p(\xi_i + \sum_{j=1}^{2r} \mathcal{A}_{ij} N_j) + \frac{5\alpha - 1}{4} p^2 \cdot N_i,$$

Moreover, using identities (61)(i) and (61)(ii), we obtain

$$\mathcal{T} \xi_i + \sum_{j=1}^{2r} u_j(\xi_i) N_j + \sum_{j=1}^{2r} \mathcal{A}_{ij}(\xi_j + \sum_{k=1}^{2r} \mathcal{A}_{jk} N_k) = p \xi_i + p \sum_{j=1}^{2r} \mathcal{A}_{ij} N_j + \frac{5\alpha - 1}{4} p^2 \cdot N_i.$$

When comparing the tangential and normal parts of both sides of this last equality, respectively, we infer the identities (67) and (68). □

By using identities (61)(i) and (61)(ii), we obtain the following remark:

Remark 8. *If $(\overline{M}, \Phi, \overline{g})$ is an almost (α, p)-golden Riemannian manifold and $X, Y \in \Gamma(TM)$, then for any $i, j \in \{1, \ldots, 2r\}$, we obtain*

$$\overline{g}(\Phi X, \Phi Y) = g(\mathcal{T}X, \mathcal{T}Y) + \sum_{i=1}^{2r} u_i(X) u_i(Y), \tag{70}$$

$$\overline{g}(\Phi N_i, \Phi N_j) = g(\xi_i, \xi_j) + \sum_{k=1}^{2r} \mathcal{A}_{ik} \mathcal{A}_{kj}, \tag{71}$$

If M is an invariant submanifold of $\overline{M}$ (i.e., $\Phi(T_x M) \subset T_x M$ and $\Phi(T_x^\perp M) \subset T_x^\perp M$ for all $x \in M$), then from identities (61), we obtain $\Phi X = \mathcal{T}X$, which implies $u_i(X) = 0$ and $\xi_i = 0$ for any $i \in \{1, 2, \ldots, 2r\}$. Therefore, using the identities (64) and (68), we obtain the following property:

Proposition 9. *Let M be an invariant submanifold of co-dimension $2r$ of the almost (α, p)-golden Riemannian manifold $(\overline{M}, \Phi, \overline{g})$, and let $\Sigma = (\mathcal{T}, g, u_i = 0, \xi_i = 0, \mathcal{A})$ be the structure induced on the submanifold M. Then, $\mathcal{T}$ is an (α, p)-golden structure on M; in other words, we have*

$$\mathcal{T}^2 X = p \mathcal{T} X + \frac{5\alpha - 1}{4} p^2 X, \tag{72}$$

for any $X \in \Gamma(TM)$, where p is a real nonzero number and $\alpha \in \{-1, 1\}$. Moreover, the quadratic matrix $\mathcal{A}$ satisfies the equality

$$\mathcal{A}^2 = p\mathcal{A} + \frac{5\alpha - 1}{4} p^2 I_{2r}, \tag{73}$$

where its entries $\mathcal{A}_{ij}$ are real functions on M ($i, j \in \{1, \ldots, 2r\}$) and I_{2r} is an identical matrix of the order $2r$.

Theorem 2. *A necessary and sufficient condition for the invariance of a submanifold M of co-dimension $2r$ in a $2m$-dimensional Riemannian manifold $(\overline{M}, \overline{g})$ endowed with an almost (α, p)-golden structure Φ is that the structure $\mathcal{T}$ on (M, g) is also an almost (α, p)-golden structure.*

Proof. If $\mathcal{T}$ is an almost (α, p)-golden structure, then from Equation (64), we obtain

$$\sum_{i=1}^{2r} u_i(X) \xi_i = 0, \tag{74}$$

for any $X \in \Gamma(TM)$. By taking the g product with X in Equation (74), we infer that

$$\sum_{i=1}^{2r} u_i(X) g(X, \xi_i) = \sum_i (u_i(X))^2 = 0,$$

which is equivalent to $u_i(X) = 0$ for every $i \in \{1, \ldots, 2r\}$, and this fact implies that M is invariant.

Conversely, if M is an invariant submanifold, then from Equation (72), we obtain that the structure $\mathcal{T}$ on (M, g) is also an almost (α, p)-golden structure. □

5. Conclusions

The world of quadratic endomorphisms of a given manifold is enriched now with a new class. If a Riemannian metric is added through a compatibility condition, then a new geometry is developed. Its submanifolds also carry remarkable structures, and new studies are expected to enrich this domain of differential geometry.

Author Contributions: C.E.H. and M.C. contributed equally to this work. All authors have read and agreed to the published version of the manuscript.

Funding: This research received no external funding.

Data Availability Statement: Not applicable.

Acknowledgments: The authors are greatly indebted to the anonymous referees for their valuable remarks, which have substantially improved the initial submission.

Conflicts of Interest: The authors declare no conflict of interest.

References

1. Hretcanu, C.E.; Crasmareanu, M. Metallic structures on Riemannian manifolds. *Rev. Union Mat. Argent.* **2013**, *54*, 15–27.
2. de Spinadel, V.W. The metallic means family and forbidden symmetries. *Int. Math. J.* **2002**, *2*, 279–288.
3. de Spinadel, V.W. The metallic means family and renormalization group techniques. *Proc. Steklov Inst. Math. Control Dyn. Syst.* **2000**, *6* (Suppl. S1), 194–209.
4. Stakhov, A.P. The generalized golden proportions, a new theory of real numbers, and ternary mirror-symmetrical arithmetic. *Chaos Solitons Fractals* **2007**, *33*, 315–334. [CrossRef]
5. Stakhov, A.P. The generalized principle of the golden section and its applications in mathematics, science, and engineering. *Chaos Solitons Fractals* **2005**, *26*, 263–289. [CrossRef]
6. Goldberg, S.I.; Yano, K. Polynomial structures on manifolds. *Kodai Math. Sem. Rep.* **1970**, *22*, 199–218. [CrossRef]
7. Goldberg, S.I.; Petridis, N.C. Differentiable solutions of algebraic equations on manifolds. *Kodai Math. Sem. Rep.* **1973**, *25*, 111–128. [CrossRef]
8. Crasmareanu, M.; Hretcanu, C.E. Golden differential geometry. *Chaos Solitons Fractals* **2008**, *38*, 1229–1238. [CrossRef]
9. Turanli, S.; Gezer, A.; Cakicioglu, H. Metallic Kähler and nearly metallic Kähler manifolds. *Int. J. Geom. Methods Mod. Phys.* **2021**, *18*, 2150146. [CrossRef]
10. Etayo, F.; deFrancisco, A.; Santamaria, R. Classification of pure metallic metric geometries. *Carpathian J. Math.* **2022**, *38*, 417–429. [CrossRef]
11. Gezer, A.; Karaman, C. Golden-Hessian structures. *Proc. Natl. Acad. Sci. India Sect. A Phys. Sci.* **2016**, *86*, 41–46. [CrossRef]
12. Etayo, F.; Santamaria, R. Classification of Almost Golden Riemannian Manifolds with Null Trace. *Mediterr. J. Math.* **2020**, *17*, 90. [CrossRef]
13. Etayo, F.; Santamaria, R.; Upadhyay, A. On the geometry of almost Golden Riemannian manifolds. *Mediterr. J. Math.* **2017**, *14*, 187. [CrossRef]
14. Etayo F.; deFrancisco A.; Santamaria, R. Unified classification of pure metric geometries. *Hacet. J. Math. Stat.* **2022**, *51*, 113–141. [CrossRef]
15. Hretcanu, C.E.; Crasmareanu, M.C. Applications of the Golden ratio on Riemannian manifolds. *Turk. J. Math.* **2009**, *33*, 179–191. [CrossRef]
16. Hretcanu, C.E.; Blaga, A.M. Submanifolds in metallic Riemannian manifolds. *Differ. Geom. Dyn. Syst.* **2018**, *20*, 83–97.
17. Torun, A.; Ozkan, M. Submanifolds of Almost-Complex Metallic Manifolds. *Mathematics* **2023**, *11*, 1172. [CrossRef]
18. Bouzir, H.; Beldjilali, G. Almost Hermitian Golden manifolds. *Balk. J. Geom. Its Appl.* **2021**, *26*, 23–32.
19. Etayo F.; Santamaria, R. Distinguished connections on ($J^2 = \pm 1$)-metric manifolds. *Arch. Math.* **2016**, *52*, 159–203.
20. Vanzura, J. Integrability conditions for polynomial structures. *Kodai Math. Sem. Rep.* **1976**, *27*, 42–50.

Disclaimer/Publisher's Note: The statements, opinions and data contained in all publications are solely those of the individual author(s) and contributor(s) and not of MDPI and/or the editor(s). MDPI and/or the editor(s) disclaim responsibility for any injury to people or property resulting from any ideas, methods, instructions or products referred to in the content.

Article

Holonomic and Non-Holonomic Geometric Models Associated to the Gibbs–Helmholtz Equation

Cristina-Liliana Pripoae [1,†], **Iulia-Elena Hirica** [2,*,†], **Gabriel-Teodor Pripoae** [2,†] **and Vasile Preda** [2,3,4,†]

1. Department of Applied Mathematics, The Bucharest University of Economic Studies, Piata Romana 6, RO-010374 Bucharest, Romania; cristinapripoae@csie.ase.ro
2. Faculty of Mathematics and Computer Science, University of Bucharest, Academiei 14, RO-010014 Bucharest, Romania; gpripoae@fmi.unibuc.ro (G.-T.P.); preda@fmi.unibuc.ro (V.P.)
3. "Gheorghe Mihoc-Caius Iacob" Institute of Mathematical Statistics and Applied Mathematics of Romanian Academy, 2. Calea 13 Septembrie, Nr.13, Sect. 5, RO-050711 Bucharest, Romania
4. "Costin C. Kiritescu" National Institute of Economic Research of Romanian Academy, 3. Calea 13 Septembrie, Nr.13, Sect. 5, RO-050711 Bucharest, Romania
* Correspondence: ihirica@fmi.unibuc.ro
† These authors contributed equally to this work.

Abstract: By replacing the internal energy with the free energy, as coordinates in a "space of observables", we slightly modify (the known three) non-holonomic geometrizations from Udriste's et al. work. The coefficients of the curvature tensor field, of the Ricci tensor field, and of the scalar curvature function still remain rational functions. In addition, we define and study a new holonomic Riemannian geometric model associated, in a canonical way, to the Gibbs–Helmholtz equation from Classical Thermodynamics. Using a specific coordinate system, we define a parameterized hypersurface in $\mathbb{R}^4$ as the "graph" of the entropy function. The main geometric invariants of this hypersurface are determined and some of their properties are derived. Using this geometrization, we characterize the equivalence between the Gibbs–Helmholtz entropy and the Boltzmann–Gibbs–Shannon, Tsallis, and Kaniadakis entropies, respectively, by means of three stochastic integral equations. We prove that some specific (infinite) families of normal probability distributions are solutions for these equations. This particular case offers a glimpse of the more general "equivalence problem" between classical entropy and statistical entropy.

Keywords: Gibbs–Helmholtz equation; free energy; pressure; volume; temperature; Boltzmann–Gibbs–Shannon entropy; heat (thermal) capacity; thermal pressure coefficient; chemical thermodynamics

MSC: 53B25; 53B50; 53B12; 58A17; 80-10

1. Introduction

1.1. Motivation

Classical Thermodynamics is conducted by the Gibbs–Helmholtz (GH) equation, which relates some macroscopic observables of a closed system: the volume, the free energy (or, alternatively, the internal energy), the pressure, the temperature, and the entropy. We can interpret it as a Pfaff equation in (an open subset of) $\mathbb{R}^5$, i.e., by equating an exterior differential one-form with zero. Its kernel is a non-integrable (non-holonomic) regular four-dimensional distribution, because it does not admit integral manifolds through all the points of $\mathbb{R}^5$. The non-holonomy forbids the standard (and canonical) application of Riemannian geometric tools on integral (sub)manifolds, so we must appeal to non-holonomic geometrizations. Better than nothing, these non-holonomic tools cannot, however, catch all the relevant information hidden in the physical model, via the associated distribution.

Our paper has two main goals. Firstly, we make a slight variation of three known Riemannian non-holonomic geometrizations of the GH equation and compare the old and new approaches. Secondly, we avoid the lack of integrability of the previous distribution by choosing other coordinates. This allows us to consider a holonomic geometrization of the GH equation, which greatly simplifies the framework.

1.2. History

At the end of the 19th Century, the Gibbs–Helmholtz (GH) equation emerged from the papers of J.W. Gibbs and H. Helmholtz and established the rigorous (mathematical) foundation of (Chemical) Thermodynamics. Its interesting story may be read in [1–5] and in the lively blog of Peter Mander [6]. The GH equation is a specific Pfaffian equation, a mathematical notion which was already defined by J.F. Pfaff 100 years before, and involves, among other observables, the so-called "thermodynamic entropy" (also known as "Gibbs-Helmholtz (GH) entropy" or "macroscopic entropy").

Approximately at the same time, L. Boltzmann (and soon after M. Planck and J.W. Gibbs) introduced another kind of entropy, suitable for Statistical Mechanics; later, Shannon adapted it for Information Theory. Today, it is known as Boltzmann–Gibbs–Shannon (BGS) entropy (also known as "Gibbs entropy", "Shannon entropy", "information entropy", or "statistical entropy") [4].

Both types of entropy notions have common epistemological roots in Carnot's papers on heat engines at the beginning of 19th Century and in Clausius's work in the mid-19th century [4]. One century after, their study split into two (apparently) divergent theories. Now, *an important open problem is to decide if the two kinds of entropy are equivalent*; in case they are, it would be interesting to establish a "dictionary" between the two theories, and to search for a single "Grand Unified Theory" of entropy. This equivalence problem is similar—in some sense—to the equivalence of the inertial and the gravitational mass in the Theory of Relativity (the "Equivalence Principle"). In the (physical, mathematical, epistemological) literature, arguments have been brought for both pro and con variants (equivalence vs. non-equivalence) [1,7–27].

The task to decide where the truth is is all the more difficult, as the mathematical methods of approach differ. Thermodynamic entropy is a deterministic notion, mainly studied by means of the GH equation, whose modelization is based on contact geometry ([28–38] and references therein) and/or on different non-holonomic associated invariants. The BGS entropy study rests on probability and statistical tools; there exist, however, some geometric objects associated to it, e.g., the Fisher metrics, the statistical manifolds, etc. (see [39–41] and references therein), but all these notions are of recent birth, when one compares them with the two-century-old Pfaffian forms. Their *long-range* relevance and applicability are still to be confirmed.

The roots of Riemannian non-holonomic geometrization can be found in the third decade of the 20th Century, with the papers of Gh. Vranceanu [42–44] and, independently, of Z. Horak (apud [45]). Some Riemannian invariants, similar to those from the holonomic known models, were associated with Pfaffian systems, which determine a non-integrable distribution D of interest in physics (especially in mechanics). Soon after, the theory evolved in many directions, notably in the theory of connections in fiber spaces of E. Cartan and C. Ehresmann.

Through a higher-dimensional analogue of Descartes' trick, a complementary orthogonal distribution $D^\perp$ w.r.t. a Riemannian metric g_D establishes an "orthogonal frame" $(D, D^\perp)$, which allows a "decomposition" in two parts; the Riemannian machinery can be now exploited, producing metric invariants. Given the distribution D, there exist an infinite number of such possible non-holonomic Riemannian models $(D, D^\perp, g_D)$ (and many more in the semi-Riemannian setting). The versatility of this approach may be an advantage, but sometimes a disadvantage, for both the glory and the limits of non-holonomic geometry. (We avoid entering here in this debate, which deserves more care and a more appropriate framework).

A highly original geometrization path for dynamical systems, via Pfaffian equations and non-holonomic geometry, is the Geometric Dynamics of C. Udriste [46]. In particular, this tool was applied also in the study of the GH equation ([28,47–51], to quote but a few).

1.3. Our Contribution

Our paper deals with three (apparently unrelated) topics: classical thermodynamics and the geometrization of the Gibbs–Helmholtz equation (via holonomic and non-holonomic models); the detailed study of a hypersurface $\mathfrak{S}$ in $\mathbb{R}^4$, from both the intrinsic and the extrinsic geometry; the equivalence problem between classical (thermodynamical) entropy and statistical entropy. The unity of the three topics consists in the double role played by the hypersurface $\mathfrak{S}$: firstly, to prove the advantages of the holonomic approach versus the non-holonomic one; secondly, to be used as a tool for characterizing analytically the (eventual) equivalence between the previous entropy notions.

In Section 2, we recall three (non-holonomic) Riemannian geometrizations of the GH equation, due to Udriste and collaborators. By replacing the internal energy with the free energy, we obtain three new analogous non-holonomic geometrizations, related to the previous ones. The new Riemannian invariants are expressed by rational functions, too.

In Section 3, we make a new *holonomic* geometrization of the GH equation, using a special parameterized hypersurface $\mathfrak{S}$ in $\mathbb{R}^5$. We calculate the matrices of the fundamental forms of this hypersurface, its mean curvatures, its principal curvatures, and some of its intrinsic invariants (geodesics, curvature coefficients, Ricci coefficients, scalar curvature). In contrast with the partial/incomplete tools offered by the non-holonomic models, the geometry of $\mathfrak{S}$ offers access to the whole Riemannian machinery, which can be used to understand and control the thermodynamic systems.

In Section 4, we use the model from Section 3 and we compare the GH entropy with the BGS, the Tsallis, and the Kaniadakis entropies, respectively, from Statistical Mechanics. Their equivalence is characterized by specific stochastic integral equations. Examples of solutions of these equations are provided.

We compare our approach with the recent result of Gao et al. [52,53], which states that (under a set of specific physical assumptions) the BGS (and, eventually, the Tsallis) entropy equals the thermodynamic entropy only for generalized Boltzmann distributions.

In Section 5, we give some thermodynamic interpretation of our results.

1.4. Conventions

Some of our definitions and results can be easily extended to deal with *generalized* Gibbs–Helmholtz equations [2,5,24]. We preferred to limit our study and keep the discourse as elementary as possible, so as not to hide the forest behind the trees.

We suppose all the physical quantities suitably normalized, so that all the equations make sense from the physics viewpoint.

2. Avatars of Three Non-Holonomic Riemannian Geometrizations for the GH Equation

Consider a closed thermodynamic system with (Gibbs) free energy G, pressure p, entropy S, temperature T, internal energy U, and volume V. We know that [28,54]

$$U = G - pV + TS. \tag{1}$$

The mutual interconnections between these observables are described by the Gibbs–Helmholtz equation

$$dG + SdT - Vdp = 0. \tag{2}$$

Via Relation (1), this equation may be written in the equivalent form

$$dU + pdV - TdS = 0. \tag{3}$$

The GH equation is one of the fundamental equations in thermodynamics, as it relates-in a subtle manner-the main observables. It is subject to many approaches, interpretations, and generalizations ([6]). We shall study it mainly from a mathematical viewpoint, maybe losing some of its physical flavor.

Define two differential one-forms $\omega := dG + SdT - Vdp$ and $\eta := dU + pdV - TdS$, on two suitable open subsets (as "configurations spaces") $\mathfrak{D}$ and $\mathfrak{E}$ in $\mathbb{R}^5$, respectively, w.r.t. coordinates (G, p, S, T, V) and (U, p, S, T, V). Then, Equations (2) and (3) can be modeled by the Pfaff equations $\omega = 0$ and $\eta = 0$, respectively, and by their associated four-dimensional (regular and non-integrable) distributions $ker\omega$ and $ker\eta$. We have

$$ker\omega = span\left\{ \frac{\partial}{\partial S}, \frac{\partial}{\partial V}, \frac{\partial}{\partial p} + V\frac{\partial}{\partial G}, \frac{\partial}{\partial T} - S\frac{\partial}{\partial G} \right\} \qquad (4)$$

and

$$ker\eta = span\left\{ \frac{\partial}{\partial p}, \frac{\partial}{\partial T}, \frac{\partial}{\partial S} + T\frac{\partial}{\partial U}, \frac{\partial}{\partial V} - p\frac{\partial}{\partial U} \right\}. \qquad (5)$$

Remark 1. *Holonomic distributions are integrable, i.e., they admit integral manifolds of maximal dimension through all the points; each such submanifold inherits a canonical induced Riemannian structure which geometrizes the solutions of the initial equation. In the non-holonomic case, the distributions lack this important property.*

The non-holonomy of the distribution $ker\omega$ (or, alternatively, $ker\eta$) is the fundamental cause of the difficulty encountered when one tries to integrate the GH equation. For this reason, empirical or more elaborate attempts were invented, and many particular cases were considered, by "slicing" the configuration space or by using idealized models (e.g., in Carnot-like attempts).

From (2), we obtain

$$S = V\frac{\partial p}{\partial T} - \frac{\partial G}{\partial T} \qquad (6)$$

and

$$V = S\frac{\partial T}{\partial p} + \frac{\partial G}{\partial p}. \qquad (7)$$

By analogy, from (3), we obtain

$$p = T\frac{\partial S}{\partial V} - \frac{\partial U}{\partial V} \qquad (8)$$

and

$$T = p\frac{\partial V}{\partial S} + \frac{\partial U}{\partial S}. \qquad (9)$$

Udriste and collaborators used the formalism based on (3) and associated to the distribution ker η three Riemannian metrics ([46–48,51] and references therein), by means of specific techniques of non-holonomic geometry. One of them is the systems of congruences method, developed by Gh. Vranceanu [44]. They considered global coordinates $(x^1, x^2, x^3, x^4, x^5) := (U, T, S, p, V)$ and they determined the respective curvature invariants (Riemann curvature, Ricci curvature, and scalar curvature) as rational functions of variables x^i, $i = \overline{1,5}$. This property eases the calculations, especially the integration of the geodesics system.

Remark 2. *An alternative and analogous method is to start from Equation (2). W.r.t. the new coordinates (G, p, S, T, V), we can obtain three analogous non-holonomic geometrizations with their corresponding Riemannian invariants. The change of coordinates is non-linear, but involves only rational functions; it follows that the previous curvature invariants are also rational functions, but of variables G, p, S, T, and V. General covariance laws establish correspondences between the curvature invariants, when calculated in these two systems of coordinates. This simple remark* might be important when, in applications, we want to consider the free energy instead of the internal energy of a system. From the theoretical viewpoint, these two formalisms associated to the equivalent forms of the Gibbs–Helmholtz Equations (2) and (3) lead to the same geometrization. This global object can be viewed, locally, in two different coordinate systems, with a "dictionary" between them.

Remark 3. Let $\mathfrak{V}$ be a domain in $\mathbb{R}^3$ of coordinates (p, G, V) (the "configurations space"). Then, the entropy function S in Formula (6) looks like a "Lagrangian" on $\mathfrak{V}$, i.e., $S: T\mathfrak{V} \to \mathbb{R}$, w.r.t. the temperature T, instead of w.r.t. time. Here, this "Lagrangian" similarity of the entropy is purely speculative, but it might be related to eventual hints in the literature (e.g., [55]).

We can determine, via formal Euler–Lagrange equations, the "stationary" curves of the system, of the form

$$T \to (p_0, G(T), V_0),$$

where both the pressure and the volume are constant. We do not enter this path, because this geometrization is also non-holonomic, even if the non-holonomy is better hidden behind the "velocities space" $T\mathfrak{V}$.

In the next section, we leave the realm of non-holonomic geometry and look for geometric properties of thermodynamic systems, with an *holonomic* associated model.

3. A Holonomic Geometrization for the GH Equation

With the previous notations, consider $\tilde{p}$ the temperature derivative of the pressure (also known as the thermal pressure coefficient [56]) and $\tilde{G}$ the heat (also known as thermal) capacity, i.e., the speed of the free energy w.r.t. T. (The notation for the heat capacity is not the usual one!) We can use Formula (6) in order to express the entropy as a function of $\tilde{p}$, $\tilde{G}$, and the volume, i.e., $S = S(\tilde{p}, \tilde{G}, V)$. Consider coordinates $(x^1, x^2, x^3) := (\tilde{p}, \tilde{G}, V)$ on an open subset $\mathfrak{U}$ of $\mathbb{R}^3$. The entropy function $S(x^1, x^2, x^3) = x^1 x^3 - x^2$ on $\mathfrak{U}$ defines a (regular, Monge-type, 3D) hypersurface in $\mathbb{R}^4$. The image of this parameterized hypersurface is a hyperquadric $\mathfrak{S}$, namely a special hypercylinder in $\mathbb{R}^4$. In Figure 1, one sees how the level sets of S foliate $\mathbb{R}^3$.

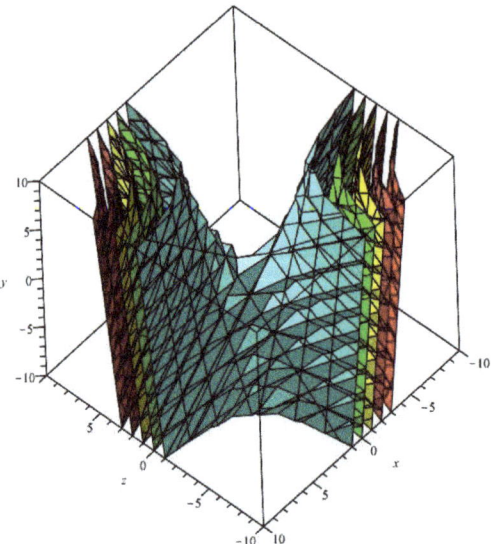

Figure 1. The level sets of S.

The first and the second fundamental forms of $\mathfrak{S}$ are, respectively,

$$(g_{ij})_{i,j=1,3} = \begin{pmatrix} 1+(x^3)^2 & -x^3 & x^1x^3 \\ -x^3 & 2 & -x^1 \\ x^1x^3 & -x^1 & 1+(x^1)^2 \end{pmatrix}, \tag{10}$$

$$(h_{ij})_{i,j=1,3} = a^{-1} \cdot \begin{pmatrix} 0 & 0 & -1 \\ 0 & 0 & 0 \\ -1 & 0 & 0 \end{pmatrix}, \tag{11}$$

where $a(x^1, x^3) := \sqrt{2 + (x^1)^2 + (x^3)^2}$. The unit normal vector field is

$$N = a^{-1} \cdot (x^3, -1, x^1, -1). \tag{12}$$

The mean curvature functions of $\mathfrak{S}$ are the coefficients of the characteristic polynomial of the second fundamental form w.r.t. the first fundamental form (Figure 2), namely

$$det(h_{ij} - tg_{ij}) = 0,$$

written

$$t^3 - 3H_1 t^2 + 3H_2 t - H_3 = 0.$$

We calculate

$$H_1 = \frac{6}{a^3} \cdot x^1 x^3, \ H_2 = -\frac{6}{a^4}, \ H_3 = 0. \tag{13}$$

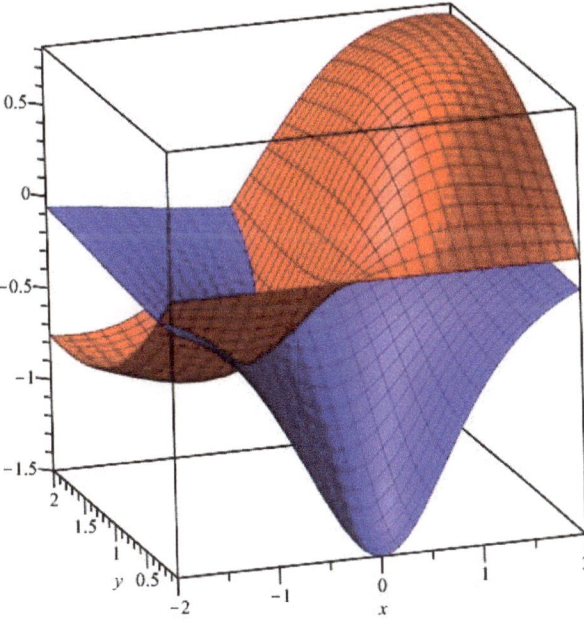

Figure 2. The first mean curvature function (red) and the second mean curvature function (blue). Notation: $x := x^1, y := x^3$.

We represent graphically, separately, the first two mean curvature functions, at large scale (only the $x^3 > 0$ zone must be retained from the graphics in Figures 3 and 4).

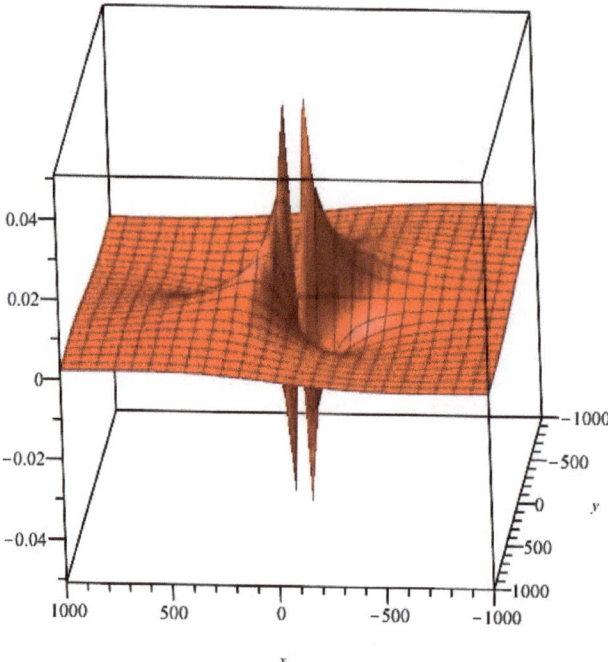

Figure 3. The first mean curvature function at large scale. Notation: $x := x^1, y := x^3$.

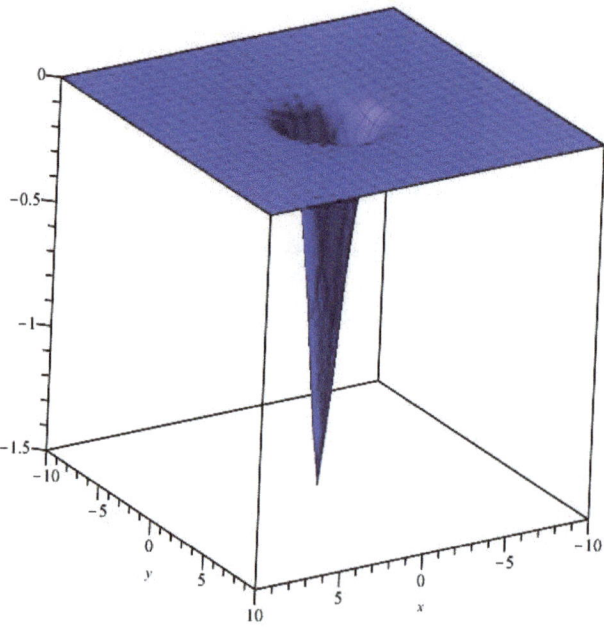

Figure 4. The second mean curvature function at large scale. Notation: $x := x^1, y := x^3$.

The roots of the previous characteristic polynomial are the principal curvature functions of $\mathfrak{S}$ (Figure 5). We calculate them:

$$\lambda_1 = \frac{1}{a^3} \cdot \left\{ x^1 x^3 + \sqrt{(2 + (x^1)^2)(2 + (x^3)^2)} \right\},$$

$$\lambda_2 = \frac{1}{a^3} \cdot \left\{ x^1 x^3 - \sqrt{(2 + (x^1)^2)(2 + (x^3)^2)} \right\},$$

$$\lambda_3 = 0.$$

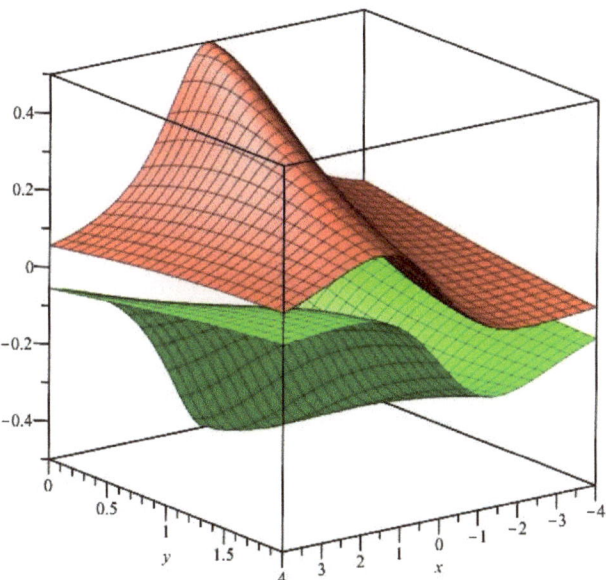

Figure 5. The first principal curvature function (red) and the second principal curvature function (green). Notation: $x := x^1$, $y := x^3$.

The mean curvature functions are symmetric expressions of the principal curvature functions. Together (and separately), they "control" the shape of the hypersurface $\mathfrak{S}$ and "measure" how much $\mathfrak{S}$ differs from a hyperplane in $\mathbb{R}^4$.

Proposition 1. *The hypersurface $\mathfrak{S}$ has the following properties:*

(i) *Its geometric invariants depend on x^1 and x^3 only.*
(ii) *It is not minimal, totally geodesic, or totally umbilical. Moreover, it has no umbilical points.*
(iii) *It has a null, a positive, and a negative smooth principal curvature function. The positive principal curvature function $\lambda_1 \leq \frac{\sqrt{2}}{2}$, with equality if and only if $x^3 = x^1 = 0$. The negative principal curvature function $\lambda_2 \geq -\frac{\sqrt{2}}{2}$, with equality if and only if $x^3 = x^1 = 0$.*
(iv) *It is asymptotically flat.*
(v) *There do not exist extremal values for H_1, which is unbounded around $(0,0)$; instead, $H_2 \leq 0$ and it has a global minimum $-\frac{3}{2}$ at $x^3 = x^1 = 0$.*

The intrinsic Riemannian geometry of $\mathfrak{S}$ can be derived from the first fundamental form only. The Riemannian manifold $(\mathfrak{S}, g)$ can be studied in an abstract way, by "forgetting" the embedding of $\mathfrak{S}$ as a hypersurface in $\mathbb{R}^4$. The (non-null) Christoffel symbols are

$$\Gamma^1_{13} = \Gamma^1_{31} = \frac{x^3}{a^2}, \ \Gamma^2_{13} = \Gamma^2_{31} = -\frac{1}{a^2}, \ \Gamma^3_{13} = \Gamma^3_{31} = \frac{x^1}{a^2}.$$

The geodesics are solutions of the following ODE system:

$$\frac{d^2x^i}{dt^2} + \Gamma^i_{jk}\frac{dx^j}{dt}\frac{dx^k}{dt} = 0, \ i = 1,2,3,$$

which may be written in detailed form:

$$\frac{d^2x^1}{dt^2} + \frac{2x^3}{a^2} \cdot \frac{dx^1}{dt} \cdot \frac{dx^3}{dt} = 0, \tag{14}$$

$$\frac{d^2x^2}{dt^2} - \frac{2}{a^2} \cdot \frac{dx^1}{dt} \cdot \frac{dx^3}{dt} = 0,$$

$$\frac{d^2x^3}{dt^2} + \frac{2x^1}{a^2} \cdot \frac{dx^1}{dt} \cdot \frac{dx^3}{dt} = 0.$$

Locally, the geodesics minimize the length of the curves with common ends. Globally, the geodesics behavior is related, in a subtle way, with curvature properties.

Remark 4. (i) By contrast with the mean and the principal curvature formulas, the previous ODE system depends (formally) on the variable x^2.

(ii) Any geodesic is uniquely determined by two initial conditions: the starting point and its velocity through it. Numerically solving ODE system (14), with initial conditions

$$x^1(0) = x^2(0) = x^3(0) = 1, \ \frac{dx^1}{dt}(0) = \frac{dx^3}{dt}(0) = 1, \ \frac{dx^2}{dt}(0) = 10,$$

and

$$x^1(0) = x^2(0) = x^3(0) = 1, \ \frac{dx^1}{dt}(0) = \frac{dx^3}{dt}(0) = 10, \ \frac{dx^2}{dt}(0) = 1,$$

respectively, produces the geodesics in Figures 6 and 7.

(iii) As the ODE system (14) is non-linear, integrating it for exact solutions is a difficult task. We consider only the non-degenerate geodesics. A general result in global Riemannian geometry assures us that all geodesics are complete ([57], p. 149, Cor.2.10). It follows that any two points of $\mathfrak{S}$ can be joined by a minimizing geodesic.

A first family of geodesics is of the form

$$x^1(t) = k_1 t + k_2, \ x^2(t) = k_3 t + k_4, \ x^3(t) = 0,$$

where k_1, k_2, k_3, and k_4 are arbitrary constants, with $(k_1)^2 + (k_3)^2 \neq 0$. Another analogous family of geodesics is

$$x^1(t) = 0, \ x^2(t) = k_5 t + k_6, \ x^3(t) = k_7 t + k_8,$$

where k_5, k_6, k_7, and k_8 are arbitrary constants, with $(k_5)^2 + (k_7)^2 \neq 0$.

Suppose $x^1 = x^1(t)$ and $x^3 = x^3(t)$ cannot be null on some open interval of the real line. Then, we have another family of geodesics, with $x^1 = x^3$; the function x^1 must satisfy an implicit equation of the form

$$x^1(t)\sqrt{(x^1(t))^2 + 1} + \ln\left(x^1(t) + \sqrt{(x^1(t))^2 + 1}\right) = k_9 t + k_{10},$$

where k_9, k_{10} are arbitrary constants. The second component of the geodesics can be recovered from the second equation in (14), as the anti-derivative

$$x^2(t) = \int \left\{ \int \left[\frac{1}{(x^1(t))^2 + 1} \cdot \left(\frac{dx^1}{dt}(t)\right)^2 \right] dt \right\} dt \ .$$

The variable x^2 will depend on two other arbitrary constants.

The two particular geodesics in Figures 6 and 7 (plotted after numerical integration) belong to this last family.

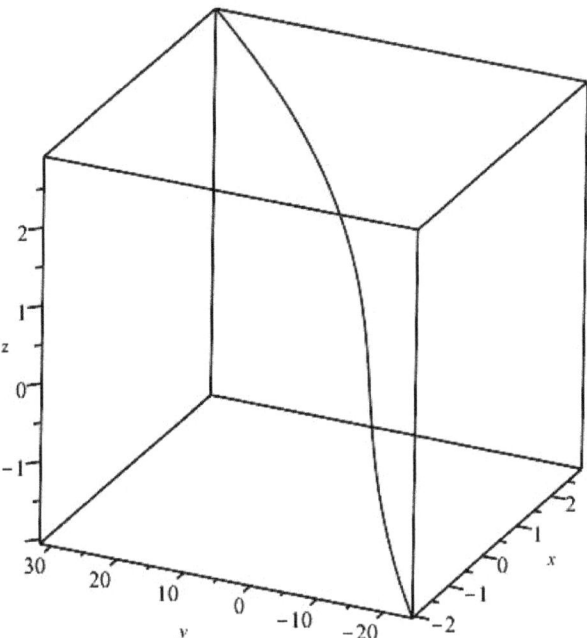

Figure 6. The first geodesic. Notation: $x := x^1, y := x^2, z := x^3$.

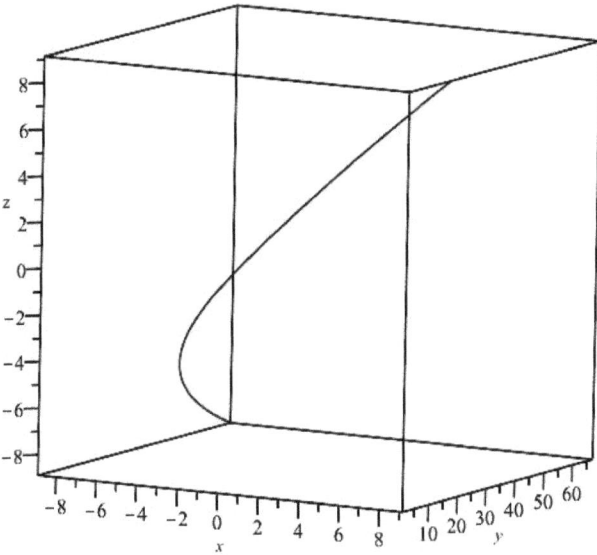

Figure 7. The second geodesic. Notation: $x := x^1, y := x^2, z := x^3$.

We calculate now the (non-null) (0,4)-Riemann curvature coefficients,

$$R_{1313} = -R_{1331} = -R_{3113} = R_{3131} = -\frac{1}{a^2},$$

the (non-null) Ricci coefficients,

$$Ric_{11} = -\frac{2+(x^3)^2}{a^4}, \; Ric_{13} = Ric_{31} = -\frac{x^1 x^3}{a^4}, \; Ric_{33} = -\frac{2+(x^1)^2}{a^4},$$

and the scalar curvature,

$$\rho = -\frac{4}{a^4}.$$

The scalar curvature function is "a trace of a trace" object, obtained by contracting the Riemann curvature tensor field twice. As a "mean of a mean", is contains information about how $\mathfrak{S}$ bends, but this information is somehow encoded twice. The eventual "reverse engineering" process is difficult; this is why finding Riemannian manifolds with prescribed properties of the scalar curvature functions is challenging.

Proposition 2. *The scalar curvature of $\mathfrak{S}$ is asymptotically flat, and is bounded $-1 \leq \rho < 0$. Its unique global minimum point is $(0,0,0)$ and $\rho(0,0,0) = -1$. Moreover, $\rho = \frac{2}{3} H_2$.*

Due to the last property, the graph of the scalar curvature is very similar to the graph of the second mean curvature, and we do not represent it in a separate figure. More interesting seems to be the foliation of $\mathbb{R}^3$ by its level sets, which are cylinders along the x^2 axis. Points on a fixed leaf correspond to thermodynamic measurements characterized by "linear/longitudinal" heat capacity (x^2) and "circular/transversal" thermal pressure (x^1) coefficient and volume (x^3).

It must be stressed that the geometry of $\mathfrak{S}$ may also have an interest per se; as stated previously, it is difficult to construct examples of Riemannian manifolds with prescribed properties of the scalar curvature function. In this case, the foliation by cylinders induced by the level sets of the scalar curvature provides exactly such a remarkable example (Figure 8).

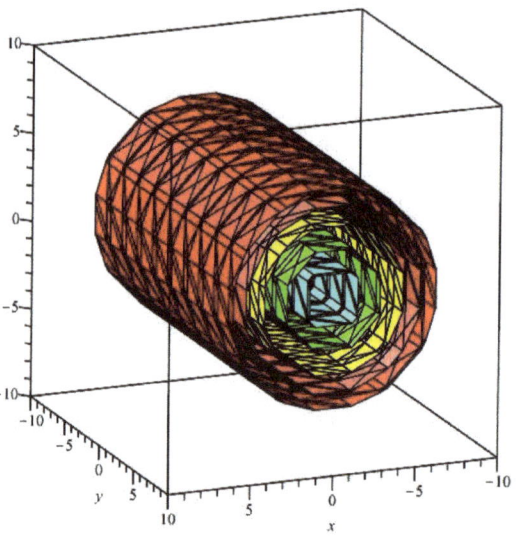

Figure 8. The level sets of ρ. Notation: $x := x^1, y := x^2, z := x^3$.

4. Characterization of the Equivalence between the GH Entropy and the BGS, the Tsallis, and the Kaniadakis Entropy

Consider a thermodynamical system as in Section 3. Let M be an open set in $\mathbb{R}^n$, $f = f(x,y)$ be a parameterized family of probability distributions (PDFs), $f : \mathfrak{U} \times M \to \mathbb{R}$, with $\int_{y \in M} f(x,y) dy = 1, f \geq 0$.

Postulate of entropy equivalence. *We suppose that the GH entropy coincides with the BGS entropy.* (For simpler calculations, the Boltzmann constant is normalized to 1).

This property is characterized by the following *equivalence equation*:

$$x^1 x^3 - x^2 + \int_{y \in M} f(x,y) \cdot \log f(x,y) dy = 0. \tag{15}$$

The first two terms describe the GH entropy (via the formalism in Section 3); the (minus) integral is the BGS entropy associated to f. This stochastic integral equation may be useful when we want to determine an unknown PDF f, suitable for a given thermodynamic model. It may act as a bridge between the classical (deterministic) setting and the statistical one.

Example 1. *Let*

$$\sigma(x) := \frac{1}{\sqrt{2\pi}} exp\left\{ x^1 x^3 - x^2 - \frac{1}{2} \right\} \tag{16}$$

and an arbitrary real valued function $\mu = \mu(x)$, defined on $\mathfrak{U}$. Consider the family of parameterized normal PDFs on the real line, given by

$$f(x,y) := \frac{1}{\sqrt{2\pi}\sigma(x)} exp\left\{ -\frac{1}{2}\left(\frac{y - \mu(x)}{\sigma(x)}\right)^2 \right\}. \tag{17}$$

A short calculation shows that f is a solution of Equation (15). We remark that the means may depend arbitrarily on the thermodynamic variables. Instead, the dispersion depends inversely proportionally on the GH entropy function.

Similar solutions of Equation (15) may be looked for w.r.t. other generalized logarithms, instead of the Neperian one. The next two examples use the Tsallis logarithm and the Kaniadakis logarithm, respectively.

Example 2. *We look for solutions for the equivalence equation*

$$x^1 x^3 - x^2 + \int_{y \in M} f(x,y) \cdot \log_q^T f(x,y) dy = 0, \tag{18}$$

which is the analogue of Equation (15), where the BGS entropy and the Neperian logarithm were replaced by the Tsallis entropy and the Tsallis q-logarithm ([41])

$$\log_q^T(z) := \frac{z^{1-q} - 1}{1 - q}, \, q \neq 1.$$

Suppose $q < 2$ and let

$$\sigma(x) := \frac{1}{\sqrt{2\pi}} (2-q)^{\frac{1}{2(q-1)}} \cdot \left[1 + (q-1)(x^1 x^3 - x^2)\right]^{\frac{1}{q-1}} \tag{19}$$

and an arbitrary real valued function $\mu = \mu(x)$, defined on $\mathfrak{U}$. Consider the family of parameterized normal PDFs on the real line, given by (17). One verifies easily, by a direct calculation, that f is a solution of Equation (18). We remark that the means may depend arbitrarily on the thermodynamic variables. The dispersion depends on the GH entropy function in a more subtle way than in Example 1.

When $q \geq 2$, some (entropy) integrals in (18) may become divergent and the previous reasoning does not work anymore.

Example 3. *We look now for solutions for the equivalence equation*

$$x^1 x^3 - x^2 + \int_{y \in M} f(x,y) \cdot \log_k^K f(x,y) dy = 0, \tag{20}$$

which is the analogue of Equation (15), where the BGS entropy and the Neperian logarithm were replaced by the Kaniadakis entropy and the Kaniadakis k-logarithm ([41])

$$\log_k^K(z) := \frac{z^k - z^{-k}}{2k}, \ k \in (-1,1), \ k \neq 0.$$

Consider

$$\sigma(x) := \frac{1}{\sqrt{2\pi}} \cdot \left\{ \frac{k\sqrt{1-k^2}(x^1 x^3 - x^2) + \sqrt{k^2(1-k^2)(x^1 x^3 - x^2)^2 + \sqrt{1-k^2}}}{\sqrt{1+k}} \right\}^{\frac{1}{k}} \tag{21}$$

and an arbitrary real valued function $\mu = \mu(x)$, *defined on* $\mathfrak{U}$. *Consider the family of parameterized normal PDFs on the real line, given by (17). A similar calculation proves f is a solution of Equation (20). We remark that the means may depend arbitrarily on the thermodynamic variables. The dispersion depends on the GH entropy function, but in a more complicated way than in Examples 1 and 2.*

Remark 5. *(i) The previous three examples suggest the following natural question: Which are the families of PDFs F (not necessarily normal !) and the generalized "logarithms"* φ *([41]), such that*

$$x^1 x^3 - x^2 + \int_{y \in M} F(x,y) \cdot \varphi(F(x,y)) dy = 0 \ ? \tag{22}$$

This equation establishes the equivalence of the thermodynamic entropy given by the first two terms and the (statistical) generalized entropy associated to the generalized "logarithm" φ. *Solving it is much more difficult, as the unknowns are both deterministic* (φ) *and stochastic (F).*

In a previous remark, we explained why we consider only the classical GH equation, and not a generalized one. In the case of generalized GH equations, the first two terms in (22) are to be replaced by another expression in, eventually, more generalized coordinates (corresponding to more thermodynamic state functions and possibly other statistical quantities). The nature of the problem remains unchanged; all complications arise only as a consequence of the complexity of calculations in a space with more dimensions.

(ii) Recently ([52,53]), Gao at al. proved that, under three specific assumptions (of physical inspiration), the only PDF in which the GBS entropy equals the (classical) thermodynamic entropy is the generalized Boltzmann distribution (i.e., a distribution of exponential type). A hint points out that the result may be extended to include the Tsallis entropy as well. This remarkable result gives a partial answer to problem (22).

However, the three assumptions of Gao significantly restrict (from the mathematical perspective) the framework, and weaker hypotheses are desirable. Moreover, hidden necessary conditions exist behind Equation (22), such as the extensivity property; it follows that the thermodynamic entropy and the statistic entropy (equal to the previous one) must be both extensive or both non-extensive (e.g., for the Tsallis and Kaniadakis entropies [58]).

(iii) We must make a clarification of terminology. Common language identifies "entropy" as a functional $E = E[f]$ *defined of the set of PDFs, with "entropy" as a specific value* $E[f_0]$ *of this functional. (At a more elementary level, this happens when we speak about "the function sint", instead of "the function sin").*

Denote the BGS, the Tsallis, and the Kaniadakis entropy functionals with E^{BGS}, E^T, *and* E^K, *respectively. Denote by* f_{BGS}, f_T, f_K *the parameterized families of PDFs obtained in the three previous examples. We showed that the thermodynamic entropy* $S = S(x)$ *coincides (as a function of x) with* $E^{BGS}[f_{BGS}(\cdot, y)]$, $E^T[f_T(\cdot, y)]$ *and* $E^K[f_K(\cdot, y)]$. *This does not mean that S (which is a function!*) *coincides with the functionals (!)* E^{BGS}, E^T, E^K. *This is the true meaning of the equivalence stated in (15) and (22).*

Remark 6. *Denote* $f = f(x,y)$ *a family of PDFs on* $\mathfrak{U} \times M$, φ *a generalized logarithm [59] and*

$$H[f](x) := -\int_{y \in M} F(x,y) \cdot \varphi(F(x,y)) dy \tag{23}$$

a parameterized family of arbitrary generalized entropy functionals. In particular, φ may be any of the Neperian, the Kaniadakis, or the Tsallis logarithms previously considered. Denote $g^{H,f}$ a Riemannian generalized Fisher metric on $\mathfrak{U}$, canonically associated to H and f [41].

The thermodynamic entropy S is called metrically equivalent with the entropy $H[f]$ if the first fundamental form g in (10) coincides with $g^{H,f}$. Variants may include the following:

- *g and $g^{H,f}$ are homothetic;*
- *g and $g^{H,f}$ are conformal;*
- *g and $g^{H,f}$ are in geodesic correspondence.*

The new "equivalence problem" can now be stated: Find H and f such that S is metrically equivalent with $H[f]$.

This equivalence of entropies is not more general than the previous one in (22), nor an extension or a particularization of it; it is of a different nature, a kind of intermediate equivalence by means of derived objects. The equivalence in (22) and the "metrical equivalence" are logically unrelated. We do not enter into further detail here, as the study requires the whole machinery behind the generalized Fisher metrics [41].

5. Thermodynamic Interpretations and Applications

The previous sections were more mathematically oriented. Now, we will focus on some physical interpretations of the holonomic model from Sections 3 and 4. Because our claims may seem too speculative to some physicists, we encourage criticism and reasoned rebuttals.

(i) First, we remark that we use somehow atypical variables, as coordinates for the "space of configurations" $\mathfrak{U}$ (in addition to the volume x^3, which is commonly and frequently used), namely the thermal pressure coefficient x^1 and the thermal capacity x^2. However, even if these variables/observables are less common in the literature, they are not completely absent (e.g., [60,61]).
As a consequence, the results and the conclusions we obtained are not covariant, because they rest in an essential manner on the particular chosen coordinates system.

(ii) The intrinsic geometry and the extrinsic geometry of the hypersurface $\mathfrak{S}$ do not depend on the variable x^2, so they are independent of the heat capacity $\tilde{G}$. Instead, the set properties of this hypersurface depend on x^2. The hypersurface $\mathfrak{S}$ may have set theoretic or differential properties which cannot be explained geometrically.
On another hand, a challenging question is the following: What thermodynamical properties may be characterized through intrinsic properties of $\mathfrak{S}$ and what through extrinsic ones? For example, as remarked previously, optimal paths joining two given states can be modeled as geodesics, which are intrinsic objects.

(iii) Our formalism may be useful when one develops a calculus on the hypersurface $\mathfrak{S}$, for example, by taking higher-order derivatives of the pressure w.r.t. temperature (see [62] for second-order ones). Geometrization of higher-order derivatives involves, in general, the use of fiber bundles over a manifold; here, the holonomy of the model proves again its superiority over an eventual non-holonomic model, where the manifold machinery is weaker.

(iv) Translations can be made between geometric and physical properties. For example, the only points where the first mean curvature function H_1 vanishes are the critical points for the pressure function (w.r.t. the temperature); the minimum value for H_2

and the "unbounded" behavior of H_1 arise only for extreme physical conditions (very small volume and thermal pressure coefficient).

The level sets for the entropy function S (see Figure 1) have deep physical meaning. We look for their intersection with the level sets of the scalar curvature function ρ (see Figure 8), which have interesting mathematical meaning. Namely, let $R \geq \sqrt{2}$ and a be a real constant. Consider the points $(x, S(x)) \in \mathfrak{S}$, such that

$$S(x) = a, \quad \rho(x) = -\frac{4}{R^2 + 2}.$$

The intersection curve of the two level sets satisfies the system of two implicit equations and an inequation

$$x^1 x^3 - x^2 = a, \quad (x^1)^2 + (x^3)^2 = R^2, \quad x^3 > 0.$$

There exists a unique $\theta \in (0, \pi)$, such that

$$x^1 = R\cos\theta, \quad x^2 = \frac{1}{2}R^2 \sin 2\theta - a, \quad x^3 = R\sin\theta.$$

The parameterized intersection curve $\theta \to (R\cos\theta, \frac{1}{2}R^2 \sin 2\theta - a, R\sin\theta)$ has the graph in Figure 9.

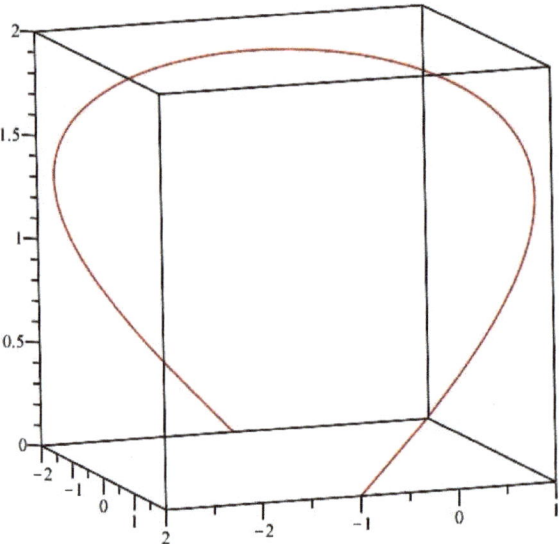

Figure 9. The intersection of the two level sets.

The second coordinate of the intersection curve (which corresponds to the heat capacity $\tilde{G}$ restricted along the intersection curve) suggests a point

$$(\frac{1}{2}R^2 \cos 2\theta, \frac{1}{2}R^2 \sin 2\theta - a),$$

situated on a virtual circle of center $(0, -a)$ and radius $\frac{R^2}{2}$. Formally, we denote $\tilde{G}^d := \frac{1}{2}R^2 \cos 2\theta$ and call it *the mate heat capacity along the intersection curve*. The following formula holds:

$$(\tilde{G}^d)^2 + (\tilde{G}^2 + a)^2 = \frac{1}{4}R^4.$$

We do not know if this quantity can be extended to a (formal, speculative, and exotic) new state variable; anyhow, it has an interesting intrinsic interpretation.

(v) The parameterized PDFs, which arise as solutions of the special stochastic equations in Section 4, are encountered in the literature, in different frameworks (see, for example, [63]). Moreover, the geometrization of such parameter spaces leads to the study of statistical manifolds and of Fisher-like Riemannian metrics in information geometry (see [39–41] and reference therein).

(vi) The ODE system (14) allows the determination of the geodesics lying on the hypersurface $\mathfrak{S}$. As pointed out in Remark 4 (iii), any geodesic local minimizes the arc length between two points, which can be interpreted as two events in the space of thermodynamic states x^1, x^2, x^3, and S. We have here a possible control tool, useful to "drive" a thermodynamic engine from a starting state to a nearby final state.

More precisely, consider the "state" in $\mathfrak{S}$ at time t_0, characterized by $\tilde{p}(t_0), \tilde{G}(t_0), V(t_0)$ and $S(t_0)$. We want to reach the "state" $(A, B, C, S(A, B, C)) \in \mathfrak{S}$, by the "shortest" path. Remark 4, (iii) ensures us that there exists a unique "minimal" geodesic

$$\gamma = \gamma(t) : [t_0, t_0 + b] \to \mathfrak{S}, \ \gamma(t_0) = (\tilde{p}(t_0), \tilde{G}(t_0), V(t_0), S(t_0)), \tag{24}$$

such that $\gamma(t_0 + b) = (A, B, C, S(A, B, C))$. Here, "minimal" refers to the Riemannian distance w.r.t. the first fundamental form, not to the Euclidean distance (as the coordinates are not position coordinates). In practice, the geodesic γ must be determined numerically, from (14).

Such an approach is, of course, determined/limited by the choice we made, by the particular Riemannian geometry we found on $\mathfrak{S}$. There exist other alternative Riemannian metrics with similar claims ([64–66]), associated to the GH equation, and a comparison of their practical efficiency and relevance deserves another detailed study.

(vii) The maximum entropy (MaxEnt) problem is a fundamental area of investigation in Statistical Mechanics and information theory. Its classical thermodynamics counterpart is less studied and, in any case, with totally different tools ([67], Ch.5); mathematical optimization with non-holonomic constraints is a difficult theory, which emerged only recently (see [68–70] and references therein).

Our holonomic geometrization allows a direct study, with geometric visualization, of (thermodynamic) entropy fluctuations, including extremum points, on subsets of the hypersurface $\mathfrak{S}$.

(viii) The geometric model in Section 3 does not take into account the (eventual) positiveness of the entropy. Such an additional condition, if necessary, restricts the framework to an open set of $\mathfrak{U}$.

(ix) Like other fundamental equations in physics, the GH equation does not remain valid outside "normal conditions", for example, for long-range interactions. Our holonomic model in Section 4 can be refined to cover scale fluctuations. As the coordinates we use are not the "spatial" ones, the Euclidean distance r (such as the length of the position vector field in spherical coordinates) no longer has applicability. We replace the r-scale by the V-scale, because there is a direct (nonlinear) proportionality between them.

Let $\nu : (0, \infty) \to (0, \infty)$ be a smooth function, strictly increasing, with the following properties:

$$\lim_{t \to \infty} \nu(t) = \infty, \ \lim_{t \to 0} \nu(t) = 0.$$

Obviously, there exists a unique t_0 such that $\nu(t_0) = 1$. Relevant examples are $\nu(t) = t^\alpha$, for a fixed positive α; $\nu(t) = a^{t^b} - 1$, for fixed positive b and $a > 1$.

Consider the ν-GH equation

$$dG + S^{(\nu)} \cdot dT - \nu(V) \cdot dp = 0.$$

We derive the formula for the *ν-entropy*

$$S^{(\nu)} = \nu(V) \cdot \tilde{p} - \tilde{G}.$$

In particular, for $\nu = id$, we obtain $S = S^{(id)}$ and we recover Formula (6).

By analogy with the computations in Section 3, we obtain a hypersurface $\mathfrak{S}^{(\nu)}$, we derive a first fundamental form $g^{(\nu)}$, a second fundamental form $h^{(\nu)}$, the mean curvature functions, the principal curvature functions, and the scalar curvature function, and we can write the equations of the geodesics.

Each member of this infinite family of models "parameterized" by ν deserves a similar study as those in Sections 4 and 5. The techniques will be similar but with distinctive outcomes. At "infinity" will dominate the long-range interactions with specific (local) entropies; near "zero", for tiny-range interactions, we shall obtain different specific entropies.

(x) The non-holonomic character of the Gibbs–Helmholtz Equation (2) (or its equivalent counterpart (1)) obstructs the description of solutions as global integral hypersurfaces in $\mathbb{R}^5$. Moreover, the versatility of the theromdynamics formalism and "idioms" hides an apparent paradox; the phase functions G, p, S, T, V depend on each other, but, when considered as coordinates, they are supposed to be independent. This is why, in the literature, one often uses a *particular* (and implicit) case; the Gibbs internal energy G is supposed to be a function of the temperature and pressure only, i.e., $G = G(p, T)$. This loss of generality seems a fair price to pay, but (unfortunately) there are more hidden additional "taxes". For example, from (2) and (6), one derives $S = -\frac{\partial G}{\partial T}$ and $\frac{\partial p}{\partial T} = 0$; it follows that the thermal pressure coefficient $\tilde{p}$ is always null!

Of course, all our previous results work also in the special case $G = G(p, T)$, where they are significantly simplified.

6. Discussion

The first part of the paper contains a short incursion into the realm of non-holonomic geometrizations of GH equations. We did not intend to develop this path, because comparing the possible approaches and further studies would take too much space. This may be an interesting project for the future. The same remark is valid for an eventual critical study about the pros and the cons of the non-holonomic modelization, when compared to the holonomic one.

The results in Section 4 originate in our belief that entropy must be described in a unified way in Classical Thermodynamics, as in statistical mechanics or information theory. We avoided the temptation to postulate it firmly, because we are aware that this hypothesis might look too speculative, from the viewpoint of both theoretical or applied scientists. Our mathematical results are expressed in a neutral approach, leaving open doors toward unlimited future conclusions. The powerful local and global differential geometric tools and, especially, the Riemannian machinery, may bring new insights concerning the abstract "phase spaces" from thermodynamics. A more ambitious goal would be a (differential geometry-based) "Grand Unifying Theory" for thermodynamics, to include the non-holonomic models for the GH equation, the holonomic ones (as such in Section 3), and—eventually—the statistical manifolds approach [39,40].

In addition to the content of Sections 4 and 5, more physical interpretations are needed, in order to confirm or to reject our claims. We must investigate if our speculative ideas correspond not only to (possible) "gedanken experiments", but also to real life thermodynamic systems with significant applications. For example, it would be interesting to know if the geodesic movement on the hypersurface $\mathfrak{S}$ corresponds to the most efficient path into the "phase space" of a thermodynamic system.

Developments may include solving the analogue of Equations (15), (18), and (20), for other remarkable families of entropies (Renyi, Sharma–Taneja–Mittal, Naudts, etc). New examples are needed, in addition to the PDF solutions of normal type ([71–74]).

Rethinking the basic thermodynamics postulates may, in particular, impose restrictions on the "equivalence problem" for entropy and forbid some PDFs to be solutions.

Equations (7)–(9) can be used in order to construct similar holonomic geometrizations of the GH equation. In these cases, one needs a completely different approach to characterize the equivalence of the GH entropy and entropies from statistical mechanics (BGS, Tsallis, Kaniadakis, etc). Instead of the "simple" stochastic integral equivalence in Equations (17), (20), and (22), one presumably will obtain more complicated stochastic functional and integral equivalence equations.

We restricted our study to the physics domain, but we must stress that there exists another active field of research, which translates (via a specific dictionary) the thermodynamical notions and results into economic ones [49–51,75,76]. For example, the internal energy, the temperature, and the pressure are translated to the growth potential, the internal politics stability, and the price level, respectively; the entropy conserves its meaning. All the contents of our paper have a direct correspondence within this economic theory, which remains to be more precisely developed in a future paper.

In several places in the paper, we emphasized the multitude of Riemannian geometries which can be associated, in various ways, to holonomic or to non-holonomic models for the GH equation. There exist at least two tools to compare any two such geometries. The first one is by means of the deformation algebra associated to the Levi–Civita connections of the respective Riemannian metrics (see [77] and references therein). The second one is the geodesic correspondence, which eventually occurs between two Riemannian manifolds and can translate the geodesic dynamics from one space into the other (see, for example, [78]). The comparison results are important in differential geometry, as they establish sufficient (and sometimes also necessary) conditions, in order that a "space" be homeomorphic, diffeomorphic, isometric, conformal, etc., with a standard one (for example, a plane or a sphere). The deformation results establish "how far" a "space" is from a standard one.

7. Conclusions

The paper reviews some known non-holonomic geometric tools and develops some new holonomic ones, in order to model the solutions of the Gibbs–Helmholtz equation from thermodynamics. Beyond the mathematical results, at the border of differential geometry with statistics, we make some speculative claims about possible applications in physics and in information theory. The key notion is the use of entropy, through both the classical and the statistical approaches. This combined study is facilitated by the choice of a new coordinate system in the phase space $\mathbb{R}^4$, parameterizing the entropy as a function depending on the thermal pressure coefficient, the heat capacity, and the volume.

Author Contributions: Conceptualization, C.-L.P., I.-E.H., G.-T.P. and V.P.; methodology, C.-L.P., I.-E.H., G.-T.P. and V.P.; validation, C.-L.P., I.-E.H., G.-T.P. and V.P.; writing—original draft preparation, C.-L.P., I.-E.H., G.-T.P. and V.P.; writing—review and editing, C.-L.P., I.-E.H., G.-T.P. and V.P.; visualization, C.-L.P., I.-E.H., G.-T.P. and V.P. All authors have read and agreed to the published version of the manuscript.

Funding: This research received no external funding.

Data Availability Statement: No new data were created.

Acknowledgments: The authors dedicate this paper to the memory of their teacher and colleague, Liviu Constantin Nicolescu (1940–2023), professor emeritus at the University of Bucharest.

Conflicts of Interest: The authors declare no conflict of interest.

References

1. Akih-Kumgeh, B. Toward Improved Understanding of the Physical Meaning of Entropy in Classical Thermodynamics. *Entropy* **2016**, *18*, 270. [CrossRef]
2. Ansermet, J.-P.; Brechet, S.D. *Principles of Thermodynamics*; Cambridge University Press: Cambridge, UK, 2019.
3. Atkins, P. *The Laws of Thermodynamics: A Very Short Introduction*; Oxford University Press: Oxford, UK, 2010.
4. Popovic, M.E. Research in Entropy Wonderland: A Review of the Entropy Concept. *Therm. Sci.* **2018**, *22*, 1163–1178. [CrossRef]

5. Saggion, A.; Faraldo, R.; Pierno, M. *Thermodynamics*; Springer: Cham, Switzerland, 2019.
6. Mander, P. Available online: https://carnotcycle.wordpress.com/ (accessed on 13 September 2023).
7. Bawden, D.; Robinson, L. "A few exciting words": Information and entropy revisited. *J. Assoc. Inf. Sci. Technol.* **2015**, *66*, 1965–1987. [CrossRef]
8. Flores Camacho, F.; Ulloa Lugo, N.; Covarrubias Martınez, H. The concept of entropy, from its origins to teachers. *Rev. Mex. Fis.* **2015**, *61*, 69–80.
9. Carnap, R. *Two Essays on Entropy*; University of California Press: Berkeley, CA, USA; Los Angeles, CA, USA, 1977.
10. Dieks, D. Is There a Unique Physical Entropy? Micro Versus Macro. In *New Challenges to Philosophy of Science. The Philosophy of Science in a European Perspective*; Andersen, H., Dieks, D., Gonzalez, W., Uebel, T., Wheeler, G., Eds.; Springer: Dordrecht, The Netherlands, 2013; Volume 4.
11. Feistel, R. Distinguishing between Clausius, Boltzmann and Pauling Entropies of Frozen Non-Equilibrium States. *Entropy* **2019**, *21*, 799. [CrossRef]
12. Gaudenzi, R. Entropy? Exercices de Style. *Entropy* **2019**, *21*, 742. [CrossRef]
13. Gujrati, P.A. On Equivalence of Nonequilibrium Thermodynamic and Statistical Entropies. *Entropy* **2015**, *17*, 710–754. [CrossRef]
14. Jauch, J.M.; Baron, J.G. Entropy, Information and Szilard's Paradox. *Helv. Phys. Acta* **1972**, *45*, 220–232.
15. Jaynes, E.T. Gibbs vs. Boltzmann Entropies. *Am. J. Phys.* **1965**, *33*, 391–398. [CrossRef]
16. Kostic, M.M. The Elusive Nature of Entropy and Its Physical Meaning. *Entropy* **2014**, *16*, 953–967. [CrossRef]
17. Lynskey, M.J. An Overview of the Physical Concept of Entropy. *J. Glob. Media Stud.* **2019**, *25*, 1–16.
18. Majernik, V. Entropy-A Universal Concept in Sciences. *Nat. Sci.* **2014**, *6*, 552–564. [CrossRef]
19. Maroney, O.J.E. The Physical Basis of the Gibbs-von Neumann entropy. *arXiv* **2008**, arXiv:0701127v2.
20. Marques, M.S.; Santana, W.S. What is entropy?—Reflections for science teaching. *Res. Soc. Dev.* **2020**, *9*, e502974344. [CrossRef]
21. Plastino, A.; Curado, E.M.F. Equivalence between maximum entropy principle and enforcing $dU = TdS$. *Phys. Rev.* **2005**, *72*, 047103.
22. Prunkl, C.E.A.; Timpson, C.G. Black Hole Entropy is Thermodynamic Entropy. *arXiv* **2019**, arXiv:1903.06276v1.
23. Prunkl, C. On the Equivalence of von Neumann and Thermodynamic Entropy. *Philos. Sci.* **2020**, *87*, 262–280. [CrossRef]
24. Serdyukov, S.I. Macroscopic Entropy of Non-Equilibrium Systems and Postulates of Extended Thermodynamics: Application to Transport Phenomena and Chemical Reactions in Nanoparticles. *Entropy* **2018**, *20*, 802. [CrossRef]
25. Swendsen, R.H. Thermodynamics, Statistical Mechanics and Entropy. *Entropy* **2017**, *19*, 603. [CrossRef]
26. Wallace, D. Gravity, Entropy, and Cosmology: In Search of Clarity. *Br. J. Philos. Sci.* **2010**, *61*, 513–540. [CrossRef]
27. Werndl, C.; Frigg, R. Entropy: A guide for the perplexed. In *Probabilities in Physics*; Beisbart, C., Hartmann, S., Eds.; Oxford University Press: Oxford, UK, 2011; pp. 115–142.
28. Badescu, V. *Modeling Thermodynamic Distance, Curvature and Fluctuations: A Geometric Approach*; Springer: Cham, Switzerland, 2016.
29. Bravetti, A. Contact Hamiltonian Dynamics: The Concept and Its Use. *Entropy* **2017**, *19*, 535. [CrossRef]
30. Entov, M.; Polterovich, L. Contact topology and non-equilibrium thermodynamics. *Nonlinearity* **2023**, *36*, 3349. [CrossRef]
31. Geiges, H. A Brief History of Contact Geometry and Topology. *Expo. Math.* **2001**, *19*, 25–53. [CrossRef]
32. Ghosh, A.; Bhamidipati, C. Contact geometry and thermodynamics of black holes in AdS spacetimes. *Phys. Rev. D* **2019**, *100*, 126020. [CrossRef]
33. Grmela, M. Contact Geometry of Mesoscopic Thermodynamics and Dynamics. *Entropy* **2014**, *16*, 1652–1686. [CrossRef]
34. Kholodenko, A.L. *Applications of Contact Geometry and Topology in Physics*; World Science Press: Singapore, 2013.
35. Kycia, R.A.; Ulan, M.; Schneider, E. *Nonlinear PDEs, Their Geometry, and Applications*; Springer: Cham, Switzerland, 2019.
36. Mrugala, R. On contact and metric structures on thermodynamic spaces. *Rims Kokyuroku* **2000**, *1142*, 167–181.
37. Schneider, E. Differential Invariants of Measurements, and Their Relation to Central Moments. *Entropy* **2020**, *22*, 1118. [CrossRef]
38. Simoes, A.A.; de Leon, M.; Valcazar, M.L.; de Diego, D.M. Contact geometry for simple thermodynamical systems with friction. *Proc. R. Soc. A* **2020**, *476*, 20200244. [CrossRef]
39. Hirica, I.E.; Pripoae, C.L.; Pripoae, G.T.; Preda, V. Affine differential control tools for statistical manifolds. *Mathematics* **2021**, *9*, 1654. [CrossRef]
40. Hirica, I.-E.; Pripoae, C.-L.; Pripoae, G.-T.; Preda, V. Conformal Control Tools for Statistical Manifolds and for g-Manifolds. *Mathematics* **2022**, *10*, 1061. [CrossRef]
41. Hirica I.-E.; Pripoae C.-L.; Pripoae, G.-T.; Preda, V. Weighted Relative Group Entropies and Associated Fisher Metrics. *Entropy* **2022**, *24*, 120. [CrossRef]
42. Nicolescu, L.; Pripoae, G.T. Gheorghe Vrănceanu—Successor of Gheorghe Țițeica at the geometry chair of the University of Bucharest. *Balkan J. Geom. Appl.* **2005**, *10*, 11–20.
43. Vranceanu, G. Les espaces non holonomes. *Mémorial Des Sci. Math.* **1936**, *76*, 70.
44. Vranceanu, G. *Leçons de Géométrie Différentielle*; Éditions de l' Académie de la République Populaire Roumaine: Bucharest, Romania, 1936.
45. Katsurada, Y. On the theory of non-holonomic systems in the Finsler space. *Tohoku Math. J.* **1951**, *2*, 140–148. [CrossRef]
46. Udriste, C. *Geometric Dynamics*; Kluwer Academic Publication: Dordrecht, Germany, 2000.
47. Stamin, C.; Udriste, C. Nonholonomic geometry of Gibbs contact structure. *U.P.B. Sci. Bull. Series A* **2010**, *72*, 153–170.
48. Stamin, C.; Udriste, C. Nonholonomic Gibbs hypersurface. *B Proc.* **2009**, *17*, 218–228.

49. Udriste, C.; Tevy, I.; Ferrara, M. Nonholonomic Economic Systems. In *Extrema with Nonholonomic Constraints*; Udriste, C., Dogaru, O., Tevy, I., Eds.; Geometry Balkan Press: Bucharest, Romania, 2002; pp. 139–150.
50. Udriste, C.; Ferrara, M.; Opris, D. *Economic Geometric Dynamics*; Geometry Balkan Press: Bucharest, Romania, 2004.
51. Udriste, C.; Ciancio, A. Interactions of nonholonomic economic systems. In Proceedings of the 3rd International Colloquium "Mathematics in Engineering and Numerical Physics", Bucharest, Romania, 7–9 October 2004; Balkan Society of Geometers, Geometry Balkan Press: Bucharest, Romania, 2005; pp. 299–303.
52. Gao, X.; Gallicchio, E.; Roitberg, A.E. The generalized Boltzmann distribution is the only distribution in which the Gibbs-Shannon entropy equals the thermodynamic entropy. *J. Chem. Phys.* **2019**, *151*, 034113. [CrossRef] [PubMed]
53. Gao, X. The Mathematics of the Ensemble Theory. *Results Phys.* **2022**, *34*, 105230. [CrossRef]
54. Blankschtein, D. *Lectures in Classical Thermodynamics with an Introduction to Statistical Mechanics*; Springer: Cham, Switzerland, 2020.
55. Haszpra, T.; Tel, T. Topological Entropy: A Lagrangian Measure of the State of the Free Atmosphere. *J. Atmos. Sci.* **2013**, *70*, 4030–4040. [CrossRef]
56. Abdulagatov, I.M.; Magee, J.W.; Polikhronidi, N.G.; Batyrova, R.G. Internal Pressure and Internal Energy of Saturated and Compressed Phases. In *Enthalpy and Internal Energy: Liquids, Solutions and Vapours*; Wilhelm, E., Letcher, T., Eds.; Royal Society of Chemistry: Cambridge, UK, 2017; pp. 411–446.
57. do Carmo, M.P. *Riemannian Geometry*; Birkhäuser: Boston, MA, USA, 1993.
58. Umarov, S.; Tsallis, C. *Mathematical Foundations of Nonextensive Statistical Mechanics*; World Scientific Press: Singapore, 2022.
59. Clenshaw, C.W.; Lozier, D.W.; Olver, F.W.J.; Turner, P.R. Generalized exponential and logarithmic functions. *Comput. Math. Appl. B* **1986**, *12*, 1091–1101. [CrossRef]
60. Chen, Y.; Li, K.; Xie, Z.Y.; Yu, J.F. Cross derivative of the Gibbs free energy: A universal and efficient method for phase transitions in classical spin models. *Phys. Rev.* **2020**, *101*, 165123. [CrossRef]
61. Liu, Y.; Liu, Y.; Drew, M.G.B. Relationship between heat capacities derived by different but connected approaches. *Am. J. Phys.* **2020**, *88*, 51–59. [CrossRef]
62. Ahlers, G. Temperature Derivative of the Pressure of ^4He at the Superfluid Transition. *J. Low Temp. Phys.* **1972**, *7*, 361–364. [CrossRef]
63. Elnaggar, M.S.; Kempf, A. Equivalence of Partition Functions Leads to Classification of Entropies and Means. *Entropy* **2012**, *14*, 1317–1342. [CrossRef]
64. Cafaro, C.; Luongo, O.; Mancini, S.; Quevedo, H. Thermodynamic length, geometric efficiency and Legendre invariance. *Phys. Stat. Mech. Appl.* **2022**, *590*, 126740. [CrossRef]
65. Scandi, M.; Perarnau-Llobet, M. Thermodynamic length in open quantum systems. *Quantum* **2019**, *3*, 197. [CrossRef]
66. Zulkowski, P.R.; Sivak, D.A.; Crooks, G.E.; DeWeese, M.R. Geometry of thermodynamic control. *Phys. Rev. E* **2012**, *86*, 041148. [CrossRef]
67. Harte, J. *Maximum Entropy and Ecology: A Theory of Abundance, Distribution, and Energetics*; Oxford University Press: Oxford, UK, 2011.
68. Lucia, U.; Grisolia, G. Non-holonomic constraints: Considerations on the least action principle also from a thermodynamic viewpoint. *Results Phys.* **2023**, *48*, 106429. [CrossRef]
69. Udriste, C.; Dogaru, O.; Ferrara, M.; Țevy, I. Nonholonomic Optimization. In *Recent Advances in Optimization*; Lecture Notes in Economics and Mathematical Systems; Seeger, A., Ed.; Springer: Berlin/Heidelberg, Germany, 2006; Volume 563, pp. 119–132.
70. Yoshimura, H.; Gay-Balmaz, F. Hamiltonian variational formulation for nonequilibrium thermodynamics of simple closed systems. *IFAC Pap. Online* **2022**, *55*, 81–85. [CrossRef]
71. Drăgan, M. Some general Gompertz and Gompertz-Makeham life expectancy models. *Analele Stiintifice Univ. Ovidius Mat.* **2022**, *30*, 117–142.
72. Iatan, I.; Drăgan, M.; Dedu, S.; Preda, V. Using Probabilistic Models for Data Compression. *Mathematics* **2022**, *10*, 3847. [CrossRef]
73. Suter, F.; Cernat, I.; Drăgan, M. Some Information Measures Properties of the GOS-Concomitants from the FGM Family. *Entropy* **2022**, *24*, 1361. [CrossRef] [PubMed]
74. Văduva, I.; Drăgan, M. On the simulation of Some Particular Discrete Distributions. *Rewiev Air Force Acad.* **2018**, *16*, 17–30. [CrossRef]
75. Ferrara, M.; Udriste, C. Area Conditions Associated to Thermodynamic and Economic Systems. In Proceedings of the 2nd International Colloquium of Mathematics in Engineering and Numerical Physics, University Politehnica of Bucharest, Bucharest, Romania, 22–27 April 2002; BSG Proceedings 8; Geometry Balkan Press: Bucharest, Romania, 2003; pp. 60–68.
76. Georgescu-Roegen, N. *The Entropy Law and the Economic Process*; Harvard University Press: Cambridge, MA, USA, 1999.
77. Nicolescu, L.; Martin, M. Einige Bemerkungen über die Deformations Algebra. *Abh. Math. Sem. Univ. Hamburg* **1979**, *49*, 244–253. [CrossRef]
78. Nicolescu, L. Sur la représentation géodésique et subgéodesique des espaces de Riemann. *An. Univ. București Matem.* **1983**, *XXXII*, 57–63.

Disclaimer/Publisher's Note: The statements, opinions and data contained in all publications are solely those of the individual author(s) and contributor(s) and not of MDPI and/or the editor(s). MDPI and/or the editor(s) disclaim responsibility for any injury to people or property resulting from any ideas, methods, instructions or products referred to in the content.

Article

Quasi-Statistical Schouten–van Kampen Connections on the Tangent Bundle

Simona-Luiza Druta-Romaniuc *

Department of Mathematics and Informatics, "Gheorghe Asachi" Technical University of Iaşi, Strada Dimitrie Mangeron, nr. 67A, 700050 Iaşi, Romania; simona-luiza.romaniuc@academic.tuiasi.ro

Abstract: We determine the general natural metrics G on the total space TM of the tangent bundle of a Riemannian manifold (M, g) such that the Schouten–van Kampen connection $\overline{\nabla}$ associated to the Levi-Civita connection of G is (quasi-)statistical. We prove that the base manifold must be a space form and in particular, when G is a natural diagonal metric, (M, g) must be locally flat. We prove that there exist one family of natural diagonal metrics and two families of proper general natural metrics such that $(TM, \overline{\nabla}, G)$ is a statistical manifold and one family of proper general natural metrics such that $(TM \setminus \{0\}, \overline{\nabla}, G)$ is a quasi-statistical manifold.

Keywords: (pseudo-)Riemannian manifold; Codazzi pair; statistical manifold; quasi-statistical manifold; Schouten–van Kampen connection; tangent bundle; general natural metric

MSC: 53B12; 53B05; 53B21

Citation: Druta-Romaniuc, S.-L. Quasi-Statistical Schouten–van Kampen Connections on the Tangent Bundle. Mathematics 2023, 11, 4614. https://doi.org/10.3390/math11224614

Academic Editor: Cristina-Elena Hretcanu

Received: 28 September 2023
Revised: 15 October 2023
Accepted: 18 October 2023
Published: 10 November 2023

Copyright: © 2023 by the authors. Licensee MDPI, Basel, Switzerland. This article is an open access article distributed under the terms and conditions of the Creative Commons Attribution (CC BY) license (https://creativecommons.org/licenses/by/4.0/).

1. Introduction

Statistical manifolds, whose points correspond to probability distributions, provide a natural framework for information geometry, which uses differential geometry in the study of probability theory and statistics and which was initiated by C. R. Rao in [1], who was the first to treat a Fisher matrix as a Riemannian metric. The notion of statistical manifold, introduced in 1987 by S. L. Lauritzen in the paper [2] and studied, e.g., in [2–32] and the references therein, has various applications in information science, neural networks, and statistical physics.

According to T. Kurose [14], a statistical manifold is a differentiable manifold endowed with a symmetric linear connection ∇ and a (pseudo-)Riemannian metric h such that the covariant derivative ∇h is totally symmetric. A couple (∇, h) with this property is called a statistical structure or a Codazzi pair, while the metric h and the connection ∇ are said to be Codazzi-coupled (see [2,9,12,23]). Alternatively, the notion of statistical manifold was defined by H. Furuhata and I. Hasegawa in [11] as a (pseudo-)Riemannian manifold endowed with a pair of torsion-free conjugate connections. For the pairs of connections compatible with a g–structure, we go back in the literature to V. Cruceanu and R. Miron [33].

A classical example of statistical manifold is a (pseudo-)Riemannian manifold (M, h) endowed with the Levi-Civita connection of the metric h. The statistical manifolds generalize the (pseudo-)Riemannian manifolds by extending the parallelism of the metric h under the Levi-Civita connection to the Codazzi coupling of the metric with a torsion-free linear connection. Moreover, relaxing the Codazzi coupling to the case when the linear connection has nonzero torsion, T. Kurose introduced in [15] the notion of statistical manifold admitting torsion, also called quasi-statistical manifold (see [17]), which is the subject of quantum information geometry.

Codazzi couplings of an affine connection with a pseudo-Riemannian metric, a nondegenerate 2-form, and a tangent bundle isomorphism on smooth manifolds and in particular on an almost (para-)Hermitian manifold (M, g, L) endowed with the 2-form ω given as

$\omega(X, Y) = g(LX, Y)$, were studied by T. Fei and J. Zhang in [9]. They proved that the Codazzi couplings of ∇ with both g and L lead to a (para-)Kähler structure, and subsequently, they defined Codazzi-(para-)Kähler manifolds as (para-)Kähler statistical manifolds. In [12], the study was extended to torsion couplings between an affine connection ∇ of nontrivial torsion and both g and L on an almost (para-)Hermitian manifold. The authors proved that the pair (∇, L) is torsion-coupled if and only if ∇ is (para-)holomorphic and the almost (para-)complex structure L is integrable. Statistical structures on almost anti-Hermitian (or Norden) manifolds were studied in [26,27] by A. Salimov and S. Turanli, who introduced the notion of anti-Kähler–Codazzi manifolds, then by L. Samereh, E. Peyghan, and I. Mihai in [28], and very recently by A. Gezer and H. Cakicioglu, who provided in [10] an alternative classification of anti-Kähler manifolds with respect to a torsion-free linear connection. Codazzi pairs on almost para-Norden manifolds were treated by S. Turanli and S. Uçan in [29]. F. Etayo et al. proved in [8] that Kähler–Codazzi type manifolds reduce to Kähler type manifolds in all the four types of (α, ε)-manifolds teated in an unified way in [34]. In [30], G. E. Vîlcu introduced the notion of para-Kähler-like statistical manifold and proved that if a manifold of this type has constant curvature in the Kurose's sense, then the statistical structure of the manifold is a Hessian structure.

Statistical structures on the tangent bundle of differentiable manifolds were treated in recent papers, such as [4,13,19,22,24].

The background of the present work is the total space TM of the tangent bundle of a Riemannian manifold (M, g), endowed with a metric G introduced by V. Oproiu in [35] as a general natural lift of the metric from the base manifold, by using Kowalski–Sekizawa's classification from [36] and the results in [37]. This metric, called a general natural metric, depends on six coefficients which are smooth real functions of the energy density t of a tangent vector y. We study the conditions under which the (pseudo-)Riemannian manifold (TM, G) endowed with the Schouten–van Kampen connection $\overline{\nabla}$ associated to the Levi-Civita connection of G is a statistical manifold admitting torsion (SMAT). A necessary condition for $(TM, \overline{\nabla}, G)$ to be a SMAT is that the base manifold is a space form. We prove that $(TM \setminus \{0\}, \overline{\nabla}, G)$ is a SMAT if and only if (M, g) has negative constant sectional curvature and the metric G depends on the energy density t, the constant sectional curvature of (M, g), an arbitrary nonzero real constant κ_2 and an arbitray smooth real function of t which is not $-\frac{\kappa_2}{2t^2}$. On the other hand, $(TM, \overline{\nabla}, G)$ is a statistical manifold (without torsion) if and only if the base manifold is locally flat and the metric G is of natural diagonal type (depending on two arbitrary nonzero smooth real functions of the energy density t and on an arbitrary nonzero real constant, satisfying the nondegenracy conditions of the metric) or a proper general natural metric with two possible expressions. In one case, the expression of G depends on an arbitrary smooth real function c_3 of t different from $\frac{const}{\sqrt{t}}$ for every $const \in \mathbb{R}$, $t > 0$, such that $c_3(0) \neq 0$, and on two arbitrary nonzero real constants whose product is different from 1. In the other case, the metric G depends only on two arbitrary smooth real functions c_2, c_3 of the energy density, such that $c_2(0)c_3(0) \neq 0$, $c_3(t) \neq \frac{const}{\sqrt{t}}$ for every $const \in \mathbb{R}$, $t > 0$. If $c_2(t) \neq \kappa(c_3(t))^2$ for every $\kappa \in \mathbb{R}$, $t \geq 0$, then the Levi-Civita connection of G is different from its associated Schouten–van Kampen connection, and hence $(TM, \overline{\nabla}, G)$ is a nontrivial statistical manifold.

The results obtained in this work lead to new examples of (quasi-)statistical structures on the tangent bundle of a Riemann manifold. Unlike the majority of previous studies (see, e.g., [4,13,19,22,24]), which produce new examples of statistical structures on the tangent bundle by lifting a given statistical structure on the base space, the present article does not assume the a priori existence of a statistical structure on the base manifold. The new structures are, thus, uncorrelated with the ones from the base, therefore constituting a more convenient geometric setting to investigate the statistical behavior in depth. Thus, new opportunities are opened for applications in information theory, machine learning, neural networks, statistical mechanics and geometry of Ricci solitons, for which we cite [38–41] and the references therein.

We mention that in the present paper the manifolds, tensor fields, and other geometric objects are considered to be smooth and the Einstein summation convention is used, the range of the indices always being $\{1, \ldots, n\}$.

2. The Schouten–van Kampen Connection of a General Natural Metric on TM Revisited

In this section, we recall some results from our previous paper [42] concerning the Schouten–van Kampen connection associated to the Levi-Civita connection of a general natural metric on the total space TM of the tangent bundle of a Riemannian manifold. For the geometry of the tangent bundle we cite the monograph [43].

Let (M, g) be a Riemannian manifold of dimension n and let $(x^i)_{i=1}^n$ and $(x^i, y^j)_{i,j=1}^n$ be the local coordinates on an open subset U of M and on $\tau^{-1}(U) \subset TM$, respectively, where $\tau : TM \to M$ is the tangent bundle of M.

Denoting, by a slight abuse, the set of all vector fields tangent to TM by TTM, we have its direct sum decomposition, that is:

$$TTM = VTM \oplus HTM, \tag{1}$$

into the vertical distribution $VTM = \ker \tau_*$ and the horizontal distribution HTM, locally generated, respectively, by $\{\frac{\partial}{\partial y^i}\}_{i=1}^n$ and $\{\frac{\delta}{\delta x_j}\}_{j=1}^n$, the horizontal generators being $\frac{\delta}{\delta x^j} = \frac{\partial}{\partial x^j} - y^l \Gamma_{lj}^h \frac{\partial}{\partial y^h}$, where Γ_{lj}^h are the Christoffel symbols of the metric g. Then, the local frame field adapted to the direct sum decomposition (1) is $\{\frac{\partial}{\partial y^i}, \frac{\delta}{\delta x^j}\}_{i,j=1}^n$, denoted also by $\{\partial_i, \delta_j\}_{i,j=1}^n$. Its Lie brackets satisfy the identities:

$$[\partial_i, \partial_j] = 0, \quad [\partial_i, \delta_j] = -\Gamma_{ij}^h \partial_h, \quad [\delta_i, \delta_j] = -R_{lij}^h y^l \partial_h, \tag{2}$$

where R_{lij}^h are components of the curvature tensor field of (M, g) in a local chart $(U, x^i)_{i=1}^n$.

The horizontal and vertical lifts of a vector field $X = X^i \frac{\partial}{\partial x^i}$ from M to TM are denoted by X^H and X^V and with respect to the adapted local frame field, they have the expressions

$$X^H = X^i \frac{\delta}{\delta x^i}, \quad X^V = X^i \frac{\partial}{\partial y^i}.$$

The kinetic energy or energy density of any tangent vector $y \in \tau^{-1}(U)$ with respect to the Riemannian metric g is given as:

$$t = \frac{1}{2}\|y\|^2 = \frac{1}{2} g_{\tau(y)}(y, y) = \frac{1}{2} g_{ik}(x) y^i y^k \geq 0. \tag{3}$$

An important tool in the geometry of the tangent bundle are the metrics constructed as natural lifts of the Riemannian metric from base manifold to the total space of the tangent bundle, classified by O. Kowalski and M. Sekizawa in [36]. By using this classification and the results in [37], V. Oproiu defined in [35] *a general natural metric* on TM, given locally as:

$$\begin{cases} G\left(\frac{\delta}{\delta x^i}, \frac{\delta}{\delta x^j}\right) = c_1 g_{ij} + d_1 g_{0i} g_{0j} = G_{ij}^{(1)} \\ G\left(\frac{\partial}{\partial y^i}, \frac{\partial}{\partial y^j}\right) = c_2 g_{ij} + d_2 g_{0i} g_{0j} = G_{ij}^{(2)} \\ G\left(\frac{\partial}{\partial y^i}, \frac{\delta}{\delta x^j}\right) = G\left(\frac{\delta}{\delta x^i}, \frac{\partial}{\partial y^j}\right) = c_3 g_{ij} + d_3 g_{0i} g_{0j} = G_{ij}^{(3)}, \end{cases} \tag{4}$$

where c_i, d_i ($i = 1, 2, 3$) are smooth real functions of the energy density on TM and $g_{0i} = g_{li} y^l$.

The invariant expression of the metric G is:

$$\begin{cases} G(X_y^H, Y_y^H) = c_1(t)g_{\tau(y)}(X,Y) + d_1(t)g_{\tau(y)}(X,y)g_{\tau(y)}(Y,y), \\ G(X_y^V, Y_y^V) = c_2(t)g_{\tau(y)}(X,Y) + d_2(t)g_{\tau(y)}(X,y)g_{\tau(y)}(Y,y), \\ G(X_y^V, Y_y^H) = c_3(t)g_{\tau(y)}(X,Y) + d_3(t)g_{\tau(y)}(X,y)g_{\tau(y)}(Y,y), \end{cases} \quad (5)$$

for all $X, Y \in \mathcal{T}_0^1(M)$, $y \in TM$, where t is the energy density of y.

The nondegeneracy conditions for the metric G are as follows:

$$c_1 c_2 - c_3^2 \neq 0, \quad (c_1 + 2td_1)(c_2 + 2td_2) - (c_3 + 2td_3)^2 \neq 0. \quad (6)$$

The metric G is positive definite if:

$$c_1 + 2td_1 > 0, \quad c_2 + 2td_2 > 0, \ (c_1 + 2td_1)(c_2 + 2td_2) - (c_3 + 2td_3)^2 > 0. \quad (7)$$

When the horizontal and vertical distributions are orthogonal with respect to the metric G, we say that G is a *metric of natural diagonal lift type* or a *natural diagonal metric* on TM (see [44]). This type of metric has the expression (5), with $c_3 = d_3 = 0$. We say that a metric given by (5) is a *proper general natural metric* if it is not a natural diagonal metric.

The matrix of the metric G with respect to the adapted local frame field $\{\delta_i, \partial_j\}_{i,j=1}^n$ and the inverse matrix are, respectively:

$$\begin{pmatrix} \left(G_{ij}^{(1)}\right) & \left(G_{ij}^{(3)}\right) \\ \left(G_{ij}^{(3)}\right) & \left(G_{ij}^{(2)}\right) \end{pmatrix}_{i,j \in \{1,\ldots,n\}}, \quad \begin{pmatrix} \left(H_{(1)}^{jk}\right) & \left(H_{(3)}^{jk}\right) \\ \left(H_{(3)}^{jk}\right) & \left(H_{(2)}^{jk}\right) \end{pmatrix}_{j,k \in \{1,\ldots,n\}},$$

where:

$$H_{(1)}^{kl} = p_1 g^{kl} + q_1 y^k y^l, \ H_{(2)}^{kl} = p_2 g^{kl} + q_2 y^k y^l, \ H_{(3)}^{kl} = p_3 g^{kl} + q_3 y^k y^l, \quad (8)$$

with:

$$p_1 = \frac{c_2}{c_1 c_2 - c_3^2}, \ p_2 = \frac{c_1}{c_1 c_2 - c_3^2}, \ p_3 = -\frac{c_3}{c_1 c_2 - c_3^2}, \quad (9)$$

$$\begin{aligned} q_1 &= -\frac{c_2 d_1 p_1 - c_3 d_3 p_1 - c_3 d_2 p_3 + c_2 d_3 p_3 + 2d_1 d_2 p_1 t - 2d_3^2 p_1 t}{(c_1 + 2d_1 t)(c_2 + 2d_2 t) - (c_3 + 2d_3 t)^2}, \\ q_2 &= \frac{(c_3 + 2d_3 t)[(d_3 p_1 + d_2 p_3)(c_1 + 2d_1 t) - (d_1 p_1 + d_3 p_3)(c_3 + 2d_3 t)]}{(c_2 + 2d_2 t)[(c_1 + 2d_1 t)(c_2 + 2d_2 t) - (c_3 + 2d_3 t)^2]} - \frac{d_2 p_2 + d_3 p_3}{c_2 + 2d_2 t}, \\ q_3 &= -\frac{(d_3 p_1 + d_2 p_3)(c_1 + 2d_1 t) - (d_1 p_1 + d_3 p_3)(c_3 + 2d_3 t)}{(c_1 + 2d_1 t)(c_2 + 2d_2 t) - (c_3 + 2d_3 t)^2}. \end{aligned} \quad (10)$$

Inspired by the Schouten–van Kampen connection associated to a linear connection on a smooth manifold with two globally complementary distributions (see [45] and [46]), we defined in [42] the Schouten–van Kampen connection $\overline{\nabla}$ associated to the Levi-Civita connection ∇ of a general natural metric G by the relation:

$$\overline{\nabla}_X Y = V \nabla_X VY + H \nabla_X HY, \quad (11)$$

for any vector fields X, Y on TM, where V and H are the projection tensor fields corresponding to VTM and HTM, respectively.

Proposition 1. (Proposition 3.1 [42]) *The Schouten–van Kampen connection $\overline{\nabla}$ associated to the Levi-Civita connection ∇ of a general natural metric G on TM has the following expression in the adapted local frame field $\{\partial_i, \delta_j\}_{i=1}^n$:*

$$\begin{cases} \overline{\nabla}_{\frac{\partial}{\partial y^i}} \frac{\partial}{\partial y^j} = Q_{ij}^h \frac{\partial}{\partial y^h}, & \overline{\nabla}_{\frac{\delta}{\delta x^i}} \frac{\partial}{\partial y^j} = \left(\Gamma_{ij}^h + \overline{U}_{ji}^h\right) \frac{\partial}{\partial y^h} \\ \overline{\nabla}_{\frac{\partial}{\partial y^i}} \frac{\delta}{\delta x^j} = U_{ij}^h \frac{\delta}{\delta x^h}, & \overline{\nabla}_{\frac{\delta}{\delta x^i}} \frac{\delta}{\delta x^j} = \left(\Gamma_{ij}^h + \overline{S}_{ij}^h\right) \frac{\delta}{\delta x^h}, \end{cases} \quad (12)$$

where Γ_{ij}^h are the Christoffel symbols of the metric g of the base manifold M:

$$\begin{cases} Q_{ij}^h = \frac{1}{2}(\partial_i G_{jk}^{(2)} + \partial_j G_{ik}^{(2)} - \partial_k G_{ij}^{(2)}) H_{(2)}^{kh} + \frac{1}{2}(\partial_i G_{jk}^{(3)} + \partial_j G_{ik}^{(3)}) H_{(3)}^{kh}, \\ U_{ij}^h = \frac{1}{2}(\partial_i G_{jk}^{(3)} - \partial_k G_{ij}^{(3)}) H_{(3)}^{kh} + \frac{1}{2}(\partial_i G_{jk}^{(1)} + R_{0jk}^l G_{li}^{(2)}) H_{(1)}^{kh}, \\ \overline{U}_{ij}^h = \frac{1}{2}(\partial_i G_{jk}^{(3)} - \partial_k G_{ij}^{(3)}) H_{(2)}^{kh} + \frac{1}{2}(\partial_i G_{jk}^{(1)} + R_{0jk}^l G_{li}^{(2)}) H_{(3)}^{kh}, \\ \overline{S}_{ij}^h = -\frac{1}{2}(\partial_k G_{ij}^{(1)} + R_{0ij}^l G_{lk}^{(2)}) H_{(3)}^{kh} + c_3 R_{i0jk} H_{(1)}^{kh}, \end{cases} \quad (13)$$

where R_{kij}^h are the components of the curvature of the base manifold and:

$$R_{0ij}^l = R_{hij}^l y^h, \quad R_{i0jk} = R_{ihjk} y^h.$$

The torsion tensor field T of the connection $\overline{\nabla}$ is defined by the formula:

$$T(X,Y) = \overline{\nabla}_X Y - \overline{\nabla}_Y X - [X,Y], \quad \forall X, Y \in \mathcal{T}_0^1(TM). \quad (14)$$

Proposition 2. *The torsion tensor field of the Schouten–van Kampen connection $\overline{\nabla}$ given in Proposition 1 has the following components with respect to the adapted local frame field $\{\partial_i, \delta_j\}_{i=1}^n$:*

$$\begin{cases} T\left(\frac{\partial}{\partial y^i}, \frac{\partial}{\partial y^j}\right) = 0, \quad T\left(\frac{\delta}{\delta x^i}, \frac{\delta}{\delta x^j}\right) = R_{0ij}^h \frac{\partial}{\partial y^h}, \\ T\left(\frac{\partial}{\partial y^i}, \frac{\delta}{\delta x^j}\right) = -T\left(\frac{\delta}{\delta x^j}, \frac{\partial}{\partial y^i}\right) = U_{ij}^h \frac{\delta}{\delta x^h} - \overline{U}_{ij}^h \frac{\partial}{\partial y^h}. \end{cases} \quad (15)$$

Proof. We showed in [42] Proposition 3.2 that the torsion tensor field of the Schouten–van Kampen connection $\overline{\nabla}$ has the components:

$$\begin{cases} T\left(\frac{\partial}{\partial y^i}, \frac{\partial}{\partial y^j}\right) = (Q_{ij}^h - Q_{ji}^h) \frac{\partial}{\partial y^h}, \\ T\left(\frac{\delta}{\delta x^i}, \frac{\delta}{\delta x^j}\right) = \left(\overline{S}_{ij}^h - \overline{S}_{ji}^h\right) \frac{\delta}{\delta x^h} + R_{0ij}^h \frac{\partial}{\partial y^h}, \\ T\left(\frac{\partial}{\partial y^i}, \frac{\delta}{\delta x^j}\right) = -T\left(\frac{\delta}{\delta x^j}, \frac{\partial}{\partial y^i}\right) = U_{ij}^h \frac{\delta}{\delta x^h} - \overline{U}_{ij}^h \frac{\partial}{\partial y^h}. \end{cases} \quad (16)$$

From the first expression in (13) it follows that Q_{ij}^h is symmetric in i and j, and hence, from (16), we have:

$$T\left(\frac{\partial}{\partial y^i}, \frac{\partial}{\partial y^j}\right) = 0.$$

By substituting into the last relation (13) the components of the metric G from (4) and the entries of the inverse matrix form (8), then using in turn (10) and (9), we obtain that:

$$\overline{S}_{ij}^h - \overline{S}_{ji}^h = \frac{c_2 c_3}{c_1 c_2 - c_3^2}\left(R_{ij0}^h + R_{j0i}^h + R_{0ij}^h\right),$$

which vanishes due to the first Bianchi identity, and hence, the second relation in (16) reduces to:

$$T\left(\frac{\delta}{\delta x^i}, \frac{\delta}{\delta x^j}\right) = R_{0ij}^h \frac{\partial}{\partial y^h}.$$

Thus, the components of the torsion tensor field of the Schouten–van Kampen connection $\overline{\nabla}$ on (TM, G) are those given in the statement. □

Theorem 1. (Theorem 3.4 [42]) *The Schouten–van Kampen connection on (TM, G), given in Proposition 1, is torsion-free if and only if the base manifold (M, g) is locally flat and the metric G has the expression:*

$$\begin{cases} G(X_y^H, Y_y^H) = \kappa_1 g_{\tau(y)}(X, Y), \\ G(X_y^V, Y_y^V) = c_2(t) g_{\tau(y)}(X, Y) + d_2(t) g_{\tau(y)}(X, y) g_{\tau(y)}(Y, y), \\ G(X_y^V, Y_y^H) = c_3(t) g_{\tau(y)}(X, Y) + c_3'(t) g_{\tau(y)}(X, y) g_{\tau(y)}(Y, y), \end{cases} \quad (17)$$

where κ_1 is a real constant and c_2, d_2, c_3 are smooth functions depending on the energy density on TM, such that one of the following two sets of conditions is satisfied:

(i) $\kappa_1 c_2 - c_3^2 \neq 0$, $\kappa_1(c_2 + 2td_2) - (c_3 + 2tc_3')^2 \neq 0$,

(ii) $\kappa_1 > 0$, $c_2 + 2td_2 > 0$, $\kappa_1(c_2 + 2td_2) - (c_3 + 2tc_3')^2 > 0$.

In the first case, G is a pseudo-Riemannian metric and in the second one it is a Riemannian metric.

Proposition 3. (Proposition 3.5 [42]) *The torsion-free Schouten–van Kampen connection characterized in Theorem 1 coincides with the Levi-Civita connection of a pseudo-Riemannian general natural metric G given by (17) if and only if the coefficients of G fall in one of the instances:*

(i) $c_3(t) = 0$, $\forall t \geq 0$, c_2, d_2 are some smooth functions of t such that:

$$\kappa_1 c_2(t) \neq 0, \quad c_2(t) + 2td_2(t) \neq 0, \quad \forall t \geq 0;$$

(ii) $c_2(t) = d_2(t) = 0$, $\forall t \geq 0$ and c_3 is an arbitrary nonzero smooth function of t, $c_3(t) \neq \frac{const}{\sqrt{t}}$, for all $const \in \mathbb{R}$ and all $t > 0$;

(iii) $c_2(t) = \kappa_2 \in \mathbb{R}$, $c_3(t) = \kappa_3 \in \mathbb{R}$, such that $\kappa_1 \kappa_2 - \kappa_3^2 \neq 0$, $d_2(t) = 0$, for all $t \geq 0$;

(iv) $c_2(t) = \kappa(c_3(t))^2$, $d_2(t) = 2\kappa c_3'(t)(c_3(t) + tc_3'(t))$, where κ is a nonzero real constant, such that $\kappa_1 \kappa \neq 1$ and c_3 is an arbitrary nonzero smooth function of t, $c_3(t) \neq \frac{const}{\sqrt{t}}$, for all $const \in \mathbb{R}$ and all $t > 0$.

If the coefficients of the metric G from Proposition 3 have the expressions (iv) extended to the situation when κ is an arbitrary real constant such that $\kappa_1 \kappa \neq 1$, then by taking $\kappa = 0$, we get the coefficients from (ii), and by taking $c_3(t) = \kappa_3 \in \mathbb{R} \setminus \{0\}$, we get the coefficients from (iii) for a proper general natural metric. Thus, we can state the following characterization of the proper general natural metrics on TM whose Levi-Civita connection coincides with the associated Schouten–van Kampen connection.

Proposition 4. *The proper general natural metrics G on TM for which the Levi-Civita connection coincides with its associated Schouten–van Kampen connection are given by (17), where c_3 is an arbitrary nonzero smooth function of t, $c_3(t) \neq \frac{const}{\sqrt{t}}$ for every $t > 0$, $const \in \mathbb{R}$, and the functions c_2 and d_2 have the particular expressions:*

$$c_2(t) = \kappa(c_3(t))^2, \quad d_2(t) = 2\kappa c_3'(t)(c_3(t) + tc_3'(t)),$$

where κ is an arbitrary real constant such that $\kappa_1 \kappa \neq 1$.

3. General Natural Metrics Torsion-Coupled with the Schouten–van Kampen Connection

Statistical manifolds, the main tool of classical information geometry, were defined in [14] as follows:

Definition 1. Let (M, h) be a pseudo-Riemannian manifold, and let ∇ be a torsion-free affine connection on M. The triplet (M, ∇, h) is called a statistical manifold if the tensor field ∇h is totally symmetric, that is:

$$(\nabla_X h)(Y, Z) = (\nabla_Y h)(X, Z), \quad \forall X, Y, Z \in \mathcal{T}_0^1(M). \tag{18}$$

A metric h and an affine connection ∇ satisfying (18) are called Codazzi-coupled. In this case, the couple (∇, h) is called a Codazzi pair or a statistical structure on M and ∇ is called a statistical connection on (M, h).

Extending the condition (18) to the case when the affine connection has nontrivial torsion, T. Kurose defined in [15] the statistical manifolds admitting torsion, also known as quasi-statistical manifolds (see [17]), which represent the subject of quantum information geometry.

Definition 2. Let (M, h) be a pseudo-Riemannian manifold, and let ∇ be an affine connection of torsion T^∇ on M. If the metric h and the connection ∇ satisfy the relation:

$$(\nabla_X h)(Y, Z) - (\nabla_Y h)(X, Z) = -h\left(T^\nabla(X, Y), Z\right), \quad \forall X, Y, Z \in \mathcal{T}_0^1(M), \tag{19}$$

then the triplet (M, ∇, h) is called a statistical manifold admitting torsion or a quasi-statistical manifold.

We say that a metric h and an affine connection ∇ with nonzero torsion T^∇ satisfying (19) are torsion-coupled. In this case the couple (∇, h) is called a statistical structure admitting torsion on M or a quasi-statistical structure on M and ∇ is called a quasi-statistical connection on (M, h).

In particular, if TM is the total space of the tangent bundle of a Riemannian manifold (M, g), endowed with a general natural metric G and with the corresponding Schouten–van Kampen connection $\overline{\nabla}$, we say that the metric G and the connection $\overline{\nabla}$ are torsion-coupled, $(\overline{\nabla}, G)$ is a statistical structure admitting torsion on TM or a quasi-statistical structure on TM, $\overline{\nabla}$ is a quasi-statistical connection on (TM, G), and the triplet $(TM, \overline{\nabla}, G)$ is a statistical manifold admitting torsion or a quasi-statistical manifold if:

$$(\overline{\nabla}_X G)(Y, Z) - (\overline{\nabla}_Y G)(X, Z) + G(T(X, Y), Z) = 0, \quad \forall X, Y, Z \in \mathcal{T}_0^1(TM), \tag{20}$$

where T is the torsion tensor field of $\overline{\nabla}$.

If the connection $\overline{\nabla}$ is torsion-free, then the relation (20) reduces to:

$$(\overline{\nabla}_X G)(Y, Z) - (\overline{\nabla}_Y G)(X, Z) = 0, \quad \forall X, Y, Z \in \mathcal{T}_0^1(TM). \tag{21}$$

If the metric G and the connection $\overline{\nabla}$ satisfy the relation (21), we say that G and $\overline{\nabla}$ are Codazzi-coupled, $(\overline{\nabla}, G)$ is a Codazzi pair or a statistical structure on TM, $\overline{\nabla}$ is a statistical connection on (TM, G) and the triplet $(TM, \overline{\nabla}, G)$ is a statistical manifold.

For simplicity of notations, we consider a $(0, 3)$-tensor field $\mathcal{T}$ on TM:

$$\mathcal{T}(X, Y, Z) = (\overline{\nabla}_X G)(Y, Z) - (\overline{\nabla}_Y G)(X, Z) + G(T(X, Y), Z), \tag{22}$$

for every $X, Y, Z \in \mathcal{T}_0^1(TM)$. Thus, the relation (20) which characterizes the statistical manifold admitting torsion $(TM, \overline{\nabla}, G)$ takes the simpler form:

$$\mathcal{T}(X, Y, Z) = 0, \quad \forall X, Y, Z \in \mathcal{T}_0^1(M). \tag{23}$$

Taking into account the expressions (15) of the torsion of $\overline{\nabla}$ and the relation (22) which gives the tensor field $\mathcal{T}$, we obtain the components of $\mathcal{T}$ with respect to the adapted local frame field $\{\delta_i, \partial_j\}_{i,j=1}^n$:

$$\mathcal{T}(\partial_i, \partial_j, \partial_k) = (\overline{\nabla}_{\partial_i} G)(\partial_j, \partial_k) - (\overline{\nabla}_{\partial_j} G)(\partial_i, \partial_k); \tag{24}$$

$$\mathcal{T}(\partial_i, \partial_j, \delta_k) = (\overline{\nabla}_{\partial_i} G)(\partial_j, \delta_k) - (\overline{\nabla}_{\partial_j} G)(\partial_i, \delta_k); \tag{25}$$

$$\mathcal{T}(\partial_i, \delta_j, \partial_k) = (\overline{\nabla}_{\partial_i} G)(\delta_j, \partial_k) - (\overline{\nabla}_{\delta_j} G)(\partial_i, \partial_k) + U_{ij}^h G_{hk}^{(3)} - \overline{U}_{ij}^h G_{hk}^{(2)}; \tag{26}$$

$$\mathcal{T}(\partial_i, \delta_j, \delta_k) = (\overline{\nabla}_{\partial_i} G)(\delta_j, \delta_k) - (\overline{\nabla}_{\delta_j} G)(\partial_i, \delta_k) + U_{ij}^h G_{hk}^{(1)} - \overline{U}_{ij}^h G_{hk}^{(3)}; \tag{27}$$

$$\mathcal{T}(\delta_i, \delta_j, \partial_k) = (\overline{\nabla}_{\delta_i} G)(\delta_j, \partial_k) - (\overline{\nabla}_{\delta_j} G)(\delta_i, \partial_k) + R_{0ij}^h G_{hk}^{(2)}; \tag{28}$$

$$\mathcal{T}(\delta_i, \delta_j, \delta_k) = (\overline{\nabla}_{\delta_i} G)(\delta_j, \delta_k) - (\overline{\nabla}_{\delta_j} G)(\delta_i, \delta_k) + R_{0ij}^h G_{hk}^{(3)}. \tag{29}$$

Proposition 5. *Let (M, g) be a connected Riemannian manifold of dimension $n > 2$ and let TM be the total space of the tangent bundle, endowed with a general natural metric G given by (5). If the metric G and the corresponding Schouten–van Kampen connection are torsion-coupled, then the base manifold is a space form when $c_2(0)c_3(0) \neq 0$ and locally flat when $c_3(t) = 0$ for every $t \geq 0$.*

Proof. By using the relations (24), (4), (12), (13), and (8), we obtain:

$$\begin{aligned}\mathcal{T}(\partial_i, \partial_j, \partial_k) = &\frac{1}{2}[(2c_3' - 2d_3 - c_1'c_3 p_1 + c_3 d_1 p_1 - 2c_3 c_3' p_3 + 2c_3 d_3 p_3 \\ &+ 2d_1 d_3 p_1 t - 2c_3' d_3 p_3 t + 2d_3^2 p_3 t + 2c_3 d_1 q_1 t - 2c_3 c_3' q_3 t \\ &+ 2c_3 d_3 q_3 t + 4d_1 d_3 q_1 t^2 - 4c_3' d_3 q_3 t^2 + 4d_3^2 q_3 t^2) \cdot \\ &(g_{jk} g_{0i} - g_{ik} g_{0j}) - c_2 c_3 p_1 (R_{lijk} - R_{ljik}) y^l \\ &+ c_2(d_3 p_1 + c_3 q_1 + 2d_3 q_1 t)(R_{likm} g_{0j} - R_{ljkm} g_{0i}) y^l y^m].\end{aligned} \tag{30}$$

The connection $\overline{\nabla}$ and the metric G are torsion-coupled if and only if the tensor field $\mathcal{T}$ vanishes, that is all its components with respect to the adapted local frame field $\{\delta_i, \partial_j\}_{i,j=1}^n$ vanish, and hence, a necessary condition for the torsion coupling between $\overline{\nabla}$ and G is $\mathcal{T}(\partial_i, \partial_j, \partial_k) = 0$. Differentiating the expression (30) with respect to the tangential coordinates y^l and taking the value of this derivative in $y = 0$, since the curvature of the base manifold does not depend on the tangent vector y, for $c_2(0)c_3(0) \neq 0$ we obtain that:

$$R_{lijk} - R_{ljik} = \left.\frac{2(1 - c_3 p_3)(c_3' - d_3) - c_3 p_1(c_1' - d_1)}{c_2 c_3 p_1}\right|_{t=0} (g_{li} g_{jk} - g_{lj} g_{ik}). \tag{31}$$

Due to the anti-symmetry of the Riemann-Christoffel tensor field in the last two arguments, the left-hand side of relation (31) becomes $R_{lijk} + R_{ljki}$, and from the first Bianchi identity it follows that:

$$R_{lkij} = c(g_{li} g_{jk} - g_{lj} g_{ik}),$$

where the function c depends on $x^1, \ldots, x^n$, only, having the expression:

$$c = -\left.\frac{2(1 - c_3 p_3)(c_3' - d_3) - c_3 p_1(c_1' - d_1)}{c_2 c_3 p_1}\right|_{t=0}.$$

Since the manifold M is connected and of dimension $n > 2$, from Schur's theorem we obtain that c is constant, i.e., M is a space form.

Now, we study the situation when $c_3(t) = 0$ for every $t \geq 0$. In this case, by using (10) and then (9), the expression (30) becomes simpler:

$$\mathcal{T}(\partial_i, \partial_j, \partial_k) = \frac{-2d_3^2 t(c_2 + c_2' t)}{c_1 c_2 + 2t(c_2 d_1 + c_1 d_2) + 4t^2(d_1 d_2 - d_3^2)}(g_{jk}g_{0i} - g_{ik}g_{0j}), \tag{32}$$

and its condition of vanishing does not involve the curvature of (M, g).

Analyzing the other components of the tensor field $\mathcal{T}$ in the same manner, we obtain:

$$\mathcal{T}(\delta_i, \delta_j, \partial_k) = \frac{d_3^2 t}{c_1 c_2 + 2t(c_2 d_1 + c_1 d_2) + 4t^2(d_1 d_2 - d_3^2)} \cdot \tag{33}$$
$$[c_1(g_{jk}g_{0i} - g_{ik}g_{0j}) + c_2(R_{hjkl}g_{0i} - R_{hikl}g_{0j})y^h y^l]$$
$$- c_2 R_{hkij} y^h,$$

whose derivative with respect to y^h computed in $y = 0$ is $c_2(0) R_{hkji}$.

Since $c_3(t) = 0$ for every $t \geq 0$, from the nondegeneracy condition (6) of the metric G it follows that $c_2(0) \neq 0$, and hence, $c_2(0) R_{hkji}$ vanishes if and only if $R_{hkji} = 0$, that is the base manifold is locally flat. □

One can easily prove the following lemma, which will be used to obtain the main results of the paper.

Lemma 1. *Let (M, g) be a Riemannian manifold of dimension $n > 2$ and α_1, α_2, α_3, α_4 be four smooth real functions of the energy density on TM. If these functions satisfy the following relation:*

$$\alpha_1(t) g_{jk} g_{0i} + \alpha_2(t) g_{ik} g_{0j} + \alpha_3(t) g_{ij} g_{0k} + \alpha_4(t) g_{0i} g_{0j} g_{0k} = 0, \forall t > 0,$$

where $g_{0i} = g_{hi} y^h$, then $\alpha_1(t) = \alpha_2(t) = \alpha_3(t) = \alpha_4(t) = 0$, for all $t \geq 0$.

Theorem 2. *Let (M, g) be a connected Riemannian manifold of dimension $n > 2$ and let the total space TM of the tangent bundle be endowed with a general natural metric G given by (5) such that $c_3(t) = 0$ for every $t \geq 0$. The following assertions are equivalent:*
(i) *The metric G and the Schouten–van Kampen connection $\overline{\nabla}$ associated to the Levi-Civita connection ∇ of G are torsion-coupled;*
(ii) *The triplet $(TM, \overline{\nabla}, G)$ is a statistical manifold;*
(iii) *The base manifold is locally flat and the metric G is of natural diagonal lift type, given by:*

$$\begin{cases} G(X_y^H, Y_y^H) = \kappa_1 g_{\tau(y)}(X, Y), \\ G(X_y^V, Y_y^V) = c_2(t) g_{\tau(y)}(X, Y) + d_2(t) g_{\tau(y)}(X, y) g_{\tau(y)}(Y, y), \\ G(X_y^V, Y_y^H) = 0, \end{cases} \tag{34}$$

for all $X, Y \in \mathcal{T}_0^1(M)$, $y \in TM$, $\kappa_1 \in \mathbb{R} \setminus \{0\}$, where c_2, d_2 are some arbitrary nonzero smooth real functions of energy density t of y such that $c_2(t) + 2t d_2(t) \neq 0$, for every $t \geq 0$;
(iv) *The Schouten–van Kampen connection $\overline{\nabla}$ coincides with the Levi-Civita connection ∇.*

Proof. According to Proposition 5, if a metric G given by (5) such that $c_3(t) = 0$ for every $t \geq 0$ is torsion-coupled with the Schouten–van Kampen connection $\overline{\nabla}$, then the base manifold (M, g) is locally flat. Thus, the expression (33) of the component $\mathcal{T}(\delta_i, \delta_j, \partial_k)$ reduces to:

$$\mathcal{T}(\delta_i, \delta_j, \partial_k) = \frac{c_1 d_3^2 t}{c_1 c_2 + 2t(c_2 d_1 + c_1 d_2) + 4t^2(d_1 d_2 - d_3^2)}(g_{jk}g_{0i} - g_{ik}g_{0j}). \tag{35}$$

Applying Lemma 1, one has $\mathcal{T}(\delta_i, \delta_j, \partial_k) = 0$ for every $t \geq 0$ if and only if $c_1 d_3^2 = 0$. Since $c_3(t) = 0$ for every $t \geq 0$, from the nondegeneracy condition (6) of the metric G it follows that $c_1(t) \neq 0$ for every $t \geq 0$, and hence, the expressions (35) of $\mathcal{T}(\delta_i, \delta_j, \partial_k)$ and (32) of $\mathcal{T}(\partial_i, \partial_j, \partial_k)$ vanish simultaneously if and only if $d_3 = 0$, i.e., the metric is of natural diagonal lift type. We compute the other components of the tensor field $\mathcal{T}$ with resect to the adapted local frame field $\{\delta_i, \partial_j\}_{i,j=1}^n$ by imposing the conditions already obtained, that is $c_3 = d_3 = 0$ and the locally flatness of the base manifold, and we have that:

$$\mathcal{T}(\partial_i, \partial_j, \delta_k) = 0,\ \mathcal{T}(\partial_i, \delta_j, \partial_k) = 0,\ \mathcal{T}(\delta_i, \delta_j, \delta_k) = 0,$$

$$\mathcal{T}(\partial_i, \delta_j, \delta_k) = \frac{1}{2}(c_1' g_{jk} g_{0i} + d_1 g_{ik} g_{0j} + d_1 g_{ij} g_{0k} + d_1' g_{0i} g_{0j} g_{0k}).$$

By using Lemma 1, it follows that $\mathcal{T}(\partial_i, \delta_j, \delta_k) = 0$ if and only if $c_1(t) = \kappa_1 \in \mathbb{R}$ and $d_1(t) = 0$ for every $t \geq 0$. For the nondegeneracy of the metric G the real constant κ_1 and the functions c_2 and $c_2 + 2t d_2$ must be nonzero. Thus, we prove that all the components of the tensor field $\mathcal{T}$ corresponding to the general natural metric G with $c_3 = 0$ vanish if and only if the base manifold (M, g) is locally flat and the metric G has the form (34). Hence, we proved the equivalence of the items (i) and (iii).

If assertion (iii) holds, i.e., the base manifold is locally flat and the metric G is given by (34), we obtain by using Theorem 1 that the Schouten–van Kampen connection $\overline{\nabla}$ associated to the Levi-Civita connection ∇ of G is torsion-free. On the other hand, we showed that (iii) is equivalent to (i), and since $\overline{\nabla}$ is torsion-free, items (i), (ii), and (iii) are equivalent. Moreover, since the metric G given by (34) is the metric from Proposition 3 (i), it follows that $\overline{\nabla}$ coincides with ∇, i.e., the items (iii) and (iv) in the statement are equivalent. □

Remark 1. *Let (M, g) be a locally flat connected Riemannian manifold of dimension $n > 2$. A natural diagonal metric whose corresponding Schouten–van Kampen connection is a statistical connection on TM depends on an arbitrary nonzero real constant and on two arbitrary nonzero smooth real functions c_2 and d_2 of the energy density t, such that $c_2(t) + 2t d_2(t) \neq 0$ for all $t \geq 0$. For every metric in this family the Levi-Civita connection and its associated Schouten–van Kampen connection are identical, and hence, there is no natural diagonal metric G on TM such that (TM, G) endowed the corresponding Schouten–van Kampen connection is a statistical manifold admitting torsion.*

Theorem 3. *Let (M, g) be a connected Riemannian manifold of dimension $n > 2$ and let TM be the total space of the tangent bundle, endowed with a proper general natural metric G given by (5) such that $c_2(0) c_3(0) \neq 0$ and with the Schouten–van Kampen connection $\overline{\nabla}$ associated to the Levi-Civita connection ∇ of G. The following assertions hold:*

(a) *$(TM, \overline{\nabla}, G)$ is a statistical manifold if and only if the base manifold (M, g) is locally flat and the metric G has one of the following expressions:*

$$(i) \begin{cases} G(X_y^H, Y_y^H) = \kappa_1 g_{\tau(y)}(X, Y), \\ G(X_y^V, Y_y^V) = \kappa_2 (c_3(t))^2 g_{\tau(y)}(X, Y) \\ \qquad + 2\kappa_2 c_3'(t)(c_3(t) + c_3'(t) t) g_{\tau(y)}(X, y) g_{\tau(y)}(Y, y), \\ G(X_y^V, Y_y^H) = c_3(t) g_{\tau(y)}(X, Y) + c_3'(t) g_{\tau(y)}(X, y) g_{\tau(y)}(Y, y), \end{cases}$$

for every $X, Y \in \mathcal{T}_0^1(TM)$, $y \in TM$, where κ_1, κ_2 are some arbitrary nonzero real constants such that $\kappa_1 \kappa_2 \neq 1$ and c_3 is an arbitrary smooth function of the energy density t of y, such that $c_3(0) \neq 0$, $c_3(t) \neq \frac{const}{\sqrt{t}}$ for all $const \in \mathbb{R}$ and all $t > 0$;

$$ii) \begin{cases} G(X_y^H, Y_y^H) = 0, \\ G(X_y^V, Y_y^V) = c_2(t) g_{\tau(y)}(X,Y) \\ \qquad + \frac{c_2'(t)c_3(t)^2 + 2c_2'(t)c_3(t)c_3'(t)t - 2c_2(t)c_3'^2(t)t}{c_3^2(t)} g_{\tau(y)}(X,y) g_{\tau(y)}(Y,y), \\ G(X_y^V, Y_y^H) = c_3(t) g_{\tau(y)}(X,Y) + c_3'(t) g_{\tau(y)}(X,y) g_{\tau(y)}(Y,y), \end{cases}$$

for every $X, Y \in \mathcal{T}_0^1(TM)$, $y \in TM$, where c_2, c_3 are some arbitrary smooth functions of the energy density t of $y \in TM$ such that $c_2(0)c_3(0) \neq 0$, $c_3(t) \neq \frac{const}{\sqrt{t}}$ for all $const \in \mathbb{R}$ and all $t > 0$.

The Levi-Civita connection ∇ of G and its associated Schouten–van Kampen connection $\overline{\nabla}$ coincide for every metric G given by i).

The connections ∇ and $\overline{\nabla}$ are different, i.e., $(TM, \overline{\nabla}, G)$ is a nontrivial statistical manifold if the metric G has the expression ii) with $c_2(t) \neq \kappa_2 c_3^2(t)$ for every $t \geq 0$ and every $\kappa_2 \in \mathbb{R}$.

(b) $(TM \setminus \{0\}, \overline{\nabla}, G)$ is a quasi-statistical manifold if and only if the base manifold (M, g) has constant sectional curvature $c < 0$ and the metric G has the following expression:

$$\begin{cases} G(X_y^H, Y_y^H) = -\frac{c\kappa_2}{t} g_{\tau(y)}(X,y) g_{\tau(y)}(Y,y), \\ G(X_y^V, Y_y^V) = \frac{\kappa_2}{t} g_{\tau(y)}(X,Y) + d_2(t) g_{\tau(y)}(X,y) g_{\tau(y)}(Y,y), \\ G(X_y^V, Y_y^H) = \pm \left[\frac{\kappa_2 \sqrt{-2c}}{\sqrt{t}} g_{\tau(y)}(X,Y) - \frac{\kappa_2 \sqrt{-2c}}{2t\sqrt{t}} (t) g_{\tau(y)}(X,y) g_{\tau(y)}(Y,y) \right], \end{cases}$$

for every $X, Y \in \mathcal{T}_0^1(TM)$, $y \in TM$, where κ_2 is an arbitrary nonzero real constant and d_2 is an arbitrary smooth real function of the energy density t of y such that $d_2(t) \neq -\frac{\kappa_2}{2t^2}$, for every $t > 0$.

Proof. Our purpose is to determine the proper general natural metrics G such that the manifold $(TM, \overline{\nabla}, G)$ is a statistical manifold admitting torsion. To this aim, we study the conditions of vanishing for all the components of the tensor field $\mathcal{T}$ given by (22) with respect to the adapted local frame field $\{\delta_i, \partial_j\}_{i,j=1}^n$.

From Proposition 5, a necessary condition for $(TM, \overline{\nabla}, G)$ to be a statistical manifold admitting torsion is that the base manifold (M, g) has constant sectional curvature c, and hence, we take from the beginning:

$$R_{kij}^h = c(\delta_i^h g_{kj} - \delta_j^h g_{ki}),$$

where δ_i^h is the Kronecker delta.

By using the expressions (24)–(29), in which we substitute the components of the metric from (4), the components of the torsion T from (15), the expressions (12) of the Schouten–van Kampen connection, its coefficients from (13), the entries of the inverse matrix H from (8) and their coefficients from (10) and (9), we obtain that the components of the tensor field $\mathcal{T}$ have the forms:

$$\mathcal{T}(\partial_i, \partial_j, \partial_k) = A_1(t)(g_{jk} g_{0i} - g_{ik} g_{0j}); \quad \mathcal{T}(\partial_i, \partial_j, \delta_k) = A_2(t)(g_{jk} g_{0i} - g_{ik} g_{0j});$$
$$\mathcal{T}(\partial_i, \delta_j, \partial_k) = A_3(t) g_{jk} g_{0i} + \widetilde{A}_3 g_{ik} g_{0j} + B_3(t) g_{ij} g_{0k} + C_3(t) g_{0i} g_{0j} g_{0k};$$
$$\mathcal{T}(\partial_i, \delta_j, \delta_k) = A_4(t) g_{jk} g_{0i} + \widetilde{A}_4 g_{ik} g_{0j} + B_4(t) g_{ij} g_{0k} + C_4(t) g_{0i} g_{0j} g_{0k};$$
$$\mathcal{T}(\delta_i, \delta_j, \partial_k) = A_5(t)(g_{jk} g_{0i} - g_{ik} g_{0j}); \quad \mathcal{T}(\delta_i, \delta_j, \delta_k) = A_6(t)(g_{jk} g_{0i} - g_{ik} g_{0j}),$$

where A_i, $i = 1, \ldots, 6$ and $\widetilde{A}_j, B_j$, $j = 3, 4$, are some rational functions depending on the coefficients of the metric G, their derivatives, the constant sectional curvature c of (M, g), and the energy density t. Since the expressions of A_i and B_i are quite long, we present here the shorter ones:

$$B_3(t) = \frac{c'_1 c_2 c_3 + c_1(c'_2 c_3 - c_2 c'_3) - c_3^2 c'_3 + (c_3^2 - c_1 c_2) d_3}{2(c_1 c_2 - c_3^2)}, \quad (36)$$

$$B_4(t) = \tfrac{1}{2}(cc_2 + d_1).$$

From Lemma 1, we have that all the components of the tensor field $\mathcal{T}$ from above vanish if and only if $A_i(t) = 0$, $i = 1, \ldots, 6$, $\widetilde{A}_j(t) = 0$, $B_j(t) = 0$, $j = 3, 4$.

From the conditions of vanishing of $B_3(t)$ and $B_4(t)$ given in (36), we obtain two necessary conditions for $(TM, \overline{\nabla}, G)$ to be a quasi-statistical manifold:

$$d_3 = \frac{c'_1 c_2 c_3 + c_1(c'_2 c_3 - c_2 c'_3) - c_3^2 c'_3}{c_1 c_2 - c_3^2}, \quad (37)$$

$$d_1 = -cc_2. \quad (38)$$

After substituting the value obtained for d_1 into the expression of $\widetilde{A}_3(t)$ this turns into:

$$\begin{aligned}
\widetilde{A}_3(t) =& (2cc_1 c_2^3 c_3 + c_1^2 c_2 c''_2 c_3 - 2cc_2^2 c_3^3 - c_1 c'_2{}^2 c_3 - 2c_1^2 c_2 c_3 d_2 \\
&+ 2c_1 c_3^3 d_2 + 2c_1^2 c_2^2 d_3 - 2c_1 c_2 c_3^2 d_3 - 4c^2 c_2^4 c_3 t - 2cc_1 c_2^2 c'_2 c_3 t \\
&+ 2cc_2 c'_2 c_3^3 t + 8cc_1 c_2^3 c_3 d_2 t - 4cc_2 c_3^3 d_2 t - 4cc_1 c_3^3 d_3 t + 2c_1^2 c_2 c'_2 d_3 t \\
&- 4cc_2^2 c_3^2 d_3 t - 2c_1 c'_2 c_3^2 d_3 t - 8c^2 c_2^3 c_3 d_2 t^2 - 4cc_1 c_2^2 c'_2 d_3 t^2 \\
&+ 4cc_2 c'_2 c_3^2 d_3 t^2 - 8cc_2^2 c_3 d_3^2 t^2)/[2(c_1 c_2 - c_3^2)(c_1 c_2 - c_3^2 \\
&- 2cc_2^2 t + 2c_1 d_2 t - 4c_3 d_3 t - 4cc_2 d_2 t^2 - 4d_3^2 t^2)],
\end{aligned} \quad (39)$$

To obtain the necessary and sufficient conditions for $\widetilde{A}_3(t) = 0$, we have to treat the following cases:

(Case I) $c_1 - 2cc_2 t \neq 0$ and $c_1 c_2 - c_3^2 \neq 2cc_2^2 t$;
(Case II) $c_1 - 2cc_2 t = 0$;
(Case III) $c_1 c_2 - c_3^2 = 2cc_2^2 t$.

Next, we study each case separately.

(Case I) When $c_1 - 2cc_2 t \neq 0$ (i.e., $c_1 + 2td_1 \neq 0$) and $c_1 c_2 - c_3^2 \neq 2cc_2^2 t$, from (39) we obtain that $\widetilde{A}_3(t) = 0$ if and only if:

$$\begin{aligned}
d_2 =& \frac{1}{2c_3(c_1 - 2cc_2 t)(c_3^2 - c_1 c_2 + 2cc_2^2 t)} \{4c^2 c_2^4 c_3 t - c_1(c_1 c_2 - c_3^2)[2c_2 d_3 \\
&+ c'_2(c_3 + 2d_3 t)] + 2cc_2\{c_1 c_2[c'_2 t(c_3 + 2d_3 t) - c_2(c_3 - 2d_3 t)] \\
&+ c_3[c_2(c_3^2 + 2c_3 d_3 t + 4d_3^2 t^2) - c'_2 c_3 t(c_3 + 2d_3 t)]\}\}.
\end{aligned} \quad (40)$$

By using (40) and then (37) and (38), we obtain that the numerators of $\widetilde{A}_4(t)$ and $A_6(t)$ become, respectively:

$$\begin{aligned}
N_{\widetilde{A}_4}(t) =& 2cc_1^3 c_2^4 - c_1^2 c'_1 c_2^2 c_3^2 - 4cc_1^2 c_3^3 c_3^2 - c_1^3 c_2 c'_2 c_3^2 + c_1 c_3^4 (c_1 c_2)' \\
&+ 2cc_1 c_2^2 c_3^4 + 2c_1^3 c_2^2 c_3 c'_3 - 2c_1^2 c_2 c_3^3 c'_3 - 4c^2 c_1^2 c_2^5 t + 2cc_1^2 c_2^3 c'_2 t \\
&+ 4c^2 c_1 c_2^4 c_3^2 t - 2cc_1^2 c_2^2 c'_2 c_3^2 t - 2cc_2 c_3^4 t(c_1 c_2)' - 4cc_1^2 c_2^3 c_3 c'_3 t \\
&+ 8cc_1 c_2^2 c_3^3 c'_3 t - 4c^2 c_1^2 c_2^4 c'_2 t^2 - 4c^2 c'_1 c_2^4 c_3^2 t^2 + 8c^2 c_1 c_2^4 c_3 c'_3 t^2,
\end{aligned} \quad (41)$$

$$N_{A_6}(t) = c_1^3 c_1' c_2^2 + 2cc_1^3 c_3^3 - 2c_1^2 c_1' c_2 c_3^2 - 2cc_1^2 c_2^2 c_3^2 + c_1 c_1' c_3^4 - 2cc_1 c_2 c_3^4 \qquad (42)$$
$$+ 2cc_3^6 - 4cc_1^2 c_1' c_3^2 t - 4c^2 c_1^2 c_2^2 t + 2cc_1^3 c_2^2 c_2' t + 6cc_1 c_1' c_2^2 c_3^2 t$$
$$- 2cc_1^2 c_2 c_2' c_3^2 t - 6cc_1' c_2 c_3^4 t + 4c^2 c_2^2 c_3^4 t - 4cc_1 c_2' c_3^4 t + 4cc_1 c_2 c_3^3 c_3' t$$
$$+ 4cc_3^5 c_3' t + 4c^2 c_1 c_1' c_2^4 t^2 - 4c^2 c_1^2 c_2^3 c_2' t^2 - 12c^2 c_1' c_2^3 c_3^2 t^2$$
$$- 4c^2 c_1 c_2^2 c_2' c_3^2 t^2 + 8c^2 c_1 c_2^3 c_3 c_3' t^2 + 8c^2 c_2^3 c_3^3 c_3' t^2.$$

Studying the simultaneous vanishing of $\widetilde{A}_4$ and A_6 we distinguish the following subcases of Case I:

(I.1) $c_3^2 \neq 2cc_2^2 t$ and $c_1 \neq 0$;
(I.2) $c_1 \neq 0$, $c > 0$ and $c_3 = \pm\sqrt{2ct} c_2$;
(I.3) $c_1 = 0$.

We treat each subcase separately.

(I.1) When $c_3^2 \neq 2cc_2^2 t$ and $c_1 \neq 0$, solving the system of equations given by $N_{\widetilde{A}_4}(t) = 0$ and $N_{A_6}(t) = 0$, we obtain that the derivatives of the functions c_1 and c_2 have the expressions:

$$c_1' = \frac{2c(c_1 c_2 c_3^2 + c_3^4 + 2c_1 c_2 c_3 c_3' t + 2c_3^3 c_3' t)}{(c_1 - 2cc_2 t)(2cc_2^2 t - c_3^2)}, \qquad (43)$$

$$c_2' = \frac{2c_2[cc_1^2 c_2^2 + cc_3^4 + c_1^2 c_3 c_3' + 2c(c_3^2 - c_1 c_2)(cc_2^2 + c_3 c_3')t + 4c^2 c_2^2 c_3 c_3' t^2]}{-c_1(c_1 - 2cc_2 t)(2cc_2^2 t - c_3^2)}. \qquad (44)$$

Substituting (43) and (44) into the expression of $\mathcal{T}(\partial_i, \delta_j, \delta_k)$, this reduces to:

$$\mathcal{T}(\partial_i, \delta_j, \delta_k) = \frac{cc_3(2c_1 c_2 + c_3^2 - 2cc_2^2 t)(c_3 + 2c_3' t)}{(c_1 - 2cc_2 t)(2cc_2^2 t - c_3^2)} g_{jk} g_{0i} \qquad (45)$$
$$+ \frac{c^2 c_2 c_3(c_3^2 + 2cc_2^2 t)(c_3 + 2c_3' t)}{c_1(c_1 - 2cc_2 t)(2cc_2^2 t - c_3^2)} g_{0i} g_{0j} g_{0k},$$

and it vanishes, according to Lemma 1, if and only if the involved coefficients vanish simultaneously. Since the metric G is proper general natural, i.e., $c_3 \neq 0, d_3 \neq 0$, the coefficient of $g_{0i} g_{0j} g_{0k}$ vanishes if and only if one of the following instances happens:

(I.1.i) $c = 0$, which together with (37), (38), (40), (43), (44) leads to:

$$c_1 = \kappa_1 \in \mathbb{R} \setminus \{0\}, \ d_1 = 0, \ c_2' = \frac{2c_2 c_3'}{c_3}, \ \text{i.e., } c_2 = \kappa_2 c_3^2, \ d_2 = 2\kappa_2 c_3'(c_3 + c_3' t), \ d_3 = c_3',$$

where κ_2 is an arbitrary nonzero real constant and c_3 is an arbitrary smooth nonzero real function of t such that $c_3(0) \neq 0$ and the nondegeneracy conditions (6) of the metric G are satisfied, i.e., $\kappa_1 \kappa_2 \neq 1$ and $(\kappa_1 \kappa_2 - 1)(c_3 + 2tc_3')^2 \neq 0$, and hence, $c_3(t) \neq \frac{const}{\sqrt{t}}$ for all $const \in \mathbb{R}$ and all $t > 0$. By substituting the values of the coefficients of the metric G obtained in Case I.1.i) and $c = 0$ into each component of the tensor field $\mathcal{T}$ with respect to the adapted local frame filed $\{\delta_i, \partial_j\}_{i,j=1}^n$, we obtain, by using Mathematica, that $\mathcal{T} = 0$. On the other hand, the obtained metric satisfies Proposition 4, and hence, the Schouten–van Kampen connection $\overline{\nabla}$ coincides with the Levi-Civita connection of the metric G, i.e., in Case (I.1.i), $(TM, \overline{\nabla}, G)$ is obviously a statistical manifold.

(I.1.ii) $c_3 + 2c_3' t = 0$, i.e., $c_3(t) = \frac{\kappa_3}{\sqrt{t}}$, for every $\kappa_3 \in \mathbb{R} \setminus \{0\}$, $t > 0$, but together with (38), (40), (37), and (43), which would imply $d_2 = -\frac{c_2}{2t}$, i.e., $c_2 + 2td_2 = 0$ and $d_3 = c_3'$, i.e., $c_3 + 2td_3 = 0$, and hence, the second nondegeneracy condition (6) of the metric G would not be satisfied.

(I.1.iii) $c_2 = 0$ does not satisfy the condition $c_2(0)c_3(0) = 0$ from the hypothesis.

(I.1.iv) $c < 0$ and $c_3^2 = -2cc_2^2 t$, which substituted into (45), turns the factor $2c_1 c_2 + c_3^2 - 2cc_2^2 t$ from the coefficient of $g_{jk} g_{0i}$ into $2c_2(c_1 - 2cc_2 t)$ and this vanishes if and only if $c_2 = 0$ (see I.1.*iii*) or $c_1 = 2cc_2t$, which together with $d_1 = -cc_2$ yields $c_1 + 2td_1 = 0$, which does not hold in Case I.

We conclude that the only favorable subcase of Case I.1 is (I.1.*i*), rended in the statement at *a* (*i*). We already showed that in Case (I.1.*i*) the Schouten–van Kampen connection $\overline{\nabla}$ coincides with the Levi-Civita connection of G.

(I.2) $c_1 \neq 0$, $c > 0$ and $c_3 = \pm\sqrt{2ct}c_2$, i.e., $c_2 = \pm\frac{c_3}{\sqrt{2ct}}$ for every $t > 0$. Substituting $c_2 = \epsilon\frac{c_3}{\sqrt{2ct}}$ (where $\epsilon = 1$ or $\epsilon = -1$) into $N_{\widetilde{A}_4}$ we obtain:

$$N_{\widetilde{A}_4}(t) = \sqrt{c}c_3[c_1(2c_1^2 - 5\epsilon c_1 c_3 \sqrt{2ct} + 10cc_3^2 t)(c_3 + 2c_3't) \\ - 2c_1' c_3 t(c_1^2 - \epsilon c_1 c_3 t\sqrt{2ct} + 4cc_3^2 t)],$$

which vanishes if and only if one of the following instances happens:

(I.2.*i*) $\begin{cases} c_1^2 - \epsilon c_1 c_3 t\sqrt{2ct} + 4cc_3^2 t = 0, \\ (2c_1^2 - 5\epsilon c_1 c_3 \sqrt{2ct} + 10cc_3^2 t)(c_3 + 2c_3' t) = 0. \end{cases}$

If $c_3 + 2c_3' t = 0$, i.e., $c_3(t) = \frac{\kappa_3}{\sqrt{t}}$ for every $t > 0$, $\kappa_3 \in \mathbb{R} \setminus \{0\}$, then the first relation in (I.2.*i*) turns into:

$$c_1^2 - \epsilon \kappa_3 \sqrt{2ct}c_1 + 4\kappa_3^2 ct = 0,$$

which is not satisfied by any real function c_1 of t.

If $2c_1^2 - 5\epsilon c_1 c_3 \sqrt{2ct} + 10cc_3^2 t = 0$, since the first relation in (I.2.*i*) holds, it follows that $3c_1^2 + 10cc_3^2 t = 0$, where $c > 0$, and hence $c_1 = c_3 = 0$, which do not satisfy neither the nondegeneracy condition (6) for the metric G nor the conditions (I.2).

(I.2.*ii*) $\begin{cases} c_1 = \kappa_1 \in \mathbb{R} \setminus \{0\}, \\ (2c_1^2 - 5\epsilon c_1 c_3 \sqrt{2ct} + 10cc_3^2 t)(c_3 + 2c_3' t) = 0. \end{cases}$

In this case, the first factor in the second relation of I.2.*ii*) becomes:

$$10ctc_3^2 - 5\epsilon\kappa_1\sqrt{2ct}c_3 + 2\kappa_1^2 \neq 0$$

for every real function c_3 of t. On the other hand, if the first relation in (I.2.*ii*) is satisfied and $c_3 + 2c_3' t = 0$, i.e., $c_3 = \frac{\kappa_3}{\sqrt{t}}$, for every $t > 0$, $\kappa_3 \in \mathbb{R} \setminus \{0\}$, by taking into account the expressions (38), (40), (37) of the coefficients d_1, d_2, d_3 and the expression of c_2 in Case I.2, it follows that:

$$(c_1 + 2td_1)(c_2 + 2td_2) - (c_3 + 2td_3)^2 = 0,$$

hence, the second nedegeneracy condition (6) is not satisfied.

(I.2.*iii*) $\begin{cases} c_1^2 - \epsilon c_1 c_3 t\sqrt{2ct} + 4cc_3^2 t \neq 0 \\ c_1' = \dfrac{2c_1^3 c_3 - 5\epsilon c_1^2 c_3^2 \sqrt{2ct} + 10cc_1 c_3^3 t + 4c_1^3 c_3' t - 10\epsilon c_1^2 c_3 c_3' t\sqrt{2ct} + 20cc_1 c_3^2 c_3' t^2}{2c_3 t(c_1^2 - \epsilon c_1 c_3 t\sqrt{2ct} + 4cc_3^2 t)}, \end{cases}$

for every $t > 0$. By using the expressions (38), (40), (37) of d_1, d_2, d_3, the expression of c_1' in Case (I.2.*iii*) and that of c_2 in Case I.2, we obtain that the component $\mathcal{T}(\delta_i, \delta_j, \delta_k)$ reduces to:

$$\mathcal{T}(\delta_i, \delta_j, \delta_k) = \frac{2\epsilon\sqrt{c}(c_1^2 - \epsilon\sqrt{2ct}c_1 c_3 + 4cc_3^2 t)}{\sqrt{t}(\sqrt{2}c_1 - 6\epsilon\sqrt{c}tc_3)} \neq 0,$$

for every c_1, c_3 nonzero smooth real functions of t. Subsequently, a general natural metric G whose coefficients satisfy Case (I.2.*iii*) is not torsion-coupled with the corresponding Schouten–van Kampen connection.

(I.3) $c_1 = 0$, which substituted into the expression of $\mathcal{T}(\partial_i, \delta_j, \delta_k)$ together with (38), (40), (37) turns the coefficient $A_4(t)$ into:

$$A_4(t) = \frac{ct(2c_2c_3' - c_2'c_3)(c_3 + 2c_3't)}{c_3(c_3 + 2tc_3') + 2cc_2t(c_2 + 2tc_2')}$$

and this vanishes if and only if one of the following situations happens:

(I.3.i) $c = 0$, which turns relation (38) into $d_1 = 0$. In this subcase, it follows that the first condition of Case I, $c_1 + 2td_1 \neq 0$ is not satisfied, and hence, the subcase (I.3.i) is not possible.

(I.3.ii) $c_3 + 2tc_3' = 0$, i.e., $c_3 = \frac{\kappa_3}{\sqrt{t}}$, for all $\kappa_3 \in \mathbb{R} \setminus \{0\}$, $t > 0$, which together with $c_1 = 0$ and the expressions (38), (40), and (37) leads to $c_2 + 2td_2 = c_3 + 2td_3 = 0$, i.e., the second nondegeneracy condition in (6) is not satisfied, and hence, there is no metric G whose coefficients satisfy Case I.3.ii).

(I.3.iii) $2c_2c_3' - c_2'c_3 = 0$, i.e., $c_2 = \kappa_2 c_3^2$, for every $\kappa_2 \in \mathbb{R} \setminus \{0\}$. Together with (38), (40), and (37), the expression obtained for c_2 yields:

$$\mathcal{T}(\partial_i, \delta_j, \delta_k) = -\frac{c\kappa_2 c_3(c_3 + 2tc_3')}{2t} g_{0i} g_{0j} g_{0k}. \tag{46}$$

The expression (46) vanishes if and only if $c = 0$ or $c_3 + 2tc_3' = 0$, relations which are not possible in Case I.3 (see the discussion from I.3.i and I.3.ii).

(Case II) When $c_1 - 2cc_2t = 0$, i.e., $c_1 + 2td_1 = 0$, by using (37), we obtain that the coefficient $B_4(t)$ from the expression of $\mathcal{T}(\partial_i, \delta_j, \delta_k)$ reduces to:

$$B_4(t) = \frac{2c^2 c_2^3}{c_3^2 - 2cc_2^2 t},$$

and hence, it vanishes if and only if one of the following subcases holds:

(II.1) $c = 0$, which due to relations (38) and (37) yields $c_1 = d_1 = 0$ and $d_3 = c_3'$, then the expression of the component $\mathcal{T}(\partial_i, \partial_j, \partial_k)$ reduces to:

$$\mathcal{T}(\partial_i, \partial_j, \partial_k) = \frac{c_2' c_3^2 - c_3^2 d_2 + 2c_2' c_3 c_3' t - 2c_2 c_3'^2 t}{c_3(c_3 + 2tc_3')} (g_{jk} g_{0i} - g_{ik} g_{0j}),$$

and according to Lemma 1 it is zero if and only if:

$$d_2 = \frac{c_2' c_3^2 + 2c_2' c_3 c_3' t - 2c_2 c_3'^2 t}{c_3^2}.$$

If the coefficients of the metric G have the expressions obtained in Case II.1 and the base manifold is locally flat, we verify by using Mathematica that all the components of the tensor field $\mathcal{T}$ with respect to the adapted local frame field $\{\delta_i, \partial_j\}_{i,j=1}^n$ vanish. The metric whose coefficients are those in Case II.1 is the metric from item $a\ ii)$ in the statement. From Theorem 1, it follows that the Schouten–van Kampen connection associated to the Levi-Civita connection of the metric G given at $a\ ii)$ is torsion-free, and since we proved that $\mathcal{T} = 0$, the triplet $(TM, \overline{\nabla}, G)$ is a statistical manifold. If in the expression $a\ (ii)$ we take $c_2(t) = \kappa(c_3(t))^2$, where κ is an arbitrary nonzero real constant, it follows that $d_2(t) = 2\kappa c_3'(t)(c_3(t) + tc_3'(t))$, and hence, the metric G satisfies Proposition 4. It follows that the Levi-Civita connection of the metric G given at $a\ ii)$ coincides with the associated Schouten–van Kampen connection only when $c_2(t) = \kappa(c_3(t))^2$ for every $t \geq 0$, $\kappa \in \mathbb{R} \setminus \{0\}$.

If the metric G has the expression from $a\ ii)$ with $c_2(t) \neq \kappa(c_3(t))^2$ for every $t \geq 0$, $\kappa \in \mathbb{R}$, then the Levi-Civita connection of G and its associated Schouten–van Kampen connection do not coincide, and hence, the statistical manifold $(TM, \overline{\nabla}, G)$ is nontrivial.

(II.2) $c_2 = 0$ doest not verify the condition $c_2(0)c_3(0) = 0$ from the hypothesis.

(Case III) When $c_1c_2 - c_3^2 = 2cc_2^2 t$, it follows from the nondegeneracy condition (6) of the metric G that the base manifold (M, g) is not locally flat, $c_2(t) \neq 0$ and $t \neq 0$, and hence, in Case III, the metric G is defined on $TM \setminus \{0\}$, the total space of the bundle of nonzero vector fields tangent to the space form (M, g). In this case, one has:

$$c_1 = \frac{c_3^2 + 2cc_2^2 t}{c_2} \qquad (47)$$

and then the expression (37) of d_3 reduces to:

$$d_3 = \frac{c_2 c_3 + 2c_2' c_3 t - c_2 c_3' t}{c_2 t}. \qquad (48)$$

Substituting the expressions (38), (47), and (48) into the expression of $\mathcal{T}(\delta_i, \delta_j, \delta_k)$, we obtain that the numerator of its coefficient is:

$$\begin{aligned} N_{A_6}(t) =& c_3^2 [8c_2^2 c_3^3 - 8cc_2^4 c_3 t + 27c_2 c_2'^2 c_3^3 t - 18c_2^2 c_3^2 c_3' t - 14cc_2^3 c_2' c_3 t^2 \\ & + 20c_2'^2 c_3^3 t^2 + 4cc_2^4 c_3' t^2 - 26c_2 c_2' c_3^2 c_3' t^2 + 8c_2^2 c_3 c_3'^2 t^2 \\ & - 8cc_2^2 c_2'^2 c_3 t^3 + 4cc_2^3 c_2' c_3' t^3 - 2c_2 c_3 d_2 t (c_3^2 + 2cc_2^2 t)]. \end{aligned}$$

To obtain necessary and sufficient conditions for $N_{A_6}(t) = 0$, we have to study two subcases of Case III:

(III.1) If $c_3^2 + 2cc_2^2 t \neq 0$, then $N_{A_6}(t) = 0$ if and only if:

$$\begin{aligned} d_2 =& (8c_2^2 c_3^3 - 8cc_2^4 c_3 t + 27c_2 c_2'^2 c_3^3 t - 18c_2^2 c_3^2 c_3' t - 14cc_2^3 c_2' c_3 t^2 \\ & + 20c_2'^2 c_3^3 t^2 + 4cc_2^4 c_3' t^2 - 26c_2 c_2' c_3^2 c_3' t^2 + 8c_2^2 c_3 c_3'^2 t^2 \\ & - 8cc_2^2 c_2'^2 c_3 t^3 + 4cc_2^3 c_2' c_3' t^3) / [2c_2 c_3 t (c_3^2 + 2cc_2^2 t)]. \end{aligned} \qquad (49)$$

Taking into account the expressions (38), (47), (48), and (49), we obtain that the numerator of the coefficient of $g_{ik}g_{0j}$ involved in the expression of $\mathcal{T}(\partial_i, \delta_j, \partial_k)$ is of the form:

$$N_{\tilde{A}_3}(t) = c_3(c_3^2 + 2cc_2^2 t)(2c_2 c_3 + 3c_2' c_3 t - 2c_2 c_3' t).$$

Since $c_3^2 + 2cc_2^2 t \neq 0$ and G is a proper general natural metric, $N_{\tilde{A}_3}(t) = 0$ if and only if:

$$c_3' = \frac{2c_2 c_3 + 3c_2' c_3 t}{2c_2 t},$$

which yields a simpler form of the coefficient of $g_{jk}g_{0i}$ in the same component of $\mathcal{T}$, namely:

$$A_3(t) = \frac{c_3(c_3^2 + 3cc_2^2 t)(c_2 + c_2' t)}{4cc_2^3 t^2}, \qquad (50)$$

while the coefficient involved in the expression of $\mathcal{T}(\partial_i, \partial_j, \delta_k)$ becomes:

$$A_2(t) = \frac{c_3(cc_2^2 t - c_3^2)(c_2 + c_2' t)}{4cc_2^3 t^2}. \qquad (51)$$

The expressions (50) and (51) vanish simultaneously if and only if $c_2 + c_2' t = 0$ or $c_3^2 + 3cc_2^2 t = cc_2^2 t - c_3^2 = 0$.

If $c_2 + c_2' t = 0$, i.e., $c_2 = \frac{\kappa_2}{t}$ for every $t > 0$, where κ_2 is an arbitrary nonzero real constant, then by taking into account (38), (47), (48) and (49) it follows that the second nondegeneracy condition (6) for the metric G is not satisfied.

If $c_3^2 + 3cc_2^2 t = cc_2^2 t - c_3^2 = 0$, i.e., $c_3^2 = cc_2^2 t = 0$, then under the condition of Case III, it follows that $c_1 c_2 - c_3^2 = 0$, i.e., the metric G is degenerate. We conclude that in

Case III.1, there is no proper general natural metric G torsion-coupled with the corresponding Schouten–van Kampen connection $\overline{\nabla}$.

(III.2) The subcase $c_3^2 + 2cc_2^2 t = 0$ holds for $c < 0$ and $t > 0$, and due to (47), it reduces to the condition $c_1 = 0$. Then, the relation (37) turns into $d_3 = c_3'$, and together with (38), it yields:

$$\mathcal{T}(\partial_i, \partial_j, \delta_k) = 0, \quad \mathcal{T}(\delta_i, \delta_j, \partial_k) = 0,$$

$$\mathcal{T}(\delta_i, \delta_j, \delta_k) = \frac{cc_3(c_3 + 2c_3' t)^2}{c_3^2 + 4c_3 c_3' t + 2cc_2^2 t + 4c_3'^2 t^2 + 4cc_2 d_2 t^2}(g_{ik}g_{0j} - g_{jk}g_{0i}).$$

Then, $\mathcal{T}(\delta_i, \delta_j, \delta_k) = 0$ if and only if $c_3(t) = \frac{\kappa_3}{\sqrt{t}}$, for every $t > 0$, $\kappa_3 \in \mathbb{R} \setminus \{0\}$.
By using (38) and the coefficients obtained in Case III.2:

$$c_1 = 0, \quad c_3 = \frac{\kappa_3}{\sqrt{t}}, \quad d_3 = -\frac{\kappa_3}{2t\sqrt{t}}, \tag{52}$$

we have:

$$\mathcal{T}(\partial_i, \partial_j, \partial_k) = \frac{c_2 + c_2' t}{2t}(g_{jk}g_{0i} - g_{ik}g_{0j}),$$

$$\mathcal{T}(\partial_i, \delta_j, \delta_k) = -\frac{c(c_2 + c_2' t)}{2t} g_{0i}g_{0j}g_{0k},$$

$$\mathcal{T}(\partial_i, \delta_j, \partial_k) = \frac{\kappa_3^2 + 2cc_2^2 t^2}{4\kappa_3 t^2 \sqrt{t}}(g_{0i}g_{0j}g_{0k} - 2t g_{ik}g_{0j}),$$

which vanish simultaneously if and only if:

$$c_2 = \frac{\kappa_2}{t}, \quad \kappa_3 = \pm \kappa_2 \sqrt{-2c}, \quad \forall t > 0, \kappa_2 \in \mathbb{R} \setminus \{0\}. \tag{53}$$

Subsequently, in Case III.2, all the components of the tensor field $\mathcal{T}$ with respect to the adapted local frame field $\{\delta_i, \partial_j\}_{i,j=1}^n$ vanish simultaneously if and only if the coefficients of the metric G satisfy the relations (38), (52), and (53) and d_2 is an arbitrary smooth real function of t, such that $d_2(t) \neq -\frac{\kappa_2}{2t^2}$, because if $d_2(t) = -\frac{\kappa_2}{2t^2}$, then the nondegeneracy condition (6) for the metric G would not be satisfied. Thus, we proved that the triplet $(TM \setminus \{0\}, \overline{\nabla}, G)$ is a statistical manifold admitting torsion if and only if the metric G has the expression given in the statement at item (b). □

Remark 2. *Let (M, g) be a locally flat connected Riemannian manifold of dimension $n > 2$. There are two families of proper general natural metrics on TM such that the Schouten–van Kampen connection associated to the Levi-Civita connection of a metric is a statistical connection on TM. One family of metrics depends on an arbitrary smooth function c_3 of the energy density t, different from $\frac{\text{const}}{\sqrt{t}}$ with const $\in \mathbb{R}$, $c_3(0) \neq 0$, and on two nonzero arbitrary real constants, provided that their product is not 1. The other family of metrics depends on two nonzero arbitrary smooth real functions c_2, c_3 of t, provided that $c_2(0)c_3(0) \neq 0$, $c_3(t) \neq \frac{\text{const}}{\sqrt{t}}$ for every $t > 0$, const $\in \mathbb{R}$. If, moreover, $c_2(t) \neq \kappa_2 c_3^2(t)$ for every $t \geq 0$, $\kappa_2 \in \mathbb{R}$, then the statistical structure on TM is nontrivial.*

Remark 3. *Let (M, g) be a connected $n > 2$–dimensional Riemannian manifold of constant sectional curvature $c < 0$. The family of proper general natural metrics on $TM \setminus \{0\}$ such that the Schouten–van Kampen connection associated to the Levi-Civita connection of a metric is a quasi-statistical connection on $TM \setminus \{0\}$ depends on the constant sectional curvature c of (M, g), the energy density t, an arbitrary nonzero real constant κ_2 and an arbitrary smooth function of t, different from $-\frac{\kappa_2}{2t^2}$.*

4. Conclusions

Investigating the quasi-statistical Schouten–van Kampen connection $\overline{\nabla}$ associated to the Levi-Civita connection of a general natural metric G given by (5) on the total space TM of the tangent bundle of a Riemannian manifold (M, g), we conclude the following:

(1) The base manifold must be a space form when $c_2(0)c_3(0) \neq 0$ and locally flat when $c_3(t) = 0$. Implicitly, when the metric G is of natural diagonal lift type, (M, g) must be locally flat.

(2) There exists one family of natural diagonal metrics such that $(TM, \overline{\nabla}, G)$ is a statistical manifold. The metrics in this family depend on two arbitrary nonzero smooth real functions of the energy density t and on an arbitrary nonzero real constant such that the nondegeneracy conditions of the metric are satisfied.

(3) When G is a proper general natural metric G on TM, $\overline{\nabla}$ is a statistical connection if and only if (M, g) is locally flat and the metric G has two possible expressions. Hence, there are two families of proper general natural metrics such that $(TM, \overline{\nabla}, G)$ is a statistical manifold. The metrics in the first family depend on two arbitrary nonzero real constants, κ_1, κ_2, and on an arbitrary smooth nonzero real function c_3 of the energy density t such that $c_3(0) \neq 0$, while the metrics in the second family depend only on two arbitrary smooth nonzero real functions of t, c_2 and c_3, for which $c_2(0)c_3(0) \neq 0$, such that the nondegeneracy conditions of the metric are satisfied in each case.

(4) If $c_2(t) \neq \kappa_2 c_3^2(t)$, then the statistical manifold $(TM, \overline{\nabla}, G)$ is nontrivial, i.e., the Levi-Civita connection is different from its associated Schouten–van Kampen connection.

(5) The manifold $(TM \setminus \{0\}, \overline{\nabla}, G)$ is quasi-statistical if and only if (M, g) has constant sectional curvature $c < 0$ and the metric G depends on c, t, on an arbitrary nonzero real constant κ_2 and on an arbitrary smooth real function of t, different from $-\frac{\kappa_2}{2t^2}$.

In a forthcoming paper we will determine the conditions under which the general natural α-structures characterized in [47] are torsion coupled (in particular Codazzi coupled) with the (quasi-)statistical Schouten–van Kampen connection $\overline{\nabla}$ associated to the Levi-Civita connection ∇ of a general natural metric G on TM. Another goal will be to characterize the para-Kähler-like statistical manifolds $(TM, \overline{\nabla}, P, G)$, where the almost product structure P and the metric G are of general natural lift type on TM.

Funding: This research received no external funding.

Data Availability Statement: No new data were created or analyzed in this study. Data sharing is not applicable to this article.

Acknowledgments: The author wants to thank Gabriel-Eduard Vîlcu for the useful discussions on the topic of the paper and the reviewers for their valuable reports, which led to the improvement of the manuscript. *This work is dedicated to the memory of Vasile Cruceanu (1931–2023).*

Conflicts of Interest: The author declares no conflict of interest.

References

1. Rao, C.R. Information and accuracy attainable in the estimation of statistical paramteters. *Bull. Calcutta Math. Soc.* **1945**, *37*, 81–91.
2. Lauritzen, S.L. Statistical manifolds. In Differential Geometry in Statistical Inference. *IMS Lect. Notes Monogr. Ser. Inst. Math. Stat.* **1987**, *10*, 163–216.
3. Amari, S.; Nagaoka, K. *Method of Information Geometry*; Oxford University Press: Oxford, UK, 2000.
4. Balan, V.; Peyghan, E.; Sharahi, E. Statistical structures on the tangent bundle of a statistical manifold with Sasaki metric. *Hacet. J. Math. Stat.* **2020**, *49*, 120–135. [CrossRef]
5. Blaga, A.M.; Chen, B.Y. Gradient solitons on statistical manifolds. *J. Geom. Phys.* **2021**, *164*, 104195. [CrossRef]
6. Chen, B.Y.; Decu, S.; Vîlcu, G.E. Inequalities for the Casorati curvature of totally real spacelike submanifolds in statistical manifolds of type para-Kähler space forms. *Entropy* **2021**, *23*, 1399. [CrossRef] [PubMed]
7. Crasmareanu, M.; Hretcanu, C. Statistical structures on metric path spaces. *Chin. Ann. Math.* **2012**, *33*, 889–902. [CrossRef]
8. Etayo, F.; Defrancisco, A.; Santamaría, R. There are no genuine Käher-Codazzi manifolds. *Int. J. Geom. Methods Mod. Phys.* **2020**, *17*, 2050044. [CrossRef]
9. Fei, T.; Zhang, J. Interaction of Codazzi couplings with (para-)Kähler geometry. *Results Math.* **2017**, *72*, 2037–2056. [CrossRef]

10. Gezer, A.; Cakicioglu, H. Notes concerning Codazzi pairs on almost anti-Hermitian manifolds. *Appl. Math. Ser. B* **2023**, *38*, 223–234. [CrossRef]
11. Furuhata, H.; Hasegawa, I. Submanifold theory in holomorphic statistical manifolds. In *Geometry of Cauchy-Riemann Submanifolds*; Dragomir, S., Hasan Shahid, M., Al-Solamy, F.R., Eds.; Springer: Singapore, 2016; pp. 179–215.
12. Grigorian, S.; Zhang, J. (Para-)holomorphic and conjugate connections on (para-)Hermitian and (para-)Kähler manifolds. *Results Math.* **2019**, *74*, 150. [CrossRef]
13. Ianuş, S. Statistical manifolds and tangent bundles. *Sci. Bull. Univ. Politech. Bucharest Ser. D* **1994**, *56*, 29–34.
14. Kurose, T. On the divergences of 1-conformally flat statistical manifolds. *Tôhoku Math. J.* **1994**, *46*, 427–433. [CrossRef]
15. Kurose, T. Statistical manifolds admitting torsion. *arXiv* **2007**, arXiv:2307.15065v. (In Japanese)
16. Loi, A.; Matta, S. Robustness of statistical manifolds. *Topol. Appl.* **2023**, *32*, 108438. [CrossRef]
17. Matsuzoe, H. Quasi-statistical manifolds and geometry of affine distributions. In *Pure and Applied Differential Geometry*; Van der Veken, J., Van de Woestyne, I., Verstraelen, L., Vrancken, L., Eds.; In Memory of Franki Dillen; Shaker: Aachen, Germany, 2013; pp. 208–214.
18. Matsuzoe, H. Statistical manifolds and geometry of estimating functions. Prospects of Differential Geometry and Its Related Fields. In Proceedings of the 3rd International Colloquium on Differential Geometry and Its Related Fields, Veliko Tarnovo, Bulgaria, 3–7 September 2013; pp. 187–202.
19. Matsuzoe, H.; Inoguchi, J. Statistical structures on tangent bundles. *Appl. Sci.* **2003**, *5*, 55–75.
20. Mihai, A.; Mihai, I. Curvature invariants for statistical submanifolds of Hessian manifolds of constant Hessian curvature. *Mathematics* **2018**, *6*, 44. [CrossRef]
21. Neacsu, C.D. On some optimal inequalities for statistical submanifolds of statistical space forms. *U. Politeh. Buch. Ser. A* **2023**, *85*, 107–118.
22. Opozda, B. On the tangent bundles of statistical manifolds. In Proceedings of the Geometric Science of Information GSI 2023, St. Malo, France, 30 August–1 September 2023.
23. Peyghan, E.; Arcuş, C. Codazzi and statistical connections on almost product manifolds. *Filomat* **2020**, *34*, 4343–4358. [CrossRef]
24. Peyghan, E.; Seifipour, D.; Gezer, A. Statistical structures on tangent bundles and tangent Lie groups. *Hacet. J. Math. Stat.* **2021**, *50*, 1140–1154. [CrossRef]
25. Peyghan, E.; Seifipour, D.; Mihai, I. Infinitesimal affine transformations and mutual curvatures on statistical manifolds and their tangent bundles. *Axioms* **2023**, *12*, 667. [CrossRef]
26. Salimov, A. On structure-preserving connections. *Period. Math. Hung.* **2018**, *77*, 69–76. [CrossRef]
27. Salimov, A.; Turanli, S. Curvature properties of anti-Kähler–Codazzi manifolds. *C. R. Acad. Sci. Paris Ser. I* **2013**, *351*, 225–227. [CrossRef]
28. Samereh, L.; Peyghan, E.; Mihai, I. On almost Norden statistical manifolds. *Entropy* **2022**, *24*, 758. [CrossRef] [PubMed]
29. Turanli, S.; Uçan, S. Interaction of Codazzi pairs with almost para Norden manifolds. *Turk. J. Math. Comput. Sci.* **2022**, *14*, 212–227. [CrossRef]
30. Vîlcu, G.E. Almost product structures on statistical manifolds and para-Kähler-like statistical submersions. *Bull. Sci. Math.* **2021**, *171*, 103018. [CrossRef]
31. Vîlcu, A.D.; Vîlcu, G.E. Statistical manifolds with almost quaternionic structures and quaternionic Kähler-like statistical submersions. *Entropy* **2015**, *17*, 6213–6228. [CrossRef]
32. Wan, J.; Xie, Z. Wintgen inequality for statistical submanifolds in statistical manifolds of constant curvature. *Ann. Mat. Pura Appl.* **2023**, *202*, 1369–1380. [CrossRef]
33. Cruceanu, V.; Miron, R. Sur les connexions compatibles à une structure métrique où presque symplectique. *Mathematica* **1967**, *9*, 245–252.
34. Etayo, F.; Santamaría, R. ($J^2 = \pm 1$)-metric manifolds. *Publ. Math. Debrecen* **2000**, *57*, 435–444. [CrossRef]
35. Oproiu, V. A generalization of natural almost Hermitian structures on the tangent bundles. *Math. J. Toyama Univ.* **1999**, *22*, 1–14.
36. Kowalski, O.; Sekizawa, M. Natural transformations of Riemannian metrics on manifolds to metrics on tangent bundles—A classification. *Bull. Tokyo Gakugei Univ.* **1988**, *40*, 1–29.
37. Janyška, J. Natural 2-forms on the tangent bundle of a Riemannian manifold. In Proceedings of the Winter School Geometry and Topology Srní, Palermo, Italy, 19 January 1992; pp. 165–174.
38. Li, Y.; Kumara, H.A.; Siddesha, M.S.; Naik, D.M. Characterization of Ricci almost soliton on Lorentzian manifolds. *Symmetry* **2023**, *15*, 1175. [CrossRef]
39. Li, Y.; Bhattacharyya, S.; Azami, S.; Saha, A.; Hui, S.K. Harnack estimation for nonlinear, Weighted, heat-type equation along geometric flow and applications. *Mathematics* **2023**, *11*, 2516. [CrossRef]
40. Li, Y.; Gupta, M.K.; Sharma, S.; Chaubey, S.K. On Ricci Curvature of a Homogeneous Generalized Matsumoto Finsler Space. *Mathematics* **2023**, *11*, 3265. [CrossRef]
41. Li, Y.; Patra, D.; Alluhaibi, N.; Mofarreh, F.; Ali, A. Geometric classifications of k-almost Ricci solitons admitting paracontact metrices. *Open Math.* **2023**, *21*, 20220610. [CrossRef]
42. Druţă-Romaniuc, S.L. General natural α-structures parallel with respect to the Schouten–Van Kampen connection on the tangent bundle. *Mediterr. J. Math.* **2022**, *19*, 195. [CrossRef]
43. Yano, K.; Ishihara, K. *Tangent and Cotangent Bundles*; M. Dekker Inc.: New York, NY, USA, 1973.

44. Oproiu, V. Some new geometric structures on the tangent bundles. *Publ. Math. Debrecen.* **1999**, *55*, 261–281. [CrossRef]
45. Schouten, J.; Van Kampen, R. Zur Einbettungs-und Krummungstheorie nichtholonomer Gebilde. *Math. Ann.* **1930**, *103*, 752–783. [CrossRef]
46. Ianuş, S. Some almost product structures on manifolds with linear connection. *Kodai Math. Sem. Rep.* **1971** *23*, 305–310.
47. Druţă-Romaniuc, S.L. General natural (α, ε)-structures. *Mediterr. J. Math.* **2018**, *15*, 228. [CrossRef]

Disclaimer/Publisher's Note: The statements, opinions and data contained in all publications are solely those of the individual author(s) and contributor(s) and not of MDPI and/or the editor(s). MDPI and/or the editor(s) disclaim responsibility for any injury to people or property resulting from any ideas, methods, instructions or products referred to in the content.

Article

Lightlike Hypersurfaces of Meta-Golden Semi-Riemannian Manifolds

Feyza Esra Erdoğan [1,*,†], **Selcen Yüksel Perktaş** [2,†], **Şerife Nur Bozdağ** [1,†] **and Bilal Eftal Acet** [2,†]

1. Department of Mathematics, Faculty of Science, Ege University, İzmir 35100, Türkiye; serife.nur.yalcin@ege.edu.tr
2. Department of Mathematics, Faculty of Science and Arts, Adıyaman University, Adıyaman 02040, Türkiye; sperktas@adiyaman.edu.tr (S.Y.P.); eacet@adiyaman.edu.tr (B.E.A.)
* Correspondence: feyza.esra.erdogan@ege.edu.tr
† These authors contributed equally to this work.

Abstract: In this research, we embark on the examination of lightlike hypersurfaces within an almost meta-Golden semi-Riemannian manifold. We investigate the properties of the induced structure on a lightlike hypersurface by meta-Golden semi-Riemannian structure. Then, we introduce invariant lightlike hypersurfaces, anti-invariant lightlike hypersurfaces and screen semi-invariant lightlike hypersurfaces of almost meta-Golden semi-Riemannian manifolds and give examples.

Keywords: Chi ratio; golden structure; meta-Golden structure; lightlike hypersurface

MSC: 53C15; 57R15

1. Introduction

It has been shown that there is a close connection between the transition from Newtonian physics to relativity mechanics and the Golden ratio. Moreover, the Golden ratio was also used to derive the special theory of relativity, Lorentz contraction of lengths and expansion of time intervals. This case reveals the research on numberless objects that satisfy the Golden ratio necessity through the world. One of the results was the view that a logarithmic spiral provides the Golden ratio. Recently, however, Barlett [1] has shown that this assertion is untrue. It was also proved that an important class of logarithmic spirals delivers the meta-Golden Chi ratio wonderfully. In [1], the same fulfillment was built around the meta-Golden Chi ratio given by $\chi = \frac{1+\sqrt{4\hat{\varphi}+5}}{2\hat{\varphi}}$, where $\hat{\varphi} = \frac{1+\sqrt{5}}{2}$.

In Riemannian (also semi-Riemannian) manifolds, different geometric structures allow important consequences to occur while investigating the geometric and differential properties of submanifolds. Manifolds with such differential geometric structures have been studied by several authors (see [2–7]).

A major shortcoming in manifold theory is the limited study of isometries between manifolds with non-positive metrics. This is a significant gap, particularly in the context of applications in physics and engineering. In fact, Riemannian submersions and isometric immersions are extensively studied topics, but degenerate cases have received scant attention due to the challenges posed by metric complexities. Nevertheless, transitioning from the non-degenerate case to the degenerate one, both in terms of applications and mathematics, holds the potential to yield more general and robust results. The degeneracy version of isometric immersions has been examined by a large group of geometers under the name of lightlike submanifolds which were firstly defined by Duggal and Bejancu [8], (see also [9–11]).

Recently, Şahin [12] introduced a new type of manifold and named it the meta-Golden Riemannian manifold. This manifold was constructed by means of the meta-Golden Chi ratio and the Golden manifolds.

In this research, we embark on the study of lightlike geometry in meta-Golden semi-Riemannian manifolds.

2. Preliminaries

A structure similar to the Golden ratio is presented as follows (see Hylebrouck [13]): From Figure 1 in [12], we obtain $\dot{\chi} = \frac{1}{\phi} + \frac{1}{\dot{\chi}}$, which suggests that $\dot{\chi}^2 - \frac{1}{\phi}\dot{\chi} - 1 = 0$. Thus, the roots are found as $\frac{\frac{1}{\phi} \mp \sqrt{4 + \frac{1}{\phi^2}}}{2}$. The correlation between the meta-Golden Chi ratio $\dot{\chi}$ and continued fractions was found in [13]. By denoting the positive and negative roots by $\dot{\chi} = \frac{\frac{1}{\phi} + \sqrt{4 + \frac{1}{\phi^2}}}{2}$ and $\ddot{\chi} = \frac{\frac{1}{\phi} - \sqrt{4 + \frac{1}{\phi^2}}}{2}$, respectively, we have [13]

$$\ddot{\chi} = \frac{1}{\phi} - \dot{\chi}, \tag{1}$$

$$\phi \dot{\chi}^2 = \phi + \dot{\chi}, \tag{2}$$

and

$$\phi \ddot{\chi}^2 = \phi + \ddot{\chi}. \tag{3}$$

In [3], it was stated that an endomorphism $\check{\beta}$ on a manifold $\check{\mathfrak{M}}^*$ is an almost Golden structure, if

$$\check{\beta}^2 \mathbb{X}_1 = \check{\beta} \mathbb{X}_1 + \mathbb{X}_1, \tag{4}$$

for $\mathbb{X}_1 \in \Gamma(T\check{\mathfrak{M}}^*)$. Hence, let $\check{g}$ be the semi-Riemannian metric on $\check{\mathfrak{M}}^*$; then, $(\check{g}, \check{\beta})$ is called an almost Golden semi-Riemannian structure if

$$\check{g}(\check{\beta}\mathbb{X}_1, \mathbb{Y}_1) = \check{g}(\mathbb{X}_1, \check{\beta}\mathbb{Y}_1), \tag{5}$$

where for $\mathbb{X}_1, \mathbb{Y}_1 \in \Gamma(T\check{\mathfrak{M}}^*)$. Therefore, $(\check{\mathfrak{M}}^*, \check{g}, \check{\beta})$ is called an almost Golden semi-Riemannian manifold. In view of (5), we obtain [3]

$$\check{g}(\check{\beta}\mathbb{X}_1, \check{\beta}\mathbb{Y}_1) = \check{g}(\mathbb{X}_1, \check{\beta}\mathbb{Y}_1) + \check{g}(\mathbb{X}_1, \mathbb{Y}_1). \tag{6}$$

Definition 1. *Let $\check{\mathfrak{I}}$ be a $(1,1)$ tensor field on an almost Golden manifold $(\check{\mathfrak{M}}^*, \check{\beta})$ which satisfies*

$$\check{\beta}\check{\mathfrak{I}}^2 \mathbb{X}_1 = \check{\beta}\mathbb{X}_1 + \check{\mathfrak{I}}\mathbb{X}_1, \tag{7}$$

for every $\mathbb{X}_1 \in \Gamma(T\check{\mathfrak{M}}^*)$. Then, $\check{\mathfrak{I}}$ is called an almost meta-Golden structure and $(\check{\mathfrak{M}}^*, \check{\beta}, \check{\mathfrak{I}})$ is called an almost meta-Golden manifold [12].

Theorem 1. *A $(1,1)$ tensor field $\check{\mathfrak{I}}$ on an almost Golden manifold $(\check{\mathfrak{M}}^*, \check{\beta})$ is an almost meta-Golden structure if*

$$\check{\mathfrak{I}}^2 = \check{\beta}\check{\mathfrak{I}} - \check{\mathfrak{I}} + I \tag{8}$$

where I is the identity map [12].

We give the following definition inspired by the definition given in [12].

Definition 2. *Let $\check{\mathfrak{I}}$ be an almost meta-Golden structure on $(\check{\mathfrak{M}}^*, \check{\beta}, \check{g})$. If $\check{\mathfrak{I}}$ is compatible with semi-Riemannian metric $\check{g}$ on $\check{\mathfrak{M}}^*$, namely,*

$$\check{g}(\check{\mathfrak{I}}\mathbb{X}_1, \mathbb{Y}_1) = \check{g}(\mathbb{X}_1, \check{\mathfrak{I}}\mathbb{Y}_1), \tag{9}$$

or

$$\check{g}(\check{\mathfrak{I}}\mathbb{X}_1, \check{\mathfrak{I}}\mathbb{Y}_1) = \check{g}(\check{\beta}\mathbb{X}_1, \check{\mathfrak{I}}\mathbb{Y}_1) - \check{g}(\mathbb{X}_1, \check{\mathfrak{I}}\mathbb{Y}_1) + \check{g}(\mathbb{X}_1, \mathbb{Y}_1), \tag{10}$$

then $(\breve{\mathfrak{M}}^*, \breve{\beta}, \breve{\mathfrak{I}}, \breve{g})$ is called an almost meta-Golden semi-Riemannian manifold where for $\mathbb{X}_1, \mathbb{Y}_1 \in \Gamma(T\breve{\mathfrak{M}}^*)$.

We note that an almost meta-Golden semi-Riemannian manifold is called a meta-Golden semi-Riemannian manifold if $\breve{\nabla}\breve{\mathfrak{I}} = 0$ where $\breve{\nabla}$ is the Levi-Civita connection of $\breve{\mathfrak{M}}^*$. In this case, we also have $\breve{\nabla}\breve{\beta} = 0$.

From here throughout the paper, an almost meta-Golden semi-Riemannian manifold (resp., meta-Golden semi-Riemannian manifold) will be denoted as AMGsR manifold (resp., MGsR manifold).

Let $\breve{\mathfrak{M}}^*$ be an $(n+2)$-dimensional semi-Riemannian manifold with index q, $0 < q < n+1$, and $\mathfrak{M}^*$ be a hypersurface of $\breve{\mathfrak{M}}^*$, with $g = \breve{g}\,|_{\mathfrak{M}^*}$. Then, $\mathfrak{M}^*$ is a lightlike hypersurface of $\breve{\mathfrak{M}}^*$, if the metric g is of rank n and the orthogonal complement $T\mathfrak{M}^{*\perp}$ of $T\mathfrak{M}^*$, given as

$$T\mathfrak{M}^{*\perp} = \bigcup_{p \in \mathfrak{M}^*} \{\mathbb{V}_p \in T_p\breve{\mathfrak{M}}^* : g_p(\mathbb{U}_p, \mathbb{V}_p) = 0, \forall\, \mathbb{U}_p \in \Gamma(T_p\mathfrak{M}^*)\},$$

is a distribution of rank 1 on $\mathfrak{M}^*$ [8]. Here, $T\mathfrak{M}^{*\perp} \subset T\mathfrak{M}^*$ and then it coincides with the distribution called the *radical distribution* given by $Rad(T\mathfrak{M}^*) = T\mathfrak{M}^* \cap T\mathfrak{M}^{*\perp}$.

A complementary bundle of $T\mathfrak{M}^{*\perp}$ in $T\mathfrak{M}^*$ is a non-degenerate distribution of constant rank $(n-1)$ over $\mathfrak{M}^*$, which is known as a *screen distribution* and demonstrated with $S(T\mathfrak{M}^*)$.

Theorem 2 ([8]). *Let $(\mathfrak{M}^*, g, S(T\mathfrak{M}^*))$ be a lightlike hypersurface of a semi-Riemannian manifold $\mathfrak{M}^*$. Then, there exists a unique rank 1 vector sub-bundle $ltr(T\mathfrak{M}^*)$ of $T\breve{\mathfrak{M}}^*$, with base space $\mathbb{N}$, such that for every non-zero section ξ of $Rad(T\mathfrak{M}^*)$ on a coordinate neighbourhood $\wp \subset \mathfrak{M}^*$, there exists a section $\mathbb{N}$ of $ltr(T\mathfrak{M}^*)$ on $\wp$ satisfying:*

$$\breve{g}(\mathbb{N}, \mathbb{W}) = 0, \quad \breve{g}(\mathbb{N}, \mathbb{N}) = 0, \quad \breve{g}(\mathbb{N}, \xi) = 1, \text{ for } \mathbb{W} \in \Gamma(S(T\mathfrak{M}^*))|_\wp.$$

Here, $ltr(T\mathfrak{M}^*)$ is called the the lightlike transversal vector bundle.

Via the previous theorem, we obtain:

$$T\mathfrak{M}^* = S(T\mathfrak{M}^*) \perp Rad(T\mathfrak{M}^*), \tag{11}$$

and

$$\begin{aligned} T\breve{\mathfrak{M}}^* &= T\mathfrak{M}^* \oplus ltr(T\mathfrak{M}^*) \\ &= S(T\mathfrak{M}^*) \perp \{Rad(T\mathfrak{M}^*) \oplus ltr(T\mathfrak{M}^*)\}. \end{aligned} \tag{12}$$

For $\mathbb{U}, \mathbb{V} \in \Gamma(T\mathfrak{M}^*)$, $\mathbb{N} \in \Gamma(ltr(T\mathfrak{M}^*))$, from the equations of Gauss and Weingarten formulas, we have

$$\breve{\nabla}_\mathbb{U}\mathbb{V} = \nabla_\mathbb{U}\mathbb{V} + h(\mathbb{U}, \mathbb{V}), \tag{13}$$

$$\breve{\nabla}_U\mathbb{N} = -A_\mathbb{N}\mathbb{U} + \nabla^t_\mathbb{U}\mathbb{N}. \tag{14}$$

3. Lightlike Hypersurfaces of Almost Meta-Golden Semi-Riemannian Manifolds

In this study, since there are both almost Golden structure and almost meta-Golden structure in AMGsR manifolds, we will obtain two structures that are induced on the lightlike hypersurface.

Throughout this paper, we will consider the structure that is induced from the almost Golden structure on the ambient manifold to the lightlike hypersurface is being an almost Golden structure and invariant, that is, $\breve{\beta}(T\mathfrak{M}^*) \subseteq T\mathfrak{M}^*$ and $\breve{\beta}(T\mathfrak{M}^{*\perp}) \subseteq T\mathfrak{M}^{*\perp}$.

Let $(\breve{\mathfrak{M}}^*, \breve{\beta}, \breve{\mathfrak{J}}, \breve{g})$ be an AMGsR manifold and $\mathfrak{M}^*$ be a lightlike hypersurface of $\breve{\mathfrak{M}}^*$. Consider a $(1,1)$ tensor field $\sharp$ and a 1-form v on $\breve{\mathfrak{M}}^*$. For any $\mathbb{X}_1 \in \Gamma(T\mathfrak{M}^*)$, we have

$$\breve{\mathfrak{J}}\mathbb{X}_1 = \sharp\mathbb{X}_1 + v(\mathbb{X}_1)N, \qquad \breve{\beta}\mathbb{X}_1 = \beta\mathbb{X}_1 + u(\mathbb{X}_1)N, \tag{15}$$

and

$$\breve{\mathfrak{J}}N = \mathbb{V} + v(N)N, \qquad \breve{\beta}N = \mathbb{U} + u(N)N, \tag{16}$$

where $\mathbb{U}, \mathbb{V} \in \Gamma(T\mathfrak{M}^*)$, $N \in \Gamma(ltr(T\mathfrak{M}^*))$, $v(.) = \breve{g}(., \breve{\mathfrak{J}}\zeta)$, $u(.) = \breve{g}(., \breve{\beta}\zeta)$ and

$$\sharp : \Gamma(T\mathfrak{M}^*) \to \Gamma(T\mathfrak{M}^*), \quad \sharp\mathbb{X}_1 = (\breve{\mathfrak{J}}\mathbb{X}_1)^\top.$$

In this case, the second parts of Equations (15) and (16) are in the form of $\breve{\beta}\mathbb{X}_1 = \beta\mathbb{X}_1$, $u(\mathbb{X}_1) = 0$ and $\mathbb{U} = 0$ due to our assumption. If $\breve{\beta}$ is applied to both sides of the second equation in (16), we have $u(N) = \phi$ and $u(N) = 1 - \phi$.

Therefore, we have the following theorem.

Theorem 3. *Let $(\breve{\mathfrak{M}}^*, \breve{\beta}, \breve{\mathfrak{J}}, \breve{g})$ be an AMGsR manifold and $\mathfrak{M}^*$ be a lightlike hypersurface of $\breve{\mathfrak{M}}^*$. In this case, we have a structure $(\beta, g, u, \mathbb{U})$ induced on $\mathfrak{M}^*$ by the almost Golden structure $\breve{\beta}$, satisfies the following equalities:*

$$\beta^2 \mathbb{X}_1 = \beta \mathbb{X}_1 + \mathbb{X}_1,$$

$$u(\beta \mathbb{X}_1) = 0,$$

$$\beta \mathbb{U} = 0,$$

$$(u(N))^2 - u(N) - 1 = 0,$$

$$g(\beta \mathbb{X}_1, \beta \mathbb{Y}_1) = g(\beta \mathbb{X}_1, \mathbb{Y}_1) + g(\mathbb{X}_1, \mathbb{Y}_1),$$

where for $\mathbb{X}_1, \mathbb{Y}_1 \in \Gamma(T\breve{\mathfrak{M}}^*)$, $N \in \Gamma(ltr(T\mathfrak{M}^*))$.

Now, we give some characterizations for the structure induced to the lightlike hypersurface from the AMGsR manifold.

Theorem 4. *Let $(\breve{\mathfrak{M}}^*, \breve{\beta}, \breve{\mathfrak{J}}, \breve{g})$ be an AMGsR manifold and $\mathfrak{M}^*$ be a lightlike hypersurface of $\breve{\mathfrak{M}}^*$. In this case, the structure $\Pi = (\sharp, \beta, g, v, \mathbb{V})$ satisfies the following equalities:*

$$\sharp^2 \mathbb{X}_1 = \beta \sharp \mathbb{X}_1 - \sharp \mathbb{X}_1 + \mathbb{X}_1 - v(\mathbb{X}_1)\mathbb{V}, \tag{17}$$

$$v(\sharp \mathbb{X}_1) = (u(N) - v(N) - I)v(\mathbb{X}_1), \tag{18}$$

$$\sharp \mathbb{V} = \beta V - (1 + v(N))\mathbb{V}, \tag{19}$$

$$(v(N))^2 = v(N)(u(N) - 1) + I - v(\mathbb{V}), \tag{20}$$

$$g(\sharp \mathbb{X}_1, \mathbb{Y}_1) = g(\mathbb{X}_1, \sharp \mathbb{Y}_1) + v(\mathbb{Y}_1)\tau(\mathbb{X}_1) - v(\mathbb{X}_1)\tau(\mathbb{Y}_1), \quad \tau(\mathbb{X}_1) = g(\mathbb{X}_1, N), \tag{21}$$

$$g(\sharp \mathbb{X}_1, \sharp \mathbb{Y}_1) = \begin{pmatrix} g(\beta \mathbb{X}_1, \sharp \mathbb{Y}_1) - g(\mathbb{X}_1, \sharp \mathbb{Y}_1) + g(\mathbb{X}_1, \mathbb{Y}_1) \\ +v(\mathbb{Y}_1)\tau(\beta \mathbb{X}_1) - v(\mathbb{Y}_1)\tau(\mathbb{X}_1) \\ -v(\mathbb{Y}_1)\zeta(\sharp \mathbb{X}_1) - v(\mathbb{X}_1)\zeta(\sharp \mathbb{Y}_1) \end{pmatrix}, \quad \zeta(\sharp \mathbb{X}_1) = g(\mathbb{X}_1, \sharp N). \tag{22}$$

Proof. If we apply $\breve{\mathfrak{J}}$ to the first part of Equation (15) and consider Equations (8), (15) and (16), we have

$$\breve{\beta}\breve{\mathfrak{J}}\mathbb{X}_1 - \breve{\mathfrak{J}}\mathbb{X}_1 + \mathbb{X}_1 = \breve{\mathfrak{J}}\sharp\mathbb{X}_1 + v(\mathbb{X}_1)\breve{\mathfrak{J}}N.$$

By using (15) and (16) in the last equation, we obtain

$$\begin{aligned}\breve{\beta}\sharp\mathbb{X}_1 + v(\mathbb{X}_1)\breve{\beta}N - \sharp\mathbb{X}_1 - v(\mathbb{X}_1)N + \mathbb{X}_1 &= \sharp^2\mathbb{X}_1 + v(\sharp\mathbb{X}_1)N \\ &\quad + v(\mathbb{X}_1)\mathbb{V} + v(N)v(\mathbb{X}_1)N,\end{aligned} \tag{23}$$

which implies

$$\begin{pmatrix} \beta\sharp\mathbb{X}_1 + v(\mathbb{X}_1)u(\mathbb{N})\mathbb{N} \\ -\sharp\mathbb{X}_1 - v(\mathbb{X}_1)\mathbb{N} + \mathbb{X}_1 \end{pmatrix} = \begin{pmatrix} \sharp^2\mathbb{X}_1 + v(\sharp\mathbb{X}_1)\mathbb{N} \\ +v(\mathbb{X}_1)\mathbb{V} + v(\mathbb{N})v(\mathbb{X}_1)\mathbb{N} \end{pmatrix}. \qquad (24)$$

If we take the tangential and transversal components of Equation (24), we obtain (17) and (18), respectively.

On the other hand, if we apply $\breve{\Im}$ to Equation (16), we have

$$\breve{\Im}^2\mathbb{N} = \breve{\Im}\mathbb{V} + v(\mathbb{N})\breve{\Im}\mathbb{N},$$

which gives

$$\beta(\mathbb{V} + v(\mathbb{N})\mathbb{N}) - (\mathbb{V} + v(\mathbb{N})\mathbb{N}) + \mathbb{N} = \sharp\mathbb{V} + v(\mathbb{V})\mathbb{N} + v(\mathbb{N})\mathbb{V} + (v(\mathbb{N}))^2\mathbb{N},$$

via (8), (15) and (16). Again, equating the tangential and transversal components of the above equation, we obtain (19) and (20), respectively. In addition, if we use (9), (15) and (16), we obtain (21). Applying (8) and (9) in (15), we find (22). □

If we use $\breve{\Im}\mathbb{X}_1$ instead of $\mathbb{X}_1$ in Equation (7), we have:

Proposition 1. *Let* $(\breve{\mathfrak{M}}^*, \breve{\beta}, \breve{\Im}, \breve{g})$ *be an MGsR manifold. Then, we have* $\bar{\nabla}\breve{\beta}\breve{\Im} = 0$.

Theorem 5. *Let* $\mathfrak{M}^*$ *be a lightlike hypersurface of an MGsR manifold* $(\breve{\mathfrak{M}}^*, \breve{\beta}, \breve{\Im}, \breve{g})$. *Then, we have*

$$(\nabla_{\mathbb{X}_1}\sharp)\mathbb{Y}_1 = v(\mathbb{Y}_1)A_\mathbb{N}\mathbb{X}_1 + B(\mathbb{X}_1, \mathbb{Y}_1)\mathbb{V}, \qquad (25)$$

$$(\nabla_{\mathbb{X}_1}v)\mathbb{Y}_1 = B(\mathbb{X}_1, \mathbb{Y}_1)v(\mathbb{N}) - B(\mathbb{X}_1, \sharp\mathbb{Y}_1)\mathbb{V} - v(\mathbb{Y}_1)\tau(\mathbb{X}_1), \qquad (26)$$

$$\nabla_{\mathbb{X}_1}\mathbb{V} = -\sharp A_\mathbb{N}\mathbb{X}_1 + \tau(\mathbb{X}_1)\mathbb{V} + v(\mathbb{N})A_\mathbb{N}\mathbb{X}_1, \qquad (27)$$

$$\mathbb{X}_1(v(\mathbb{N})) = -B(\mathbb{X}_1, \mathbb{V}) - v(A_\mathbb{N}\mathbb{X}_1). \qquad (28)$$

Proof. Since $\bar{\nabla}\breve{\Im} = 0$, by using (15) and (16) and Gauss–Weingarten formulas, we write

$$\begin{pmatrix} \nabla_{\mathbb{X}_1}\sharp\mathbb{Y}_1 + B(\mathbb{X}_1, \sharp\mathbb{Y}_1)\mathbb{N} \\ +\mathbb{X}_1(v(\mathbb{Y}_1))\mathbb{N} - v(\mathbb{X}_1)A_\mathbb{N}\mathbb{X}_1 \end{pmatrix} = \begin{pmatrix} \sharp\nabla_{\mathbb{X}_1}\mathbb{Y}_1 + v(\nabla_{\mathbb{X}_1}\mathbb{Y}_1)\mathbb{N} \\ +B(\mathbb{X}_1, \mathbb{Y}_1)\mathbb{V} + B(\mathbb{X}_1, \mathbb{Y}_1)v(\mathbb{N})\mathbb{N} \end{pmatrix},$$

for $\mathbb{X}_1, \mathbb{Y}_1 \in \Gamma(T\mathfrak{M}^*)$.

If the tangential and transversal parts of the above equation are equalized, we find (25) and (26). In a similar way, for $\mathbb{X}_1 \in \Gamma(T\mathfrak{M}^*)$, $\mathbb{N} \in \Gamma(ltrT\mathfrak{M}^*)$, if we use $\bar{\nabla}\breve{\Im} = 0$, the Equations (15) and (16) and also Gauss–Weingarten formulas, we obtain

$$\begin{pmatrix} \nabla_{\mathbb{X}_1}\mathbb{V} + B(\mathbb{X}_1, \mathbb{V})\mathbb{N} + \mathbb{X}_1(v(\mathbb{N}))\mathbb{N} \\ -v(\mathbb{N})A_\mathbb{N}\mathbb{X}_1 + v(\mathbb{N})\tau(\mathbb{X}_1)\mathbb{V} \end{pmatrix} = \begin{pmatrix} -\sharp A_\mathbb{N}\mathbb{X}_1 - v(A_\mathbb{N}\mathbb{X}_1)\mathbb{N} \\ +\tau(\mathbb{X}_1)\mathbb{V} + v(\mathbb{N})\tau(\mathbb{X}_1)\mathbb{V} \end{pmatrix}.$$

Therefore, if the tangential and transversal parts of above equation are equalized, we find the Equations (27) and (28). □

Theorem 6. *Let* $(\breve{\mathfrak{M}}^*, \breve{\beta}, \breve{\Im}, \breve{g})$ *be an MGsR manifold and* $\mathfrak{M}^*$ *be a lightlike hypersurface of* $\breve{\mathfrak{M}}^*$. *Then, we have the following equations:*

$$\nabla\beta = 0,$$
$$B(\mathbb{X}_1, \beta\mathbb{Y}_1) = B(\mathbb{X}_1, \mathbb{Y}_1)u(\mathbb{N}),$$
$$\beta A_\mathbb{N}\mathbb{X}_1 = u(\mathbb{N})A_\mathbb{N}\mathbb{X}_1,$$
$$\mathbb{X}_1(u(\mathbb{N})) = 0.$$

Now, using $\bar{\nabla}\check{\beta}\Im = 0$, we can give the following theorem regarding the conditions provided by the structures reduced on the lightlike hypersurface of the MGsR manifold $(\check{\mathfrak{M}}^*, \check{\beta}, \Im, \check{g})$.

Theorem 7. *Let $(\check{\mathfrak{M}}^*, \check{\beta}, \Im, \check{g})$ be an MGsR manifold and $\mathfrak{M}^*$ be a lightlike hypersurface of $\check{\mathfrak{M}}^*$. Then, we have*

$$(\nabla_{\mathbb{X}_1} \beta\sharp)\mathbb{Y}_1 = B(\mathbb{X}_1, \mathbb{Y}_1)\beta\mathbb{V} - v(\mathbb{Y}_1)u(\mathbb{N})A_\mathbb{N}\mathbb{X}_1,$$

$$u(\mathbb{N})(\nabla_{\mathbb{X}_1} v)\mathbb{Y}_1 = -B(\mathbb{X}_1, \beta\sharp\mathbb{Y}_1) - v(\mathbb{Y}_1)u(\mathbb{N})\tau(\mathbb{X}_1)$$
$$+ B(\mathbb{X}_1, \mathbb{Y}_1)v(\mathbb{N})u(\mathbb{N}),$$

$$\nabla_{\mathbb{X}_1} \beta\mathbb{V} = \beta\nabla_{\mathbb{X}_1}\mathbb{V} = v(\mathbb{N})u(\mathbb{N})A_\mathbb{N}\mathbb{X}_1 - \beta\sharp A_\mathbb{N}\mathbb{X}_1 + \tau(\mathbb{X}_1)\beta\mathbb{V},$$

$$\mathbb{X}_1(v(\mathbb{N}))u(\mathbb{N}) = -v(A_\mathbb{N}\mathbb{X}_1)u(\mathbb{N}) - B(\mathbb{X}_1, \beta\mathbb{V}) - v(\mathbb{N})u(\mathbb{N})\tau(\mathbb{X}_1).$$

Proof. For $\mathbb{X}_1, \mathbb{Y}_1 \in \Gamma(T\mathfrak{M}^*)$, $\mathbb{N} \in \Gamma(ltrT\mathfrak{M}^*)$, if we use $\bar{\nabla}\check{\beta}\Im = 0$ and Equations (15) and (16), we have

$$\begin{pmatrix} \nabla_{\mathbb{X}_1}\beta\sharp\mathbb{Y}_1 + B(\mathbb{X}_1, \beta\sharp\mathbb{Y}_1)\mathbb{N} \\ +[\mathbb{X}_1(v(\mathbb{Y}_1))u(\mathbb{N}) + v(\mathbb{Y}_1)\mathbb{X}_1(u(\mathbb{N}))]\mathbb{N} \\ -v(\mathbb{Y}_1)u(\mathbb{N})A_\mathbb{N}\mathbb{X}_1 \\ +v(\mathbb{Y}_1)u(\mathbb{N})\tau(\mathbb{X}_1)\mathbb{N} \end{pmatrix} = \begin{pmatrix} \beta\sharp\nabla_{\mathbb{X}_1}\mathbb{Y}_1 + v(\nabla_{\mathbb{X}_1}\mathbb{Y}_1)u(\mathbb{N})\mathbb{N} \\ +B(\mathbb{X}_1, \mathbb{Y}_1)\beta\mathbb{V} \\ +B(\mathbb{X}_1, \mathbb{Y}_1)v(\mathbb{N})u(\mathbb{N})\mathbb{N} \end{pmatrix}.$$

By taking the tangential and transversal parts of this equation, the first two of the equations specified in the theorem are obtained. For $\mathbb{X}_1 \in \Gamma(T\mathfrak{M}^*)$, $\mathbb{N} \in \Gamma(ltrT\mathfrak{M}^*)$, by using $\bar{\nabla}\check{\beta}\Im = 0$ and Equations (15) and (16), we obtain

$$\begin{pmatrix} \nabla_{\mathbb{X}_1}\beta\mathbb{V} + B(\mathbb{X}_1, \beta\mathbb{V})\mathbb{N} \\ +[\mathbb{X}_1(v(\mathbb{N}))u(\mathbb{N}) + v(\mathbb{N})\mathbb{X}_1(u(\mathbb{N}))]\mathbb{N} \\ -v(\mathbb{N})u(\mathbb{N})A_\mathbb{N}\mathbb{X}_1 \\ +v(\mathbb{N})u(\mathbb{N})\tau(\mathbb{X}_1)\mathbb{N} \end{pmatrix} = \begin{pmatrix} -\beta\sharp A_\mathbb{N}\mathbb{X}_1 - v(A_\mathbb{N}\mathbb{X}_1)u(\mathbb{N})\mathbb{N} \\ +\tau(\mathbb{X}_1)\beta\mathbb{V} + \tau(\mathbb{X}_1)v(\mathbb{N})\mathbb{V} \\ +\tau(\mathbb{X}_1)v^2(\mathbb{N})\mathbb{N} \end{pmatrix},$$

which implies that the last two of the equations specified in the theorem are obtained. Thus, the proof is completed. □

Now, we define some special lightlike hypersurfaces.

Definition 3. *Let $(\check{\mathfrak{M}}^*, \check{\beta}, \Im, \check{g})$ be an AMGsR manifold and $\mathfrak{M}^*$ be a lightlike hypersurface of $\check{\mathfrak{M}}^*$. Then,*

1. *if $\check{\beta}\Im(T\mathfrak{M}^*) \subset T\mathfrak{M}^*$, $\mathfrak{M}^*$ is called as an invariant,*
2. *If $\check{\beta}\Im(Rad(T\mathfrak{M}^*)) \subset S(T\mathfrak{M}^*)$ and $\check{\beta}\Im(ltrT\mathfrak{M}^*) \subset S(T\mathfrak{M}^*)$, $\mathfrak{M}^*$ is called a screen semi-invariant,*
3. *If $\check{\beta}\Im(Rad(T\mathfrak{M}^*)) \subset ltrT\mathfrak{M}^*$, $\mathfrak{M}^*$ is called a radical anti-invariant,*

lightlike hypersurface.

Example 1. *Let $\check{\mathfrak{M}}^* = \mathbb{R}_1^5$ be an almost Golden semi-Riemannian manifold with a coordinate system $(x_1, x_2, x_3, x_4, x_5)$, a semi-Euclidean metric $\check{g}$ of signature $(-, +, +, +, +)$ and an almost Golden structure defined by*

$$\check{\beta}(x_1, x_2, x_3, x_4, x_5) = (\phi x_1, \phi x_2, \phi x_3, (1-\phi)x_4, (1-\phi)x_5).$$

Also, we define a $(1,1)$ tensor field $\Im$ on $\check{\mathfrak{M}}^*$ by

$$\Im(x_1, x_2, x_3, x_4, x_5) = (\dot{\chi}x_1, \dot{\chi}x_2, \dot{\chi}x_3, -\tilde{\chi}x_4, -\tilde{\chi}x_5),$$

where $\tilde{\chi} = \frac{\varphi + \sqrt{\varphi^2+4}}{2}$ and $\tilde{\chi}^2 = \varphi\tilde{\chi} + I$, (I is an identity map.)
One can see that $\tilde{\mathfrak{S}}$ satisfies (8)–(10) which imply that $(\breve{\mathfrak{M}}^*, \breve{\beta}, \tilde{\mathfrak{S}}, \breve{g})$ is an AMGsR manifold. Now, we consider a hypersurface $\mathfrak{M}^*$ of $\breve{\mathfrak{M}}^*$ given by

$$x_1 = u_3, \quad x_2 = -(\sin\alpha)u_1 + (\cos\alpha)u_3,$$

$$x_3 = (\cos\alpha)u_1 + (\sin\alpha)u_3, \quad x_4 = u_2, \quad x_5 = u_4.$$

Then, $T\mathfrak{M}^*$ is spanned by

$$\mathbb{Z}_1 = -\sin\alpha\frac{\partial}{\partial x_2} + \cos\alpha\frac{\partial}{\partial x_3}, \quad \mathbb{Z}_2 = \frac{\partial}{\partial x_4},$$

$$\mathbb{Z}_3 = \frac{\partial}{\partial x_1} + \cos\alpha\frac{\partial}{\partial x_2} + \sin\alpha\frac{\partial}{\partial x_3}, \quad \mathbb{Z}_4 = \frac{\partial}{\partial x_5}.$$

So, $\mathfrak{M}^*$ is a lightlike hypersurface of $\breve{\mathfrak{M}}^*$. In this case, $Rad(T\mathfrak{M}^*)$ and $S(T\mathfrak{M}^*)$ are given by

$$Rad(T\mathfrak{M}^*) = Span\{\mathbb{Z}_3\},$$

and

$$S(T\mathfrak{M}^*) = Span\{\mathbb{Z}_1, \mathbb{Z}_2, \mathbb{Z}_4\},$$

respectively, where $\breve{\beta}\mathbb{Z}_4 = (1-\varphi)\mathbb{Z}_4 \in \Gamma(S(T\mathfrak{M}^*))$, $\breve{\beta}\mathbb{Z}_3 = \varphi\mathbb{Z}_3 \in \Gamma(Rad(T\mathfrak{M}^*))$, $\breve{\beta}\mathbb{Z}_1 = \varphi\mathbb{Z}_1 \in \Gamma(S(T\mathfrak{M}^*))$ and $\breve{\beta}\mathbb{Z}_2 = (1-\varphi)\mathbb{Z}_2 \in \Gamma(S(T\mathfrak{M}^*))$. Thus, $Rad(T\mathfrak{M}^*)$ and $S(T\mathfrak{M}^*)$ are $\breve{\beta}$-invariant distributions. Also, we obtain

$$ltr(T\mathfrak{M}^*) = Span\left\{\mathbb{N} = \frac{1}{2}\left(-\frac{\partial}{\partial x_1} + \cos\alpha\frac{\partial}{\partial x_2} + \sin\alpha\frac{\partial}{\partial x_3}\right)\right\},$$

and $\breve{\beta}\mathbb{N} = \varphi\mathbb{N} \in \Gamma(ltr(T\mathfrak{M}^*))$, which imply that $\mathfrak{M}^*$ is a $\breve{\beta}$-invariant lightlike hypersurface of $\breve{\mathfrak{M}}^*$. Since

$$\tilde{\mathfrak{S}}\mathbb{Z}_1 = \tilde{\chi}\mathbb{Z}_1 \in \Gamma(S(T\mathfrak{M}^*)), \quad \tilde{\mathfrak{S}}\mathbb{Z}_2 = -\tilde{\chi}\mathbb{Z}_2 \in \Gamma(S(T\mathfrak{M}^*)),$$

$$\tilde{\mathfrak{S}}\mathbb{Z}_4 = -\tilde{\chi}\mathbb{Z}_4 \in \Gamma(S(T\mathfrak{M}^*)), \quad \tilde{\mathfrak{S}}\mathbb{Z}_3 = \tilde{\chi}\mathbb{Z}_3 \in \Gamma(Rad(T\mathfrak{M}^*)),$$

and

$$\tilde{\mathfrak{S}}\mathbb{N} = \tilde{\chi}\mathbb{N} \in \Gamma(ltr(T\mathfrak{M}^*)).$$

Then, $\mathfrak{M}^*$ is an invariant lightlike hypersurface of an AMGsR manifold $\breve{\mathfrak{M}}^*$.

Theorem 8. *Let $(\breve{\mathfrak{M}}^*, \breve{\beta}, \tilde{\mathfrak{S}}, \breve{g})$ be an AMGsR manifold and $\mathfrak{M}^*$ be a lightlike hypersurface of $\breve{\mathfrak{M}}^*$. Then, the followings are equivalent;*

1. *$\mathfrak{M}^*$ is $\tilde{\mathfrak{S}}$-invariant, so $\breve{\beta}\tilde{\mathfrak{S}}$ is invariant;*
2. *v vanishes on $\mathfrak{M}^*$;*
3. *$\sharp$ is an almost meta-Golden structure on $\mathfrak{M}^*$.*

Proof. We know that if $\mathfrak{M}^*$ is $\tilde{\mathfrak{S}}$-invariant, then for any $\mathbb{X}_1 \in \Gamma(T\mathfrak{M}^*)$ we write $\tilde{\mathfrak{S}}\mathbb{X}_1 = \sharp\mathbb{X}_1$. From (15), we obtain $v(\mathbb{X}_1) = 0$. Conversely, if v vanishes on $\mathfrak{M}^*$, then (1) is satisfied. Hence, (1)$\iff$(2). The necessary and sufficient condition for $v = 0$ on $\mathfrak{M}^*$ is that $\tilde{\mathfrak{S}}\mathbb{X}_1 = \sharp\mathbb{X}_1$. Then, we obtain

$$\sharp^2\mathbb{X}_1 = \beta\sharp\mathbb{X}_1 - \sharp\mathbb{X}_1 + \mathbb{X}_1.$$

Here, we also have

$$g(\sharp\mathbb{X}_1, \mathbb{Y}_1) = g(\mathbb{X}_1, \sharp\mathbb{Y}_1).$$

Therefore, $\sharp$ is an almost meta-Golden structure on $\mathfrak{M}^*$. □

Theorem 9. *There is no radical anti-invariant lightlike hypersurface of an AMGsR manifold.*

Proof. Let $(\breve{\mathfrak{M}}^*, \breve{\beta}, \breve{\mathfrak{F}}, \breve{g})$ be an AMGsR manifold and $\mathfrak{M}^*$ be a radical anti-invariant lightlike hypersurface of $\breve{\mathfrak{M}}^*$. From the definition of radical anti-invariant lightlike hypersurface, for any $\zeta \in \Gamma(Rad(T\mathfrak{M}^*))$, we have $\breve{\mathfrak{F}}\zeta \in \Gamma(ltr(T\mathfrak{M}^*))$, which implies

$$\breve{g}(\breve{\mathfrak{F}}\zeta, \breve{\mathfrak{F}}\zeta) = 0, \quad \breve{g}(\breve{\mathfrak{F}}\zeta, \breve{\mathfrak{F}}N) \neq 0, \quad \breve{g}(\breve{\mathfrak{F}}N, \breve{\mathfrak{F}}N) = 0.$$

Therefore, there is no radical anti-invariant lightlike hypersurface. □

4. Screen Semi-Invariant Lightlike Hypersurfaces of Almost Meta-Golden Semi-Riemannian Manifolds

Let $(\breve{\mathfrak{M}}^*, \breve{\beta}, \breve{\mathfrak{F}}, \breve{g})$ be an $(m+2)$-dimensional AMGsR manifold and $(\mathfrak{M}^*, g)$ be a screen semi-invariant lightlike hypersurface of $\breve{\mathfrak{M}}^*$. Taking $D_T = \sharp Rad(T\mathfrak{M}^*)$, $D_\perp = \sharp ltr(T\mathfrak{M}^*)$ and $D = D_\circ \perp Rad(T\mathfrak{M}^*) \perp \sharp Rad(T\mathfrak{M}^*)$, we have the following decompositions:

$$S(T\mathfrak{M}^*) = D_\circ \perp (D_T \oplus D_\perp), \tag{29}$$

$$T\mathfrak{M}^* = D \oplus D_\perp, \tag{30}$$

$$T\breve{\mathfrak{M}}^* = D \oplus D_\perp \oplus ltr(T\mathfrak{M}^*), \tag{31}$$

where $D_\circ$ is an $(m-2)$-dimensional distribution, $\mathbb{V} = \breve{\mathfrak{F}}N$ and $\mathbb{Z} = \breve{\mathfrak{F}}\zeta$.

Example 2. Let $\breve{\mathfrak{M}}^* = \mathbb{R}_2^5$ be a semi-Riemannian manifold with coordinate system $(x_1, x_2, x_3, x_4, x_5)$ and signature $(-, +, -, +, +)$. Taking an almost Golden structure

$$\breve{\beta}(x_1, x_2, x_3, x_4, x_5) = (\phi x_1, \phi x_2, \phi x_3, \phi x_4, \phi x_5),$$

with a meta-Golden structure

$$\breve{\mathfrak{F}}(x_1, x_2, x_3, x_4, x_5) = (\ddot{\chi} x_1, \ddot{\chi} x_2, \ddot{\chi} x_3, \ddot{\chi} x_4, \ddot{\chi} x_5),$$

then $(\mathbb{R}_2^5, \breve{\beta}, \breve{\mathfrak{F}}, \breve{g})$ is an AMGsR manifold.

Now, we consider a hypersurface $\mathfrak{M}^*$ of $\breve{\mathfrak{M}}^*$ given by

$$x_5 = \ddot{\chi} x_1 + \ddot{\chi} x_2 + x_3,$$

Then, $T\mathfrak{M}^*$ is spanned by $\{\mathbb{Z}_1, \mathbb{Z}_2, \mathbb{Z}_3, \mathbb{Z}_4\}$, where

$$\mathbb{Z}_1 = \frac{\partial}{\partial x_1} + \ddot{\chi} \frac{\partial}{\partial x_5}, \quad \mathbb{Z}_2 = \frac{\partial}{\partial x_2} + \ddot{\chi} \frac{\partial}{\partial x_5},$$

$$\mathbb{Z}_3 = \frac{\partial}{\partial x_3} + \frac{\partial}{\partial x_5}, \quad \mathbb{Z}_4 = \frac{\partial}{\partial x_4}.$$

So, $\mathfrak{M}^*$ is a 1-lightlike hypersurface of $\breve{\mathfrak{M}}^*$ with

$$Rad(T\mathfrak{M}^*) = Span\{\zeta = \ddot{\chi}\frac{\partial}{\partial x_1} - \ddot{\chi}\frac{\partial}{\partial x_2} - \frac{\partial}{\partial x_3} - \frac{\partial}{\partial x_5}\},$$

and

$$S(T\mathfrak{M}^*) = Span\{\mathbb{W}_1, \mathbb{W}_2, \mathbb{W}_3\},$$

where

$$\mathbb{W}_1 = \frac{\partial}{\partial x_4}, \quad \mathbb{W}_2 = -\ddot{\chi}\frac{\partial}{\partial x_1} + \ddot{\chi}\frac{\partial}{\partial x_2} + \frac{\partial}{\partial x_3} + \frac{\partial}{\partial x_5},$$

$$\mathbb{W}_3 = -\ddot{\chi}\frac{\partial}{\partial x_1} - \ddot{\chi}\frac{\partial}{\partial x_2} + \frac{\partial}{\partial x_3} - \frac{\partial}{\partial x_5}.$$

Then, we write $D_T = Span\{\mathbb{W}_2\}$ and $D_\perp = Span\{\mathbb{W}_3\}$. Also, we obtain

$$ltr(T\mathfrak{M}^*) = Span\left\{\mathbb{N} = \frac{1}{2(1-\ddot{\chi}^2)}\left(\ddot{\chi}\frac{\partial}{\partial x_1} + \ddot{\chi}\frac{\partial}{\partial x_2} - \frac{\partial}{\partial x_3} + \frac{\partial}{\partial x_5}\right)\right\},$$

which implies that $\mathfrak{M}^*$ is a $\check{\beta}$–invariant lightlike hypersurface of $\ddot{\mathfrak{M}}^*$. Furthermore, we obtain

$$\check{\mathfrak{I}}\xi = \ddot{\chi}\mathbb{W}_2 \in \Gamma(D_T),$$

$$\check{\mathfrak{I}}\mathbb{N} = \frac{\ddot{\chi}}{2(1-\ddot{\chi}^2)}\mathbb{W}_3 \in \Gamma(D_\perp).$$

Therefore, $\mathfrak{M}^*$ is a screen semi-invariant lightlike hypersurface of $(\mathbb{R}_2^5, \check{\beta}, \check{\mathfrak{I}}, \check{g})$.

Proposition 2. *Let $\mathfrak{M}^*$ be a screen semi-invariant lightlike hypersurface of an AMGsR manifold $(\ddot{\mathfrak{M}}^*, \check{\beta}, \check{\mathfrak{I}}, \check{g})$. Then, for $\mathbb{X}_1, \mathbb{Y}_1 \in \Gamma(T\mathfrak{M}^*)$, $\mathbb{V} \in \Gamma(D_\perp)$ and $\mathbb{Z} \in \Gamma(D_T)$, we have*

$$v(\sharp\mathbb{X}_1) = v(\mathbb{X}_1)(u(\mathbb{N}) + I),$$

$$\sharp v = \beta v - v,$$

$$v(\mathbb{V}) = 1, \qquad (32)$$

$$u(\mathbb{N})(\nabla_{\mathbb{X}_1}v)\mathbb{Y}_1 = -B(\mathbb{X}_1, \beta\sharp\mathbb{Y}_1) - v(\mathbb{Y}_1)u(\mathbb{N})\tau(\mathbb{X}_1),$$

$$\nabla_{\mathbb{X}_1}\beta\mathbb{V} = -\beta\sharp A_\mathbb{N}\mathbb{X}_1 + \tau(\mathbb{X}_1)\beta\mathbb{V},$$

$$v(A_\mathbb{N}\mathbb{X}_1)u(\mathbb{N}) = -B(\mathbb{X}_1, \beta\mathbb{V}),$$

$$(\nabla_{\mathbb{X}_1}v)\mathbb{Y}_1 = -B(\mathbb{X}_1, \sharp\mathbb{Y}_1) - v(\mathbb{Y}_1)\tau(\mathbb{X}_1),$$

$$B(\mathbb{X}_1, \sharp\mathbb{Y}_1) = \frac{1}{u(\mathbb{N})}B(\mathbb{X}_1, \beta\sharp\mathbb{Y}_1),$$

$$(\nabla_{\mathbb{X}_1}\beta\sharp)\mathbb{Y}_1 = B(\mathbb{X}_1, \mathbb{Y}_1)\beta\mathbb{V},$$

$$u(A_\mathbb{N}\mathbb{X}_1)u(\mathbb{N}) = C(\mathbb{X}_1, \sharp\xi)u(\mathbb{N}) = -B(\mathbb{X}_1, \beta\mathbb{V}),$$

$$B(\mathbb{X}_1, \mathbb{V}) = -C(\mathbb{X}_1, \mathbb{Z}), \qquad (33)$$

$$\nabla_{\mathbb{X}_1}\mathbb{Z} = -\sharp A^*_\xi \mathbb{X}_1 - \tau(\mathbb{X}_1)\mathbb{Z},$$

$$C(\mathbb{X}_1, \mathbb{V}) = 0. \qquad (34)$$

Corollary 1. *Let $(\ddot{\mathfrak{M}}^*, \check{\beta}, \check{\mathfrak{I}}, \check{g})$ be an AMGsR manifold and $\mathfrak{M}^*$ be a screen semi-invariant lightlike hypersurface of $\ddot{\mathfrak{M}}^*$. Then, for $\mathbb{X}_1, \mathbb{Z} \in \Gamma(T\mathfrak{M}^*)$, we have*

$$B(\mathbb{X}_1, \mathbb{Z}) = 0. \qquad (35)$$

Corollary 2. *There is no D_T–valued component of A^*_ξ in a screen semi-invariant lightlike hypersurface of an AMGsR manifold.*

Proof. In view of (35), we state

$$B(\mathbb{X}_1, \mathbb{Z}) = -g(A^*_\xi \mathbb{X}_1, \check{\mathfrak{I}}\xi) = -g(A^*_\xi \mathbb{X}_1, \mathbb{Z}) = 0,$$

for $\mathbb{X}_1, \mathbb{Z} \in \Gamma(T\mathfrak{M}^*)$, which gives our assertion. □

Corollary 3. *There is no $D_\perp$– valued component of $A_\mathbb{N}$ in a screen semi-invariant lightlike hypersurface of an AMGsR manifold.*

Proof. In view of (34), we write

$$C(\mathbb{X}_1, \mathbb{V}) = -g(A_\mathbb{N}\mathbb{X}_1, \check{\Im}\mathbb{N}) = -g(A_\mathbb{N}\mathbb{X}_1, \mathbb{V}) = 0,$$

which completes the proof. □

Proposition 3. *Let $(\breve{\mathfrak{M}}^*, \breve{\beta}, \check{\Im}, \breve{g})$ be an AMGsR manifold and $\mathfrak{M}^*$ be a screen semi-invariant lightlike hypersurface of $\breve{\mathfrak{M}}^*$. Then, for the distribution $D_\circ$, we have $\check{\Im}D_\circ \subset S(T\mathfrak{M}^*)$.*

Proof. For $\mathbb{X}_1 \in \Gamma(D_\circ)$, $\xi \in \Gamma(Rad(T\mathfrak{M}^*))$ and $\mathbb{N} \in \Gamma(ltr(T\mathfrak{M}^*))$, we obtain

$$\breve{g}(\check{\Im}\mathbb{X}_1, \xi) = \breve{g}(\mathbb{X}_1, \check{\Im}\xi) = 0,$$

and

$$\breve{g}(\check{\Im}\mathbb{X}_1, \mathbb{N}) = \breve{g}(\mathbb{X}_1, \check{\Im}\mathbb{N}) = 0.$$

Moreover, for $\mathbb{V} \in \Gamma(D_\perp)$ and $\mathbb{Z} \in \Gamma(D_T)$, we obtain

$$\breve{g}(\check{\Im}\mathbb{X}_1, \mathbb{V}) = \breve{g}(\mathbb{X}_1, \check{\Im}\mathbb{V}) = \breve{g}(\mathbb{X}_1, \check{\Im}^2\mathbb{N})$$
$$= \breve{g}(\mathbb{X}_1, \breve{\beta}\check{\Im}\mathbb{N} - \check{\Im}\mathbb{N} + \mathbb{N})$$
$$= \breve{g}(\breve{\beta}\mathbb{X}_1, \check{\Im}\mathbb{N})$$

and

$$\breve{g}(\check{\Im}\mathbb{X}_1, \mathbb{Z}) = \breve{g}(\mathbb{X}_1, \check{\Im}\mathbb{Z}) = \breve{g}(\mathbb{X}_1, \check{\Im}^2\xi)$$
$$= \breve{g}(\mathbb{X}_1, \breve{\beta}\check{\Im}\xi - \check{\Im}\xi + \xi)$$
$$= \breve{g}(\breve{\beta}\mathbb{X}_1, \check{\Im}\xi).$$

So, there is no component of $\check{\Im}\mathbb{X}_1$ on $ltr(T\mathfrak{M}^*)$ and $Rad(T\mathfrak{M}^*)$. □

Corollary 4. *Let $\mathfrak{M}^*$ be a screen semi-invariant lightlike hypersurface of an AMGsR manifold $(\breve{\mathfrak{M}}^*, \breve{\beta}, \check{\Im}, \breve{g})$. Then, $D_\circ$ is an $\check{\Im}$-invariant distribution.*

Theorem 10. *Let $(\breve{\mathfrak{M}}^*, \breve{\beta}, \check{\Im}, \breve{g})$ be an AMGsR manifold and $\mathfrak{M}^*$ be a screen semi-invariant lightlike hypersurface of $\breve{\mathfrak{M}}^*$. Then, the vector field $\mathbb{Z}$ is parallel on $\mathfrak{M}^*$ if $B(\mathbb{X}_1, \mathbb{Y}_1) = -g(\check{\Im}A_\xi^*\mathbb{X}_1, \breve{\beta}\mathbb{Y}_1)$ and $\tau = 0$.*

Proof. Assume that the vector field $\mathbb{Z}$ is parallel. From (25), for $\mathbb{X}_1 \in \Gamma(T\mathfrak{M}^*)$, we obtain

$$\nabla_{\mathbb{X}_1}\mathbb{Z} = -\check{\Im}A_\xi^*\mathbb{X}_1 - \tau(\mathbb{X}_1)\mathbb{Z} = 0. \tag{36}$$

Applying $\check{\Im}$ to (36) and using (15) with (16), we obtain

$$-\check{\Im}^2 A_\xi^*\mathbb{X}_1 - \tau(\mathbb{X}_1)\check{\Im}^2\xi = -\breve{\beta}\check{\Im}A_\xi^*\mathbb{X}_1 + \check{\Im}A_\xi^*\mathbb{X}_1 - A_\xi^*\mathbb{X}_1$$
$$- \tau(\mathbb{X}_1)\breve{\beta}\check{\Im}\xi + \tau(\mathbb{X}_1)\check{\Im}\xi - \tau(\mathbb{X}_1)\xi. \tag{37}$$

From (36) with (37), we arrive at

$$-\breve{\beta}\check{\Im}A_\xi^*\mathbb{X}_1 - A_\xi^*\mathbb{X}_1 - \tau(\mathbb{X}_1)\breve{\beta}\check{\Im}\xi - \tau(\mathbb{X}_1)\xi = 0,$$

which gives $\tau = 0$ and $\breve{\beta}\check{\Im}A_\xi^*\mathbb{X}_1 = -A_\xi^*\mathbb{X}_1$. So, the proof is completed. □

Theorem 11. *Let $\mathfrak{M}^*$ be a screen semi-invariant lightlike hypersurface of an AMGsR manifold $(\breve{\mathfrak{M}}^*, \breve{\beta}, \check{\Im}, \breve{g})$ and the vector field $\mathbb{Z}$ be parallel on $\mathfrak{M}^*$. Then, either $\sharp$ or $\mathbb{V}$ are parallel on $\mathfrak{M}^*$ if $B(\mathbb{X}_1, \mathbb{V}) = 0$ and $A_\mathbb{N}\mathbb{X}_1 = 0$.*

Proof. Assume that $\sharp$ is parallel on $\mathfrak{M}^*$. From (25), for $\mathbb{X}_1, \mathbb{Y}_1 \in \Gamma(T\mathfrak{M}^*)$, we obtain

$$0 = (\nabla_{\mathbb{X}_1}\sharp)\mathbb{Y}_1 = v(\mathbb{Y}_1)A_\mathbb{N}\mathbb{X}_1 + B(\mathbb{X}_1,\mathbb{Y}_1)\mathbb{V},$$

from which we have

$$B(\mathbb{X}_1,\mathbb{Y}_1)\mathbb{V} = -v(\mathbb{Y}_1)A_\mathbb{N}\mathbb{X}_1. \tag{38}$$

Since $\mathbb{Z}$ is parallel, we state

$$\check{g}(\check{\Im} A_\zeta^* \mathbb{X}_1, \check{\beta}\mathbb{Y}_1)\mathbb{V} = v(\mathbb{Y}_1)A_\mathbb{N}\mathbb{X}_1.$$

In the last equation, replacing $\mathbb{Y}_1$ with $\mathbb{V}$ and using (32), we obtain

$$\check{g}(\check{\Im} A_\zeta^* \mathbb{X}_1, \check{\beta}\mathbb{V})\mathbb{V} = v(\mathbb{V})A_\mathbb{N}\mathbb{X}_1 = A_\mathbb{N}\mathbb{X}_1,$$

which gives

$$\check{g}(\check{\Im} A_\zeta^* \mathbb{X}_1, \check{\beta}\mathbb{V}) = g(A_\mathbb{N}\mathbb{X}_1, \mathbb{V}) = C(\mathbb{X}_1, \mathbb{V}).$$

By use of (34), we obtain $B(\mathbb{X}_1, \mathbb{V}) = 0$.

Similarly suppose that $\mathbb{V}$ is parallel on $\mathfrak{M}^*$, i.e., $\nabla_{\mathbb{X}_1}\mathbb{V} = 0$. So, we write

$$-\sharp A_\mathbb{N}\mathbb{X}_1 + \tau(\mathbb{X}_1)\mathbb{V} = 0,$$

from which

$$-\check{\Im} A_\mathbb{N}\mathbb{X}_1 + v(A_\mathbb{N}\mathbb{X}_1)\mathbb{N} + \tau(\mathbb{X}_1)\mathbb{V} = 0. \tag{39}$$

Applying $\check{\Im}$ to (39) and using (15), we obtain

$$\begin{aligned}0 &= -\check{\Im}^2 A_\mathbb{N}\mathbb{X}_1 + v(A_\mathbb{N}\mathbb{X}_1)\check{\Im}\mathbb{N} + \tau(\mathbb{X}_1)\check{\Im}\mathbb{V} \\ &= -\beta\sharp A_\mathbb{N}\mathbb{X}_1 + \sharp A_\mathbb{N}\mathbb{X}_1 - A_\mathbb{N}\mathbb{X}_1 \\ &\quad + (v(A_\mathbb{N}\mathbb{X}_1) - \tau(\mathbb{X}_1))\mathbb{V} \\ &\quad + ((1-u(\mathbb{N})v(A_\mathbb{N}\mathbb{X}_1) + \tau(\mathbb{X}_1))\mathbb{N}.\end{aligned} \tag{40}$$

From (39) with (40), we arrive at

$$-\beta\sharp A_\mathbb{N}\mathbb{X}_1 - A_\mathbb{N}\mathbb{X}_1 + v(A_\mathbb{N}\mathbb{X}_1)\mathbb{V} + ((1-u(\mathbb{N})v(A_\mathbb{N}\mathbb{X}_1) + \tau(\mathbb{X}_1))\mathbb{N} = 0. \tag{41}$$

From (41), we obtain

$$\begin{aligned}-\beta\sharp A_\mathbb{N}\mathbb{X}_1 - A_\mathbb{N}\mathbb{X}_1 + v(A_\mathbb{N}\mathbb{X}_1)\mathbb{V} &= 0, \\ (1-u(\mathbb{N}))v(A_\mathbb{N}\mathbb{X}_1) + \tau(\mathbb{X}_1) &= 0.\end{aligned} \tag{42}$$

Since $\mathbb{Z}$ is parallel, we know that $\tau(\mathbb{X}_1) = 0$, which gives rise to $A_\mathbb{N}\mathbb{X}_1 = 0$, via (42). So, the proof is completed. □

Theorem 12. *Let $\mathfrak{M}^*$ be a screen semi-invariant lightlike hypersurface of an AMGsR manifold $(\check{\mathfrak{M}}^*, \check{\beta}, \check{\Im}, \check{g})$. If $\sharp$ is parallel with respect to the induced connection ∇ on $\mathfrak{M}^*$, then D is parallel with respect to ∇. Furthermore, $\mathfrak{M}^*$ has $\mathfrak{M}_1 \times \mathfrak{M}_2$ local product structure, where $\mathfrak{M}_1$ is a null curve tangent to $\check{\Im}ltr(T\mathfrak{M}^*)$ and $\mathfrak{M}_2$ is a leaf of distribution D.*

Proof. Assume that $\sharp$ is parallel with respect to the induced connection ∇ on $\mathfrak{M}^*$. D is parallel with respect to ∇ if and only if

$$g(\nabla_{\mathbb{X}_1}\zeta, \check{\Im}\zeta) = g(\nabla_{\mathbb{X}_1}\check{\Im}\zeta, \check{\Im}\zeta) = g(\nabla_{\mathbb{X}_1}\mathbb{Y}_1, \check{\Im}\zeta) = 0, \tag{43}$$

for $\mathbb{X}_1 \in \Gamma(T\mathfrak{M}^*)$ and $\mathbb{Y}_1 \in \Gamma(D_\circ)$. From (13)–(15), we obtain

$$g(\nabla_{\mathbb{X}_1}\xi, \check{\Im}\xi) = g(\check{\Im}\nabla_{\mathbb{X}_1}\xi, \xi) = g(\nabla_{\mathbb{X}_1}\check{\Im}\xi, \xi) = B(\mathbb{X}_1, \mathbb{Z}), \quad g(\nabla_{\mathbb{X}_1}\check{\Im}\xi, \check{\Im}\xi) = 0, \quad (44)$$

and

$$\begin{aligned}
g(\nabla_{\mathbb{X}_1}\mathbb{Y}_1, \check{\Im}\xi) &= g(\bar{\nabla}_{\mathbb{X}_1}\mathbb{Y}_1, \check{\Im}\xi) \\
&= g(\check{\Im}\bar{\nabla}_{\mathbb{X}_1}\mathbb{Y}_1, \xi) \\
&= g(\bar{\nabla}_{\mathbb{X}_1}\check{\Im}\mathbb{Y}_1, \xi) \\
&= -g(\check{\Im}\mathbb{Y}_1, \bar{\nabla}_{\mathbb{X}_1}\xi) \\
&= g(\check{\Im}\mathbb{Y}_1, A^*_{\mathbb{X}_1}\xi) \\
&= B(\mathbb{X}_1, \check{\Im}\mathbb{Y}_1).
\end{aligned} \quad (45)$$

From (35), we know that $B(\mathbb{X}_1, \mathbb{Z}) = 0$. By use of (38), we obtain

$$B(\mathbb{X}_1, \check{\Im}\mathbb{Y}_1)\mathbb{V} = -v(\check{\Im}\mathbb{Y}_1)A_\mathbb{N}\mathbb{X}_1 = 0.$$

If we consider this equation in (45), we obtain the proof of our assertion. □

Definition 4. *Let $(\tilde{\mathfrak{M}}^*, \check{\beta}, \check{\Im}, \check{g})$ be an AMGsR manifold and $\mathfrak{M}^*$ be a lightlike hypersurface of $\tilde{\mathfrak{M}}^*$. If the second fundamental form B of $\mathfrak{M}^*$ satisfies*

$$B(\mathbb{X}_1, \mathbb{Y}_1) = 0, \quad \mathbb{X}_1, \mathbb{Y}_1 \in \Gamma(D_\perp),$$

then we say that $\mathfrak{M}^*$ is a $D_\perp$- totally geodesic lightlike hypersurface.

Definition 5. *Let $(\tilde{\mathfrak{M}}^*, \check{\beta}, \check{\Im}, \check{g})$ be an AMGsR manifold and $\mathfrak{M}^*$ be a screen semi-invariant lightlike hypersurface of $\tilde{\mathfrak{M}}^*$. If the second fundamental form B of $\mathfrak{M}^*$ satisfies*

$$B(\mathbb{X}_1, \mathbb{Y}_1) = 0, \quad \mathbb{X}_1 \in \Gamma(D), \mathbb{Y}_1 \in \Gamma(D_\perp),$$

then $\mathfrak{M}^*$ is called a mixed geodesic lightlike hypersurface.

Theorem 13. *Let $\mathfrak{M}^*$ be a screen semi-invariant lightlike hypersurface of an AMGsR manifold $(\tilde{\mathfrak{M}}^*, \check{\beta}, \check{\Im}, \check{g})$. Then, the following assertions are equivalent:*

(i) $\mathfrak{M}^*$ is a mixed geodesic lightlike hypersurface.
(ii) There is no D_T-valued component of $A_\mathbb{N}$.
(iii) There is no $D_\perp$-valued component of A^*_ξ.

Proof. Suppose that $\mathfrak{M}^*$ is a mixed geodesic lightlike hypersurface. Then from (33), for $\mathbb{X}_1 \in \Gamma(D), \mathbb{V} \in \Gamma(D_\perp)$ and $\mathbb{Z} \in \Gamma(D_T)$, we have

$$B(\mathbb{X}_1, \mathbb{V}) = -C(\mathbb{X}_1, \mathbb{Z}) = -g(A_\mathbb{N}\mathbb{X}_1, \mathbb{Z}) = 0$$

which implies the equivalence of (i) and (ii).

The equivalence of (ii) and (iii) follows from

$$B(\mathbb{X}_1, \mathbb{V}) = -C(\mathbb{X}_1, \mathbb{Z}) \Rightarrow -g(A_\mathbb{N}\mathbb{X}_1, \mathbb{Z}) = g(A^*_\xi\mathbb{X}_1, \mathbb{V}) = 0,$$

which completes the proof. □

Theorem 14. *Let $(\tilde{\mathfrak{M}}^*, \check{\beta}, \check{\Im}, \check{g})$ be an AMGsR manifold and $\mathfrak{M}^*$ be a screen semi-invariant lightlike hypersurface of $\tilde{\mathfrak{M}}^*$. Then, the distribution D is integrable if and only if*

$$B(\check{\Im}\mathbb{Y}_1, \check{\Im}\mathbb{X}_1) = B(\mathbb{X}_1, \check{\Im}\check{\beta}\mathbb{Y}_1) - B(\mathbb{X}_1, \check{\Im}\mathbb{Y}_1) + B(\mathbb{X}_1, \mathbb{Y}_1), \quad (46)$$

for any $\mathbb{X}_1, \mathbb{Y}_1 \in \Gamma(D)$.

Proof. It is known that, for $\mathbb{X}_1 \in \Gamma(D)$, if the D is invariant then $\check{\mathfrak{J}}\mathbb{X}_1 \in \Gamma(D)$. So the D is integrable if and only if
$$v([\check{\mathfrak{J}}\mathbb{X}_1, \mathbb{Y}_1]) = 0.$$

From the above equation, we obtain

$$\begin{aligned}
v([\check{\mathfrak{J}}\mathbb{X}_1, \mathbb{Y}_1]) &= g([\check{\mathfrak{J}}\mathbb{X}_1, \mathbb{Y}_1], \check{\mathfrak{J}}\xi) \\
&= g(\bar{\nabla}_{\check{\mathfrak{J}}\mathbb{X}_1} \mathbb{Y}_1, \check{\mathfrak{J}}\xi) - g(\bar{\nabla}_{\mathbb{Y}_1} \check{\mathfrak{J}}\mathbb{X}_1, \check{\mathfrak{J}}\xi) \\
&= g(\bar{\nabla}_{\check{\mathfrak{J}}\mathbb{X}_1} \check{\mathfrak{J}}\mathbb{Y}_1, \xi) - g(\check{\mathfrak{J}}\bar{\nabla}_{\mathbb{Y}_1} \mathbb{X}_1, \check{\mathfrak{J}}\xi) \\
&= g(\nabla_{\check{\mathfrak{J}}\mathbb{X}_1} \check{\mathfrak{J}}\mathbb{Y}_1 + B(\check{\mathfrak{J}}\mathbb{X}_1, \check{\mathfrak{J}}\mathbb{Y}_1)N, \xi) \\
&\quad - g(\nabla_{\mathbb{X}_1} \check{\mathfrak{J}}\check{\beta}\mathbb{Y}_1, \xi) + g(\nabla_{\mathbb{X}_1} \check{\mathfrak{J}}\mathbb{Y}_1, \xi) - g(\nabla_{\mathbb{X}_1} \mathbb{Y}_1, \xi) \\
&= B(\check{\mathfrak{J}}\mathbb{Y}_1, \check{\mathfrak{J}}\mathbb{X}_1) - B(\mathbb{X}_1, \check{\mathfrak{J}}\check{\beta}\mathbb{Y}_1) \\
&\quad + B(\mathbb{X}_1, \check{\mathfrak{J}}\mathbb{Y}_1) - B(\mathbb{X}_1, \mathbb{Y}_1),
\end{aligned}$$

which gives (46). □

Theorem 15. *Let $(\bar{\mathfrak{M}}^*, \check{\beta}, \check{\mathfrak{J}}, \check{g})$ be an AMGsR manifold and $\mathfrak{M}^*$ be a screen semi-invariant lightlike hypersurface of $\bar{\mathfrak{M}}^*$. Then, the following assertions are equivalent:*

(i) The distribution D is parallel.
(ii) The distribution D is totally geodesic.
(iii) $(\nabla_{\mathbb{X}_1} \sharp)\mathbb{Y}_1 = 0$, for any $\mathbb{X}_1, \mathbb{Y}_1 \in \Gamma(D)$.

Proof. The distribution D is parallel if for any $\mathbb{X}_1, \mathbb{Y}_1 \in \Gamma(D)$ and $\mathbb{Z} \in \Gamma(D_T)$
$$v(\nabla_{\mathbb{X}_1} \mathbb{Y}_1) = 0.$$

From the above equation, we obtain

$$\begin{aligned}
v(\nabla_{\mathbb{X}_1} \mathbb{Y}_1) &= g(\nabla_{\mathbb{X}_1} \mathbb{Y}_1, \check{\mathfrak{J}}\xi) \\
&= g(\bar{\nabla}_{\mathbb{X}_1} \mathbb{Y}_1, \check{\mathfrak{J}}\xi) \\
&= g(\check{\mathfrak{J}}\bar{\nabla}_{\mathbb{X}_1} \mathbb{Y}_1, \xi) \\
&= g(\bar{\nabla}_{\mathbb{X}_1} \check{\mathfrak{J}}\mathbb{Y}_1, \xi) \\
&= B(\mathbb{X}_1, \check{\mathfrak{J}}\mathbb{Y}_1)
\end{aligned}$$

which gives the equivalence of (i) and (ii).

In view of (25), the equivalence of (ii) and (iii) follows from
$$(\nabla_{\mathbb{X}_1} \sharp)\mathbb{Y}_1 = v(\mathbb{Y}_1) A_N \mathbb{X}_1 + B(\mathbb{X}_1, \mathbb{Y}_1) \mathbb{V} \Rightarrow (\nabla_{\mathbb{X}_1} \sharp)\mathbb{Y}_1 = B(\mathbb{X}_1, \mathbb{Y}_1) \mathbb{V},$$

which completes the proof. □

Theorem 16. *Let $(\bar{\mathfrak{M}}^*, \check{\beta}, \check{\mathfrak{J}}, \check{g})$ be an AMGsR manifold and $\mathfrak{M}^*$ be a screen semi-invariant lightlike hypersurface of $\bar{\mathfrak{M}}^*$. Then, $\mathfrak{M}^*$ is totally geodesic if for any $\mathbb{X}_1 \in \Gamma(T\mathfrak{M}^*)$, $\mathbb{Y}_1 \in \Gamma(D)$ and $\mathbb{V} \in \Gamma(D_\perp)$*

$$(\nabla_{\mathbb{X}_1} \sharp)\mathbb{Y}_1 = 0, \tag{47}$$

$$(\nabla_{\mathbb{X}_1} \sharp)\mathbb{V} = A_N \mathbb{X}_1. \tag{48}$$

Proof. Suppose that $\mathfrak{M}^*$ is totally geodesic; then for $\mathbb{Y}_1 \in \Gamma(D)$, we obtain
$$v(\mathbb{Y}_1) = g(\mathbb{Y}_1, \check{\mathfrak{J}}\xi) = g(\check{\mathfrak{J}}\mathbb{Y}_1, \xi) = 0.$$

From (25), we have
$$(\nabla_{\mathbb{X}_1}\sharp)\mathbb{Y}_1 = v(\mathbb{Y}_1)A_\mathbb{N}\mathbb{X}_1 + B(\mathbb{X}_1,\mathbb{Y}_1)\mathbb{V} = 0.$$

Similarly, for $\mathbb{V} \in \Gamma(D_\perp)$, we have $v(\mathbb{V}) = 1$. In Equation (25), replacing $\mathbb{Y}_1$ by $\mathbb{V}$, we obtain
$$(\nabla_{\mathbb{X}_1}\sharp)\mathbb{V} = v(\mathbb{V})A_\mathbb{N}\mathbb{X}_1 + B(\mathbb{X}_1,\mathbb{V})\mathbb{V} = A_\mathbb{N}\mathbb{X}_1.$$

Conversely, we suppose that Equations (47) and (48) are satisfied. In view of decomposition (30), for any $\mathbb{Y}_1 \in \Gamma(T\mathfrak{M}^*)$ we find a function f such that $\mathbb{Y}_1 = \mathbb{Y}_d + f\mathbb{V}$, where $\mathbb{Y}_d \in \Gamma(D)$. So we write
$$B(\mathbb{X}_1,\mathbb{Y}_1) = B(\mathbb{X}_1,\mathbb{Y}_d) + fB(\mathbb{X}_1,\mathbb{V}). \tag{49}$$

In (25), replacing $\mathbb{Y}$ with $\mathbb{Y}_d$ and using (47), we obtain
$$0 = (\nabla_{\mathbb{X}_1}\sharp)\mathbb{Y}_d$$
$$= v(\mathbb{Y}_d)A_\mathbb{N}\mathbb{X}_1 + B(\mathbb{X}_1,\mathbb{Y}_d)\mathbb{V},$$

which gives $B(\mathbb{X}_1,\mathbb{Y}_d) = 0$.

Similarly in (25), replacing $\mathbb{Y}$ with $\mathbb{V}$ and using (48), we have
$$0 = (\nabla_{\mathbb{X}_1}\sharp)\mathbb{V}$$
$$= v(\mathbb{V})A_\mathbb{N}\mathbb{X}_1 + B(\mathbb{X}_1,\mathbb{V})\mathbb{V}$$
$$= A_\mathbb{N}\mathbb{X}_1 + B(\mathbb{X}_1,\mathbb{V})\mathbb{V}$$

which implies $B(\mathbb{X}_1,\mathbb{V}) = 0$. So, from (49) we arrive at $B(\mathbb{X}_1,\mathbb{Y}_1) = 0$. This completes the proof. □

Theorem 17. *Let $\mathfrak{M}^*$ be a totally umbilic screen semi-invariant lightlike hypersurface of an AMGsR manifold $(\breve{\mathfrak{M}}^*, \breve{\beta}, \breve{\Im}, \breve{g})$. Then, $\mathfrak{M}^*$ is totally geodesic on $\breve{\mathfrak{M}}^*$.*

Proof. Suppose that $\mathfrak{M}^*$ is a totally umbilic screen semi-invariant lightlike hypersurface of $\breve{\mathfrak{M}}^*$. From (35), for any $\mathbb{X}_1 \in \Gamma(T\mathfrak{M}^*)$ we have
$$B(\mathbb{X}_1,\mathbb{Z}) = \lambda g(\mathbb{X}_1,\mathbb{Z}).$$

Replacing $\mathbb{X}_1$ with $\mathbb{V}$ in the last equation, we obtain
$$B(\mathbb{V},\mathbb{Z}) = \lambda g(\mathbb{V},\mathbb{Z}) = 0,$$

which yields $\lambda = 0$. In this case, we obtain $B = 0$. □

Theorem 18. *Let $(\breve{\mathfrak{M}}^*, \breve{\beta}, \breve{\Im}, \breve{g})$ be an AMGsR manifold and $\mathfrak{M}^*$ be a screen semi-invariant lightlike hypersurface of $\breve{\mathfrak{M}}^*$. Then, if screen distribution $S(T\mathfrak{M}^*)$ is totally umbilic, then $S(T\mathfrak{M}^*)$ is totally geodesic.*

Proof. Suppose that $S(T\mathfrak{M}^*)$ is totally umbilic. From (34), for any $\mathbb{X}_1 \in \Gamma(T\mathfrak{M}^*)$, we have
$$C(\mathbb{X}_1,\mathbb{V}) = \delta g(\mathbb{X}_1,\mathbb{V}).$$

Replacing $\mathbb{X}_1$ with $\mathbb{Z}$ in the above equation, we obtain
$$C(\mathbb{Z},\mathbb{V}) = \delta g(\mathbb{Z},\mathbb{V}) = 0,$$

which gives $\delta = 0$. In this case, we obtain $C = 0$. So, the proof is completed. □

5. Conclusions

In this study, we found structures reduced from the meta-Golden structure of an almost meta-Golden semi-Riemannian manifold onto the tangent and transversal bundles of the lightlike hypersurface. We gave the definitions of invariant, anti-invariant and screen semi-invariant lightlike hypersurfaces of the meta-Golden semi-Riemannian manifold. We have obtained the necessary and sufficient conditions for the distributions of these hypersurfaces to be integrable and totally geodesic.

Working with manifolds with a polynomial structure with constant coefficients allows the definition of many results from classical algebra and geometry, tools that make calculations and proofs simpler (tensor fields, 1-forms, reduced structures, etc.). For example, the fundamental theorem of algebra states that any polynomial with complex coefficients is factored by linear equations, and this result is used to prove that certain manifolds are topologically equivalent to a sphere. These types of manifolds are also important for the differential geometry of manifolds because the properties offered by these structures make geometric structures and curves much easier to examine and understand.

Hypersurfaces and submanifolds are special types of general manifolds and have certain geometric properties. These structures allow the achievement of more specific and meaningful results in mathematical analysis. Submanifolds represent situations where certain parts of the manifold have flatter and simpler geometry. This is important for its flattenability and minimalism properties. Submanifolds provide the ability to better model and understand physical phenomena. For example, they can be used to model physical quantities such as time, which is a submanifold of spacetime. Hypersurfaces and submanifolds are widely used in physics, engineering, computer science and other applications. For example, these structures are frequently encountered concepts in fields such as image processing, graphic design and data analysis. In physics, the integrability of distributions of submanifolds of a manifold provides the ability to better model and understand physical phenomena. It is particularly important for the analysis of physical quantities such as energy distributions or currents on submanifolds of spacetime. An integrable surface provides advantages in calculating center of gravity, moment and similar quantities. Such calculations are important in engineering and physics, especially for analyzing the geometric properties of objects. The concept of parallelism plays an important role in fields such as differential geometry on manifolds and general relativity. For example, it is important in physics, especially in the general theory of relativity, for describing the trajectories of objects in a gravitational field.

Author Contributions: F.E.E., S.Y.P., Ş.N.B. and B.E.A. contributed equally to this work. All authors have read and agreed to the published version of the manuscript.

Funding: This research received no external funding.

Data Availability Statement: Data are contained within the article.

Conflicts of Interest: The authors declare no conflict of interest.

References

1. Barlett, C. Nautilus spirals and the meta-Golden ratio Chi. *Nexus Netw. J.* **2019**, *21*, 641–656. [CrossRef]
2. Goldberg, S.I.; Yano, K. Polynomial structures on manifolds. *Kodai Math. Sem. Rep.* **1970**, *22*, 199–218. [CrossRef]
3. Crasmareanu, M.; Hretcanu, C.E. Golden differential geometry. *Chaos Solitons Fractals* **2008**, *38*, 1229–1238. [CrossRef]
4. Gezer, A.; Cengiz, N.; Salimov, A. On integrability of Golden Riemannian structures. *Turk. J. Math.* **2013**, *37*, 693–703. [CrossRef]
5. Şahin, B. Almost poly-Norden manifolds. *Int. J. Maps Math.* **2018**, *1*, 68–79.
6. Erdoğan, F.E.; Yüksel Perktaş, S.; Acet, B.E.; Bozdağ, Ş.N. Lightlike hypersurfaces of almost Norden Golden semi-Riemannian manifolds. *Facta Univ. Ser. Math. Inform.* **2022**, *37*, 813–828.
7. Hretcanu, C.E.; Crasmareanu, M. Applications of the golden ratio on Riemannian manifolds. *Turk. J. Math.* **2009**, *33*, 179–191. [CrossRef]
8. Duggal, K.L.; Bejancu, A. *Lightlike Submanifolds of Semi-Riemannian Manifolds and Applications*; Mathematics and Its Applications; Kluwer Publisher: Alphen aan den Rijn, The Netherlands, 1996.
9. Duggal, K.L.; Şahin, B. *Differential Geometry of Lightlike Submanifolds*; Frontiers in Mathematics: Lausanne, Switzerland, 2010.

10. Duggal, K.L.; Şahin, B. Generalized Cauchy-Riemann lightlike submanifolds of Kaehler manifolds. *Acta Math. Hungar.* **2006**, *112*, 107–130. [CrossRef]
11. Duggal, K.L.; Şahin, B. Lightlike submanifolds of indefinite Sasakian manifolds. *Int. J. Math. Math. Sci.* **2007**, *2007*, 57585. [CrossRef]
12. Şahin, F.; Şahin, B. Meta-Golden Riemannian manifolds. *Math. Meth. Appl. Sci.* **2022**, *45*, 10491–10501. [CrossRef]
13. Huylebrouck, D. The meta-Golden ratio Chi. In Proceedings of the Bridges 2014: Mathematics, Music, Art, Architecture, Culture, Seoul, Republic of Korea, 14–19 August 2014; pp. 151–158.

Disclaimer/Publisher's Note: The statements, opinions and data contained in all publications are solely those of the individual author(s) and contributor(s) and not of MDPI and/or the editor(s). MDPI and/or the editor(s) disclaim responsibility for any injury to people or property resulting from any ideas, methods, instructions or products referred to in the content.

MDPI
St. Alban-Anlage 66
4052 Basel
Switzerland
www.mdpi.com

Mathematics Editorial Office
E-mail: mathematics@mdpi.com
www.mdpi.com/journal/mathematics

Disclaimer/Publisher's Note: The statements, opinions and data contained in all publications are solely those of the individual author(s) and contributor(s) and not of MDPI and/or the editor(s). MDPI and/or the editor(s) disclaim responsibility for any injury to people or property resulting from any ideas, methods, instructions or products referred to in the content.